Family Business

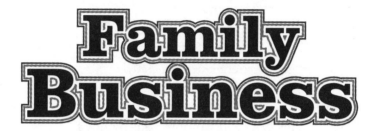

Other For Better or For Worse® Collections

Graduation: A Time for Change
The Big 5-0
Sunshine and Shadow
Middle Age Spread
Growing Like a Weed
Love Just Screws Everything Up
Starting from Scratch
"There Goes My Baby!"
Things Are Looking Up . . .
What, Me Pregnant?
If This Is a Lecture, How Long Will It Be?
Pushing 40
It's All Downhill from Here
Keep the Home Fries Burning
The Last Straw
Just One More Hug
"It Must Be Nice to Be Little"
Is This "One of Those Days," Daddy?
I've Got the One-More-Washload Blues . . .

Retrospectives

All About April
The Lives Behind the Lines: 20 Years of For Better or For Worse
Remembering Farley: A Tribute to the Life of Our Favorite Cartoon Dog
It's the Thought that Counts . . . Fifteenth Anniversary Collection
A Look Inside . . . For Better or For Worse: The 10th Anniversary Collection

Little Books

Isn't He Beautiful?
Isn't She Beautiful?
Wags and Kisses
A Perfect Christmas

Family Business

A *For Better or For Worse*® Collection by Lynn Johnston

Andrews McMeel
Publishing

Kansas City

For Better or For Worse® is distributed by United Feature Syndicate.

Family Business copyright © 2002 by Lynn Johnston Productions, Inc. All rights reserved. Printed in the United States of America. No part of this book may be used or reproduced in any manner whatsoever without written permission except in the case of reprints in the context of reviews. For permission information, write Lynn Johnston Productions, 304 MacPherson Drive, Corbeil, Ontario, Canada POH IKO.

www.FBorFW.com

02 03 04 05 06 BAH 10 9 8 7 6 5 4 3 2 1

ISBN: 0-7407-2669-2

Library of Congress Control Number: 2002107478

──── **ATTENTION: SCHOOLS AND BUSINESSES** ────

Andrews McMeel books are available at quantity discounts with bulk purchase for educational, business, or sales promotional use. For information, please write to: Special Sales Department, Andrews McMeel Publishing, 4520 Main Street, Kansas City, Missouri 64111.

*"This book is dedicated,
with thanks,
to all the booksellers
who have supported my work
so generously for so many years."*

Lynn Johnston

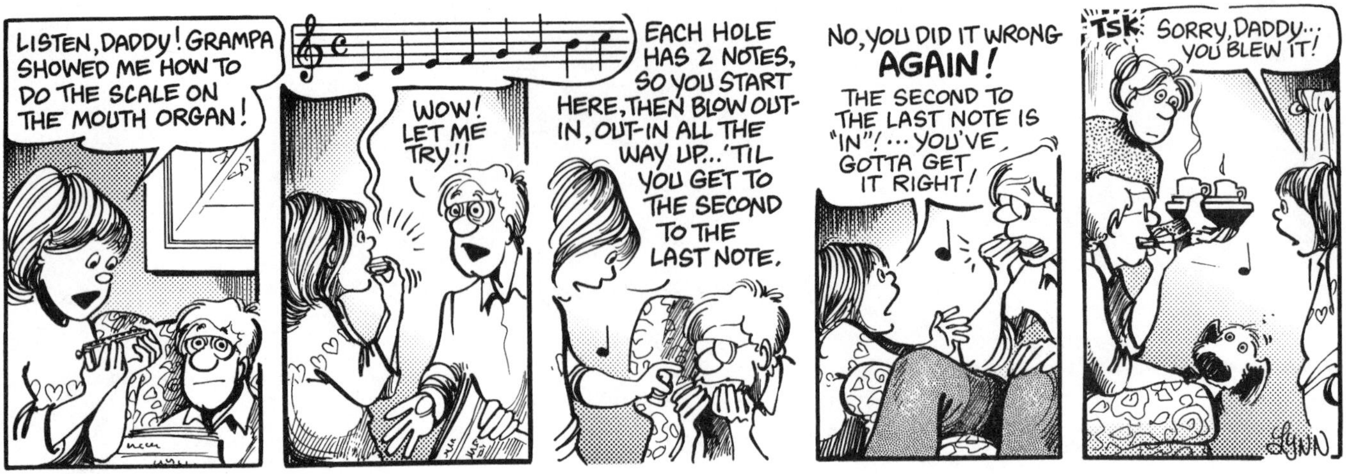
LISTEN, DADDY! GRAMPA SHOWED ME HOW TO DO THE SCALE ON THE MOUTH ORGAN!
WOW! LET ME TRY!!
EACH HOLE HAS 2 NOTES, SO YOU START HERE, THEN BLOW OUT-IN, OUT-IN ALL THE WAY UP...'TIL YOU GET TO THE SECOND TO THE LAST NOTE.
NO, YOU DID IT WRONG AGAIN!
THE SECOND TO THE LAST NOTE IS "IN"!... YOU'VE GOTTA GET IT RIGHT!
TSK
SORRY, DADDY... YOU BLEW IT!

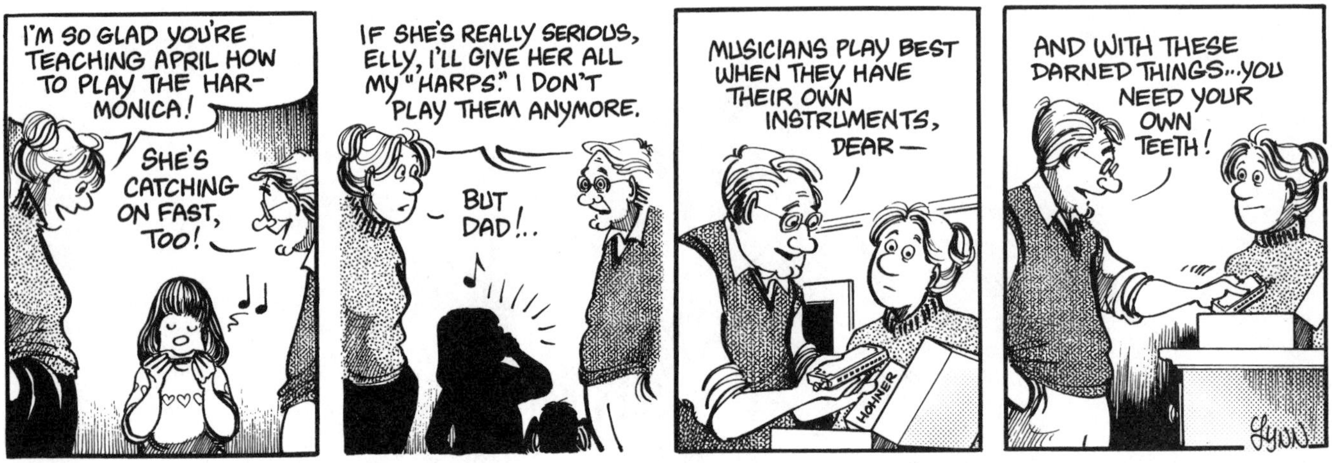
I'M SO GLAD YOU'RE TEACHING APRIL HOW TO PLAY THE HAR-MONICA!
SHE'S CATCHING ON FAST, TOO!
IF SHE'S REALLY SERIOUS, ELLY, I'LL GIVE HER ALL MY "HARPS." I DON'T PLAY THEM ANYMORE.
BUT DAD!..
MUSICIANS PLAY BEST WHEN THEY HAVE THEIR OWN INSTRUMENTS, DEAR —
HOHNER
AND WITH THESE DARNED THINGS...YOU NEED YOUR OWN TEETH!

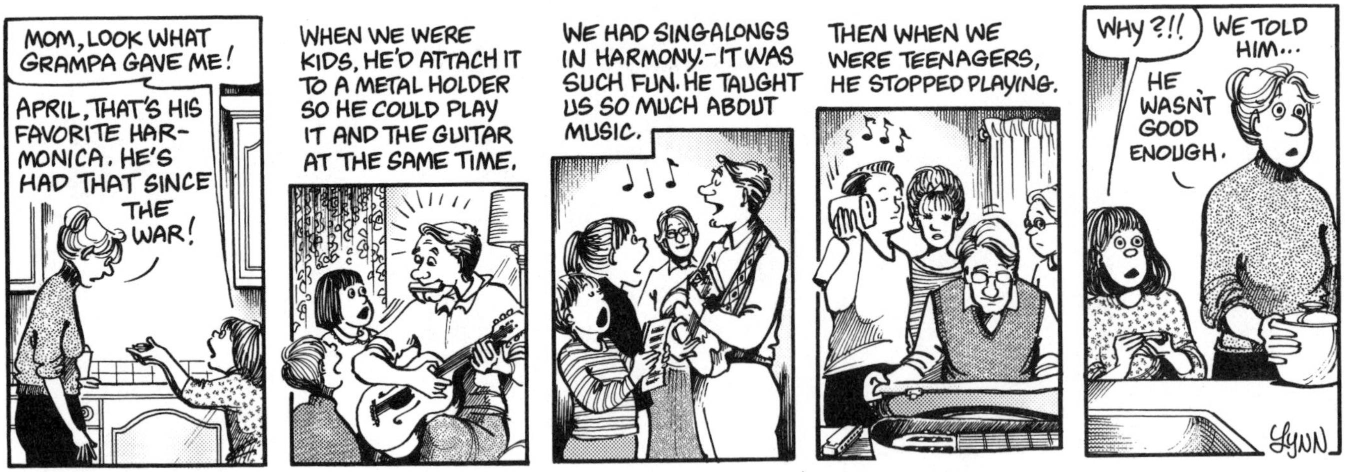
MOM, LOOK WHAT GRAMPA GAVE ME!
APRIL, THAT'S HIS FAVORITE HAR-MONICA. HE'S HAD THAT SINCE THE WAR!
WHEN WE WERE KIDS, HE'D ATTACH IT TO A METAL HOLDER SO HE COULD PLAY IT AND THE GUITAR AT THE SAME TIME.
WE HAD SING-ALONGS IN HARMONY.- IT WAS SUCH FUN. HE TAUGHT US SO MUCH ABOUT MUSIC.
THEN WHEN WE WERE TEENAGERS, HE STOPPED PLAYING.
WHY?!!
WE TOLD HIM...
HE WASN'T GOOD ENOUGH.

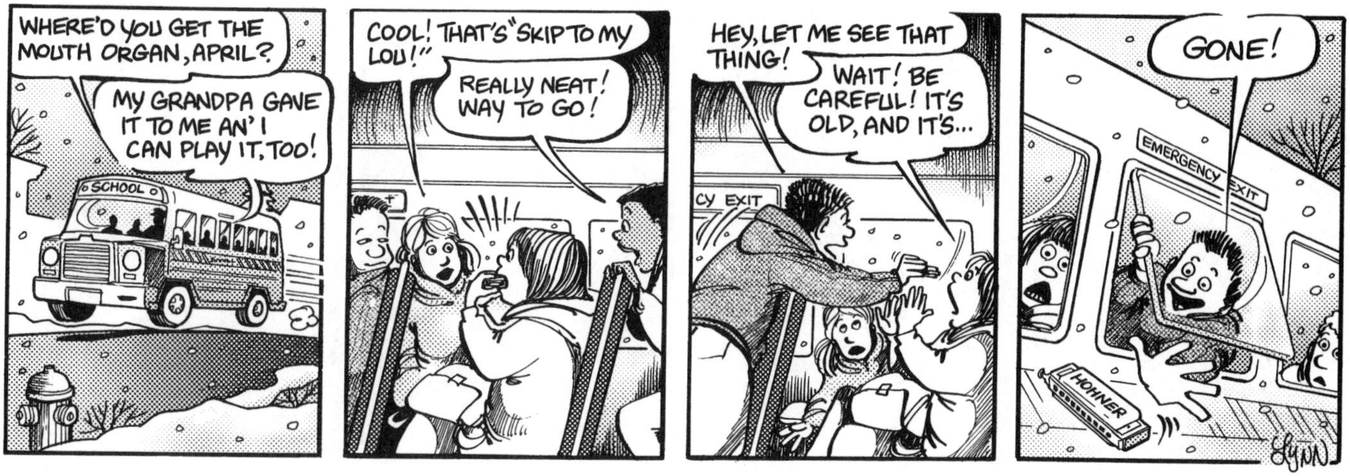
WHERE'D YOU GET THE MOUTH ORGAN, APRIL?
MY GRANDPA GAVE IT TO ME AN' I CAN PLAY IT, TOO!
SCHOOL
COOL! THAT'S "SKIP TO MY LOU!"
REALLY NEAT! WAY TO GO!
HEY, LET ME SEE THAT THING!
WAIT! BE CAREFUL! IT'S OLD, AND IT'S...
CY EXIT
GONE!
EMERGENCY EXIT
HOHNER
LYNN

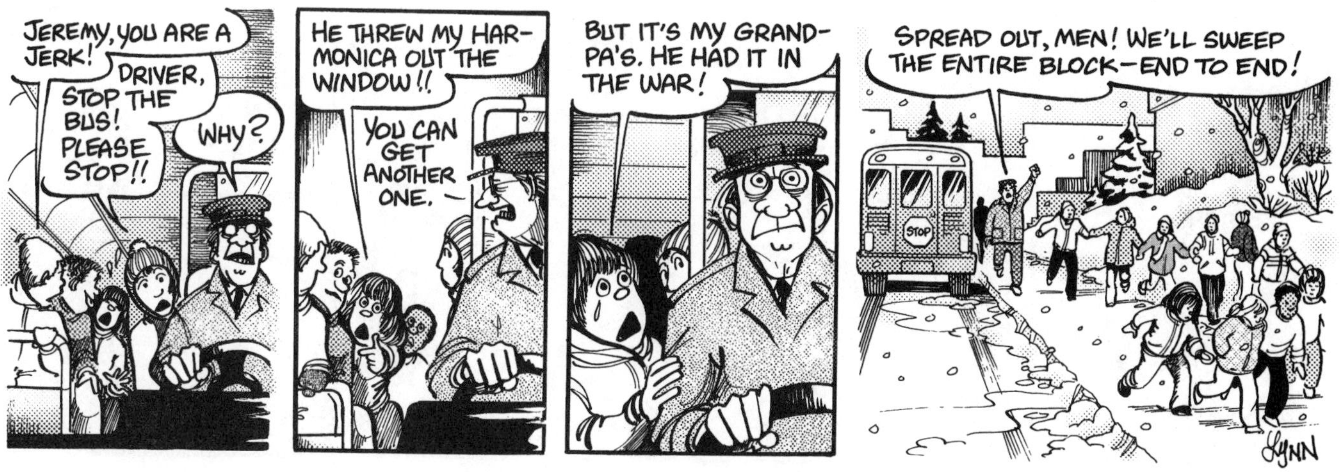
JEREMY, YOU ARE A JERK!
DRIVER, STOP THE BUS! PLEASE STOP!!
WHY?
HE THREW MY HARMONICA OUT THE WINDOW!!
YOU CAN GET ANOTHER ONE.
BUT IT'S MY GRANDPA'S. HE HAD IT IN THE WAR!
SPREAD OUT, MEN! WE'LL SWEEP THE ENTIRE BLOCK—END TO END!
STOP
LYNN

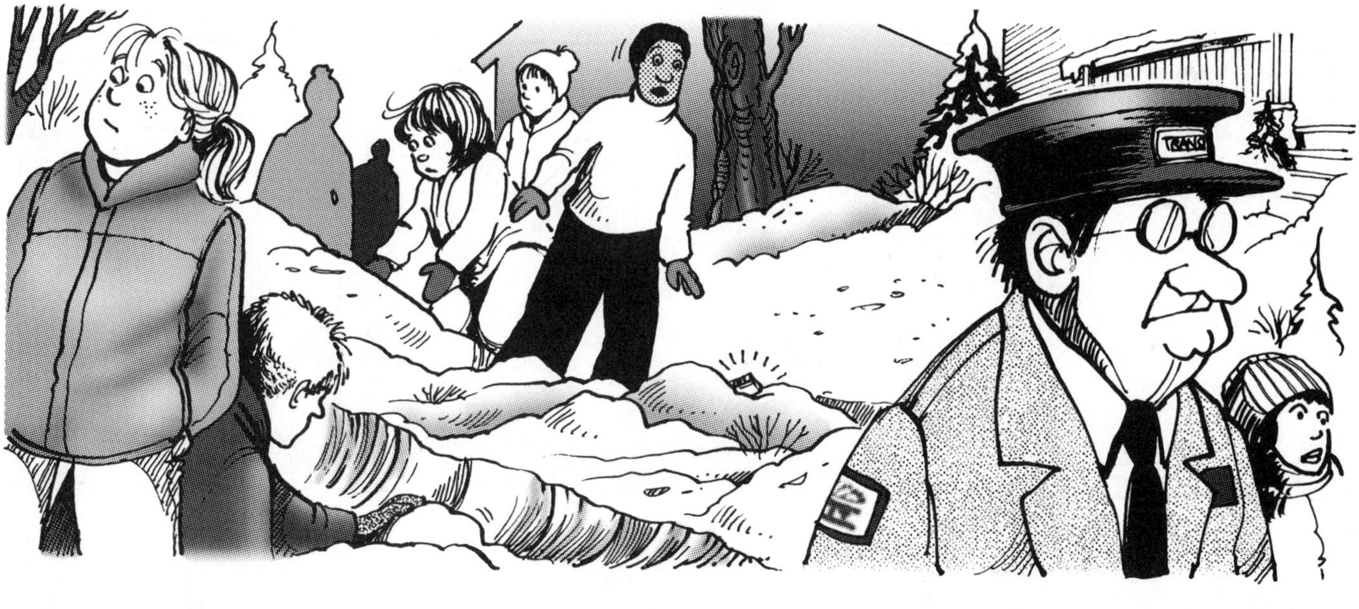

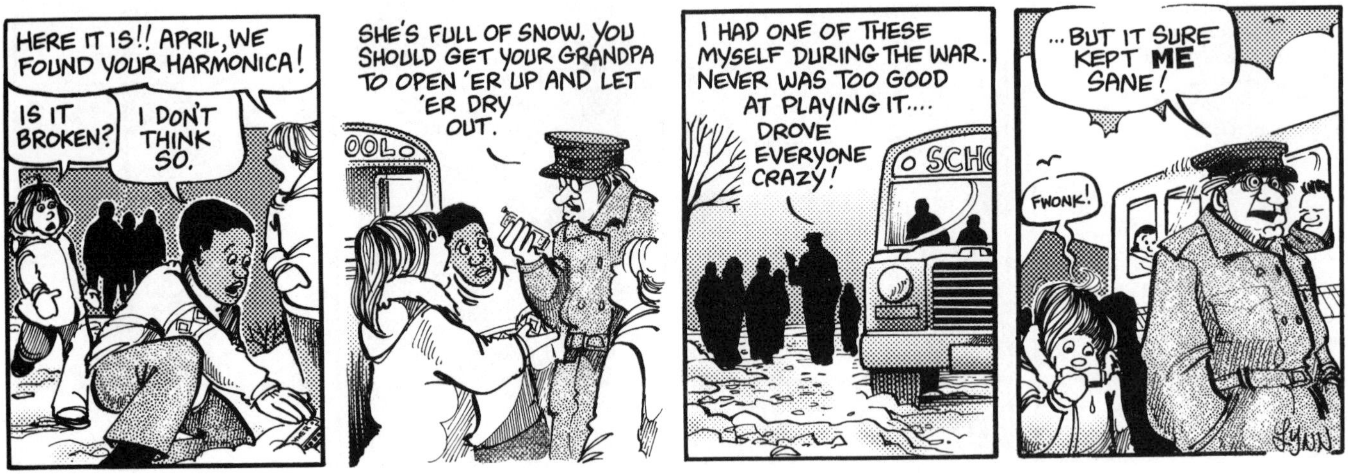
HERE IT IS!! APRIL, WE FOUND YOUR HARMONICA!
IS IT BROKEN?
I DON'T THINK SO.
SHE'S FULL OF SNOW. YOU SHOULD GET YOUR GRANDPA TO OPEN 'ER UP AND LET 'ER DRY OUT.
I HAD ONE OF THESE MYSELF DURING THE WAR. NEVER WAS TOO GOOD AT PLAYING IT....
DROVE EVERYONE CRAZY!
...BUT IT SURE KEPT ME SANE!
FWONK!
LYNN

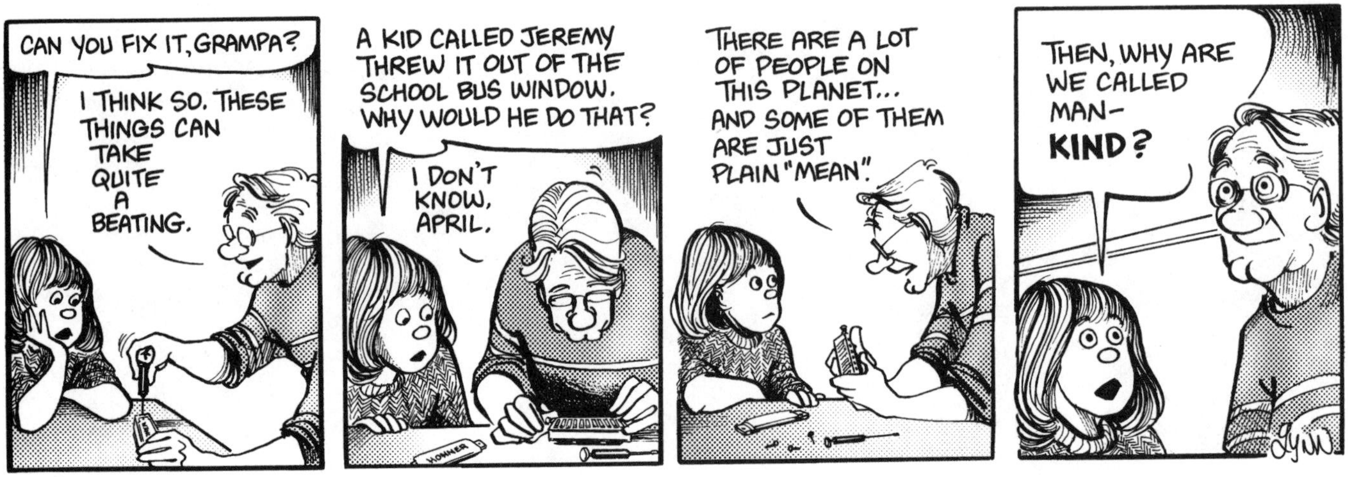
CAN YOU FIX IT, GRAMPA?
I THINK SO. THESE THINGS CAN TAKE QUITE A BEATING.
A KID CALLED JEREMY THREW IT OUT OF THE SCHOOL BUS WINDOW. WHY WOULD HE DO THAT?
I DON'T KNOW, APRIL.
THERE ARE A LOT OF PEOPLE ON THIS PLANET... AND SOME OF THEM ARE JUST PLAIN "MEAN".
THEN, WHY ARE WE CALLED MAN-KIND?
LYNN

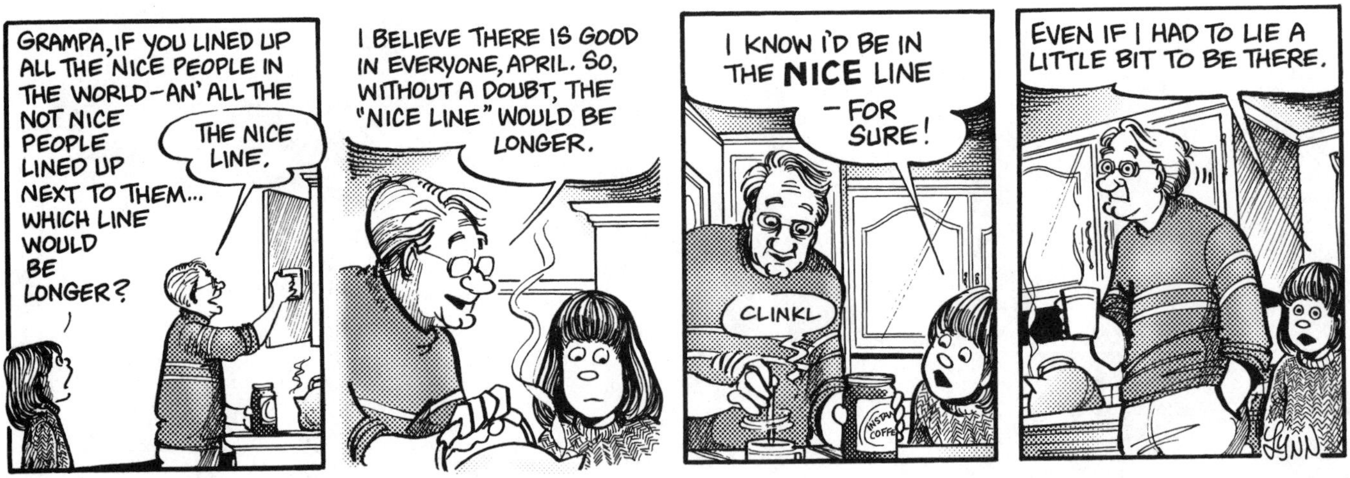
GRAMPA, IF YOU LINED UP ALL THE NICE PEOPLE IN THE WORLD–AN' ALL THE NOT NICE PEOPLE LINED UP NEXT TO THEM... WHICH LINE WOULD BE LONGER?
THE NICE LINE.
I BELIEVE THERE IS GOOD IN EVERYONE, APRIL. SO, WITHOUT A DOUBT, THE "NICE LINE" WOULD BE LONGER.
I KNOW I'D BE IN THE NICE LINE
–FOR SURE!
CLINKL
INSTANT COFFEE
EVEN IF I HAD TO LIE A LITTLE BIT TO BE THERE.
LYNN

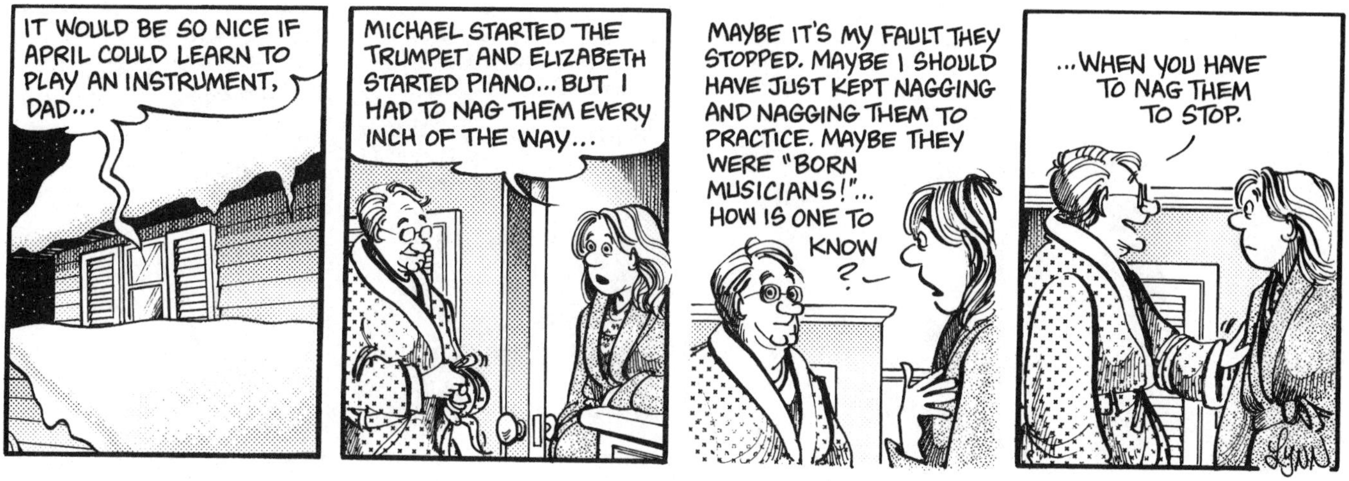
IT WOULD BE SO NICE IF APRIL COULD LEARN TO PLAY AN INSTRUMENT, DAD...
MICHAEL STARTED THE TRUMPET AND ELIZABETH STARTED PIANO... BUT I HAD TO NAG THEM EVERY INCH OF THE WAY...
MAYBE IT'S MY FAULT THEY STOPPED. MAYBE I SHOULD HAVE JUST KEPT NAGGING AND NAGGING THEM TO PRACTICE. MAYBE THEY WERE "BORN MUSICIANS!"... HOW IS ONE TO KNOW?
...WHEN YOU HAVE TO NAG THEM TO STOP.
LYNN

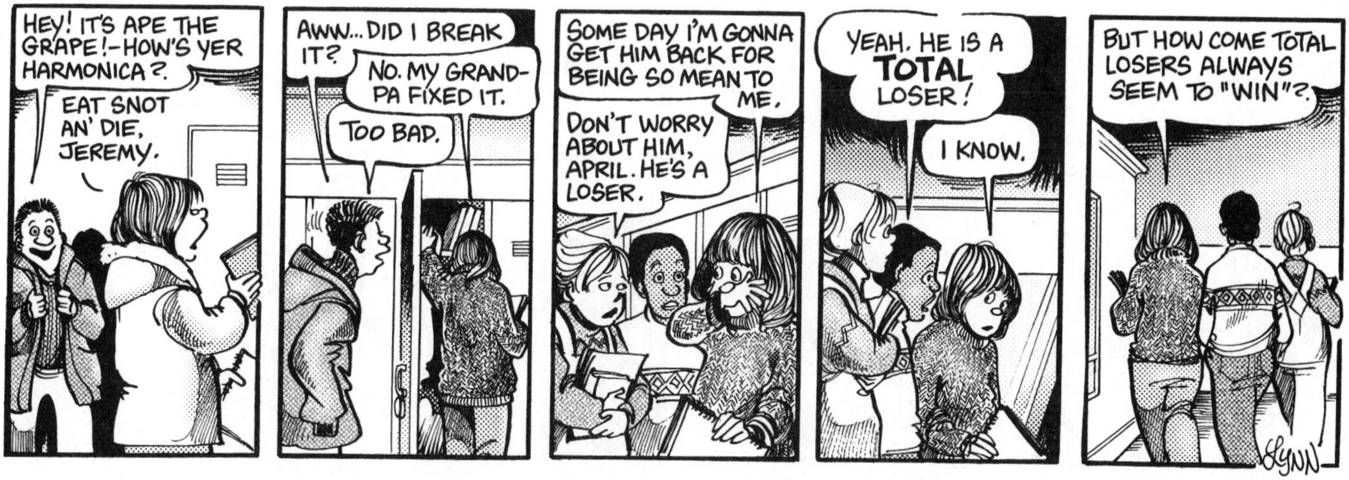
HEY! IT'S APE THE GRAPE!–HOW'S YER HARMONICA?
EAT SNOT AN' DIE, JEREMY.
AWW... DID I BREAK IT?
NO. MY GRAND-PA FIXED IT.
TOO BAD.
SOME DAY I'M GONNA GET HIM BACK FOR BEING SO MEAN TO ME.
DON'T WORRY ABOUT HIM, APRIL. HE'S A LOSER.
YEAH. HE IS A TOTAL LOSER!
I KNOW.
BUT HOW COME TOTAL LOSERS ALWAYS SEEM TO "WIN"?
LYNN

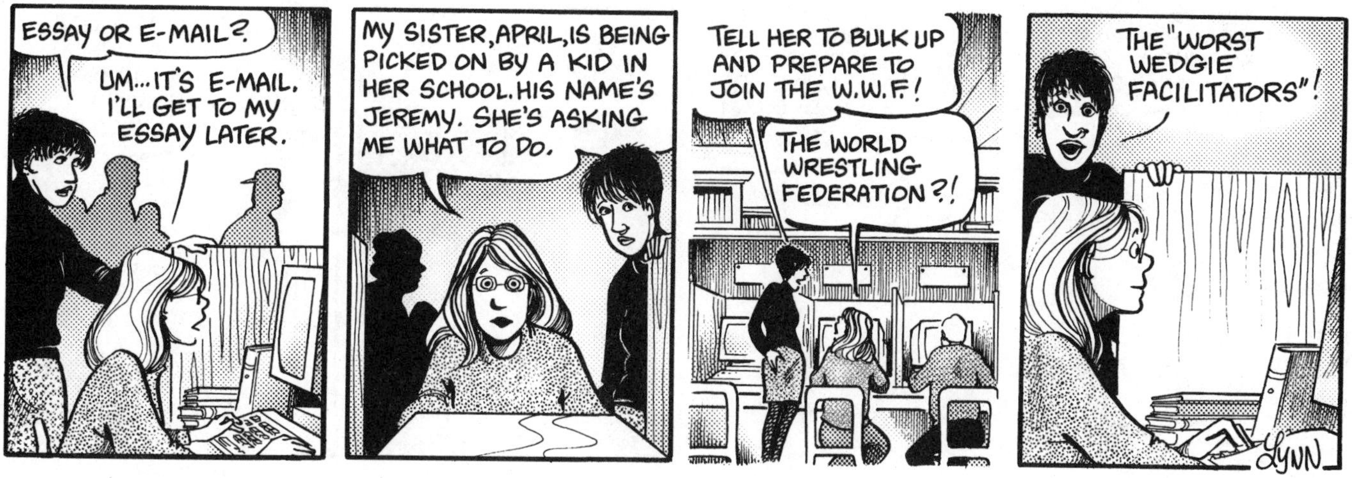
ESSAY OR E-MAIL?
UM... IT'S E-MAIL. I'LL GET TO MY ESSAY LATER.
MY SISTER, APRIL, IS BEING PICKED ON BY A KID IN HER SCHOOL. HIS NAME'S JEREMY. SHE'S ASKING ME WHAT TO DO.
TELL HER TO BULK UP AND PREPARE TO JOIN THE W.W.F!
THE WORLD WRESTLING FEDERATION?!
THE "WORST WEDGIE FACILITATORS"!
LYNN

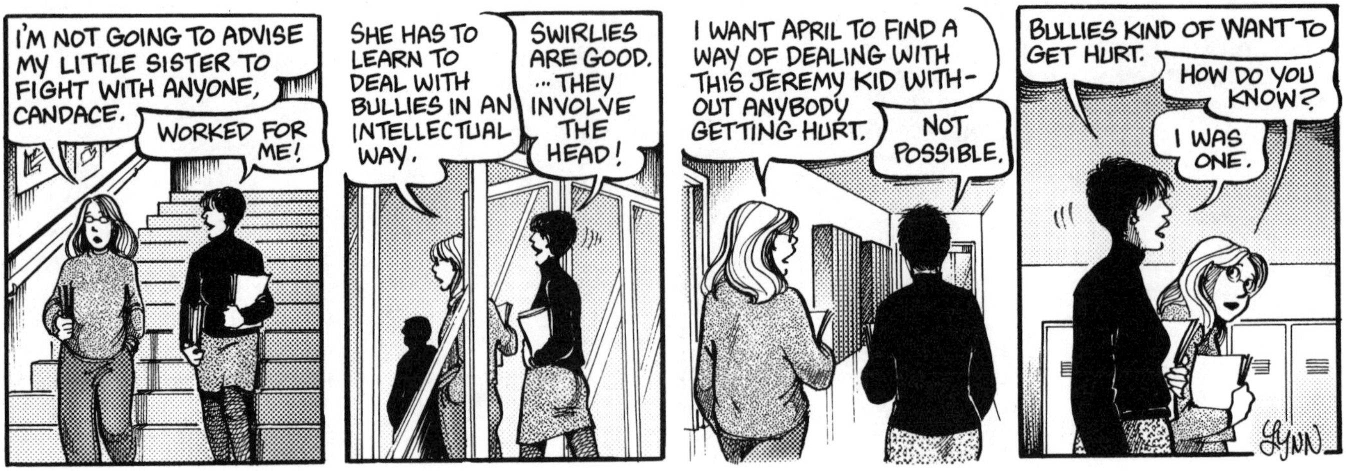
I'M NOT GOING TO ADVISE MY LITTLE SISTER TO FIGHT WITH ANYONE, CANDACE.
WORKED FOR ME!
SHE HAS TO LEARN TO DEAL WITH BULLIES IN AN INTELLECTUAL WAY.
SWIRLIES ARE GOOD. ...THEY INVOLVE THE HEAD!
I WANT APRIL TO FIND A WAY OF DEALING WITH THIS JEREMY KID WITHOUT ANYBODY GETTING HURT.
NOT POSSIBLE.
BULLIES KIND OF WANT TO GET HURT.
HOW DO YOU KNOW?
I WAS ONE.
LYNN

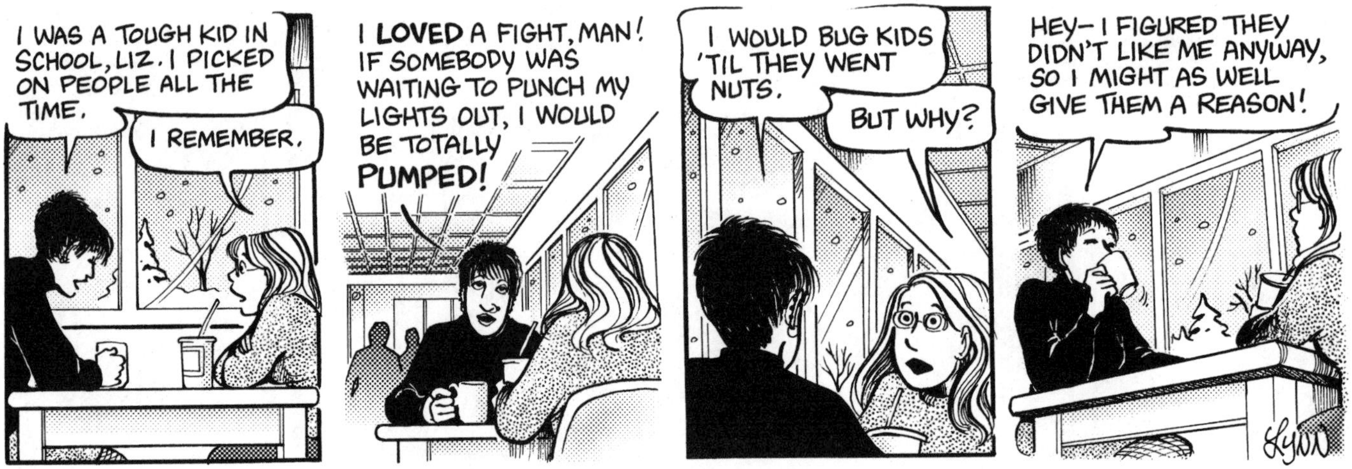
I WAS A TOUGH KID IN SCHOOL, LIZ. I PICKED ON PEOPLE ALL THE TIME.
I REMEMBER.
I LOVED A FIGHT, MAN! IF SOMEBODY WAS WAITING TO PUNCH MY LIGHTS OUT, I WOULD BE TOTALLY PUMPED!
I WOULD BUG KIDS 'TIL THEY WENT NUTS.
BUT WHY?
HEY– I FIGURED THEY DIDN'T LIKE ME ANYWAY, SO I MIGHT AS WELL GIVE THEM A REASON!
LYNN

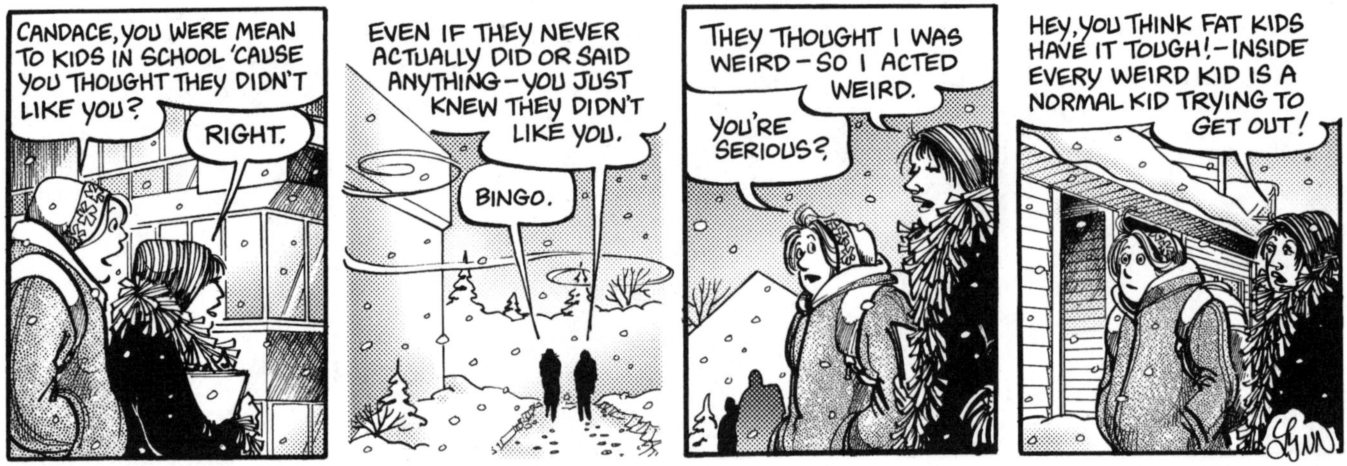
CANDACE, YOU WERE MEAN TO KIDS IN SCHOOL 'CAUSE YOU THOUGHT THEY DIDN'T LIKE YOU?
RIGHT.
EVEN IF THEY NEVER ACTUALLY DID OR SAID ANYTHING – YOU JUST KNEW THEY DIDN'T LIKE YOU.
BINGO.
THEY THOUGHT I WAS WEIRD – SO I ACTED WEIRD.
YOU'RE SERIOUS?
HEY, YOU THINK FAT KIDS HAVE IT TOUGH! – INSIDE EVERY WEIRD KID IS A NORMAL KID TRYING TO GET OUT!
LYNN

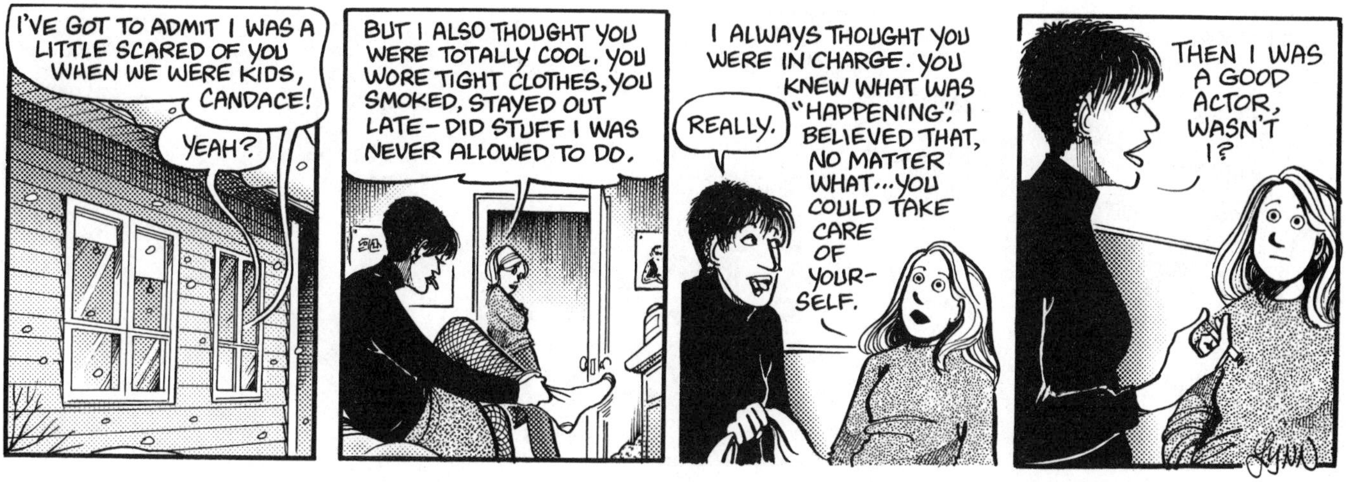
I'VE GOT TO ADMIT I WAS A LITTLE SCARED OF YOU WHEN WE WERE KIDS, CANDACE!
YEAH?
BUT I ALSO THOUGHT YOU WERE TOTALLY COOL. YOU WORE TIGHT CLOTHES, YOU SMOKED, STAYED OUT LATE – DID STUFF I WAS NEVER ALLOWED TO DO.
I ALWAYS THOUGHT YOU WERE IN CHARGE. YOU KNEW WHAT WAS "HAPPENING". I BELIEVED THAT, NO MATTER WHAT... YOU COULD TAKE CARE OF YOURSELF.
REALLY.
THEN I WAS A GOOD ACTOR, WASN'T I?
LYNN

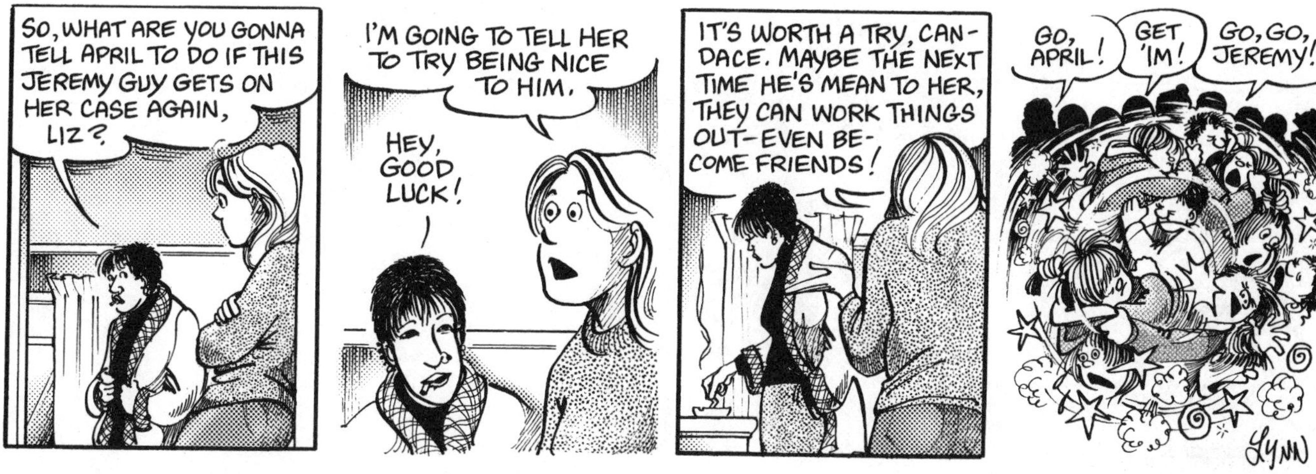
SO, WHAT ARE YOU GONNA TELL APRIL TO DO IF THIS JEREMY GUY GETS ON HER CASE AGAIN, LIZ?
I'M GOING TO TELL HER TO TRY BEING NICE TO HIM.
HEY, GOOD LUCK!
IT'S WORTH A TRY, CANDACE. MAYBE THE NEXT TIME HE'S MEAN TO HER, THEY CAN WORK THINGS OUT – EVEN BECOME FRIENDS!
GO, APRIL!
GET 'IM!
GO, GO, JEREMY!
LYNN

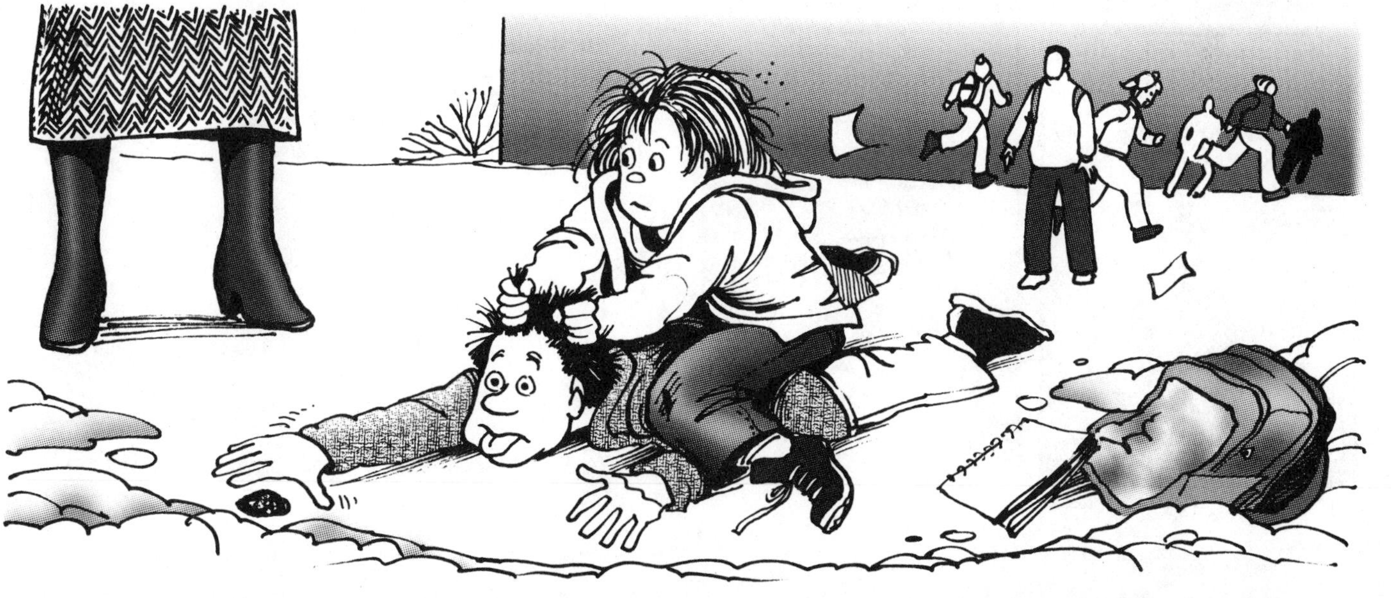

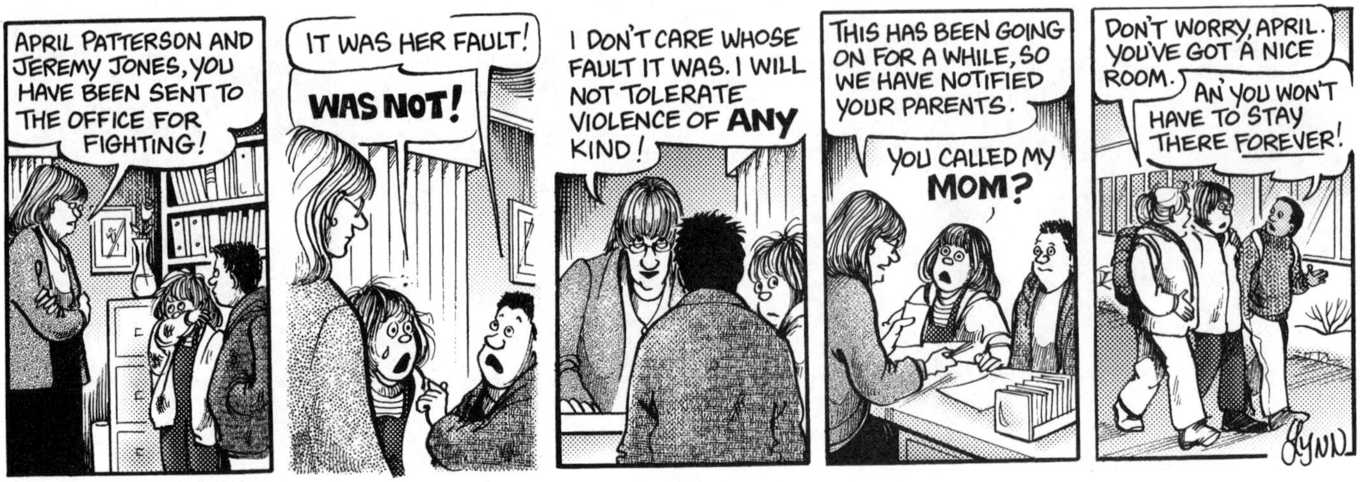
APRIL PATTERSON AND JEREMY JONES, YOU HAVE BEEN SENT TO THE OFFICE FOR FIGHTING!
IT WAS HER FAULT!
WAS NOT!
I DON'T CARE WHOSE FAULT IT WAS. I WILL NOT TOLERATE VIOLENCE OF ANY KIND!
THIS HAS BEEN GOING ON FOR A WHILE, SO WE HAVE NOTIFIED YOUR PARENTS.
YOU CALLED MY MOM?
DON'T WORRY, APRIL. YOU'VE GOT A NICE ROOM.
AN' YOU WON'T HAVE TO STAY THERE FOREVER!
LYNN

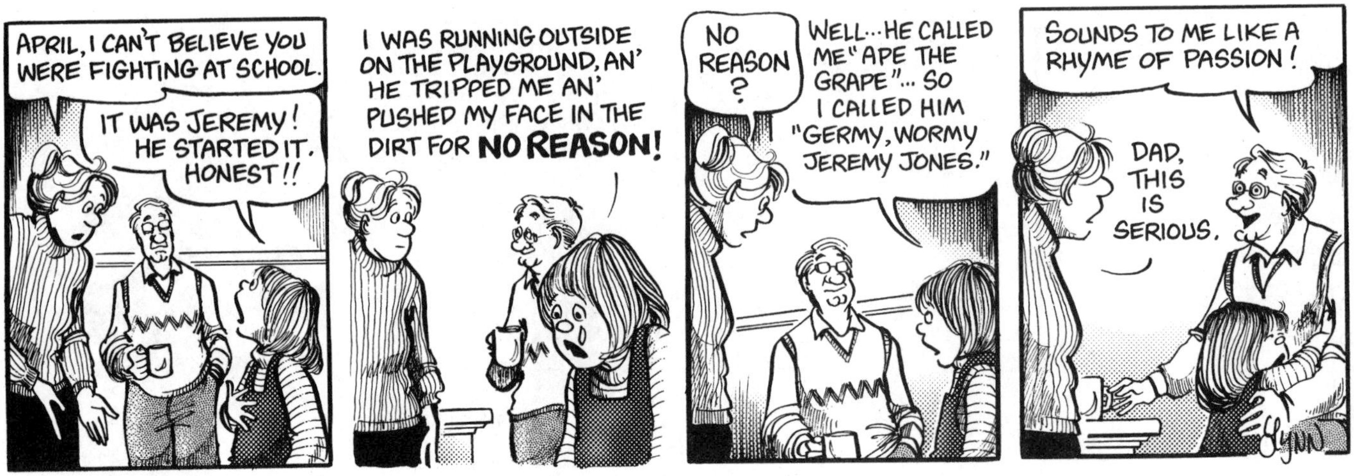
APRIL, I CAN'T BELIEVE YOU WERE FIGHTING AT SCHOOL.
IT WAS JEREMY! HE STARTED IT. HONEST!!
I WAS RUNNING OUTSIDE ON THE PLAYGROUND, AN' HE TRIPPED ME AN' PUSHED MY FACE IN THE DIRT FOR NO REASON!
NO REASON?
WELL... HE CALLED ME "APE THE GRAPE"... SO I CALLED HIM "GERMY, WORMY JEREMY JONES."
SOUNDS TO ME LIKE A RHYME OF PASSION!
DAD, THIS IS SERIOUS.
LYNN

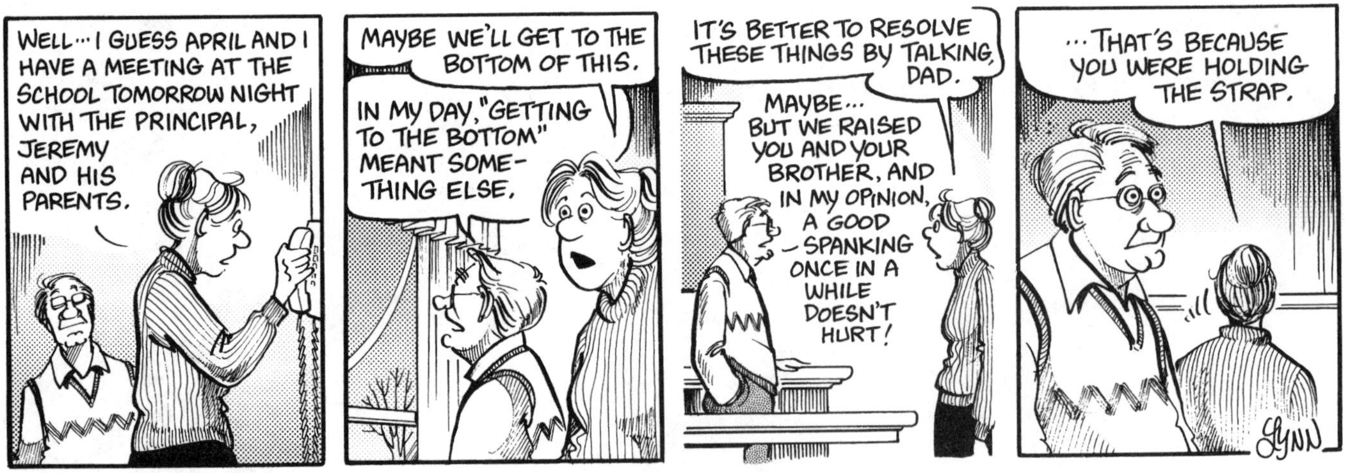
WELL... I GUESS APRIL AND I HAVE A MEETING AT THE SCHOOL TOMORROW NIGHT WITH THE PRINCIPAL, JEREMY AND HIS PARENTS.
MAYBE WE'LL GET TO THE BOTTOM OF THIS.
IN MY DAY, "GETTING TO THE BOTTOM" MEANT SOMETHING ELSE.
IT'S BETTER TO RESOLVE THESE THINGS BY TALKING, DAD.
MAYBE... BUT WE RAISED YOU AND YOUR BROTHER, AND IN MY OPINION, A GOOD SPANKING ONCE IN A WHILE DOESN'T HURT!
...THAT'S BECAUSE YOU WERE HOLDING THE STRAP.
LYNN

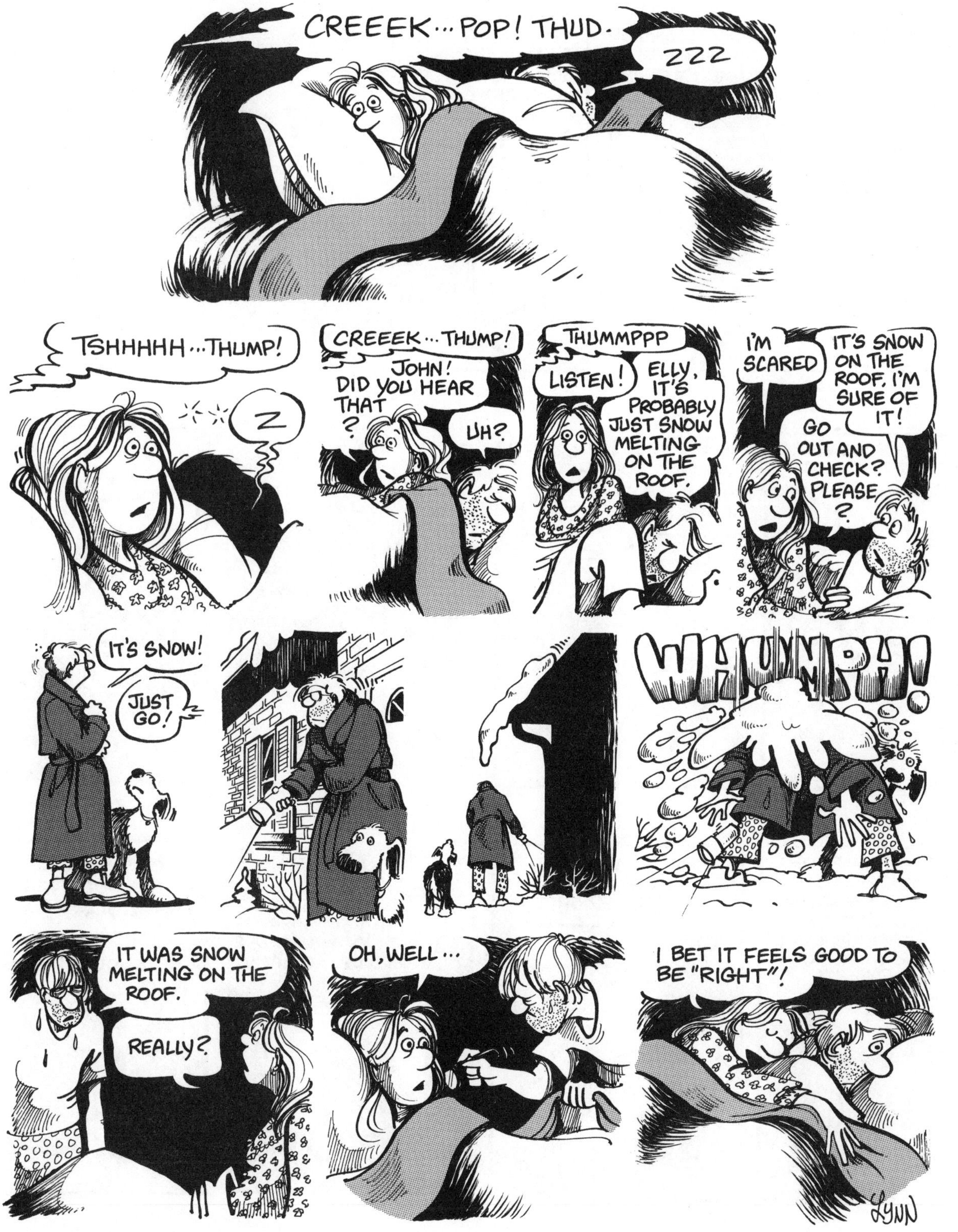
CREEEK...POP! THUD.
ZZZ
TSHHHHH...THUMP!
Z
CREEEK...THUMP!
JOHN! DID YOU HEAR THAT?
UH?
THUMMPPP
LISTEN!
ELLY, IT'S PROBABLY JUST SNOW MELTING ON THE ROOF.
I'M SCARED
IT'S SNOW ON THE ROOF. I'M SURE OF IT!
GO OUT AND CHECK? PLEASE?
IT'S SNOW!
JUST GO!
WHUUMPH!
IT WAS SNOW MELTING ON THE ROOF.
REALLY?
OH, WELL...
I BET IT FEELS GOOD TO BE "RIGHT"!
LYNN

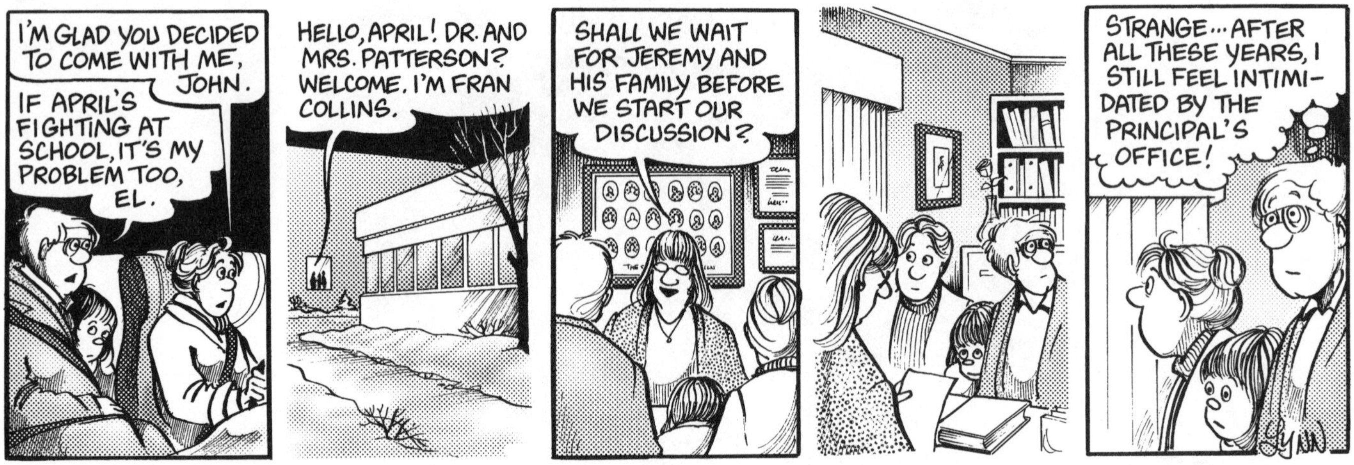
I'M GLAD YOU DECIDED TO COME WITH ME, JOHN.
IF APRIL'S FIGHTING AT SCHOOL, IT'S MY PROBLEM TOO, EL.
HELLO, APRIL! DR. AND MRS. PATTERSON? WELCOME. I'M FRAN COLLINS.
SHALL WE WAIT FOR JEREMY AND HIS FAMILY BEFORE WE START OUR DISCUSSION?
STRANGE... AFTER ALL THESE YEARS, I STILL FEEL INTIMIDATED BY THE PRINCIPAL'S OFFICE!
LYNN

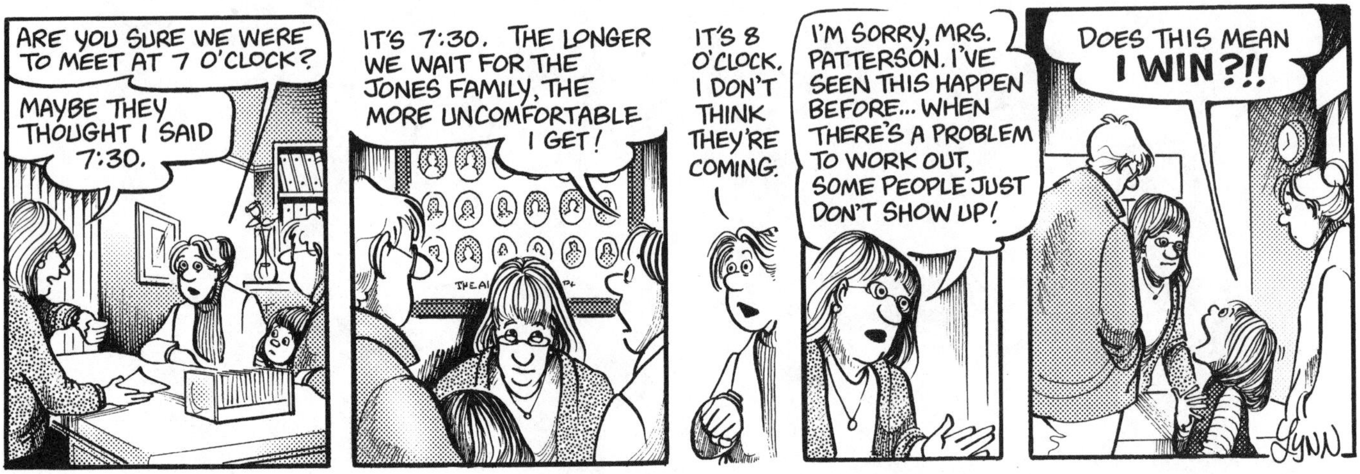
ARE YOU SURE WE WERE TO MEET AT 7 O'CLOCK?
MAYBE THEY THOUGHT I SAID 7:30.
IT'S 7:30. THE LONGER WE WAIT FOR THE JONES FAMILY, THE MORE UNCOMFORTABLE I GET!
IT'S 8 O'CLOCK. I DON'T THINK THEY'RE COMING.
I'M SORRY, MRS. PATTERSON. I'VE SEEN THIS HAPPEN BEFORE... WHEN THERE'S A PROBLEM TO WORK OUT, SOME PEOPLE JUST DON'T SHOW UP!
DOES THIS MEAN I WIN?!!
LYNN

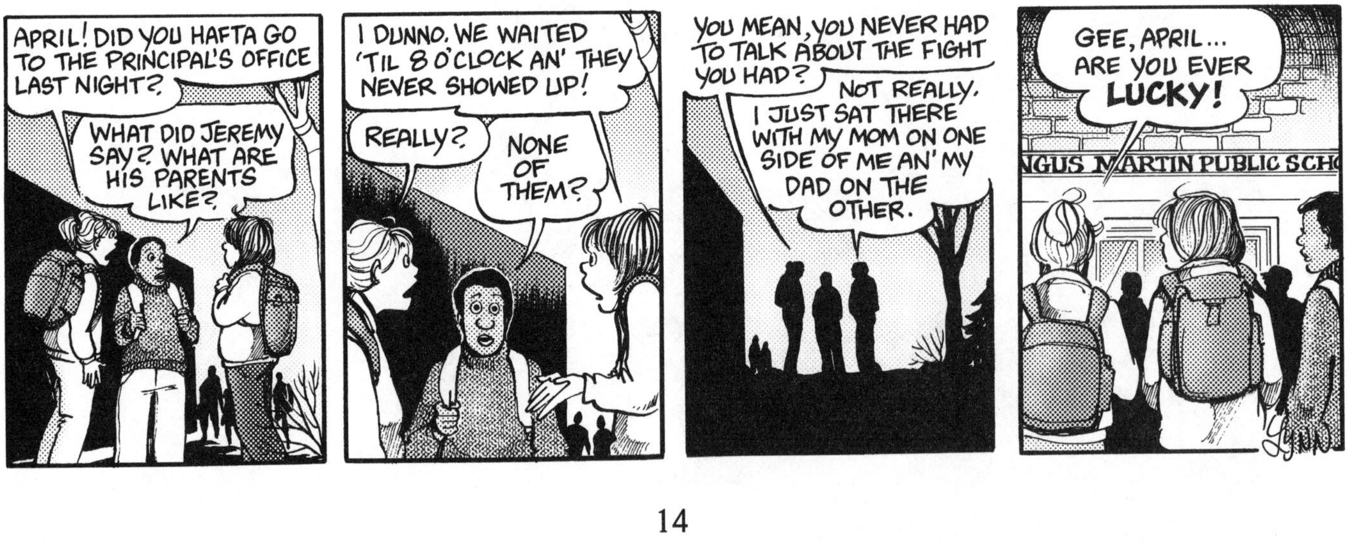
APRIL! DID YOU HAFTA GO TO THE PRINCIPAL'S OFFICE LAST NIGHT?
WHAT DID JEREMY SAY? WHAT ARE HIS PARENTS LIKE?
I DUNNO. WE WAITED 'TIL 8 O'CLOCK AN' THEY NEVER SHOWED UP!
REALLY?
NONE OF THEM?
YOU MEAN, YOU NEVER HAD TO TALK ABOUT THE FIGHT YOU HAD?
NOT REALLY. I JUST SAT THERE WITH MY MOM ON ONE SIDE OF ME AN' MY DAD ON THE OTHER.
GEE, APRIL... ARE YOU EVER LUCKY!
NGUS MARTIN PUBLIC SCH
LYNN

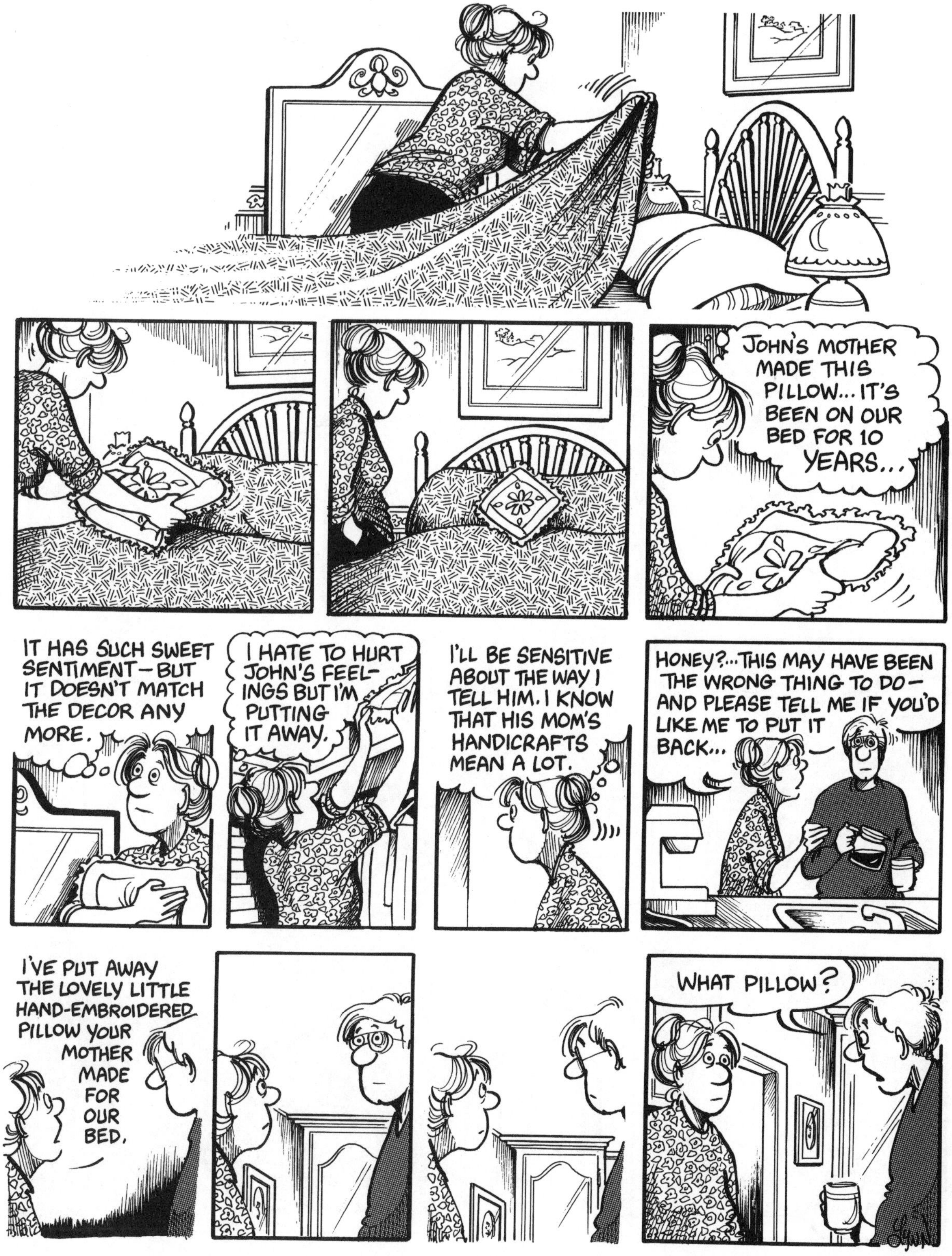

JOHN'S MOTHER MADE THIS PILLOW... IT'S BEEN ON OUR BED FOR 10 YEARS...
IT HAS SUCH SWEET SENTIMENT—BUT IT DOESN'T MATCH THE DECOR ANY MORE.
I HATE TO HURT JOHN'S FEEL-INGS BUT I'M PUTTING IT AWAY.
I'LL BE SENSITIVE ABOUT THE WAY I TELL HIM. I KNOW THAT HIS MOM'S HANDICRAFTS MEAN A LOT.
HONEY?...THIS MAY HAVE BEEN THE WRONG THING TO DO—AND PLEASE TELL ME IF YOU'D LIKE ME TO PUT IT BACK...
I'VE PUT AWAY THE LOVELY LITTLE HAND-EMBROIDERED PILLOW YOUR MOTHER MADE FOR OUR BED.
WHAT PILLOW?

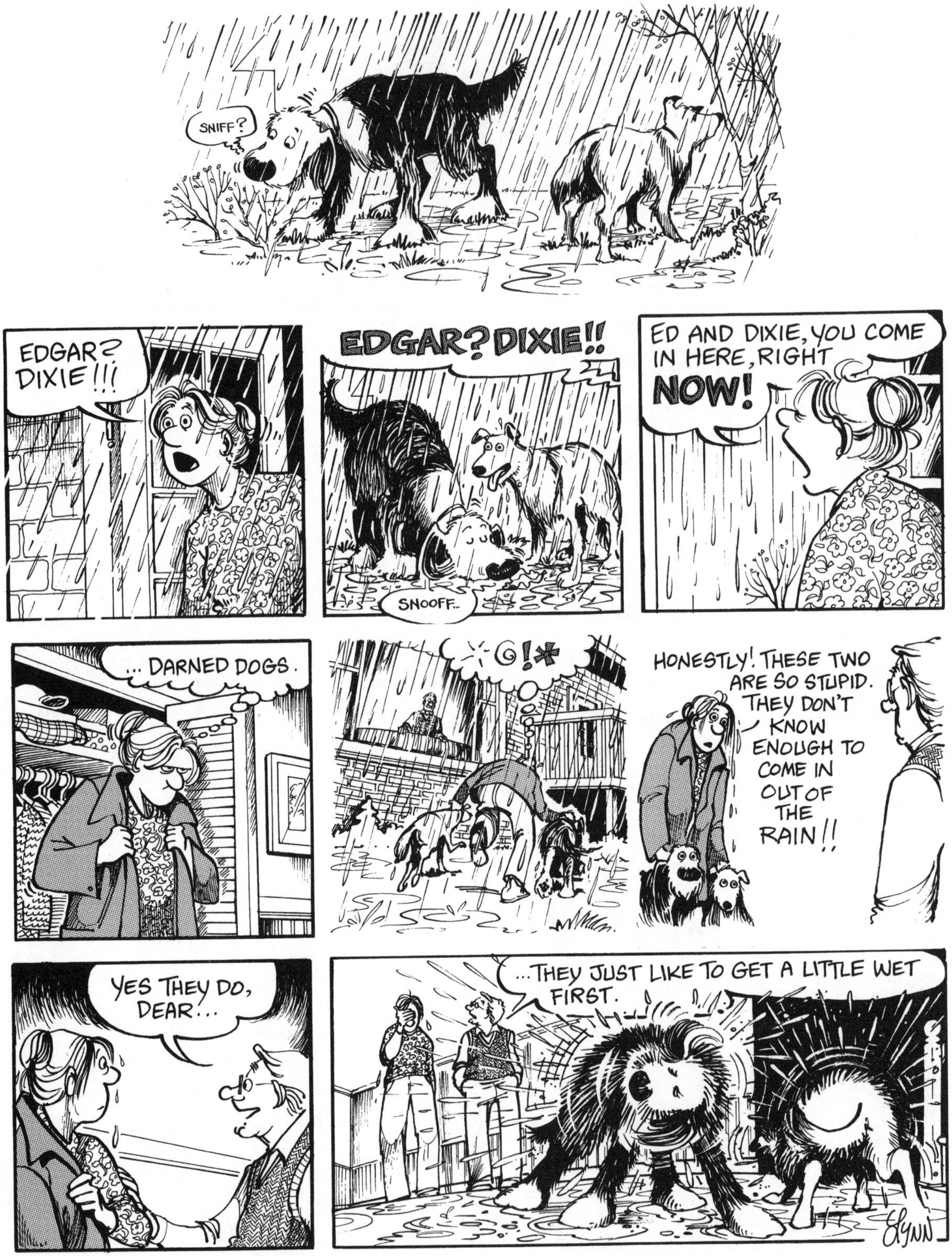
SNIFF?
EDGAR? DIXIE!!!
EDGAR? DIXIE!!
SNOOFF..
ED AND DIXIE, YOU COME IN HERE, RIGHT NOW!
... DARNED DOGS.
!*
HONESTLY! THESE TWO ARE SO STUPID. THEY DON'T KNOW ENOUGH TO COME IN OUT OF THE RAIN!!
YES THEY DO, DEAR...
...THEY JUST LIKE TO GET A LITTLE WET FIRST.
LYNN

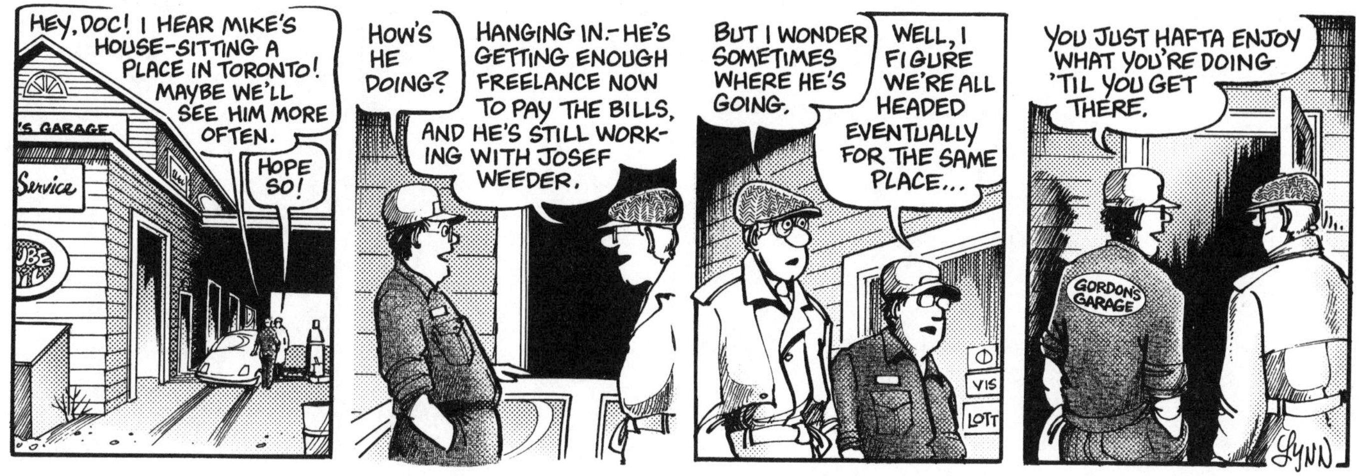

HEY, DOC! I HEAR MIKE'S HOUSE-SITTING A PLACE IN TORONTO! MAYBE WE'LL SEE HIM MORE OFTEN.
HOPE SO!
Service
HOW'S HE DOING?
HANGING IN.- HE'S GETTING ENOUGH FREELANCE NOW TO PAY THE BILLS, AND HE'S STILL WORKING WITH JOSEF WEEDER.
BUT I WONDER SOMETIMES WHERE HE'S GOING.
WELL, I FIGURE WE'RE ALL HEADED EVENTUALLY FOR THE SAME PLACE...
YOU JUST HAFTA ENJOY WHAT YOU'RE DOING 'TIL YOU GET THERE.
GORDON'S GARAGE
LYNN

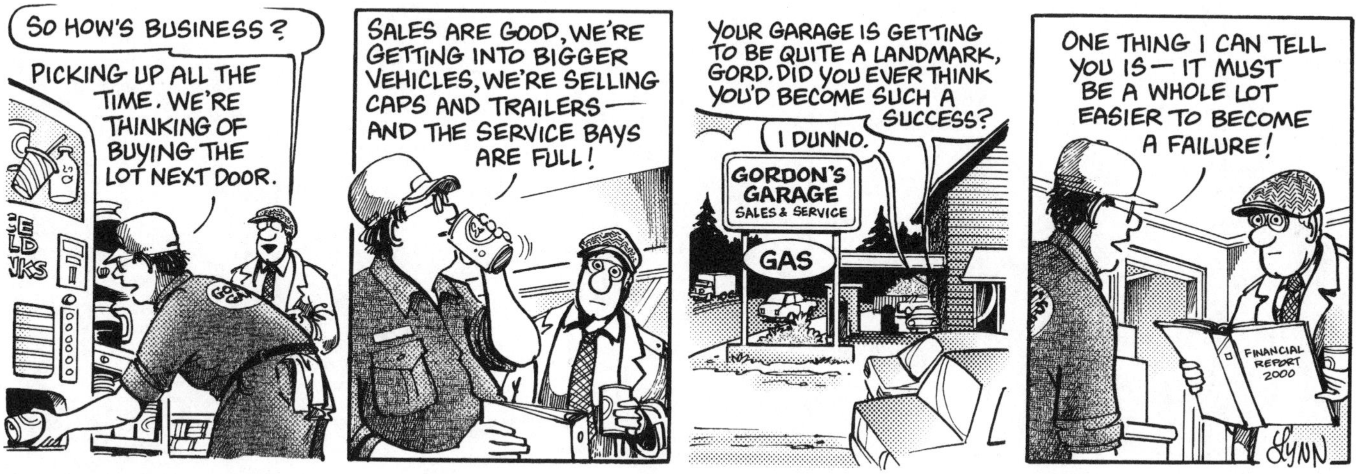

SO HOW'S BUSINESS?
PICKING UP ALL THE TIME. WE'RE THINKING OF BUYING THE LOT NEXT DOOR.
SALES ARE GOOD, WE'RE GETTING INTO BIGGER VEHICLES, WE'RE SELLING CAPS AND TRAILERS— AND THE SERVICE BAYS ARE FULL!
YOUR GARAGE IS GETTING TO BE QUITE A LANDMARK, GORD. DID YOU EVER THINK YOU'D BECOME SUCH A SUCCESS?
I DUNNO.
GORDON'S GARAGE
SALES & SERVICE
GAS
ONE THING I CAN TELL YOU IS— IT MUST BE A WHOLE LOT EASIER TO BECOME A FAILURE!
FINANCIAL REPORT 2000
LYNN

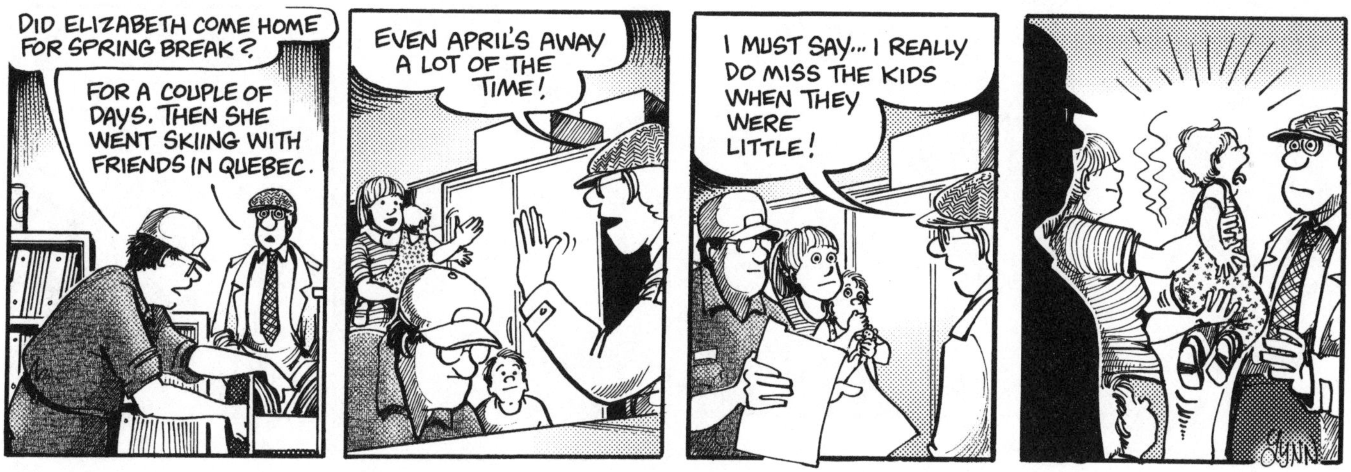

DID ELIZABETH COME HOME FOR SPRING BREAK?
FOR A COUPLE OF DAYS. THEN SHE WENT SKIING WITH FRIENDS IN QUEBEC.
EVEN APRIL'S AWAY A LOT OF THE TIME!
I MUST SAY... I REALLY DO MISS THE KIDS WHEN THEY WERE LITTLE!
LYNN

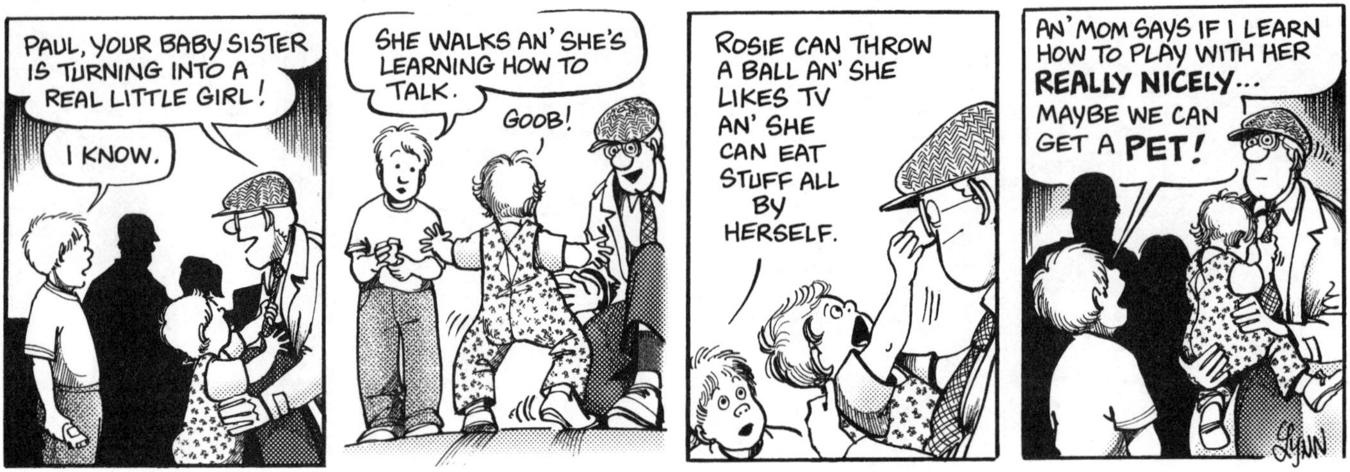
PAUL, YOUR BABY SISTER IS TURNING INTO A REAL LITTLE GIRL!
I KNOW.
SHE WALKS AN' SHE'S LEARNING HOW TO TALK.
GOOB!
ROSIE CAN THROW A BALL AN' SHE LIKES TV AN' SHE CAN EAT STUFF ALL BY HERSELF.
AN' MOM SAYS IF I LEARN HOW TO PLAY WITH HER **REALLY NICELY**... MAYBE WE CAN GET A **PET!**
LYNN

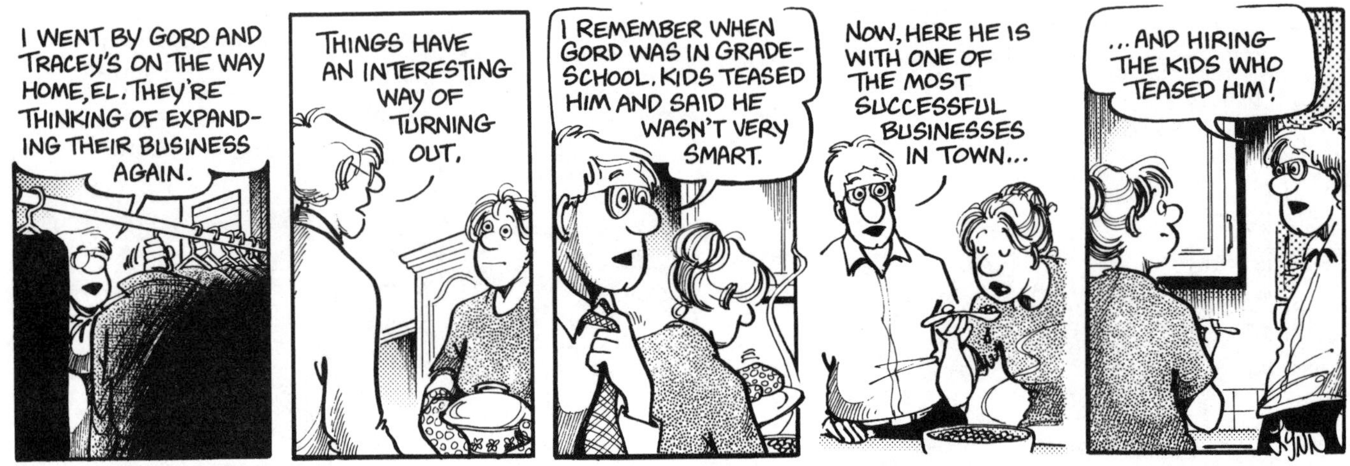
I WENT BY GORD AND TRACEY'S ON THE WAY HOME, EL. THEY'RE THINKING OF EXPANDING THEIR BUSINESS AGAIN.
THINGS HAVE AN INTERESTING WAY OF TURNING OUT.
I REMEMBER WHEN GORD WAS IN GRADE-SCHOOL. KIDS TEASED HIM AND SAID HE WASN'T VERY SMART.
NOW, HERE HE IS WITH ONE OF THE MOST SUCCESSFUL BUSINESSES IN TOWN...
...AND HIRING THE KIDS WHO TEASED HIM!
LYNN

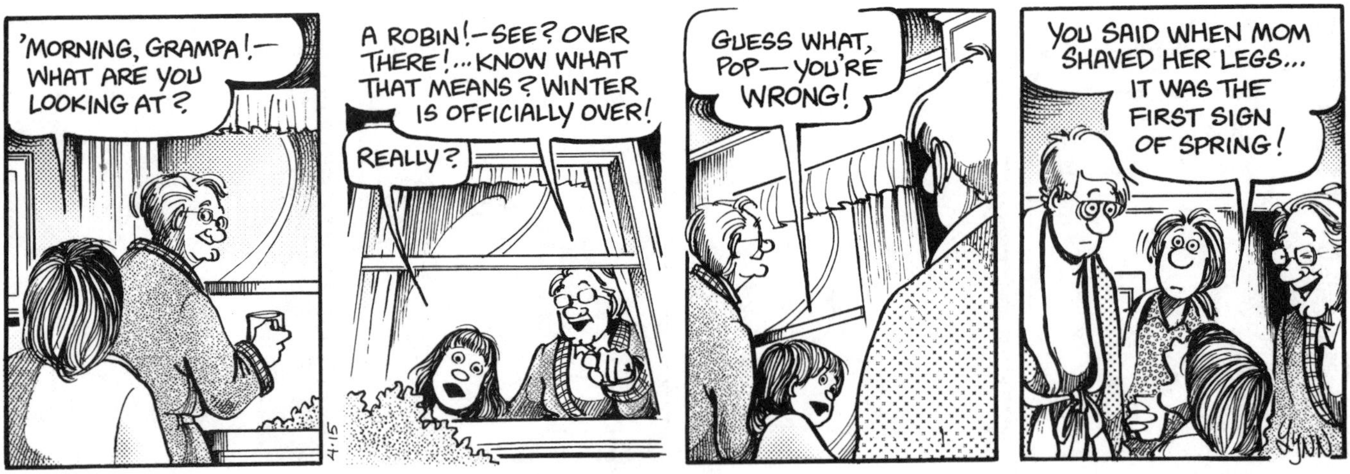
'MORNING, GRAMPA!— WHAT ARE YOU LOOKING AT?
A ROBIN!—SEE? OVER THERE!... KNOW WHAT THAT MEANS? WINTER IS OFFICIALLY OVER!
REALLY?
4-15
GUESS WHAT, POP— YOU'RE WRONG!
YOU SAID WHEN MOM SHAVED HER LEGS... IT WAS THE FIRST SIGN OF SPRING!
LYNN

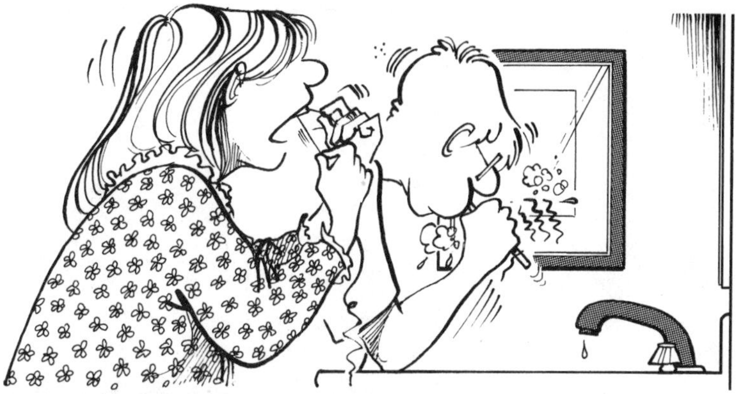

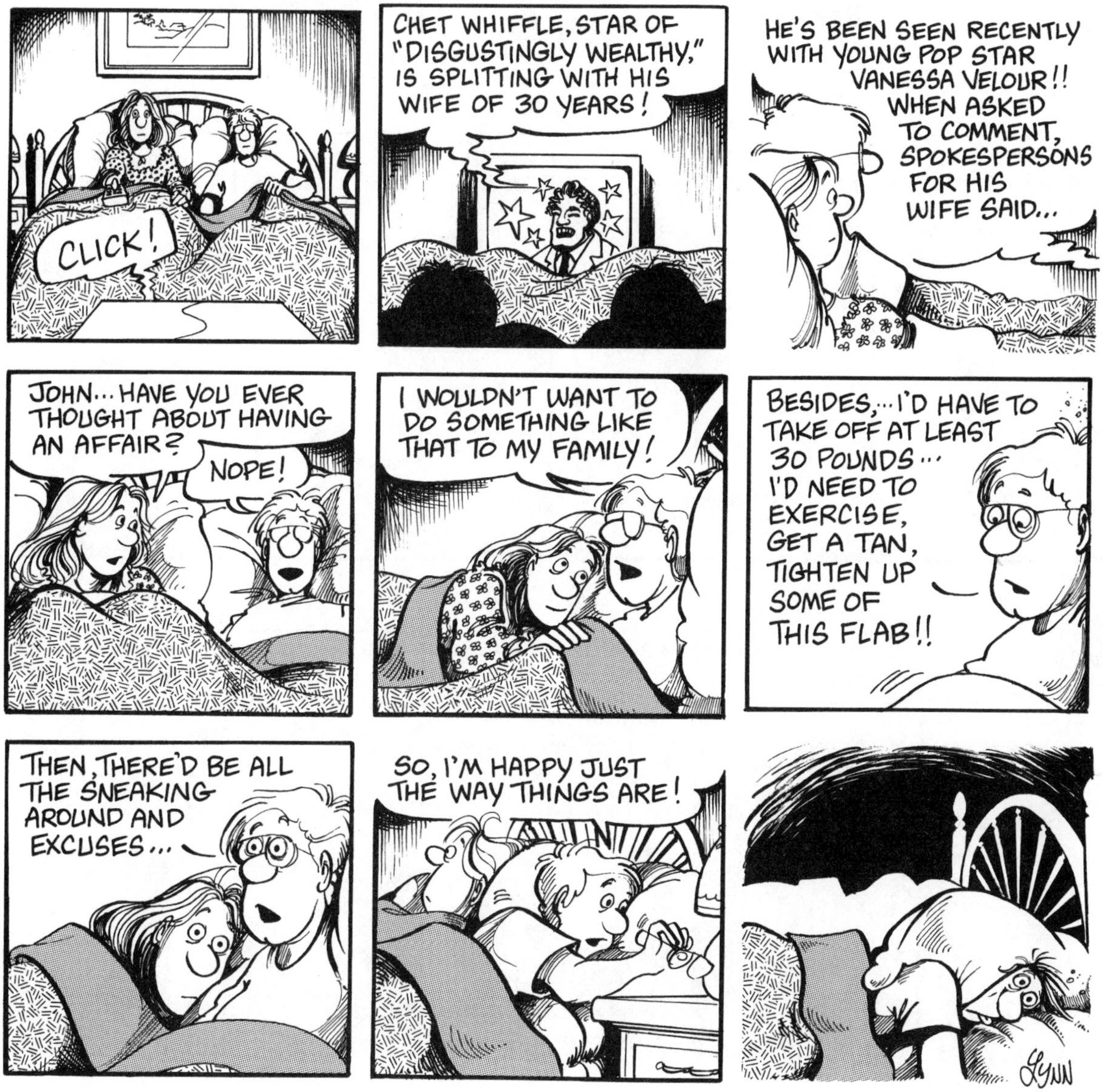

CLICK!
CHET WHIFFLE, STAR OF "DISGUSTINGLY WEALTHY," IS SPLITTING WITH HIS WIFE OF 30 YEARS!
HE'S BEEN SEEN RECENTLY WITH YOUNG POP STAR VANESSA VELOUR!! WHEN ASKED TO COMMENT, SPOKESPERSONS FOR HIS WIFE SAID...
JOHN... HAVE YOU EVER THOUGHT ABOUT HAVING AN AFFAIR?
NOPE!
I WOULDN'T WANT TO DO SOMETHING LIKE THAT TO MY FAMILY!
BESIDES,... I'D HAVE TO TAKE OFF AT LEAST 30 POUNDS... I'D NEED TO EXERCISE, GET A TAN, TIGHTEN UP SOME OF THIS FLAB!!
THEN, THERE'D BE ALL THE SNEAKING AROUND AND EXCUSES...
SO, I'M HAPPY JUST THE WAY THINGS ARE!
LYNN

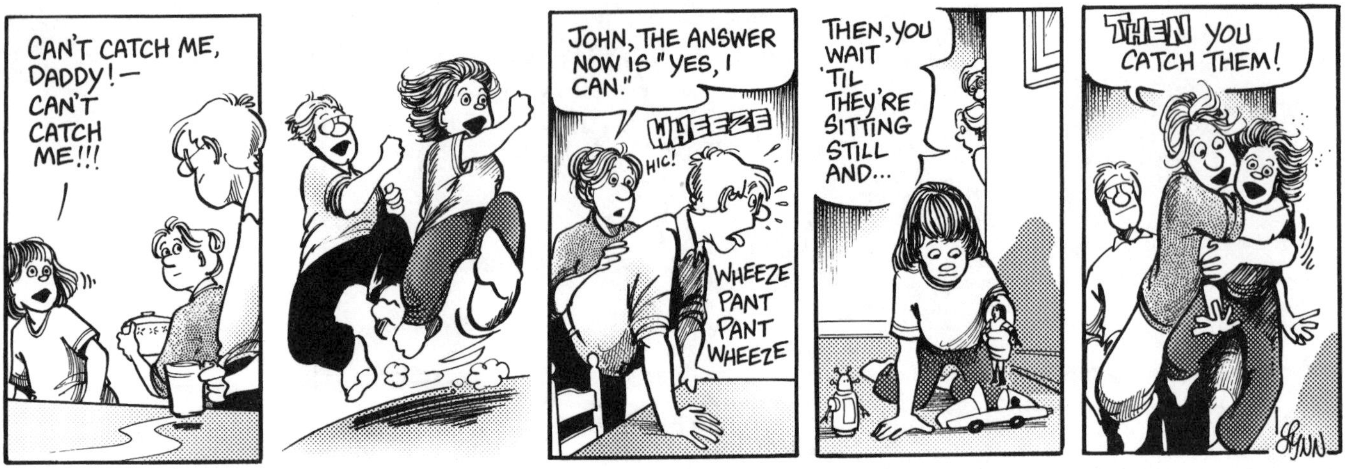
CAN'T CATCH ME, DADDY!— CAN'T CATCH ME!!!
JOHN, THE ANSWER NOW IS "YES, I CAN."
WHEEZE
HIC!
WHEEZE PANT PANT WHEEZE
THEN, YOU WAIT 'TIL THEY'RE SITTING STILL AND...
THEN YOU CATCH THEM!

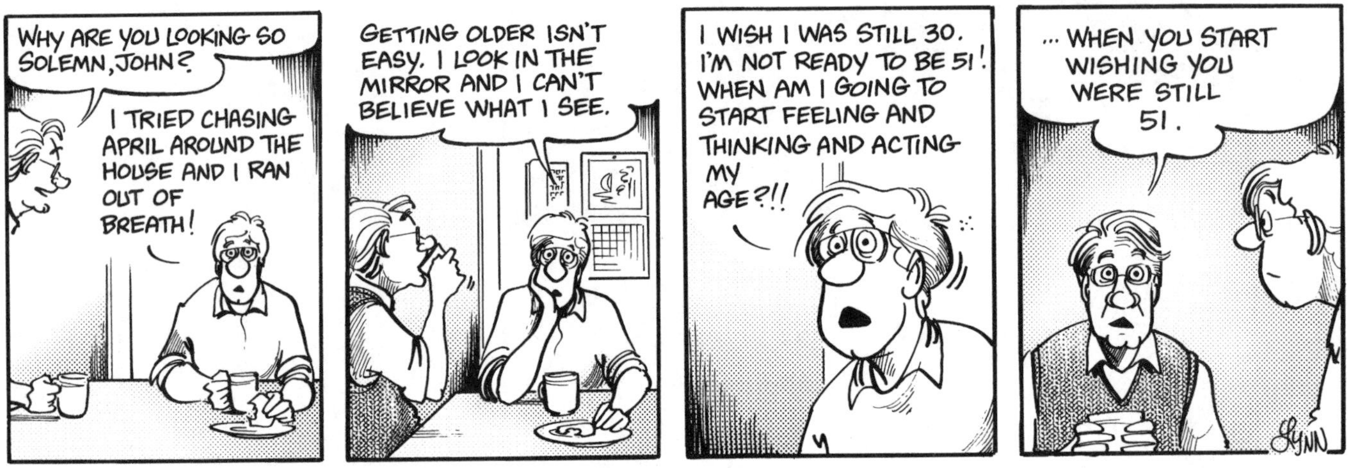
WHY ARE YOU LOOKING SO SOLEMN, JOHN?
I TRIED CHASING APRIL AROUND THE HOUSE AND I RAN OUT OF BREATH!
GETTING OLDER ISN'T EASY. I LOOK IN THE MIRROR AND I CAN'T BELIEVE WHAT I SEE.
I WISH I WAS STILL 30. I'M NOT READY TO BE 51! WHEN AM I GOING TO START FEELING AND THINKING AND ACTING MY AGE?!!
...WHEN YOU START WISHING YOU WERE STILL 51.

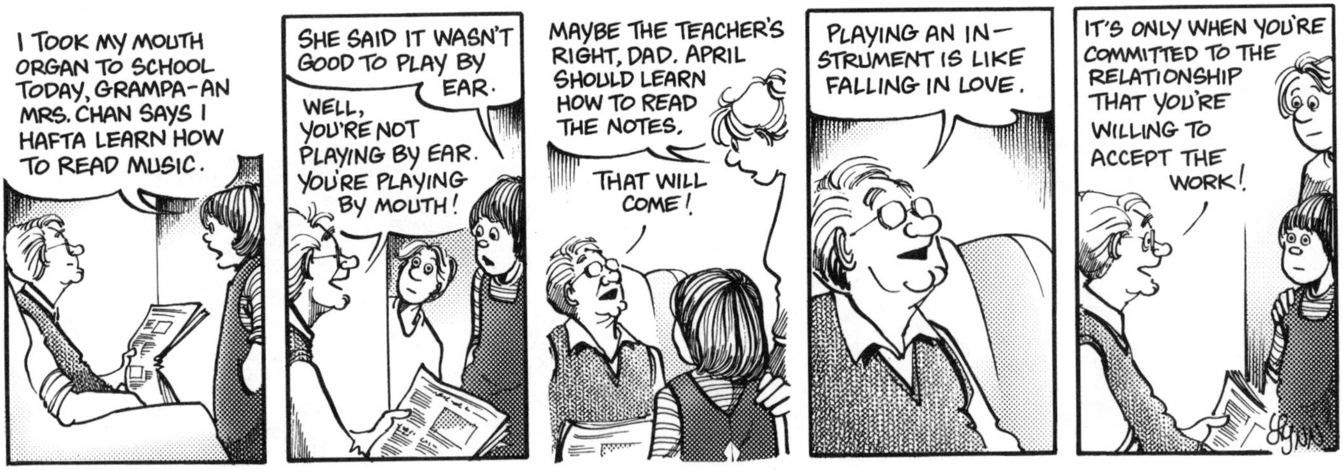
I TOOK MY MOUTH ORGAN TO SCHOOL TODAY, GRAMPA—AN MRS. CHAN SAYS I HAFTA LEARN HOW TO READ MUSIC.
SHE SAID IT WASN'T GOOD TO PLAY BY EAR.
WELL, YOU'RE NOT PLAYING BY EAR. YOU'RE PLAYING BY MOUTH!
MAYBE THE TEACHER'S RIGHT, DAD. APRIL SHOULD LEARN HOW TO READ THE NOTES.
THAT WILL COME!
PLAYING AN IN—STRUMENT IS LIKE FALLING IN LOVE.
IT'S ONLY WHEN YOU'RE COMMITTED TO THE RELATIONSHIP THAT YOU'RE WILLING TO ACCEPT THE WORK!

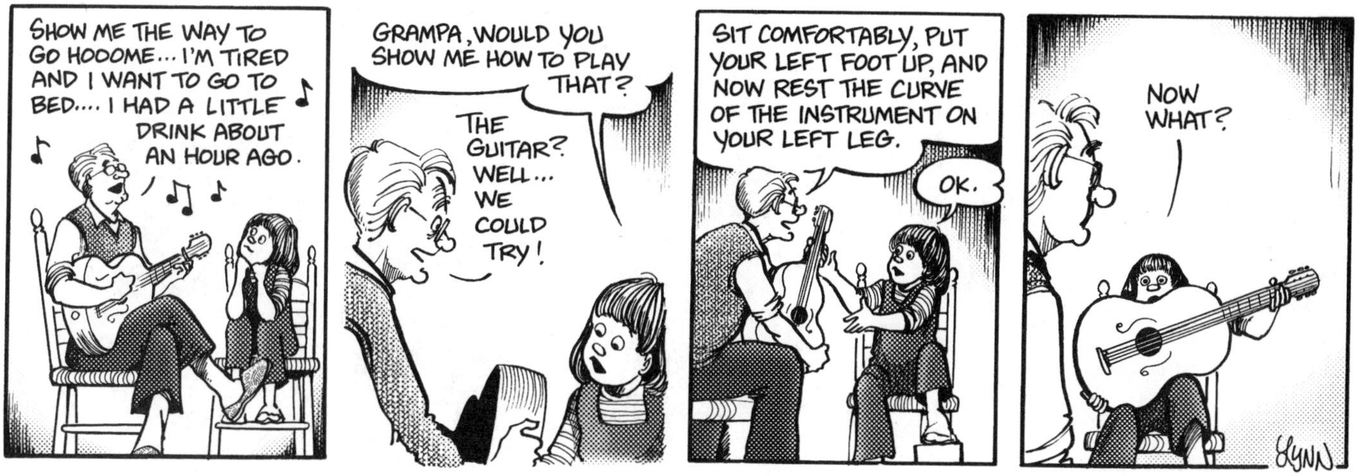
SHOW ME THE WAY TO GO HOOOME... I'M TIRED AND I WANT TO GO TO BED.... I HAD A LITTLE DRINK ABOUT AN HOUR AGO.
GRAMPA, WOULD YOU SHOW ME HOW TO PLAY THAT?
THE GUITAR? WELL... WE COULD TRY!
SIT COMFORTABLY, PUT YOUR LEFT FOOT UP, AND NOW REST THE CURVE OF THE INSTRUMENT ON YOUR LEFT LEG.
OK.
NOW WHAT?

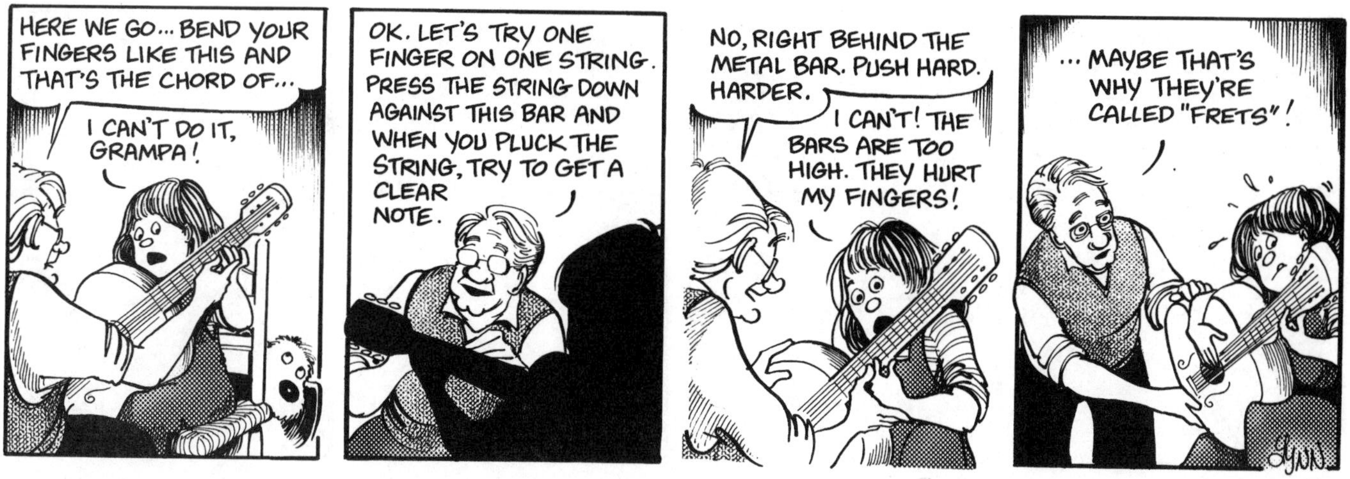
HERE WE GO... BEND YOUR FINGERS LIKE THIS AND THAT'S THE CHORD OF...
I CAN'T DO IT, GRAMPA!
OK. LET'S TRY ONE FINGER ON ONE STRING. PRESS THE STRING DOWN AGAINST THIS BAR AND WHEN YOU PLUCK THE STRING, TRY TO GET A CLEAR NOTE.
NO, RIGHT BEHIND THE METAL BAR. PUSH HARD. HARDER.
I CAN'T! THE BARS ARE TOO HIGH. THEY HURT MY FINGERS!
... MAYBE THAT'S WHY THEY'RE CALLED "FRETS"!

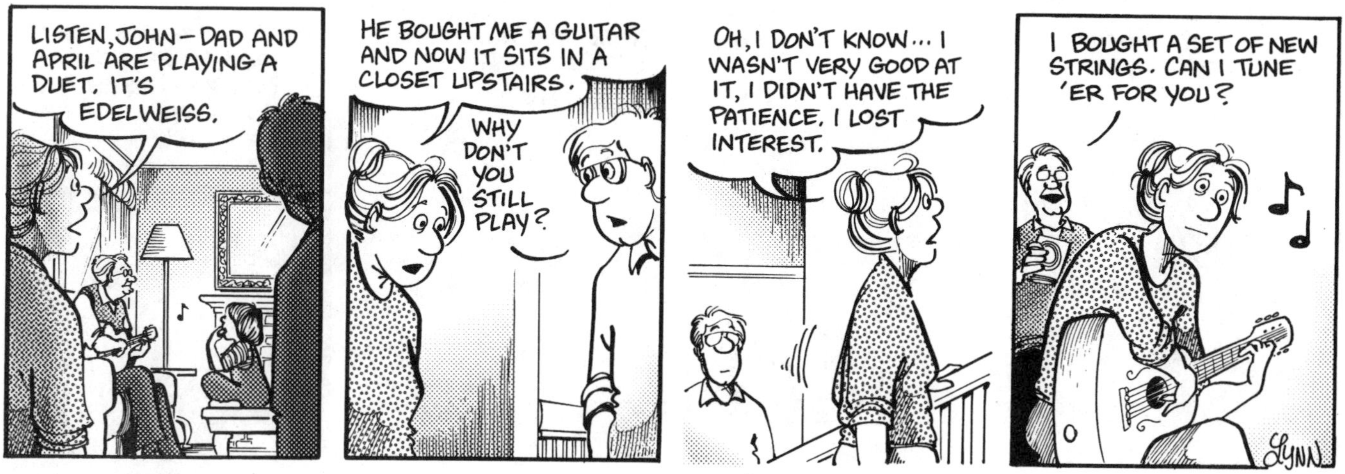
LISTEN, JOHN – DAD AND APRIL ARE PLAYING A DUET. IT'S EDELWEISS.
HE BOUGHT ME A GUITAR AND NOW IT SITS IN A CLOSET UPSTAIRS.
WHY DON'T YOU STILL PLAY?
OH, I DON'T KNOW... I WASN'T VERY GOOD AT IT, I DIDN'T HAVE THE PATIENCE, I LOST INTEREST.
I BOUGHT A SET OF NEW STRINGS. CAN I TUNE 'ER FOR YOU?

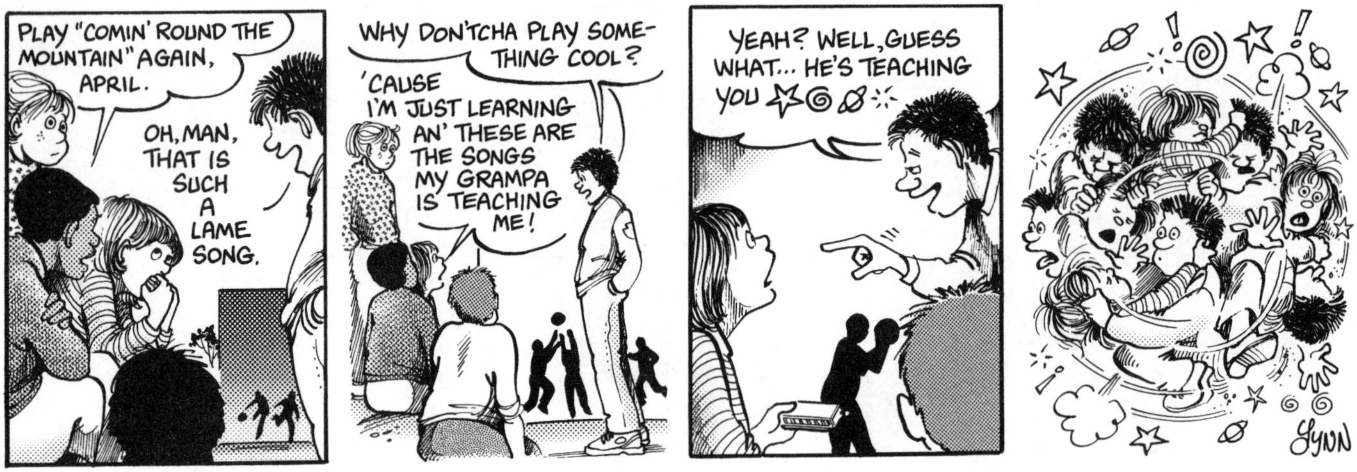
PLAY "COMIN' ROUND THE MOUNTAIN" AGAIN, APRIL.
OH, MAN, THAT IS SUCH A LAME SONG.
WHY DON'TCHA PLAY SOMETHING COOL?
'CAUSE I'M JUST LEARNING AN' THESE ARE THE SONGS MY GRAMPA IS TEACHING ME!
YEAH? WELL, GUESS WHAT... HE'S TEACHING YOU
LYNN

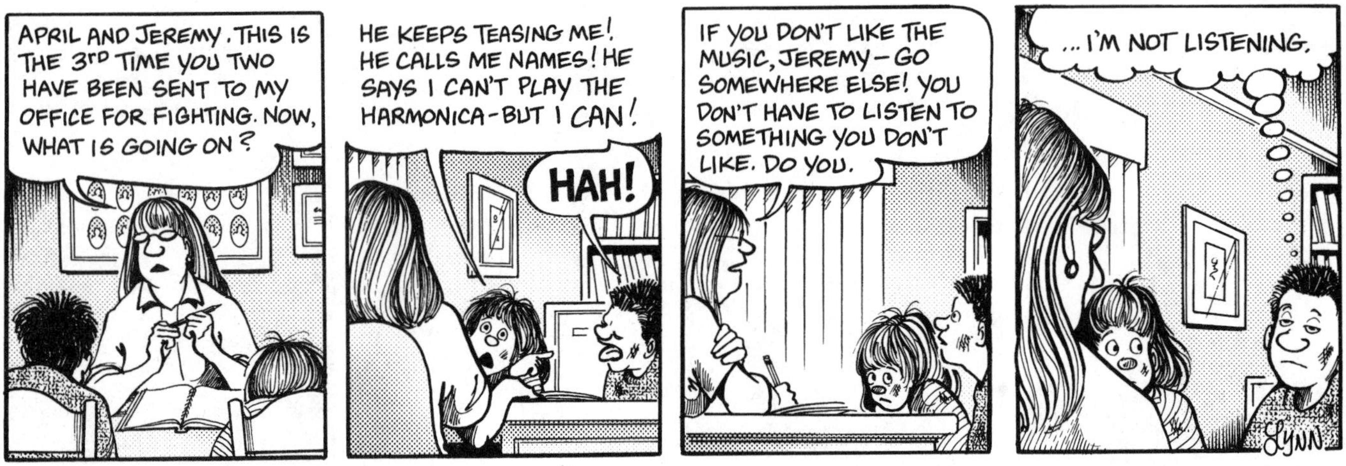
APRIL AND JEREMY. THIS IS THE 3RD TIME YOU TWO HAVE BEEN SENT TO MY OFFICE FOR FIGHTING. NOW, WHAT IS GOING ON?
HE KEEPS TEASING ME! HE CALLS ME NAMES! HE SAYS I CAN'T PLAY THE HARMONICA-BUT I CAN!
HAH!
IF YOU DON'T LIKE THE MUSIC, JEREMY-GO SOMEWHERE ELSE! YOU DON'T HAVE TO LISTEN TO SOMETHING YOU DON'T LIKE. DO YOU.
...I'M NOT LISTENING.
LYNN

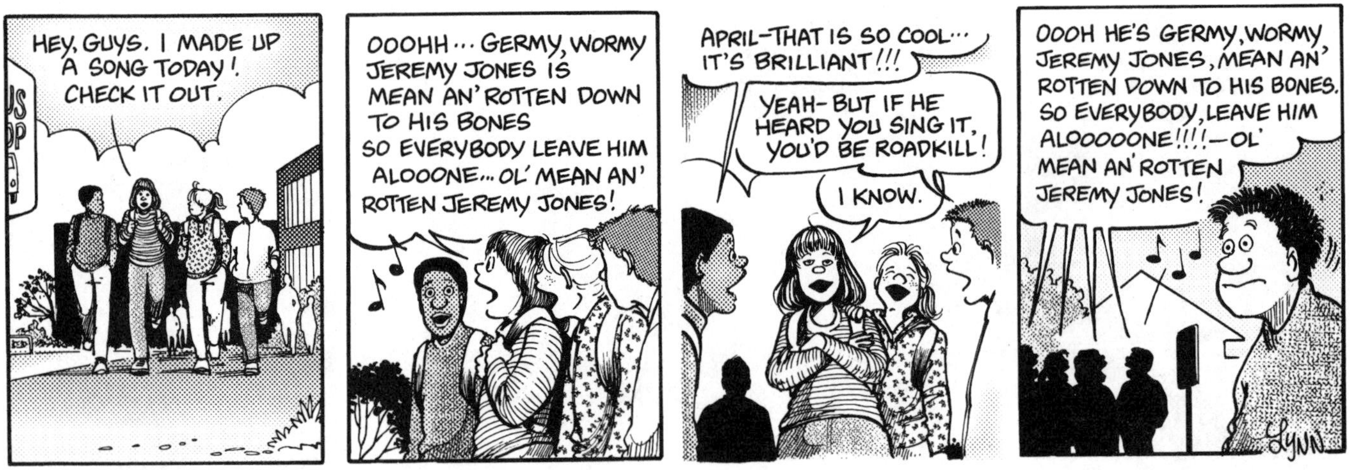
HEY, GUYS. I MADE UP A SONG TODAY! CHECK IT OUT.
OOOHH... GERMY, WORMY JEREMY JONES IS MEAN AN' ROTTEN DOWN TO HIS BONES SO EVERYBODY LEAVE HIM ALOOONE... OL' MEAN AN' ROTTEN JEREMY JONES!
APRIL-THAT IS SO COOL... IT'S BRILLIANT!!!
YEAH-BUT IF HE HEARD YOU SING IT, YOU'D BE ROADKILL!
I KNOW.
OOOH HE'S GERMY, WORMY JEREMY JONES, MEAN AN' ROTTEN DOWN TO HIS BONES. SO EVERYBODY, LEAVE HIM ALOOOOONE!!!!-OL' MEAN AN' ROTTEN JEREMY JONES!
LYNN

Panel 1: YOU PEOPLE ARE HERE IN MY OFFICE BECAUSE THERE IS A SONG GOING AROUND THE SCHOOL ABOUT JEREMY JONES,—I ASSUME YOU KNOW THE SONG I AM TALKING ABOUT!!!

UH...

Panel 2: I KNOW YOU'VE ALL HAD TROUBLE GETTING ALONG WITH HIM, BUT A SONG LIKE THIS IS NOT GOING TO MAKE THINGS BETTER.

Panel 3: IF I HEAR ANY OF YOU SINGING THE "JEREMY JONES SONG" AGAIN, THERE WILL BE SERIOUS TROUBLE, DO YOU UNDERSTAND?

YES! UH-HUH! WE DO!

Panel 4: MISS COLLINS? THOSE GUYS WERE HUMMING AT ME!!!

Panel 5: WE'RE REALLY IN TROUBLE NOW, APRIL. 'CAUSE JEREMY TOLD THE PRINCIPAL WE WERE SINGING "THE SONG"

Panel 6: YEAH!—AN' ALSO HE HAS FRIENDS WHO ARE ON HIS SIDE! WE'RE GONNA BE FIGHTING WITH THESE GUYS AN' IT'S ALL BECAUSE OF YOU!

Panel 7: BUT HE STARTED IT! HE STARTED EVERYTHING! HE HIT ME AN' SAID MEAN STUFF!—ALL I DID WAS MAKE UP A SONG!!!

Panel 8: WHY DOESN'T HE JUST MAKE UP A SONG ABOUT ME?!!

Panel 9: 'CAUSE THE ONLY THING HE KNOWS HOW TO MAKE UP IS HIS FIST!

Panel 10: MOM? LISTEN, APRIL! I CAN STILL PLAY "WILDWOOD FLOWER"!

Panel 11: MOM, I MADE UP A SONG ABOUT JEREMY JONES AN' EVERYBODY AT SCHOOL IS SINGING IT AN' JEREMY'S GOT A BUNCH OF FRIENDS AN' THEY WANNA PUNCH ME OUT!

Panel 12: HONEY, THAT'S AWFUL!!! WHEN YOU MAKE UP A SONG, IT SHOULD LIFT SPIRITS UP, MAKE BAD FEELINGS GO AWAY—IT SHOULD MAKE PEOPLE FEEL BETTER!

I KNOW.

Panel 13: THIS ONE MADE ME FEEL GREAT!!!

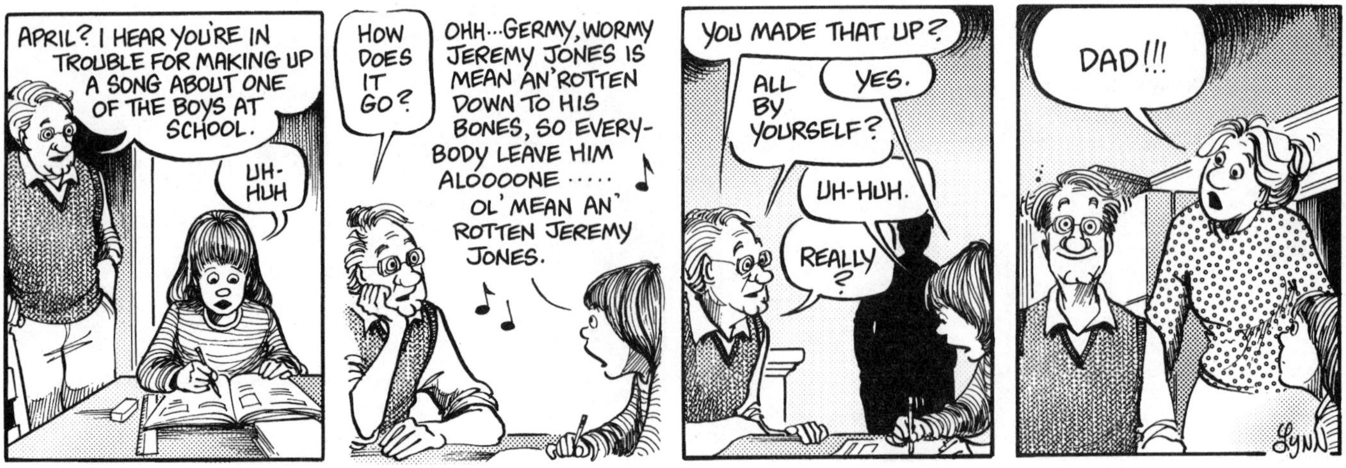
APRIL? I HEAR YOU'RE IN TROUBLE FOR MAKING UP A SONG ABOUT ONE OF THE BOYS AT SCHOOL.
UH-HUH
HOW DOES IT GO?
OHH...GERMY, WORMY JEREMY JONES IS MEAN AN' ROTTEN DOWN TO HIS BONES, SO EVERY-BODY LEAVE HIM ALOOOONE..... OL' MEAN AN' ROTTEN JEREMY JONES.
YOU MADE THAT UP?
YES.
ALL BY YOURSELF?
UH-HUH.
REALLY?
DAD!!!
LYNN

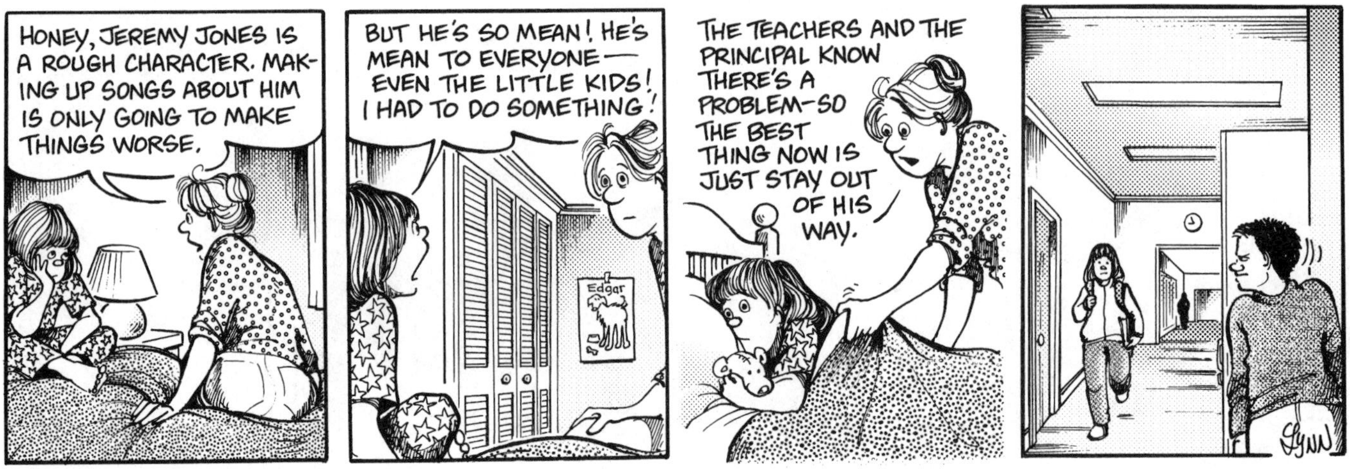
HONEY, JEREMY JONES IS A ROUGH CHARACTER. MAKING UP SONGS ABOUT HIM IS ONLY GOING TO MAKE THINGS WORSE.
BUT HE'S SO MEAN! HE'S MEAN TO EVERYONE— EVEN THE LITTLE KIDS! I HAD TO DO SOMETHING!
Edgar
THE TEACHERS AND THE PRINCIPAL KNOW THERE'S A PROBLEM—SO THE BEST THING NOW IS JUST STAY OUT OF HIS WAY.
LYNN

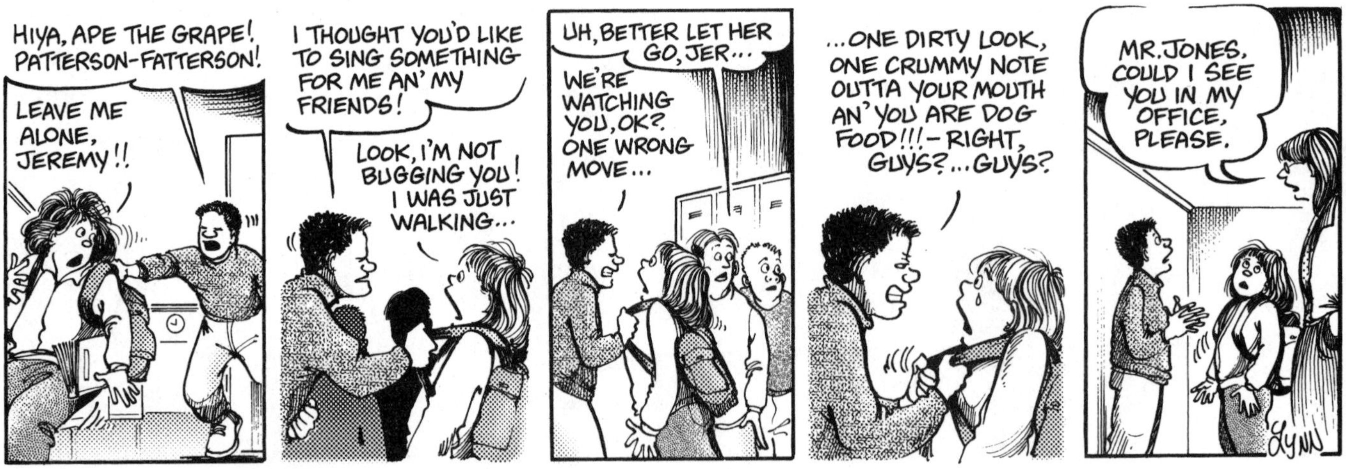
HIYA, APE THE GRAPE! PATTERSON-FATTERSON!
LEAVE ME ALONE, JEREMY!!
I THOUGHT YOU'D LIKE TO SING SOMETHING FOR ME AN' MY FRIENDS!
LOOK, I'M NOT BUGGING YOU! I WAS JUST WALKING...
UH, BETTER LET HER GO, JER...
WE'RE WATCHING YOU, OK? ONE WRONG MOVE...
...ONE DIRTY LOOK, ONE CRUMMY NOTE OUTTA YOUR MOUTH AN' YOU ARE DOG FOOD!!!—RIGHT, GUYS?...GUYS?
MR. JONES, COULD I SEE YOU IN MY OFFICE, PLEASE.
LYNN

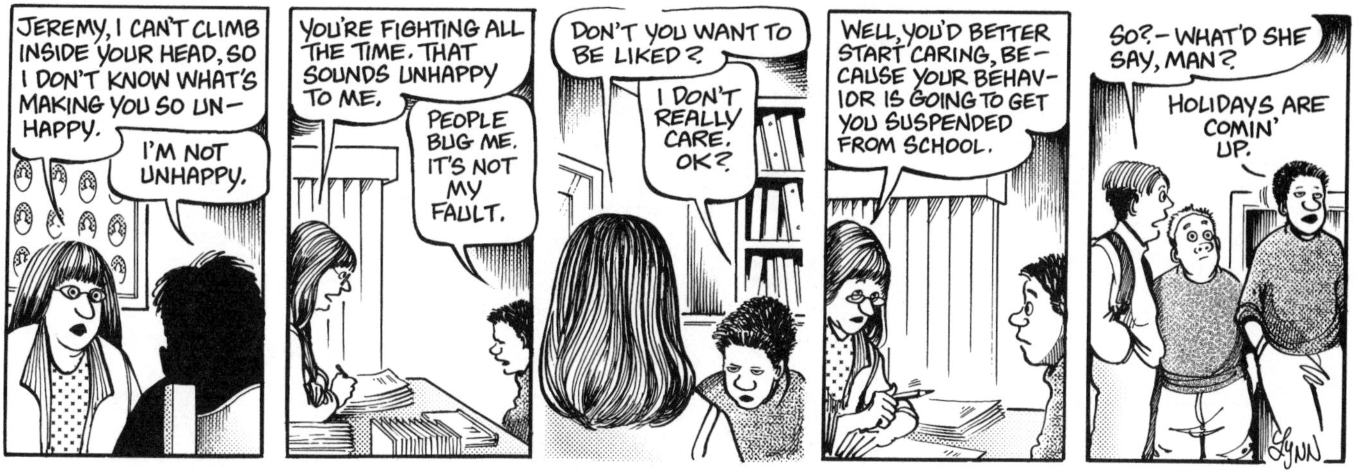
JEREMY, I CAN'T CLIMB INSIDE YOUR HEAD, SO I DON'T KNOW WHAT'S MAKING YOU SO UNHAPPY.
I'M NOT UNHAPPY.
YOU'RE FIGHTING ALL THE TIME. THAT SOUNDS UNHAPPY TO ME.
PEOPLE BUG ME. IT'S NOT MY FAULT.
DON'T YOU WANT TO BE LIKED?
I DON'T REALLY CARE. OK?
WELL, YOU'D BETTER START CARING, BECAUSE YOUR BEHAVIOR IS GOING TO GET YOU SUSPENDED FROM SCHOOL.
SO?– WHAT'D SHE SAY, MAN?
HOLIDAYS ARE COMIN' UP.
LYNN

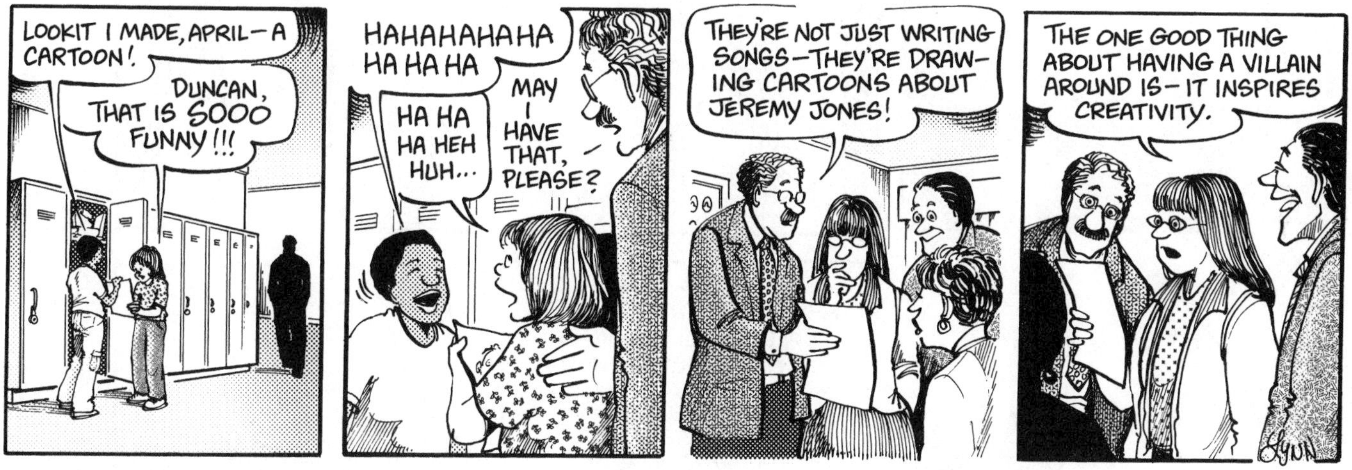
LOOKIT I MADE, APRIL– A CARTOON!
DUNCAN, THAT IS SOOO FUNNY!!!
HAHAHAHAHA HA HA HA HA
HA HA HA HEH HUH...
MAY I HAVE THAT, PLEASE?
THEY'RE NOT JUST WRITING SONGS– THEY'RE DRAWING CARTOONS ABOUT JEREMY JONES!
THE ONE GOOD THING ABOUT HAVING A VILLAIN AROUND IS– IT INSPIRES CREATIVITY.
LYNN

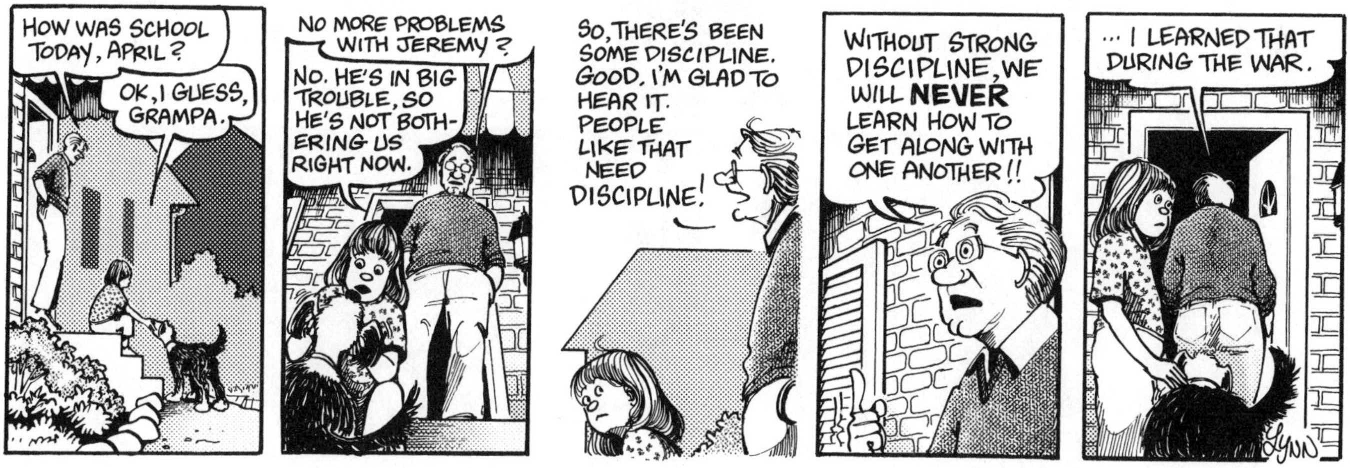
HOW WAS SCHOOL TODAY, APRIL?
OK, I GUESS, GRAMPA.
NO MORE PROBLEMS WITH JEREMY?
NO. HE'S IN BIG TROUBLE, SO HE'S NOT BOTHERING US RIGHT NOW.
SO, THERE'S BEEN SOME DISCIPLINE. GOOD. I'M GLAD TO HEAR IT. PEOPLE LIKE THAT NEED DISCIPLINE!
WITHOUT STRONG DISCIPLINE, WE WILL NEVER LEARN HOW TO GET ALONG WITH ONE ANOTHER!!
... I LEARNED THAT DURING THE WAR.
LYNN

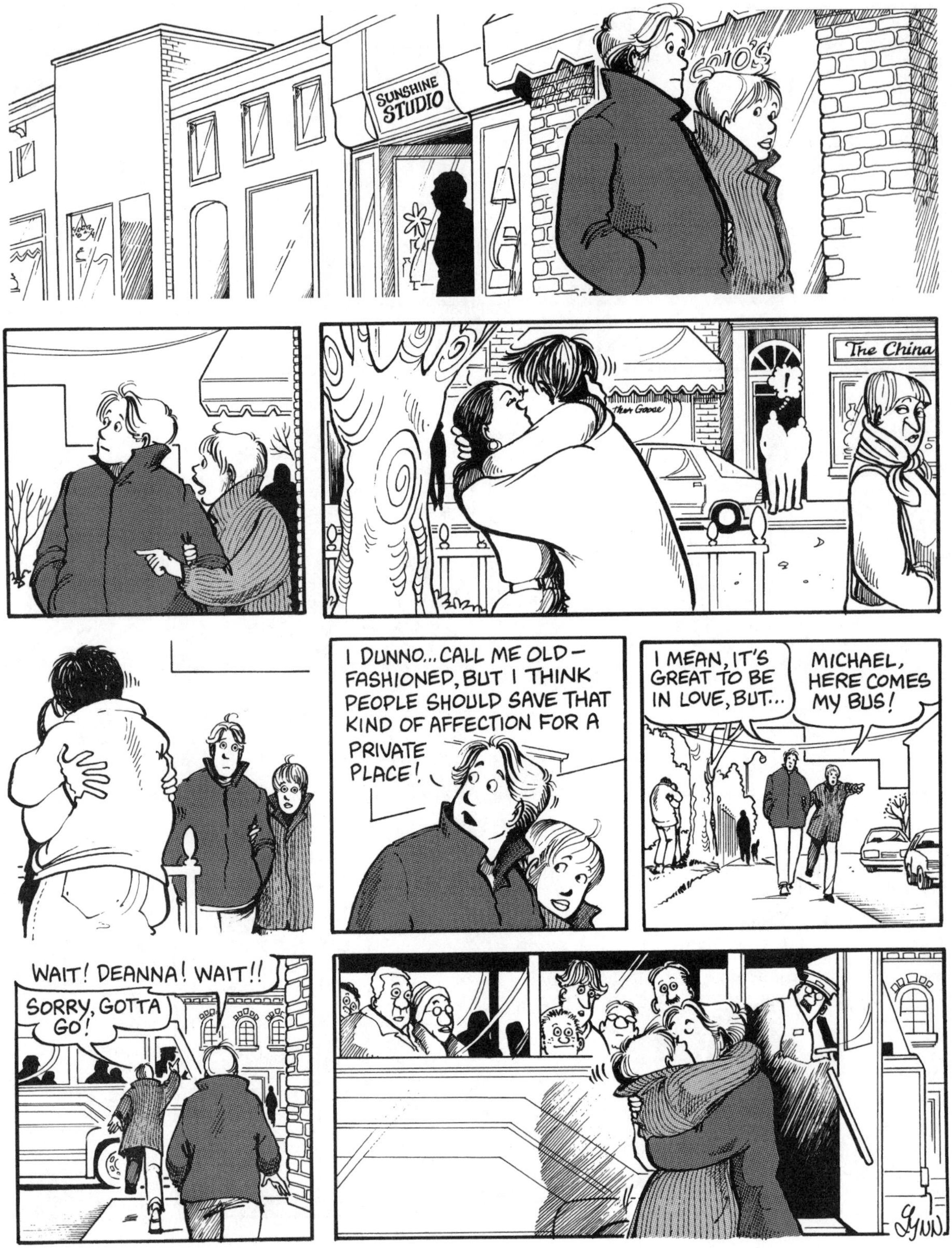
SUNSHINE STUDIO
The China
I DUNNO... CALL ME OLD-FASHIONED, BUT I THINK PEOPLE SHOULD SAVE THAT KIND OF AFFECTION FOR A PRIVATE PLACE!
I MEAN, IT'S GREAT TO BE IN LOVE, BUT...
MICHAEL, HERE COMES MY BUS!
WAIT! DEANNA! WAIT!!
SORRY, GOTTA GO!
LYNN

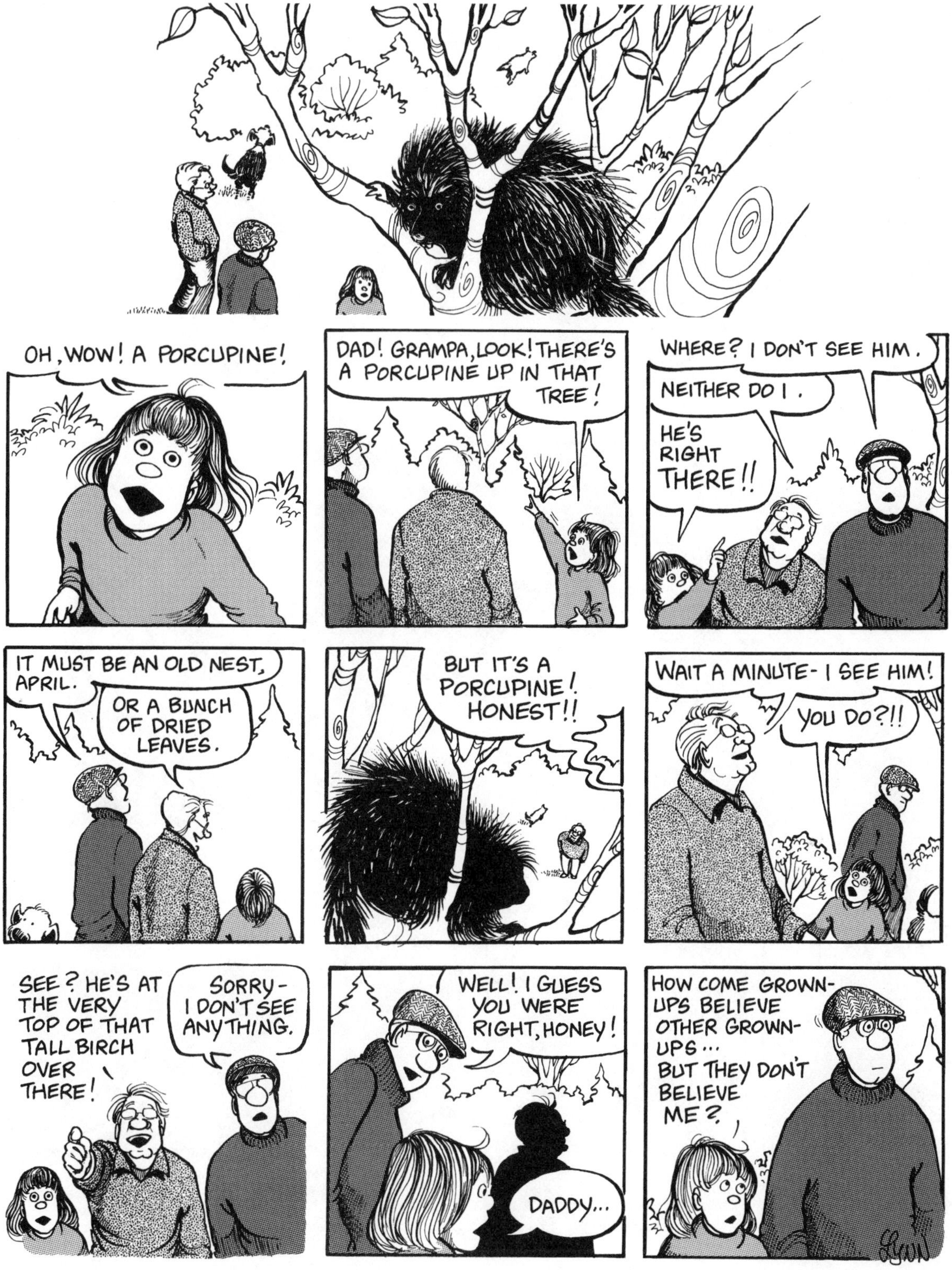
OH, WOW! A PORCUPINE!
DAD! GRAMPA, LOOK! THERE'S A PORCUPINE UP IN THAT TREE!
WHERE? I DON'T SEE HIM.
NEITHER DO I.
HE'S RIGHT THERE!!
IT MUST BE AN OLD NEST, APRIL.
OR A BUNCH OF DRIED LEAVES.
BUT IT'S A PORCUPINE! HONEST!!
WAIT A MINUTE- I SEE HIM!
YOU DO?!!
SEE? HE'S AT THE VERY TOP OF THAT TALL BIRCH OVER THERE!
SORRY- I DON'T SEE ANYTHING.
WELL! I GUESS YOU WERE RIGHT, HONEY!
DADDY...
HOW COME GROWN-UPS BELIEVE OTHER GROWN-UPS... BUT THEY DON'T BELIEVE ME?
LYNN

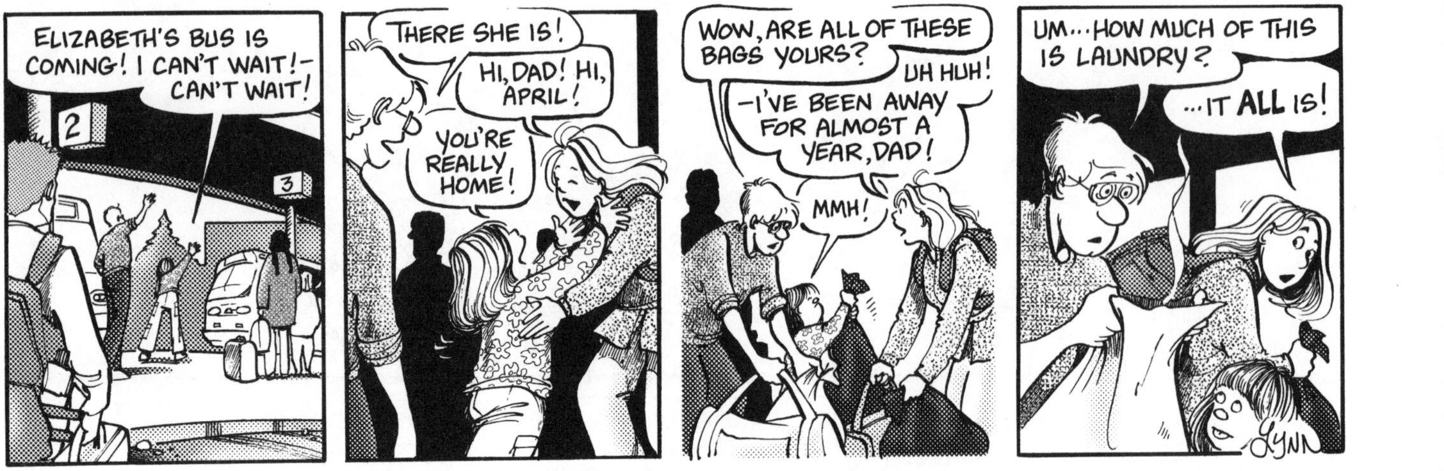
ELIZABETH'S BUS IS COMING! I CAN'T WAIT!– CAN'T WAIT!
2
3
THERE SHE IS!
HI, DAD! HI, APRIL!
YOU'RE REALLY HOME!
WOW, ARE ALL OF THESE BAGS YOURS?
UH HUH!
–I'VE BEEN AWAY FOR ALMOST A YEAR, DAD!
MMH!
UM... HOW MUCH OF THIS IS LAUNDRY?
...IT **ALL** IS!

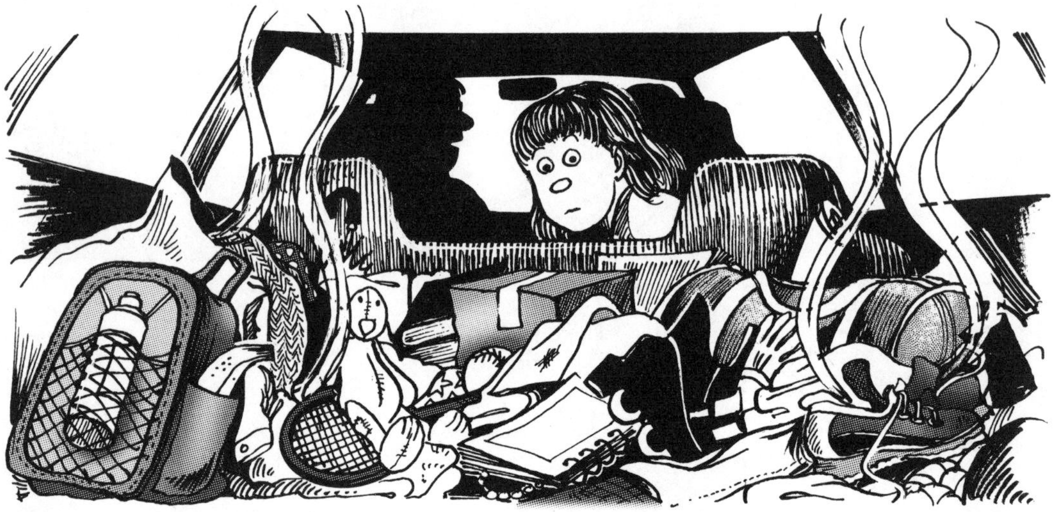

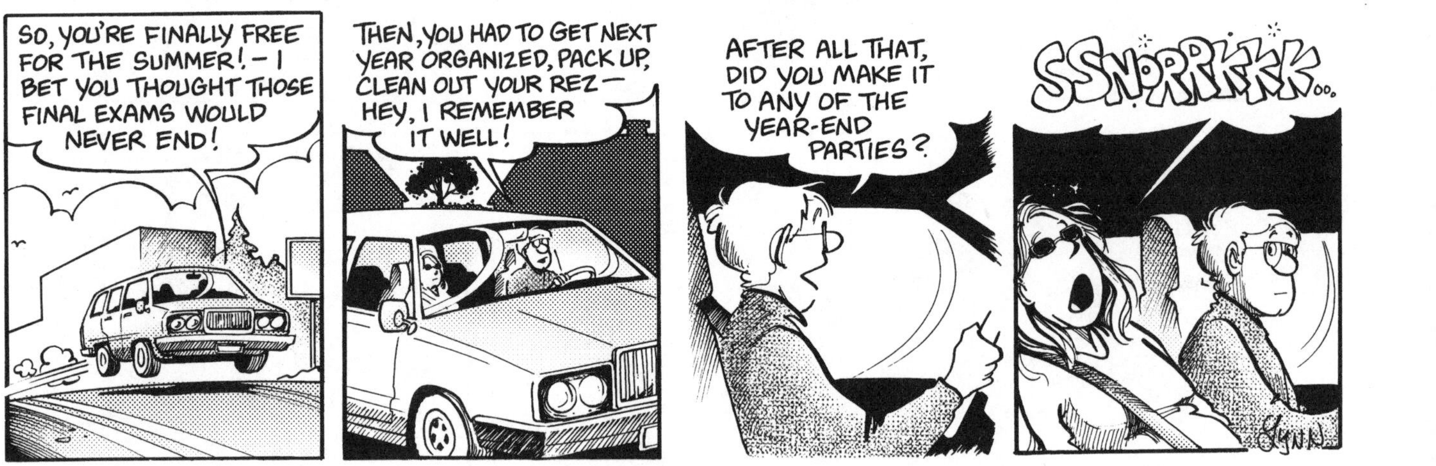
SO, YOU'RE FINALLY FREE FOR THE SUMMER! – I BET YOU THOUGHT THOSE FINAL EXAMS WOULD NEVER END!
THEN, YOU HAD TO GET NEXT YEAR ORGANIZED, PACK UP, CLEAN OUT YOUR REZ– HEY, I REMEMBER IT WELL!
AFTER ALL THAT, DID YOU MAKE IT TO ANY OF THE YEAR-END PARTIES?
SSNORRKKK...

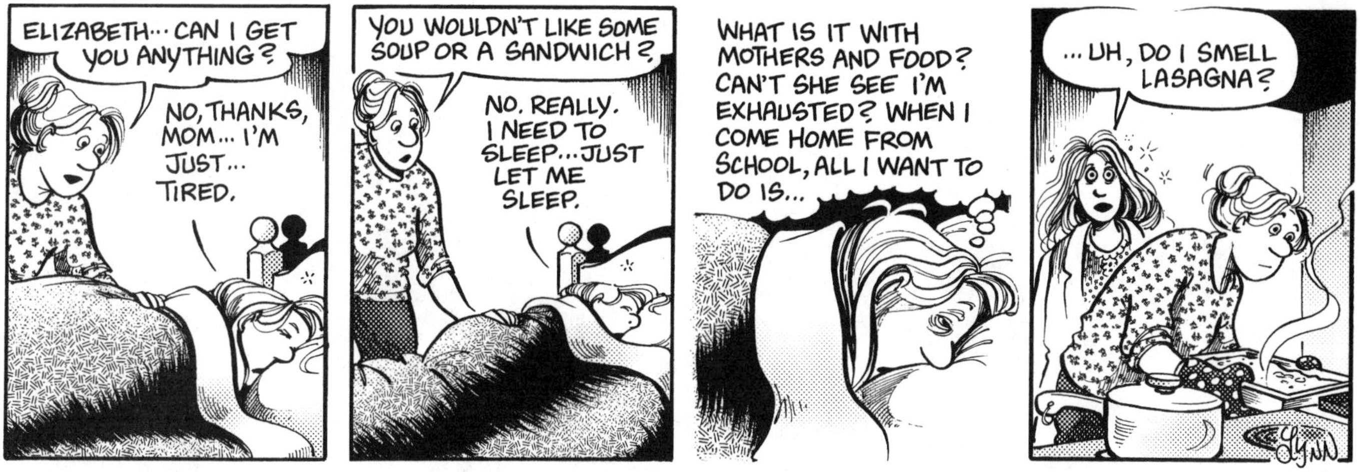
ELIZABETH... CAN I GET YOU ANYTHING?
NO, THANKS, MOM... I'M JUST... TIRED.
YOU WOULDN'T LIKE SOME SOUP OR A SANDWICH?
NO. REALLY. I NEED TO SLEEP... JUST LET ME SLEEP.
WHAT IS IT WITH MOTHERS AND FOOD? CAN'T SHE SEE I'M EXHAUSTED? WHEN I COME HOME FROM SCHOOL, ALL I WANT TO DO IS...
... UH, DO I SMELL LASAGNA?
LYNN

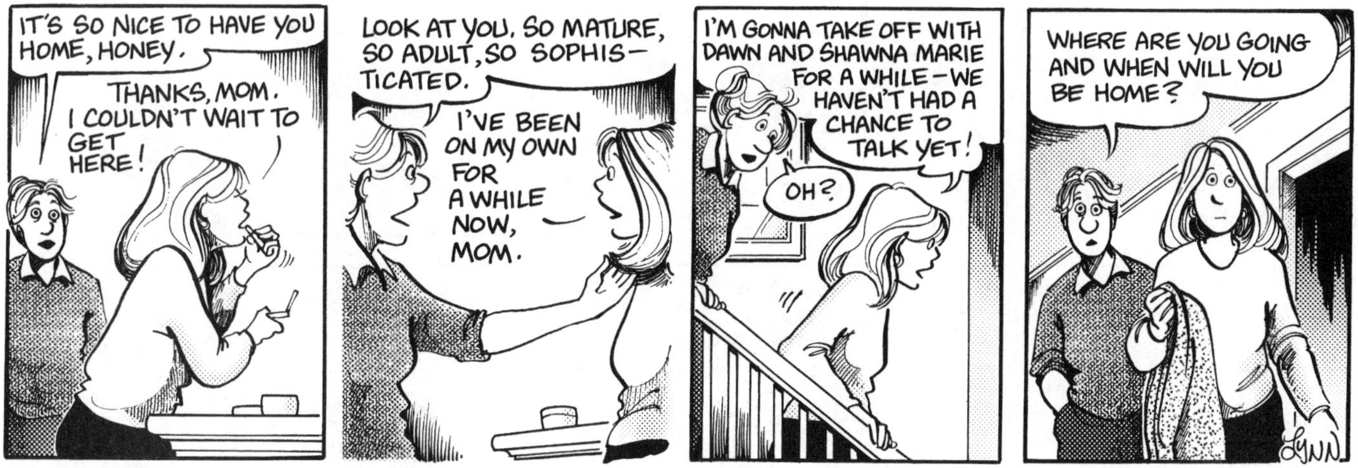
IT'S SO NICE TO HAVE YOU HOME, HONEY.
THANKS, MOM. I COULDN'T WAIT TO GET HERE!
LOOK AT YOU. SO MATURE, SO ADULT, SO SOPHIS-TICATED.
I'VE BEEN ON MY OWN FOR A WHILE NOW, MOM.
I'M GONNA TAKE OFF WITH DAWN AND SHAWNA MARIE FOR A WHILE – WE HAVEN'T HAD A CHANCE TO TALK YET!
OH?
WHERE ARE YOU GOING AND WHEN WILL YOU BE HOME?
LYNN

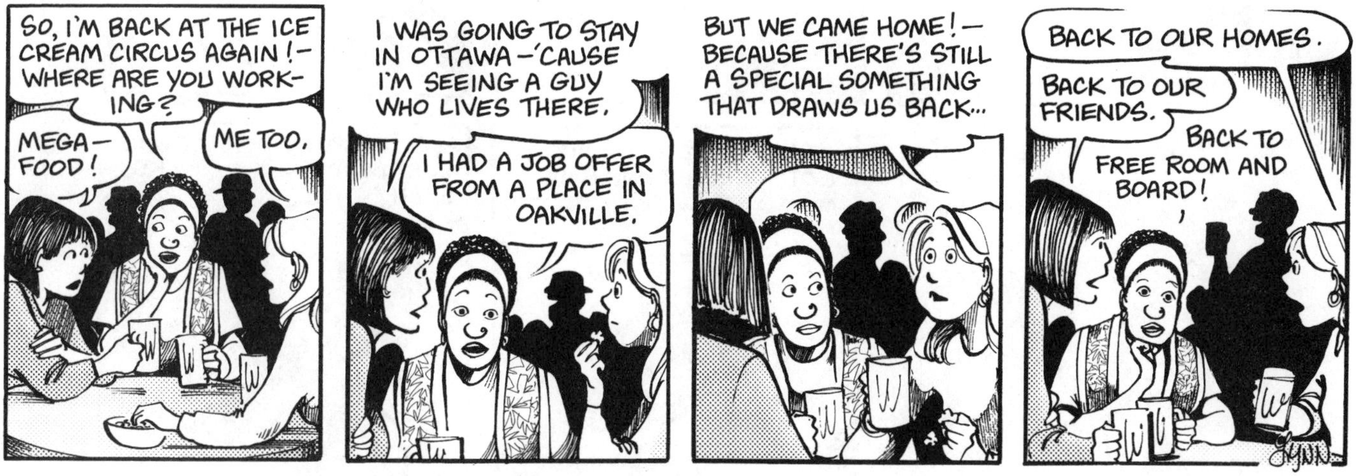
SO, I'M BACK AT THE ICE CREAM CIRCUS AGAIN! – WHERE ARE YOU WORK-ING?
MEGA-FOOD!
ME TOO.
I WAS GOING TO STAY IN OTTAWA – 'CAUSE I'M SEEING A GUY WHO LIVES THERE.
I HAD A JOB OFFER FROM A PLACE IN OAKVILLE.
BUT WE CAME HOME! – BECAUSE THERE'S STILL A SPECIAL SOMETHING THAT DRAWS US BACK...
BACK TO OUR HOMES.
BACK TO OUR FRIENDS.
BACK TO FREE ROOM AND BOARD!
LYNN

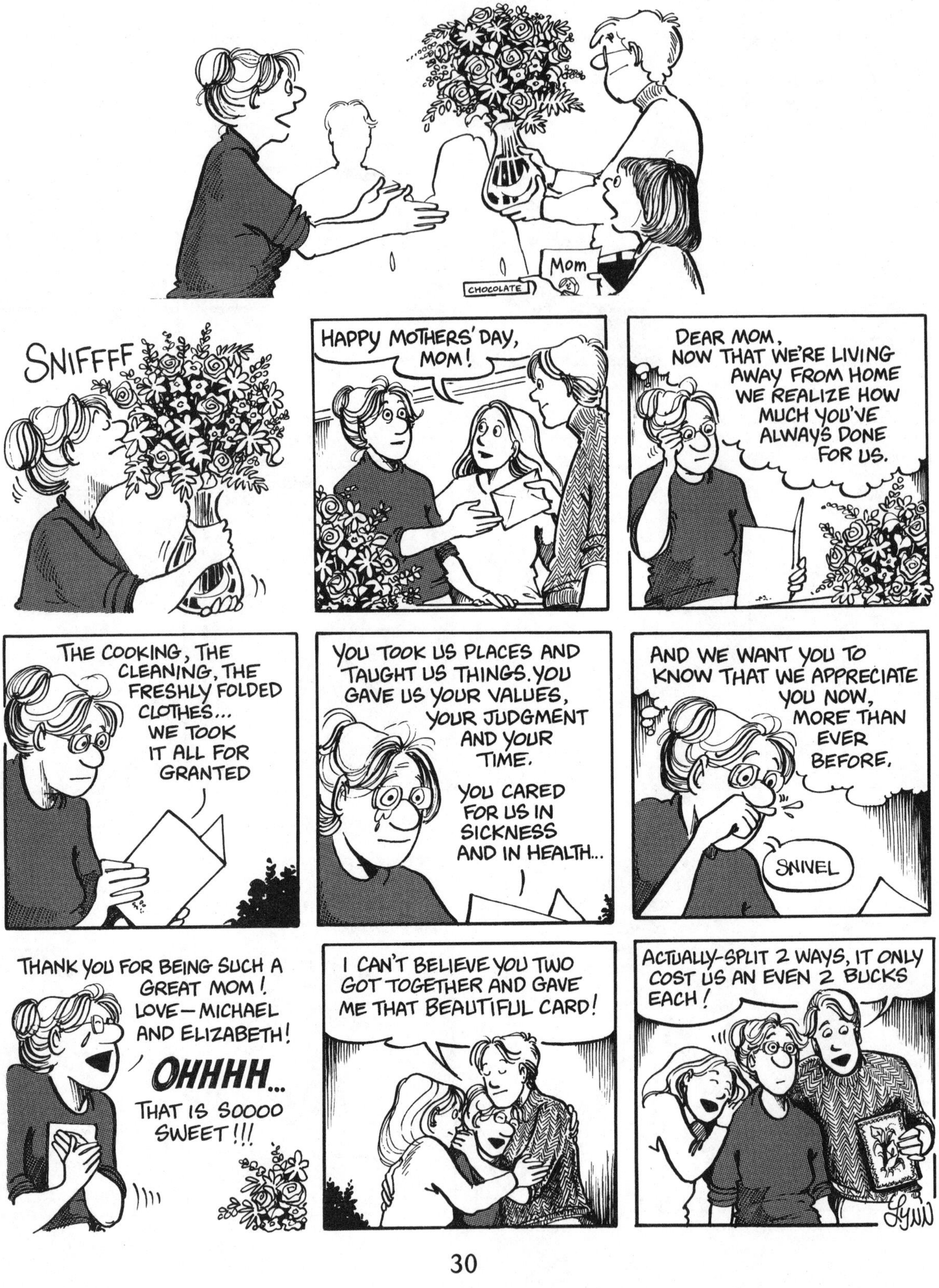

Mom
CHOCOLATE
SNIFFFF
HAPPY MOTHERS' DAY, MOM!
DEAR MOM, NOW THAT WE'RE LIVING AWAY FROM HOME WE REALIZE HOW MUCH YOU'VE ALWAYS DONE FOR US.
THE COOKING, THE CLEANING, THE FRESHLY FOLDED CLOTHES... WE TOOK IT ALL FOR GRANTED
YOU TOOK US PLACES AND TAUGHT US THINGS. YOU GAVE US YOUR VALUES, YOUR JUDGMENT AND YOUR TIME.
YOU CARED FOR US IN SICKNESS AND IN HEALTH...
AND WE WANT YOU TO KNOW THAT WE APPRECIATE YOU NOW, MORE THAN EVER BEFORE.
SNIVEL
THANK YOU FOR BEING SUCH A GREAT MOM! LOVE—MICHAEL AND ELIZABETH!
OHHHH...
THAT IS SOOOO SWEET!!!
I CAN'T BELIEVE YOU TWO GOT TOGETHER AND GAVE ME THAT BEAUTIFUL CARD!
ACTUALLY-SPLIT 2 WAYS, IT ONLY COST US AN EVEN 2 BUCKS EACH!
Lynn

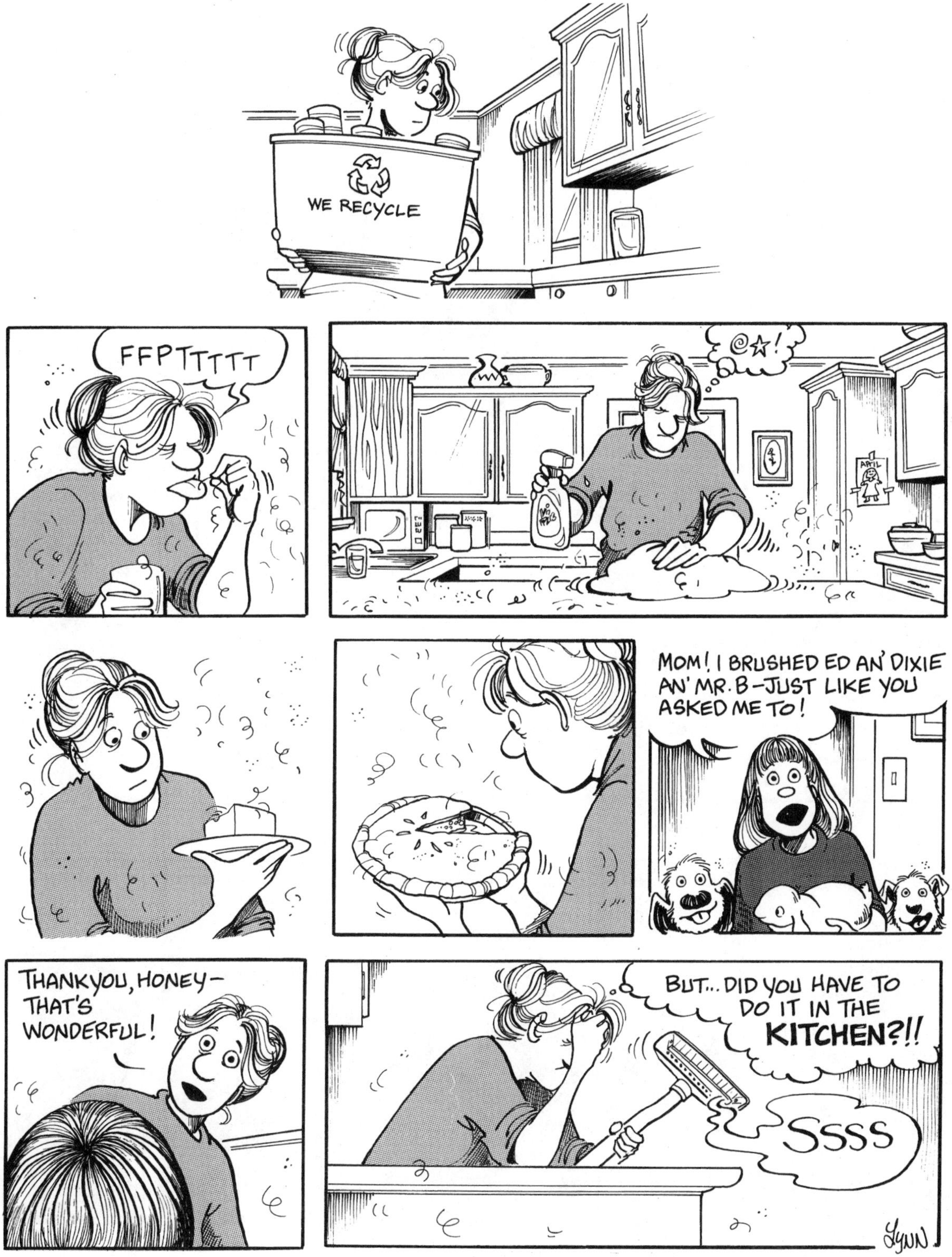
WE RECYCLE
FFPTTTTTT
@☆!
MOM! I BRUSHED ED AN' DIXIE AN' MR. B—JUST LIKE YOU ASKED ME TO!
THANKYOU, HONEY—THAT'S WONDERFUL!
BUT... DID YOU HAVE TO DO IT IN THE **KITCHEN?!!**
SSSS
LYNN

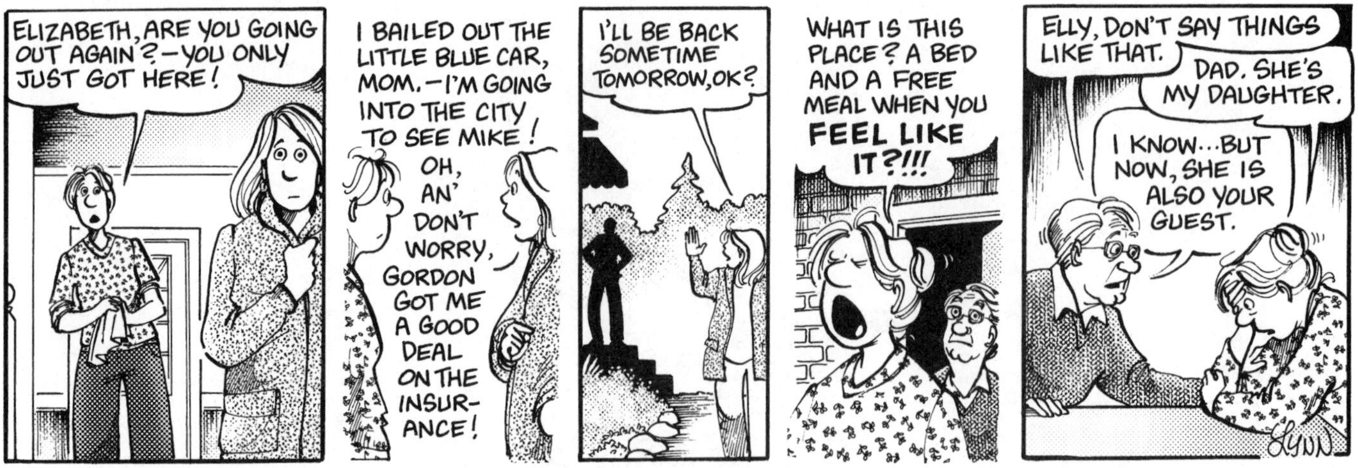
ELIZABETH, ARE YOU GOING OUT AGAIN?—YOU ONLY JUST GOT HERE!
I BAILED OUT THE LITTLE BLUE CAR, MOM.—I'M GOING INTO THE CITY TO SEE MIKE!
OH, AN' DON'T WORRY, GORDON GOT ME A GOOD DEAL ON THE INSURANCE!
I'LL BE BACK SOMETIME TOMORROW, OK?
WHAT IS THIS PLACE? A BED AND A FREE MEAL WHEN YOU **FEEL LIKE IT?!!!**
ELLY, DON'T SAY THINGS LIKE THAT.
DAD. SHE'S MY DAUGHTER.
I KNOW...BUT NOW, SHE IS ALSO YOUR GUEST.
LYNN

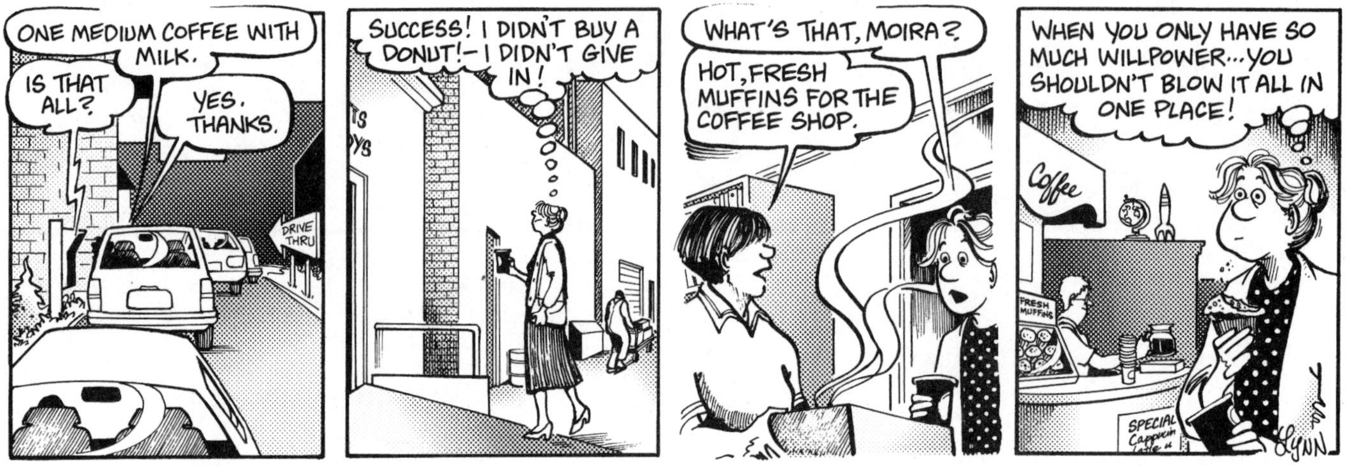
ONE MEDIUM COFFEE WITH MILK.
IS THAT ALL?
YES. THANKS.
DRIVE THRU
SUCCESS! I DIDN'T BUY A DONUT!—I DIDN'T GIVE IN!
WHAT'S THAT, MOIRA?
HOT, FRESH MUFFINS FOR THE COFFEE SHOP.
WHEN YOU ONLY HAVE SO MUCH WILLPOWER...YOU SHOULDN'T BLOW IT ALL IN ONE PLACE!
Coffee
FRESH MUFFINS
SPECIAL
LYNN

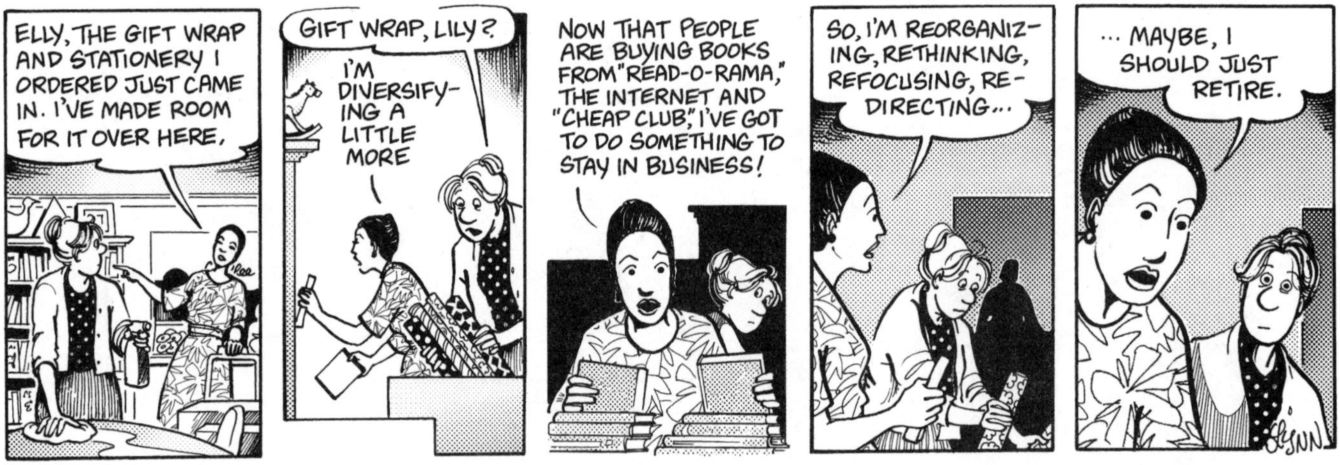
ELLY, THE GIFT WRAP AND STATIONERY I ORDERED JUST CAME IN. I'VE MADE ROOM FOR IT OVER HERE.
GIFT WRAP, LILY?
I'M DIVERSIFYING A LITTLE MORE
NOW THAT PEOPLE ARE BUYING BOOKS FROM "READ-O-RAMA," THE INTERNET AND "CHEAP CLUB," I'VE GOT TO DO SOMETHING TO STAY IN BUSINESS!
SO, I'M REORGANIZING, RETHINKING, REFOCUSING, REDIRECTING...
...MAYBE, I SHOULD JUST RETIRE.
LYNN

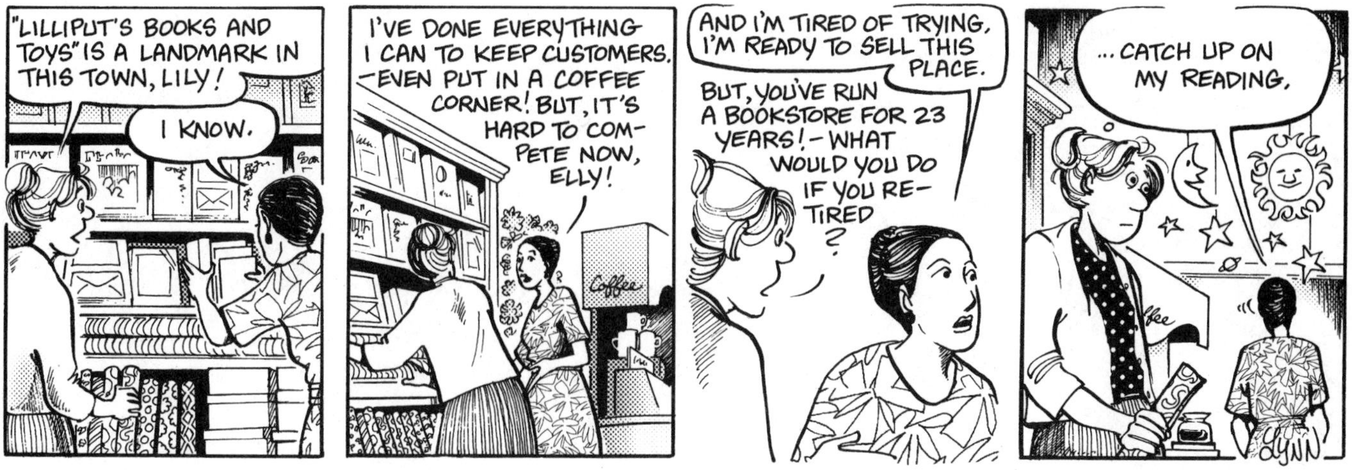
"LILLIPUT'S BOOKS AND TOYS" IS A LANDMARK IN THIS TOWN, LILY!
I KNOW.
I'VE DONE EVERYTHING I CAN TO KEEP CUSTOMERS. —EVEN PUT IN A COFFEE CORNER! BUT, IT'S HARD TO COMPETE NOW, ELLY!
Coffee
AND I'M TIRED OF TRYING, I'M READY TO SELL THIS PLACE.
BUT, YOU'VE RUN A BOOKSTORE FOR 23 YEARS! — WHAT WOULD YOU DO IF YOU RETIRED?
... CATCH UP ON MY READING.

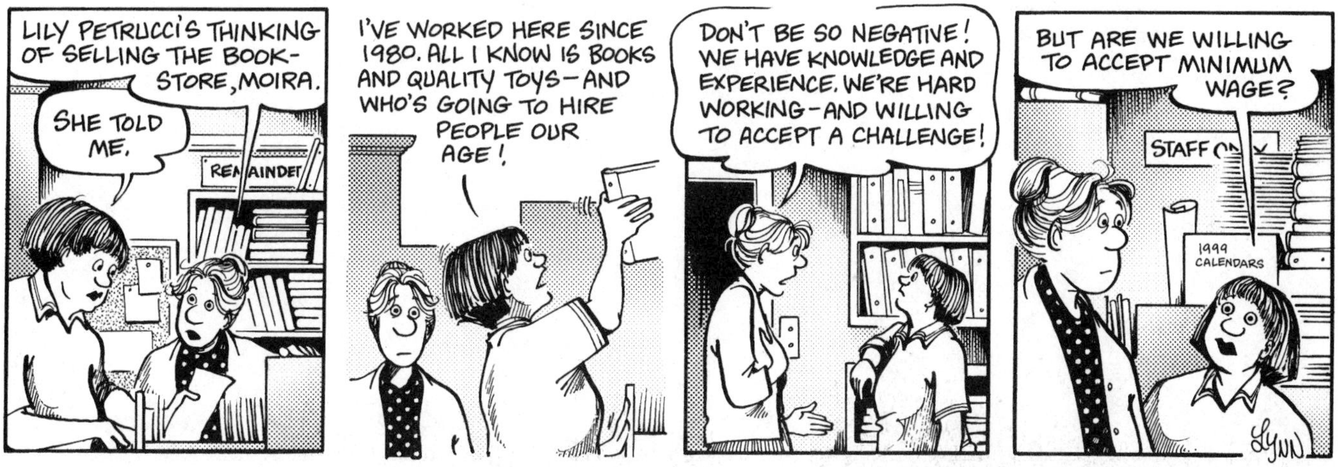
LILY PETRUCCI'S THINKING OF SELLING THE BOOKSTORE, MOIRA.
SHE TOLD ME.
I'VE WORKED HERE SINCE 1980. ALL I KNOW IS BOOKS AND QUALITY TOYS — AND WHO'S GOING TO HIRE PEOPLE OUR AGE!
DON'T BE SO NEGATIVE! WE HAVE KNOWLEDGE AND EXPERIENCE. WE'RE HARD WORKING — AND WILLING TO ACCEPT A CHALLENGE!
BUT ARE WE WILLING TO ACCEPT MINIMUM WAGE?
1999 CALENDARS

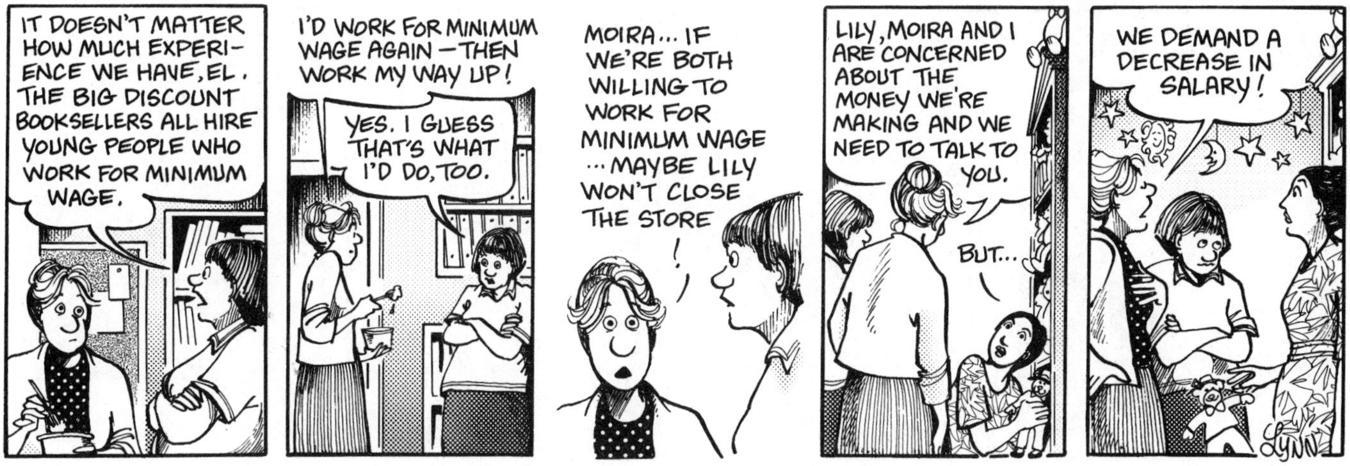
IT DOESN'T MATTER HOW MUCH EXPERIENCE WE HAVE, EL. THE BIG DISCOUNT BOOKSELLERS ALL HIRE YOUNG PEOPLE WHO WORK FOR MINIMUM WAGE.
I'D WORK FOR MINIMUM WAGE AGAIN — THEN WORK MY WAY UP!
YES. I GUESS THAT'S WHAT I'D DO, TOO.
MOIRA... IF WE'RE BOTH WILLING TO WORK FOR MINIMUM WAGE ... MAYBE LILY WON'T CLOSE THE STORE!
LILY, MOIRA AND I ARE CONCERNED ABOUT THE MONEY WE'RE MAKING AND WE NEED TO TALK TO YOU.
BUT...
WE DEMAND A DECREASE IN SALARY!

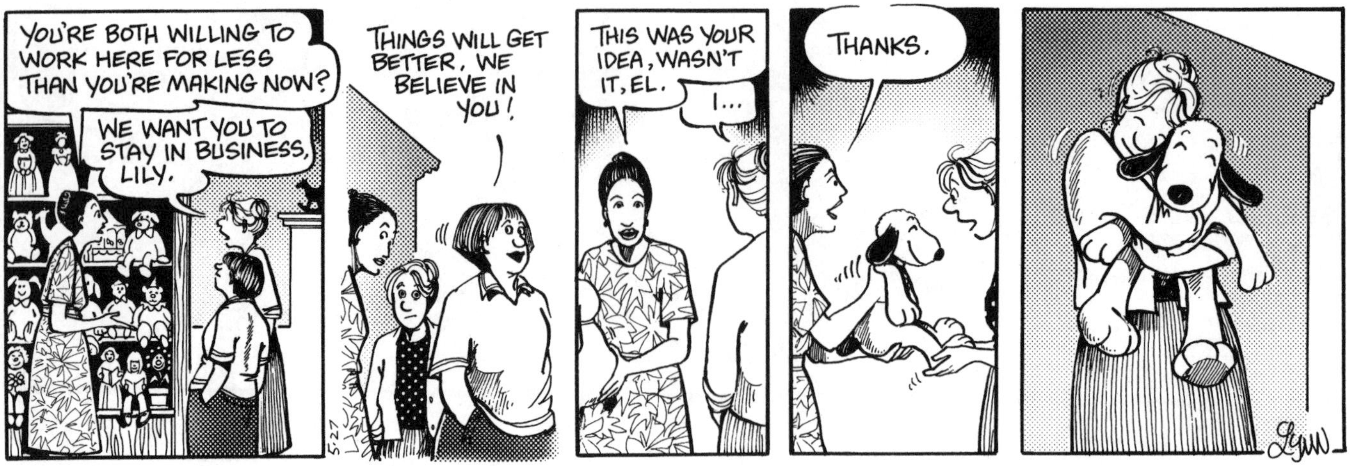
YOU'RE BOTH WILLING TO WORK HERE FOR LESS THAN YOU'RE MAKING NOW?
WE WANT YOU TO STAY IN BUSINESS, LILY.
THINGS WILL GET BETTER, WE BELIEVE IN YOU!
THIS WAS YOUR IDEA, WASN'T IT, EL.
I...
THANKS.

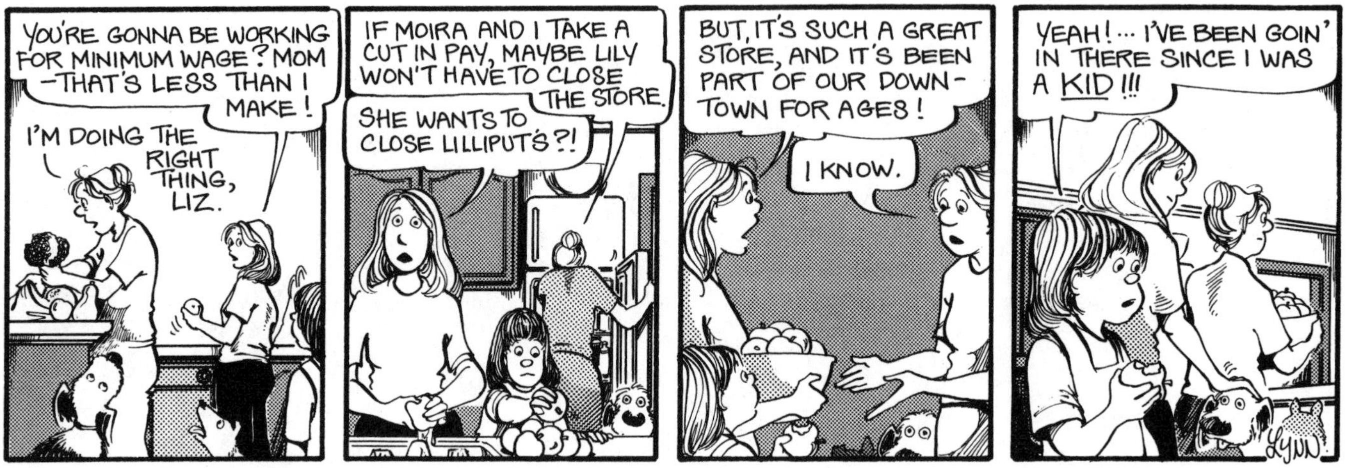
YOU'RE GONNA BE WORKING FOR MINIMUM WAGE? MOM —THAT'S LESS THAN I MAKE!
I'M DOING THE RIGHT THING, LIZ.
IF MOIRA AND I TAKE A CUT IN PAY, MAYBE LILY WON'T HAVE TO CLOSE THE STORE.
SHE WANTS TO CLOSE LILLIPUT'S?!
BUT, IT'S SUCH A GREAT STORE, AND IT'S BEEN PART OF OUR DOWN-TOWN FOR AGES!
I KNOW.
YEAH! ... I'VE BEEN GOIN' IN THERE SINCE I WAS A KID!!!

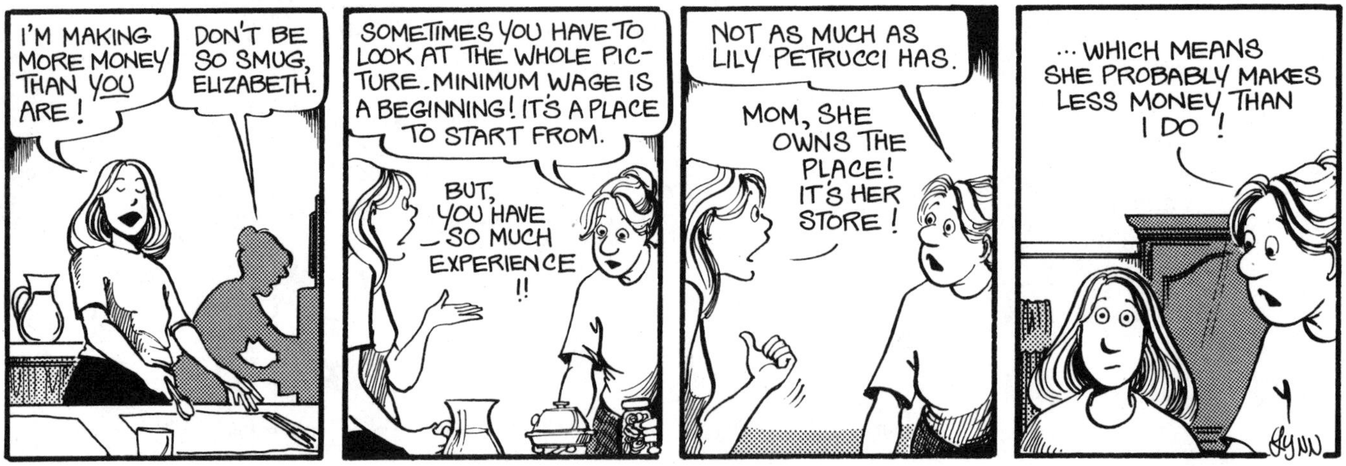
I'M MAKING MORE MONEY THAN YOU ARE!
DON'T BE SO SMUG, ELIZABETH.
SOMETIMES YOU HAVE TO LOOK AT THE WHOLE PIC-TURE. MINIMUM WAGE IS A BEGINNING! IT'S A PLACE TO START FROM.
BUT, YOU HAVE SO MUCH EXPERIENCE!!
NOT AS MUCH AS LILY PETRUCCI HAS.
MOM, SHE OWNS THE PLACE! IT'S HER STORE!
... WHICH MEANS SHE PROBABLY MAKES LESS MONEY THAN I DO!

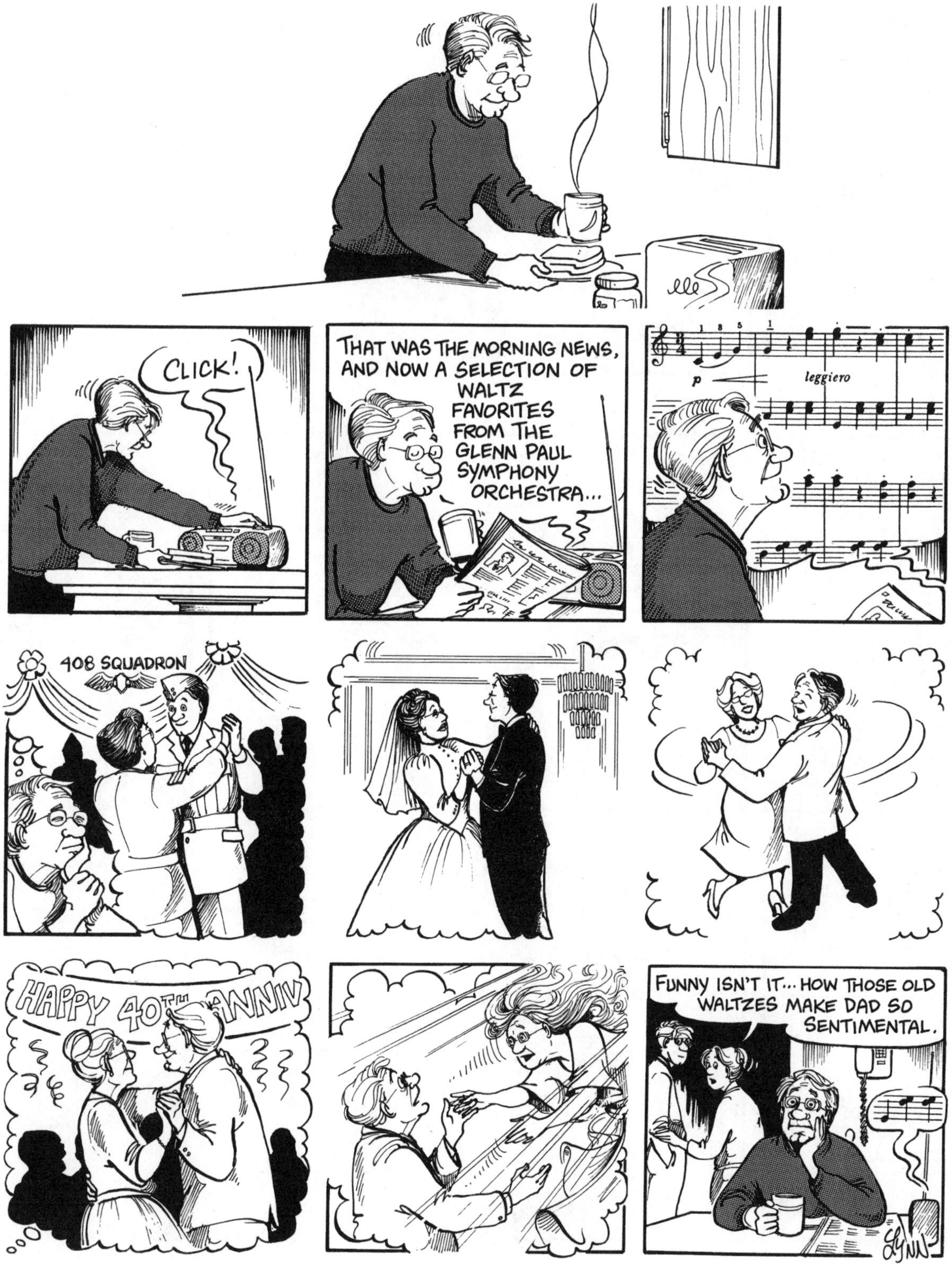
CLICK!
THAT WAS THE MORNING NEWS, AND NOW A SELECTION OF WALTZ FAVORITES FROM THE GLENN PAUL SYMPHONY ORCHESTRA...
p
leggiero
408 SQUADRON
HAPPY 40TH ANNIV
FUNNY ISN'T IT... HOW THOSE OLD WALTZES MAKE DAD SO SENTIMENTAL.
LYNN

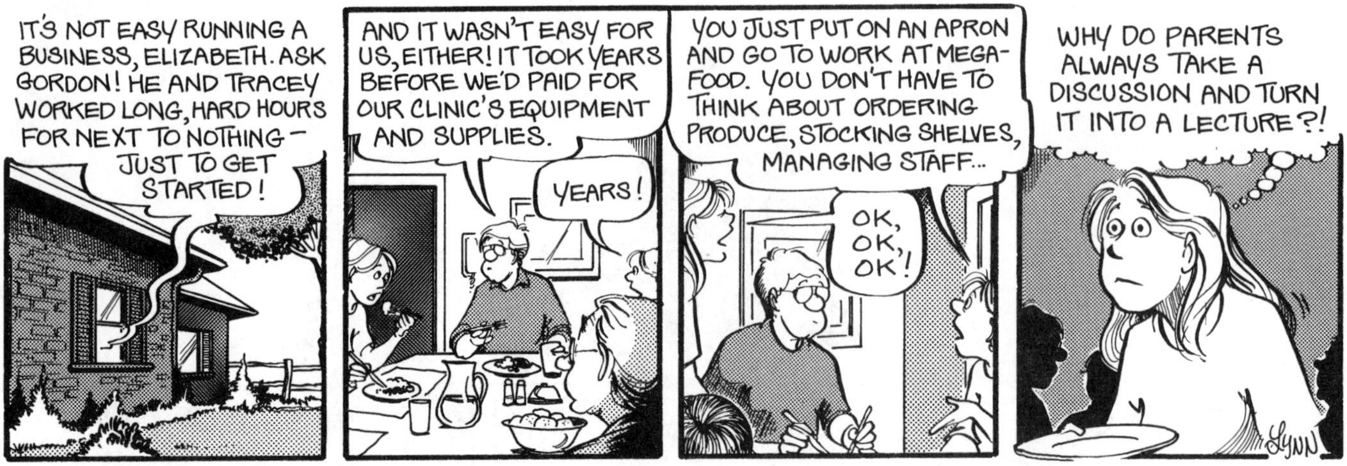
IT'S NOT EASY RUNNING A BUSINESS, ELIZABETH. ASK GORDON! HE AND TRACEY WORKED LONG, HARD HOURS FOR NEXT TO NOTHING— JUST TO GET STARTED!
AND IT WASN'T EASY FOR US, EITHER! IT TOOK YEARS BEFORE WE'D PAID FOR OUR CLINIC'S EQUIPMENT AND SUPPLIES.
YEARS!
YOU JUST PUT ON AN APRON AND GO TO WORK AT MEGA-FOOD. YOU DON'T HAVE TO THINK ABOUT ORDERING PRODUCE, STOCKING SHELVES, MANAGING STAFF...
OK, OK, OK!
WHY DO PARENTS ALWAYS TAKE A DISCUSSION AND TURN IT INTO A LECTURE?!
LYNN

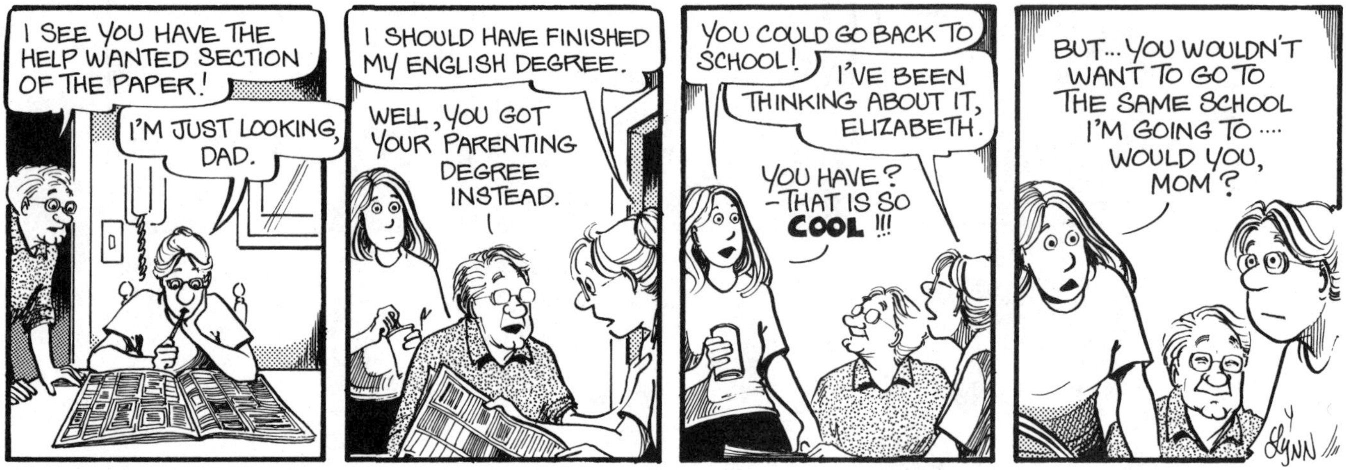
I SEE YOU HAVE THE HELP WANTED SECTION OF THE PAPER!
I'M JUST LOOKING, DAD.
I SHOULD HAVE FINISHED MY ENGLISH DEGREE.
WELL, YOU GOT YOUR PARENTING DEGREE INSTEAD.
YOU COULD GO BACK TO SCHOOL!
I'VE BEEN THINKING ABOUT IT, ELIZABETH.
YOU HAVE? —THAT IS SO **COOL**!!!
BUT... YOU WOULDN'T WANT TO GO TO THE SAME SCHOOL I'M GOING TO.... WOULD YOU, MOM?
LYNN

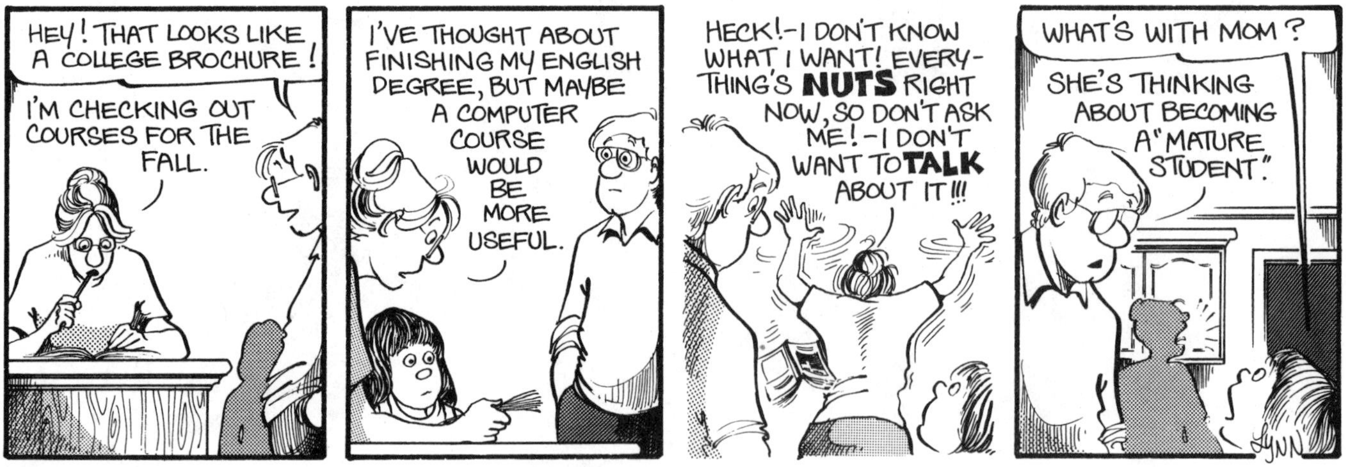
HEY! THAT LOOKS LIKE A COLLEGE BROCHURE!
I'M CHECKING OUT COURSES FOR THE FALL.
I'VE THOUGHT ABOUT FINISHING MY ENGLISH DEGREE, BUT MAYBE A COMPUTER COURSE WOULD BE MORE USEFUL.
HECK!—I DON'T KNOW WHAT I WANT! EVERY-THING'S **NUTS** RIGHT NOW, SO DON'T ASK ME!—I DON'T WANT TO **TALK** ABOUT IT!!!
WHAT'S WITH MOM?
SHE'S THINKING ABOUT BECOMING A "MATURE STUDENT."
LYNN

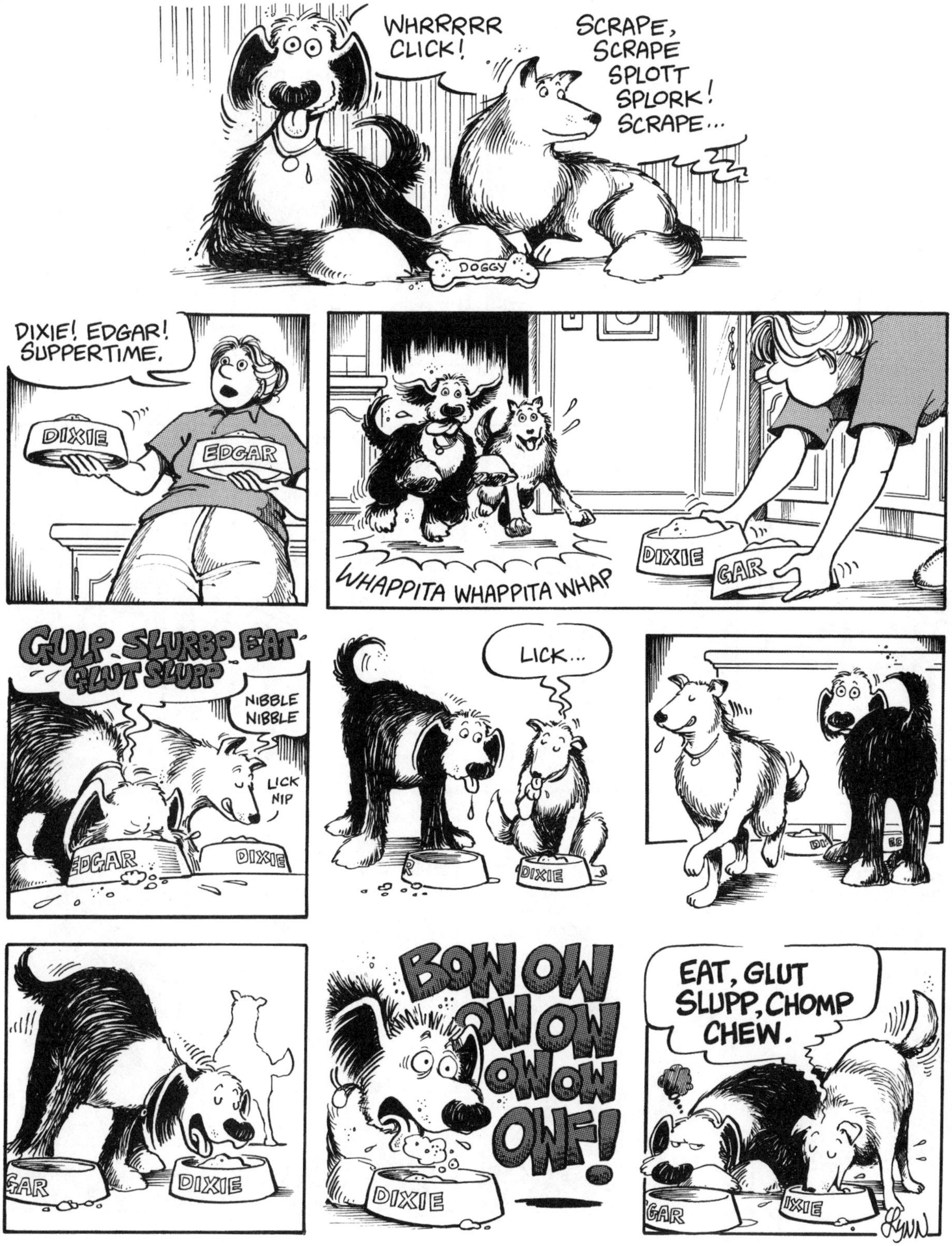
WHRRRRR CLICK!
SCRAPE, SCRAPE SPLOTT SPLORK! SCRAPE...
DOGGY
DIXIE! EDGAR! SUPPERTIME.
DIXIE
EDGAR
WHAPPITA WHAPPITA WHAP
DIXIE
GAR
GULP SLURRP EAT GLUT SLUPP
NIBBLE NIBBLE
LICK NIP
EDGAR
DIXIE
LICK...
DIXIE
GAR
DIXIE
BOW OW OW OW OW OW ONF!
DIXIE
EAT, GLUT SLUPP, CHOMP CHEW.
GAR
IXIE
Lynn

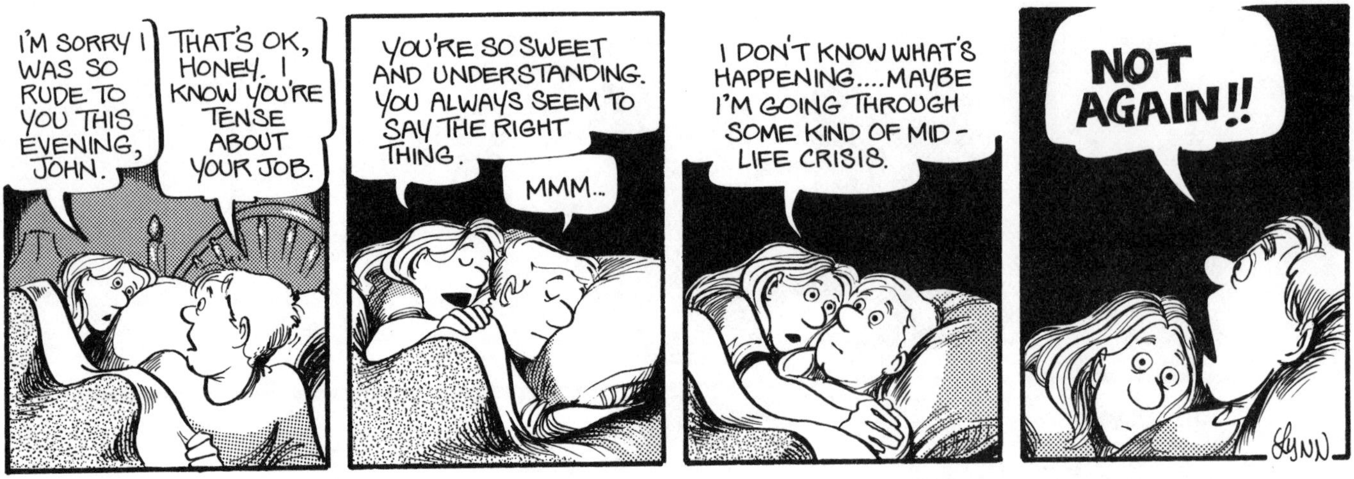
I'M SORRY I WAS SO RUDE TO YOU THIS EVENING, JOHN.
THAT'S OK, HONEY. I KNOW YOU'RE TENSE ABOUT YOUR JOB.
YOU'RE SO SWEET AND UNDERSTANDING. YOU ALWAYS SEEM TO SAY THE RIGHT THING.
MMM...
I DON'T KNOW WHAT'S HAPPENING....MAYBE I'M GOING THROUGH SOME KIND OF MID-LIFE CRISIS.
NOT AGAIN!!
LYNN

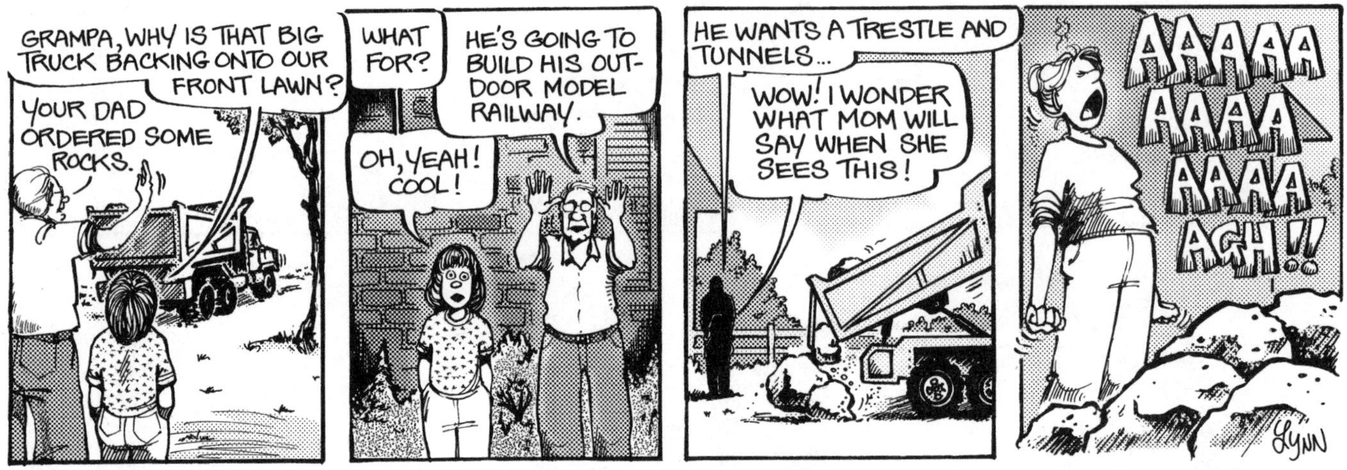
GRAMPA, WHY IS THAT BIG TRUCK BACKING ONTO OUR FRONT LAWN?
YOUR DAD ORDERED SOME ROCKS.
WHAT FOR?
HE'S GOING TO BUILD HIS OUT-DOOR MODEL RAILWAY.
OH, YEAH! COOL!
HE WANTS A TRESTLE AND TUNNELS...
WOW! I WONDER WHAT MOM WILL SAY WHEN SHE SEES THIS!
AAAAA AAAA AAAA AGH!!
LYNN

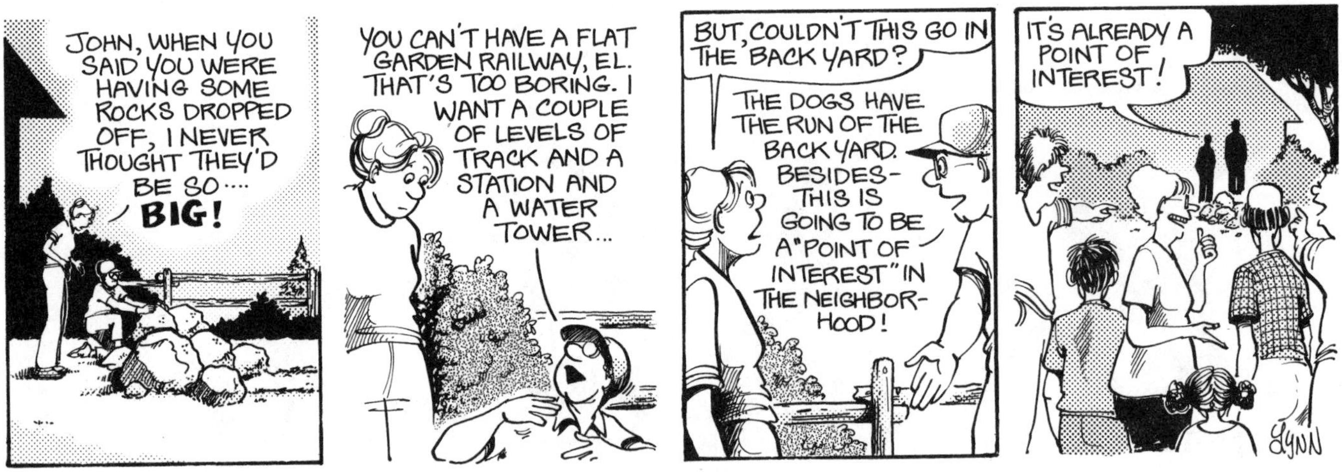
JOHN, WHEN YOU SAID YOU WERE HAVING SOME ROCKS DROPPED OFF, I NEVER THOUGHT THEY'D BE SO.... BIG!
YOU CAN'T HAVE A FLAT GARDEN RAILWAY, EL. THAT'S TOO BORING. I WANT A COUPLE OF LEVELS OF TRACK AND A STATION AND A WATER TOWER...
BUT, COULDN'T THIS GO IN THE BACK YARD?
THE DOGS HAVE THE RUN OF THE BACK YARD. BESIDES - THIS IS GOING TO BE A "POINT OF INTEREST" IN THE NEIGHBOR-HOOD!
IT'S ALREADY A POINT OF INTEREST!
LYNN

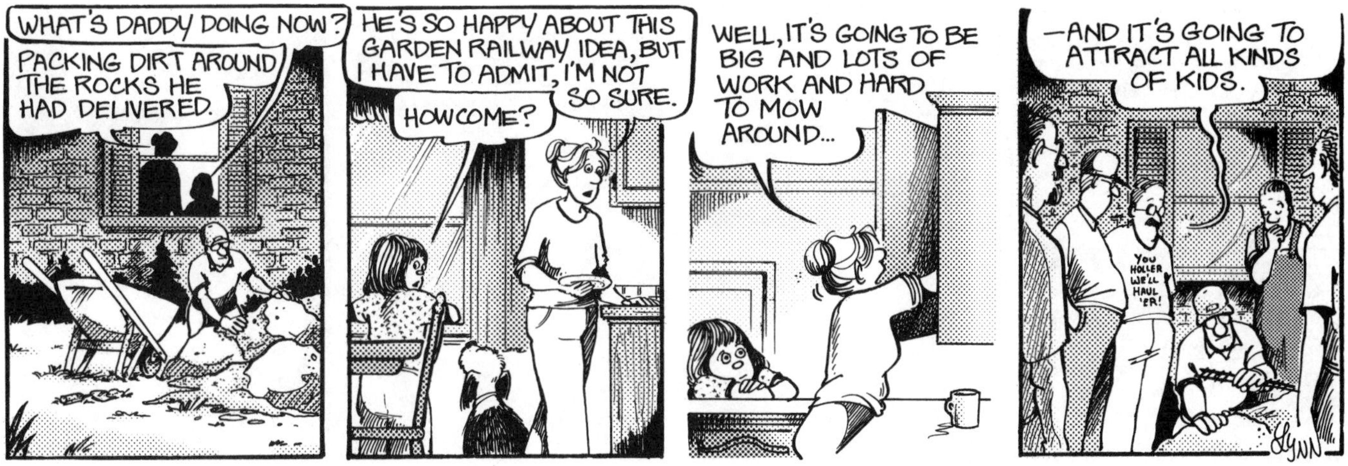
WHAT'S DADDY DOING NOW?
PACKING DIRT AROUND THE ROCKS HE HAD DELIVERED.
HE'S SO HAPPY ABOUT THIS GARDEN RAILWAY IDEA, BUT I HAVE TO ADMIT, I'M NOT SO SURE.
HOW COME?
WELL, IT'S GOING TO BE BIG AND LOTS OF WORK AND HARD TO MOW AROUND...
—AND IT'S GOING TO ATTRACT ALL KINDS OF KIDS.
YOU HOLLER WE'LL HAUL 'ER!
LYNN

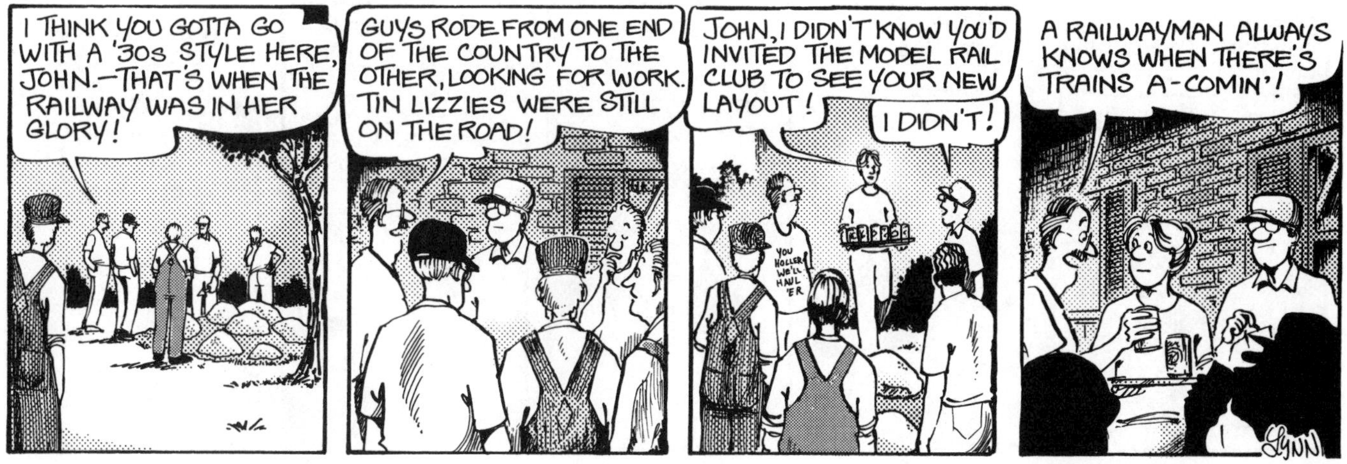
I THINK YOU GOTTA GO WITH A '30s STYLE HERE, JOHN.—THAT'S WHEN THE RAILWAY WAS IN HER GLORY!
GUYS RODE FROM ONE END OF THE COUNTRY TO THE OTHER, LOOKING FOR WORK. TIN LIZZIES WERE STILL ON THE ROAD!
JOHN, I DIDN'T KNOW YOU'D INVITED THE MODEL RAIL CLUB TO SEE YOUR NEW LAYOUT!
I DIDN'T!
YOU HOLLER WE'LL HAUL 'ER
A RAILWAYMAN ALWAYS KNOWS WHEN THERE'S TRAINS A-COMIN'!
LYNN

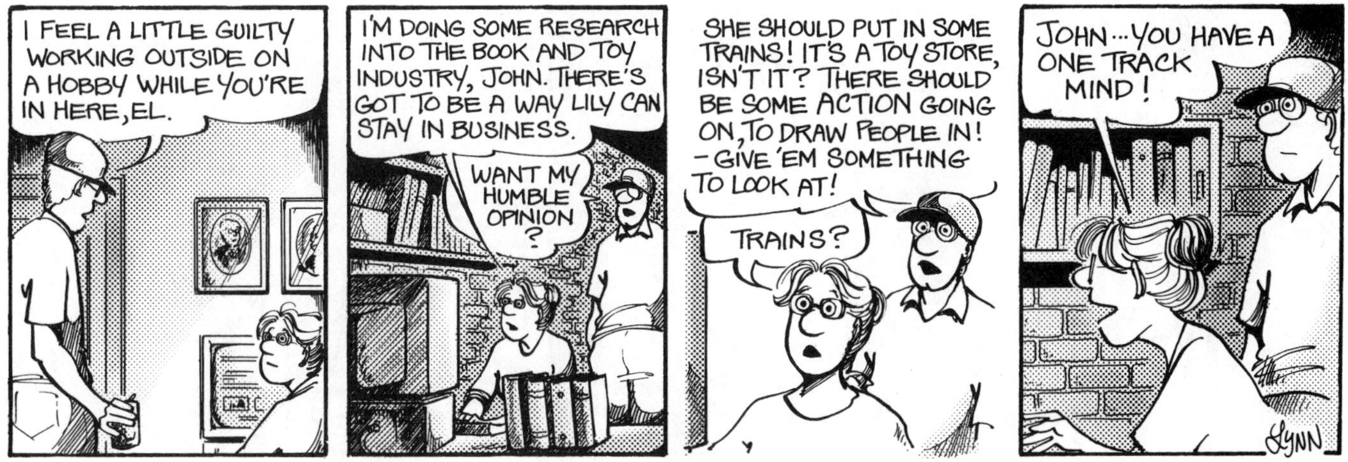
I FEEL A LITTLE GUILTY WORKING OUTSIDE ON A HOBBY WHILE YOU'RE IN HERE, EL.
I'M DOING SOME RESEARCH INTO THE BOOK AND TOY INDUSTRY, JOHN. THERE'S GOT TO BE A WAY LILY CAN STAY IN BUSINESS.
WANT MY HUMBLE OPINION?
SHE SHOULD PUT IN SOME TRAINS! IT'S A TOY STORE, ISN'T IT? THERE SHOULD BE SOME ACTION GOING ON, TO DRAW PEOPLE IN! —GIVE 'EM SOMETHING TO LOOK AT!
TRAINS?
JOHN... YOU HAVE A ONE TRACK MIND!
LYNN

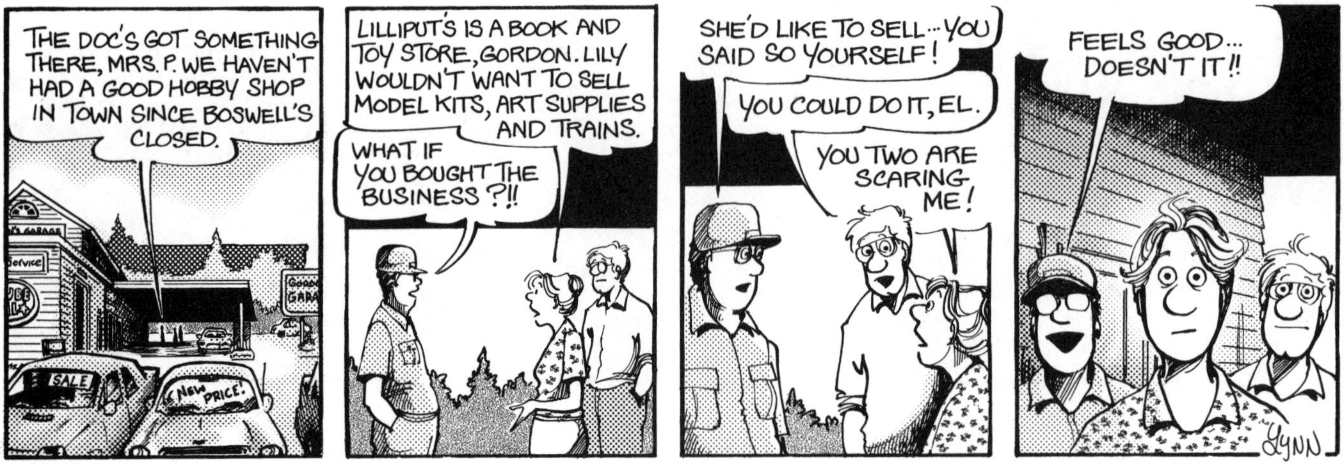
THE DOC'S GOT SOMETHING THERE, MRS. P. WE HAVEN'T HAD A GOOD HOBBY SHOP IN TOWN SINCE BOSWELL'S CLOSED.
SALE
NEW PRICE!
LILLIPUT'S IS A BOOK AND TOY STORE, GORDON. LILY WOULDN'T WANT TO SELL MODEL KITS, ART SUPPLIES AND TRAINS.
WHAT IF YOU BOUGHT THE BUSINESS ?!!
SHE'D LIKE TO SELL... YOU SAID SO YOURSELF!
YOU COULD DO IT, EL.
YOU TWO ARE SCARING ME!
FEELS GOOD... DOESN'T IT!!
LYNN

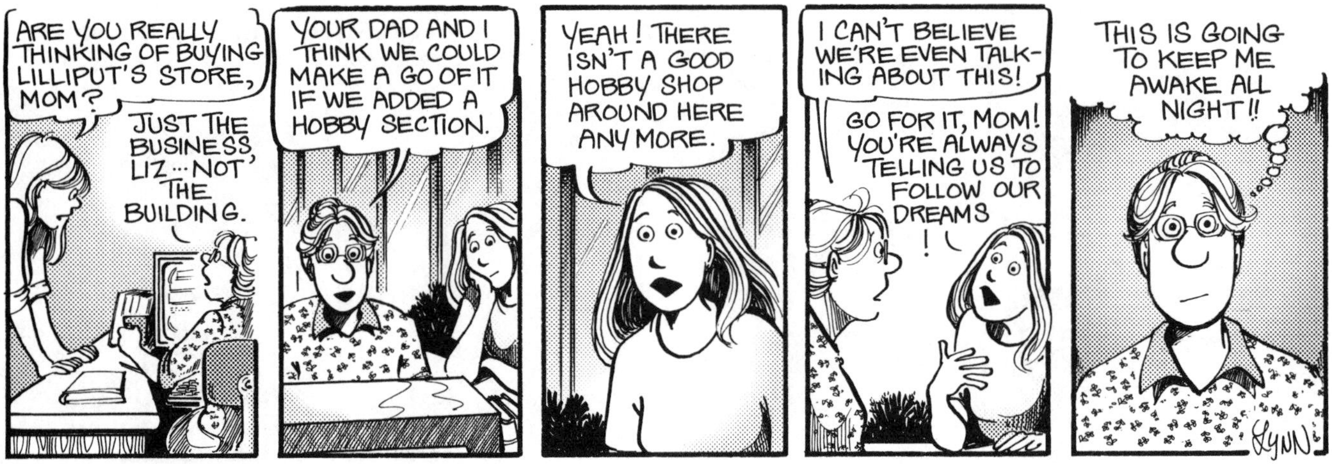
ARE YOU REALLY THINKING OF BUYING LILLIPUT'S STORE, MOM?
JUST THE BUSINESS, LIZ... NOT THE BUILDING.
YOUR DAD AND I THINK WE COULD MAKE A GO OF IT IF WE ADDED A HOBBY SECTION.
YEAH! THERE ISN'T A GOOD HOBBY SHOP AROUND HERE ANY MORE.
I CAN'T BELIEVE WE'RE EVEN TALKING ABOUT THIS!
GO FOR IT, MOM! YOU'RE ALWAYS TELLING US TO FOLLOW OUR DREAMS
THIS IS GOING TO KEEP ME AWAKE ALL NIGHT!!
LYNN

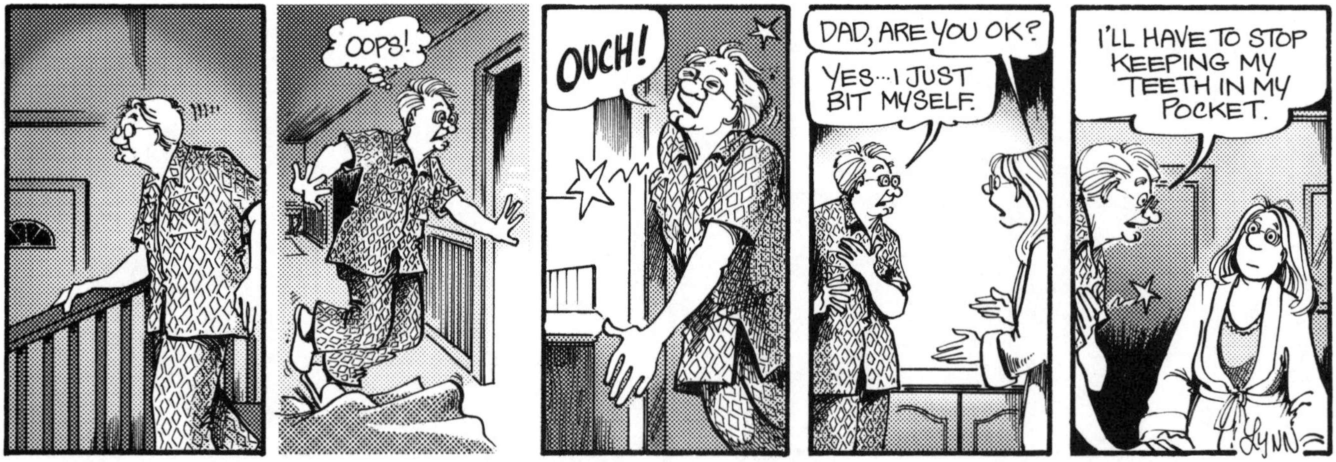
OOPS!
OUCH!
DAD, ARE YOU OK?
YES... I JUST BIT MYSELF.
I'LL HAVE TO STOP KEEPING MY TEETH IN MY POCKET.
LYNN

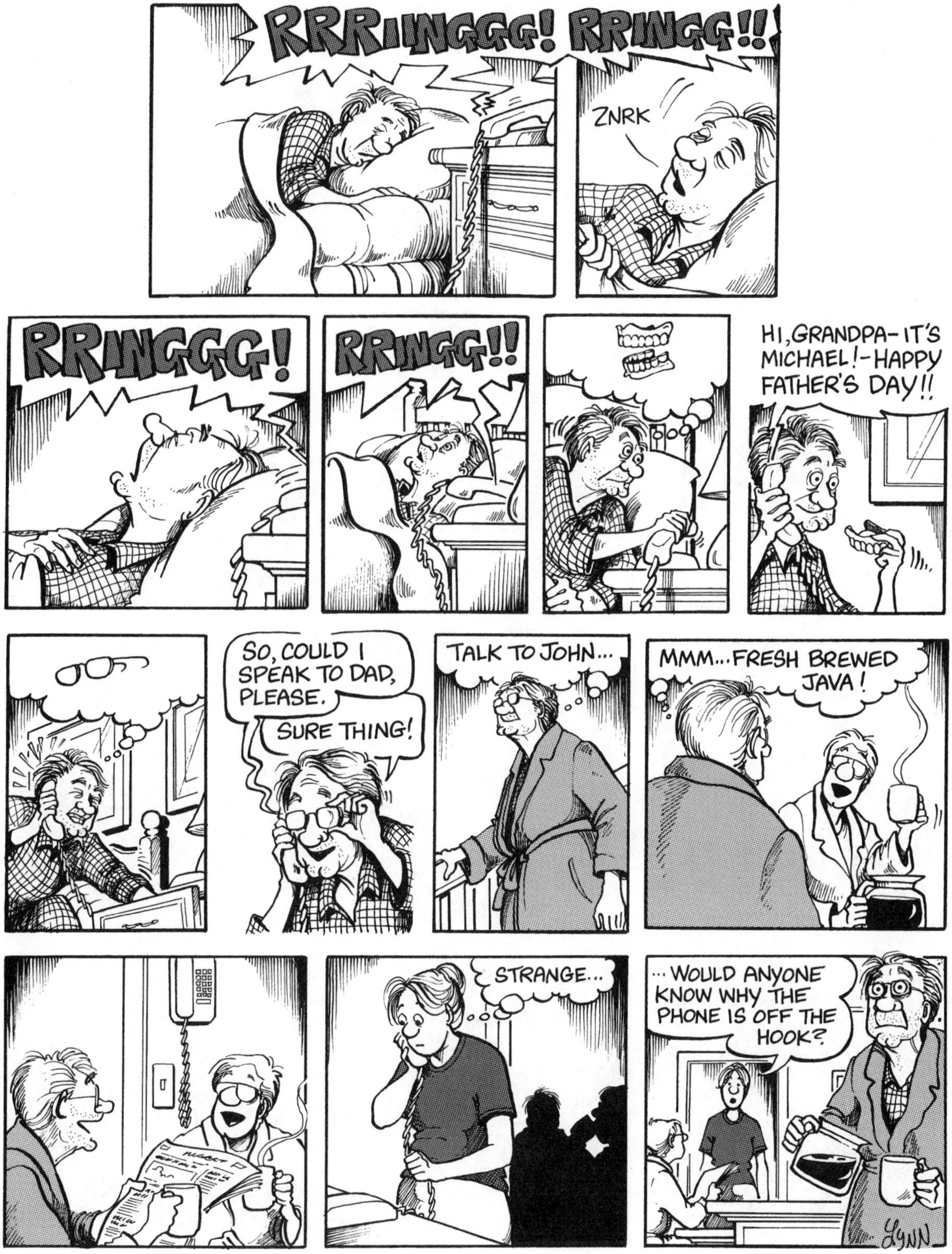
RRRIINGGG! RRINGG!!
ZNRK
RRINGGG!
RRINGG!!
HI, GRANDPA- IT'S MICHAEL! -HAPPY FATHER'S DAY!!
SO, COULD I SPEAK TO DAD, PLEASE.
SURE THING!
TALK TO JOHN...
MMM... FRESH BREWED JAVA!
STRANGE...
...WOULD ANYONE KNOW WHY THE PHONE IS OFF THE HOOK?
LYNN

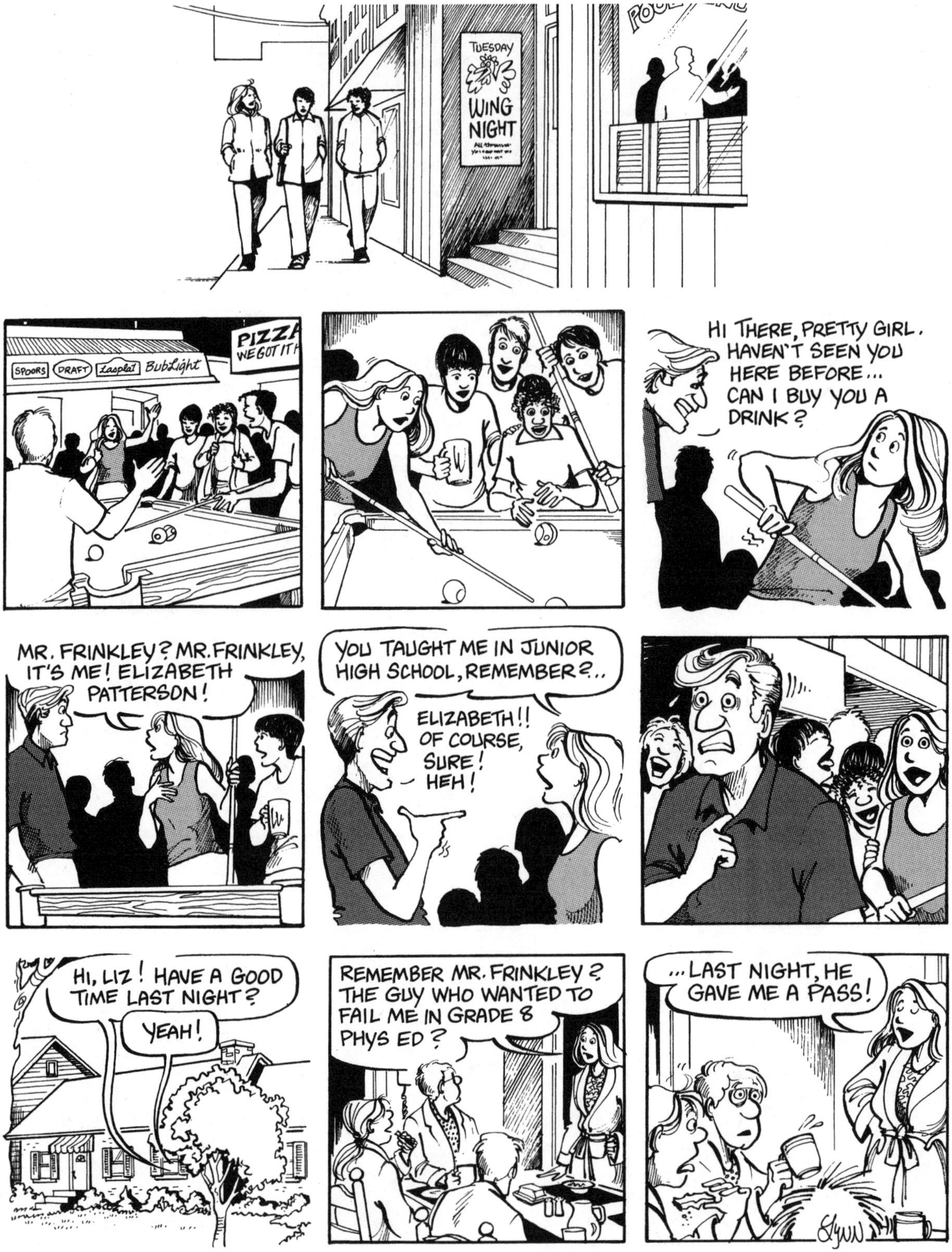
TUESDAY
WING NIGHT
PIZZA
WE GOT IT
SPOORS
DRAFT
HI THERE, PRETTY GIRL. HAVEN'T SEEN YOU HERE BEFORE... CAN I BUY YOU A DRINK?
MR. FRINKLEY? MR. FRINKLEY, IT'S ME! ELIZABETH PATTERSON!
YOU TAUGHT ME IN JUNIOR HIGH SCHOOL, REMEMBER?..
ELIZABETH!! OF COURSE, SURE! HEH!
HI, LIZ! HAVE A GOOD TIME LAST NIGHT?
YEAH!
REMEMBER MR. FRINKLEY? THE GUY WHO WANTED TO FAIL ME IN GRADE 8 PHYS ED?
...LAST NIGHT, HE GAVE ME A PASS!

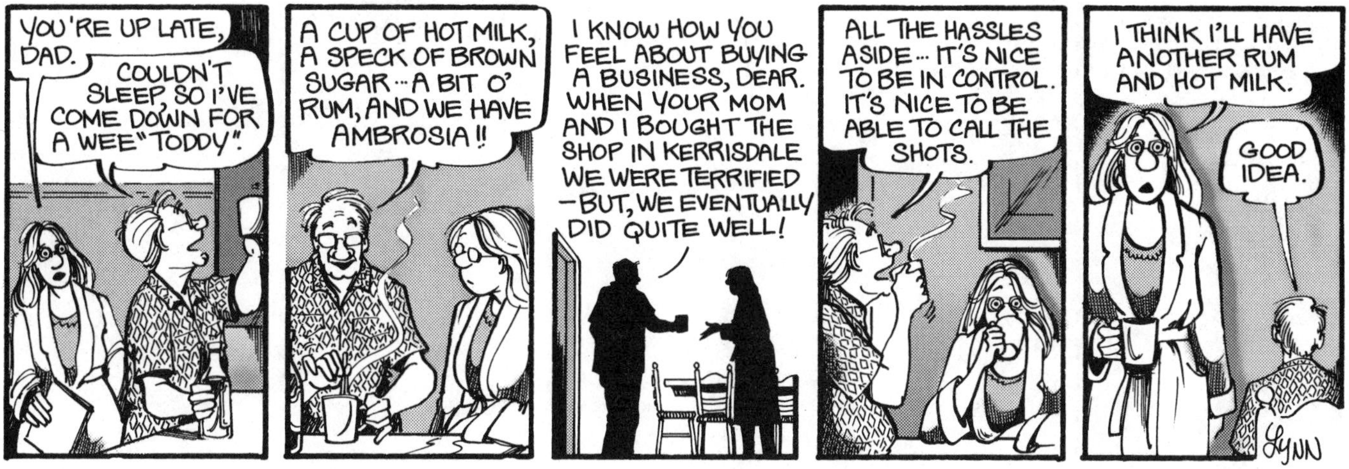
YOU'RE UP LATE, DAD.
COULDN'T SLEEP, SO I'VE COME DOWN FOR A WEE "TODDY".
A CUP OF HOT MILK, A SPECK OF BROWN SUGAR ... A BIT O' RUM, AND WE HAVE AMBROSIA !!
I KNOW HOW YOU FEEL ABOUT BUYING A BUSINESS, DEAR. WHEN YOUR MOM AND I BOUGHT THE SHOP IN KERRISDALE WE WERE TERRIFIED —BUT, WE EVENTUALLY DID QUITE WELL!
ALL THE HASSLES ASIDE ... IT'S NICE TO BE IN CONTROL. IT'S NICE TO BE ABLE TO CALL THE SHOTS.
I THINK I'LL HAVE ANOTHER RUM AND HOT MILK.
GOOD IDEA.
LYNN

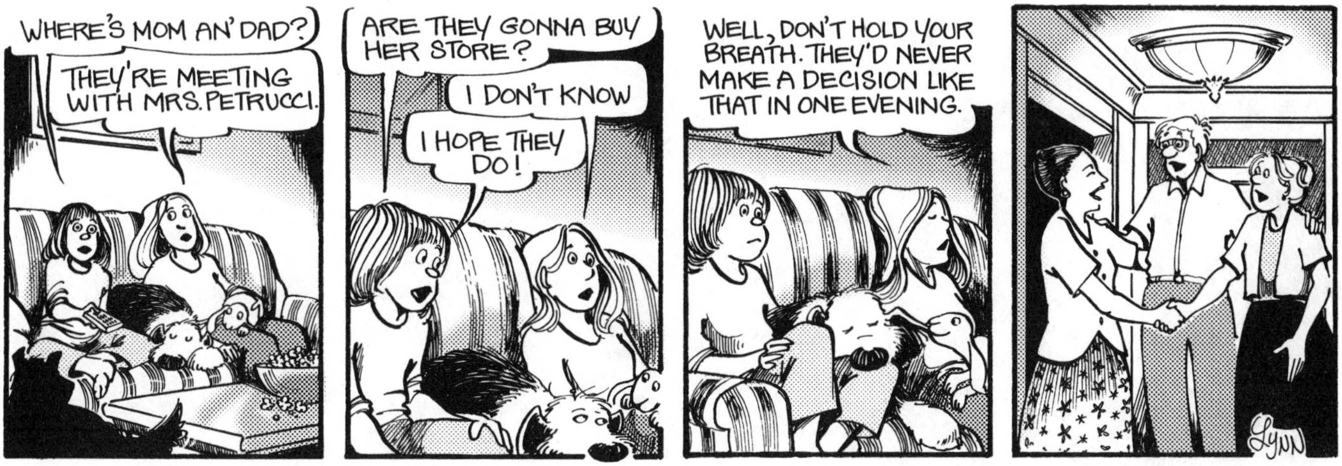
WHERE'S MOM AN' DAD?
THEY'RE MEETING WITH MRS. PETRUCCI.
ARE THEY GONNA BUY HER STORE?
I DON'T KNOW
I HOPE THEY DO!
WELL, DON'T HOLD YOUR BREATH. THEY'D NEVER MAKE A DECISION LIKE THAT IN ONE EVENING.
LYNN

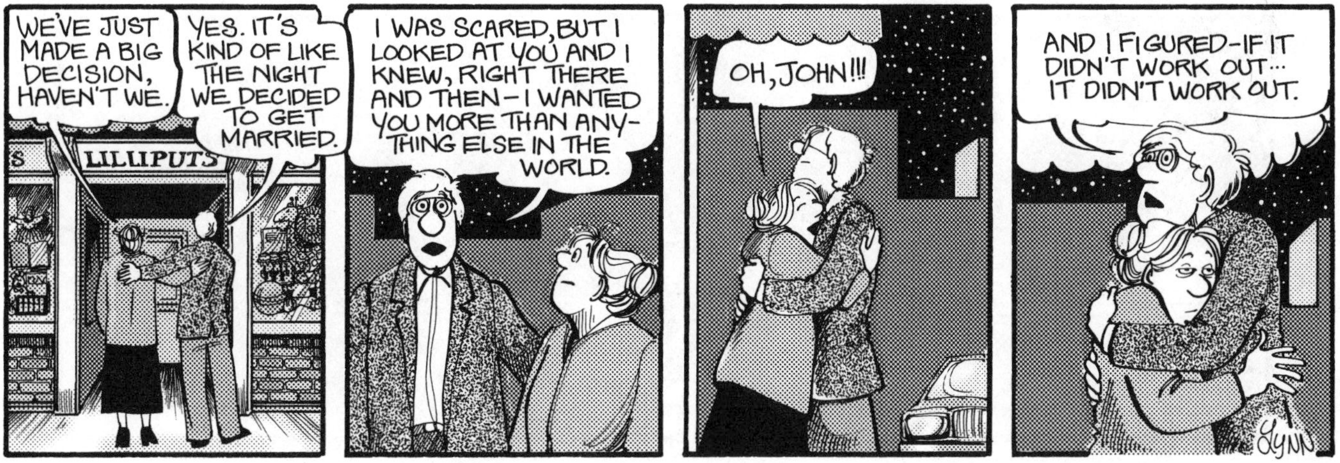
WE'VE JUST MADE A BIG DECISION, HAVEN'T WE.
YES. IT'S KIND OF LIKE THE NIGHT WE DECIDED TO GET MARRIED.
LILLIPUTS
I WAS SCARED, BUT I LOOKED AT YOU AND I KNEW, RIGHT THERE AND THEN — I WANTED YOU MORE THAN ANYTHING ELSE IN THE WORLD.
OH, JOHN!!!
AND I FIGURED—IF IT DIDN'T WORK OUT ... IT DIDN'T WORK OUT.
LYNN

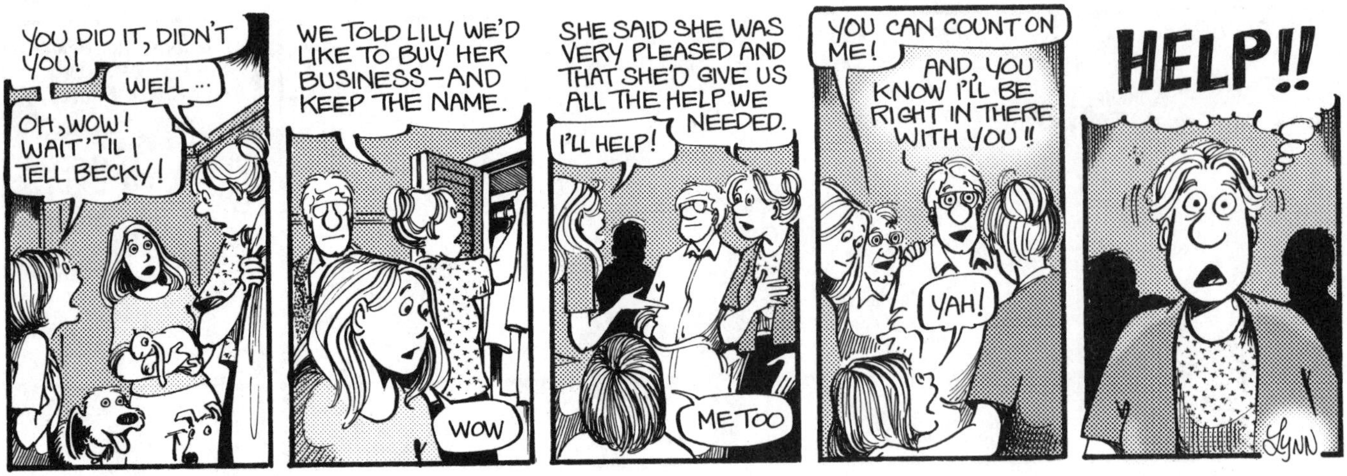
YOU DID IT, DIDN'T YOU!
WELL...
OH, WOW! WAIT 'TIL I TELL BECKY!
WE TOLD LILY WE'D LIKE TO BUY HER BUSINESS—AND KEEP THE NAME.
WOW
SHE SAID SHE WAS VERY PLEASED AND THAT SHE'D GIVE US ALL THE HELP WE NEEDED.
I'LL HELP!
ME TOO
YOU CAN COUNT ON ME!
AND, YOU KNOW I'LL BE RIGHT IN THERE WITH YOU !!
YAH!
HELP!!
LYNN

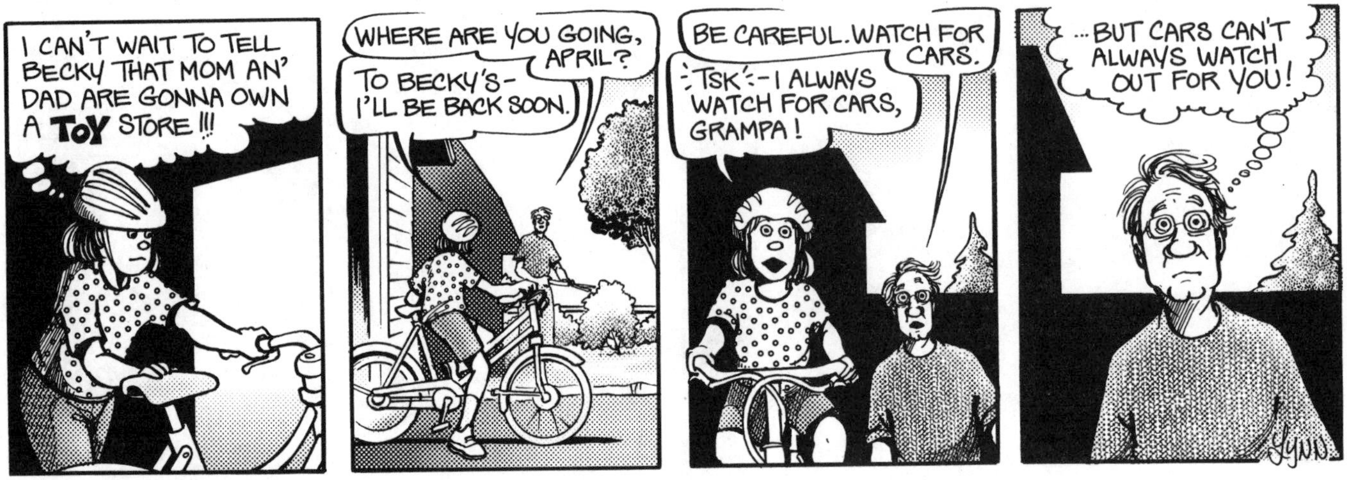
I CAN'T WAIT TO TELL BECKY THAT MOM AN' DAD ARE GONNA OWN A TOY STORE !!!
WHERE ARE YOU GOING, APRIL?
TO BECKY'S- I'LL BE BACK SOON.
BE CAREFUL. WATCH FOR CARS.
TSK - I ALWAYS WATCH FOR CARS, GRAMPA!
...BUT CARS CAN'T ALWAYS WATCH OUT FOR YOU!
LYNN

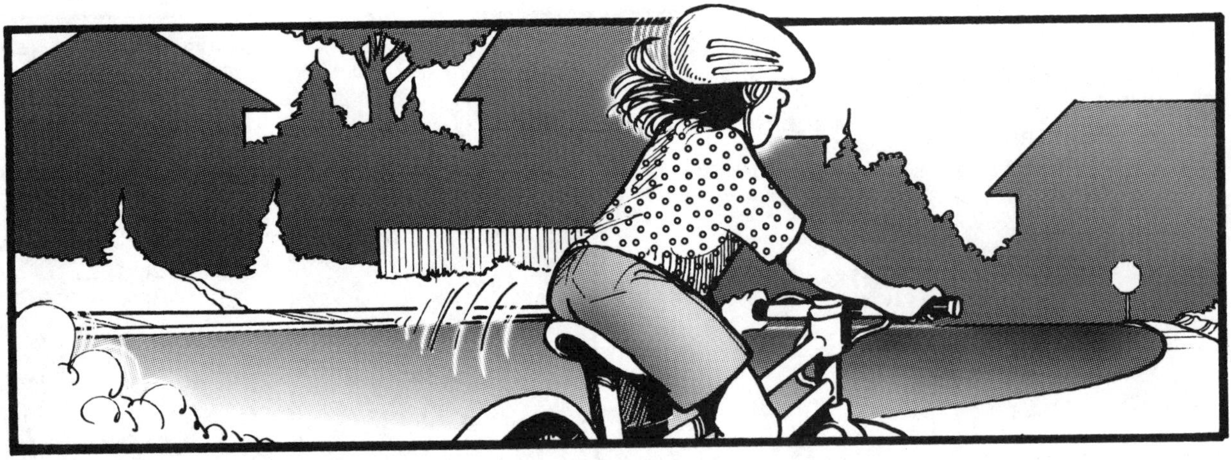

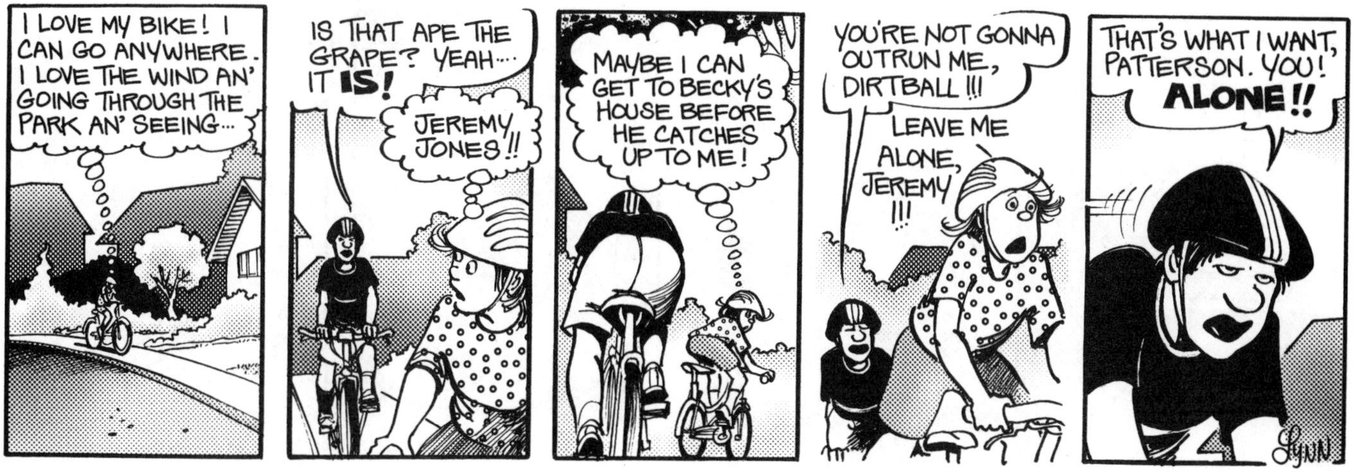
I LOVE MY BIKE! I CAN GO ANYWHERE. I LOVE THE WIND AN' GOING THROUGH THE PARK AN' SEEING...
IS THAT APE THE GRAPE? YEAH.... IT **IS**!
JEREMY JONES!!
MAYBE I CAN GET TO BECKY'S HOUSE BEFORE HE CATCHES UP TO ME!
YOU'RE NOT GONNA OUTRUN ME, DIRTBALL!!!
LEAVE ME ALONE, JEREMY!!!
THAT'S WHAT I WANT, PATTERSON. YOU! **ALONE!!**
LYNN

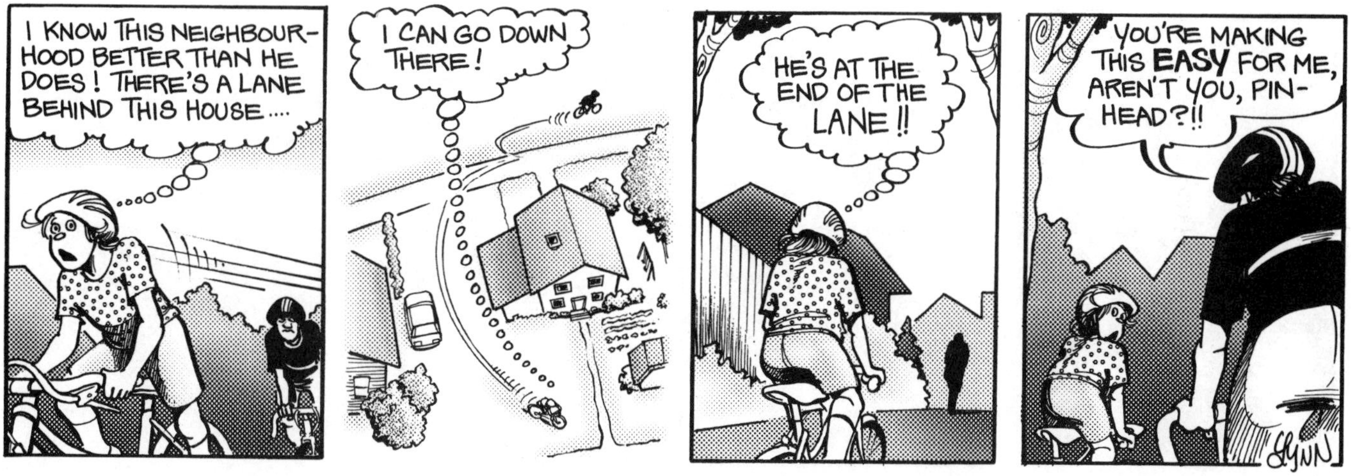
I KNOW THIS NEIGHBOURHOOD BETTER THAN HE DOES! THERE'S A LANE BEHIND THIS HOUSE....
I CAN GO DOWN THERE!
HE'S AT THE END OF THE LANE!!
YOU'RE MAKING THIS **EASY** FOR ME, AREN'T YOU, PINHEAD?!!
LYNN

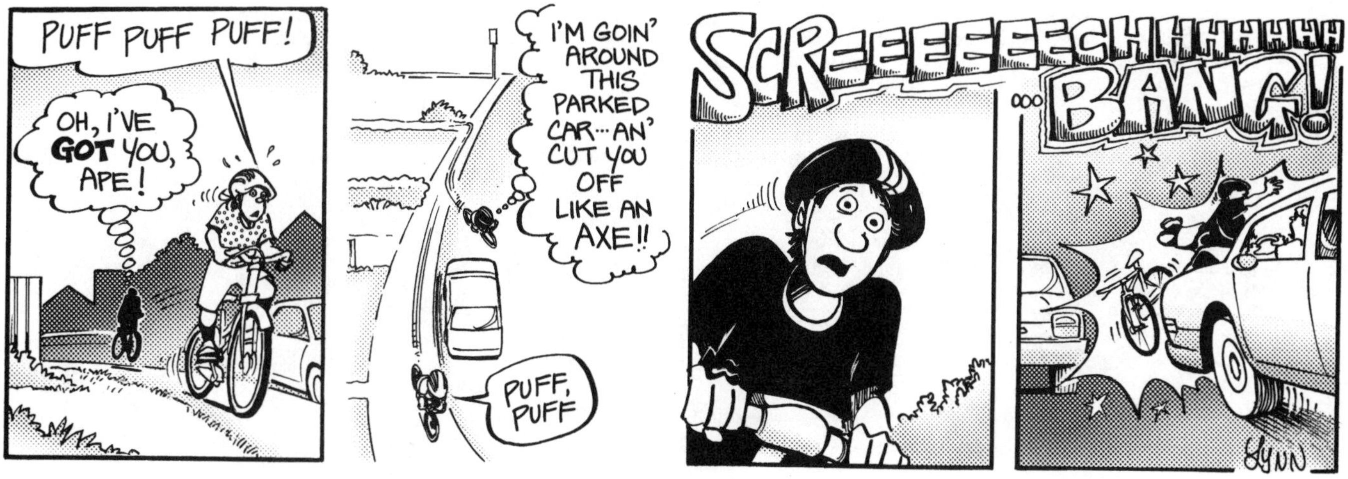
PUFF PUFF PUFF!
OH, I'VE **GOT** YOU, APE!
I'M GOIN' AROUND THIS PARKED CAR... AN' CUT YOU OFF LIKE AN AXE!!
PUFF, PUFF
SCREEEEEEECHHHHHHHH
...BANG!
LYNN

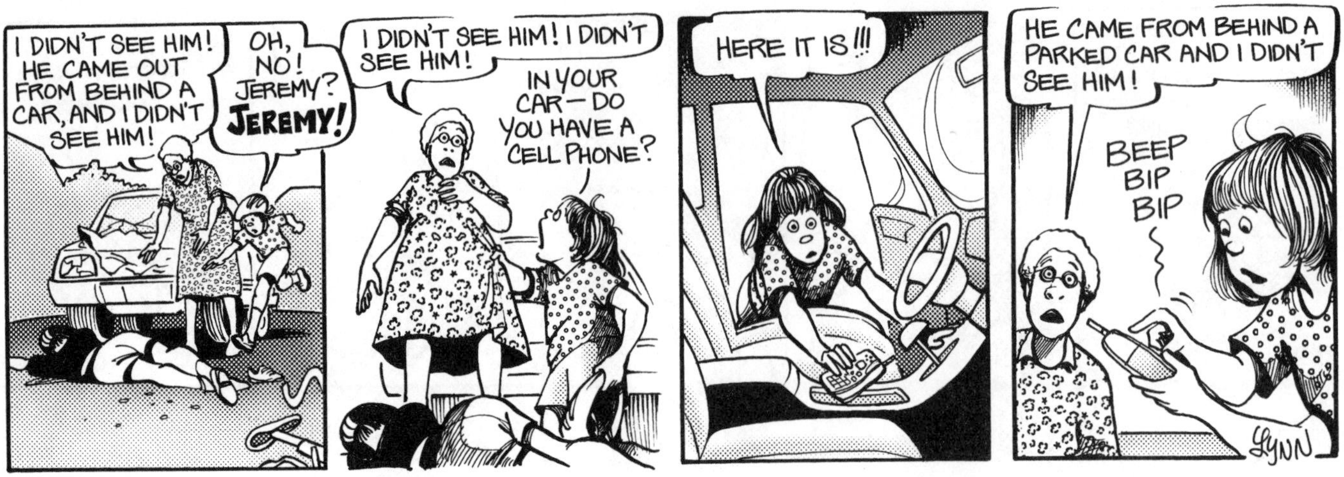
I DIDN'T SEE HIM! HE CAME OUT FROM BEHIND A CAR, AND I DIDN'T SEE HIM!
OH, NO! JEREMY? JEREMY!
I DIDN'T SEE HIM! I DIDN'T SEE HIM!
IN YOUR CAR— DO YOU HAVE A CELL PHONE?
HERE IT IS!!!
HE CAME FROM BEHIND A PARKED CAR AND I DIDN'T SEE HIM!
BEEP BIP BIP
LYNN

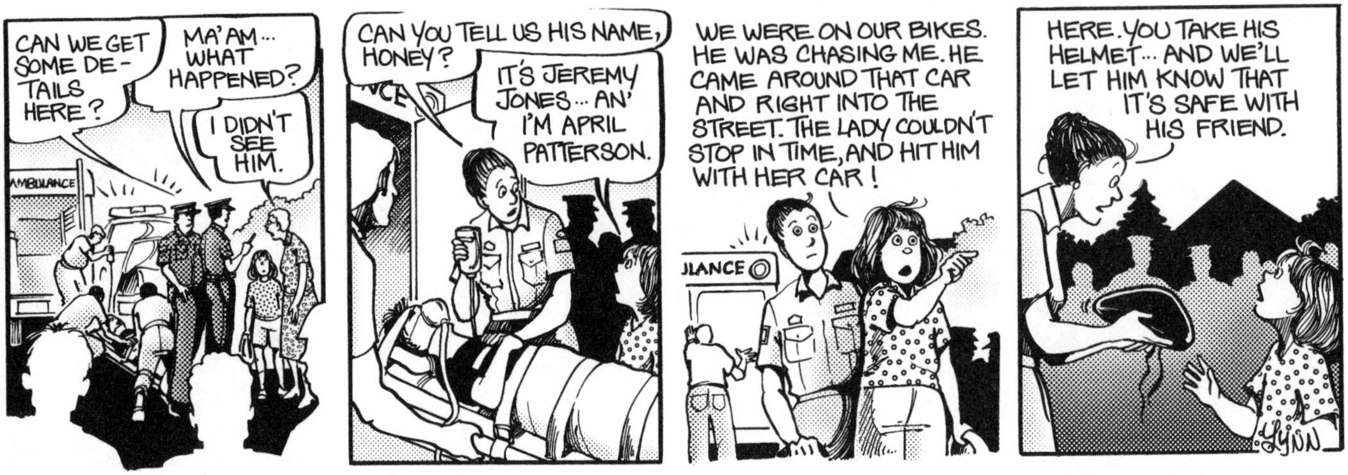
CAN WE GET SOME DE-TAILS HERE?
MA'AM... WHAT HAPPENED?
I DIDN'T SEE HIM.
AMBULANCE
CAN YOU TELL US HIS NAME, HONEY?
IT'S JEREMY JONES... AN' I'M APRIL PATTERSON.
WE WERE ON OUR BIKES. HE WAS CHASING ME. HE CAME AROUND THAT CAR AND RIGHT INTO THE STREET. THE LADY COULDN'T STOP IN TIME, AND HIT HIM WITH HER CAR!
HERE. YOU TAKE HIS HELMET... AND WE'LL LET HIM KNOW THAT IT'S SAFE WITH HIS FRIEND.
LYNN

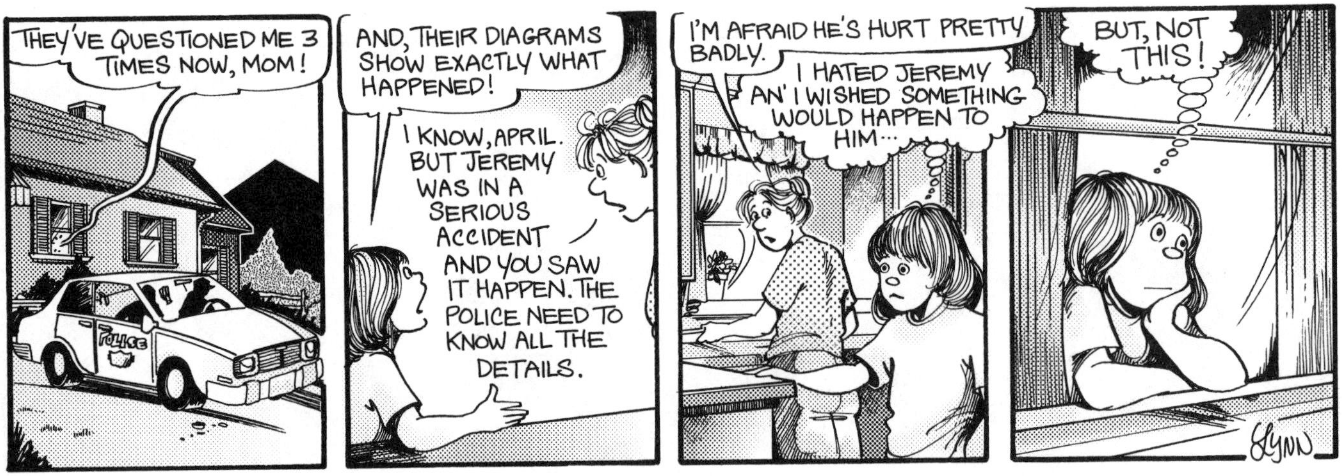
THEY'VE QUESTIONED ME 3 TIMES NOW, MOM!
POLICE
AND, THEIR DIAGRAMS SHOW EXACTLY WHAT HAPPENED!
I KNOW, APRIL. BUT JEREMY WAS IN A SERIOUS ACCIDENT AND YOU SAW IT HAPPEN. THE POLICE NEED TO KNOW ALL THE DETAILS.
I'M AFRAID HE'S HURT PRETTY BADLY.
I HATED JEREMY AN' I WISHED SOMETHING WOULD HAPPEN TO HIM...
BUT, NOT THIS!
LYNN

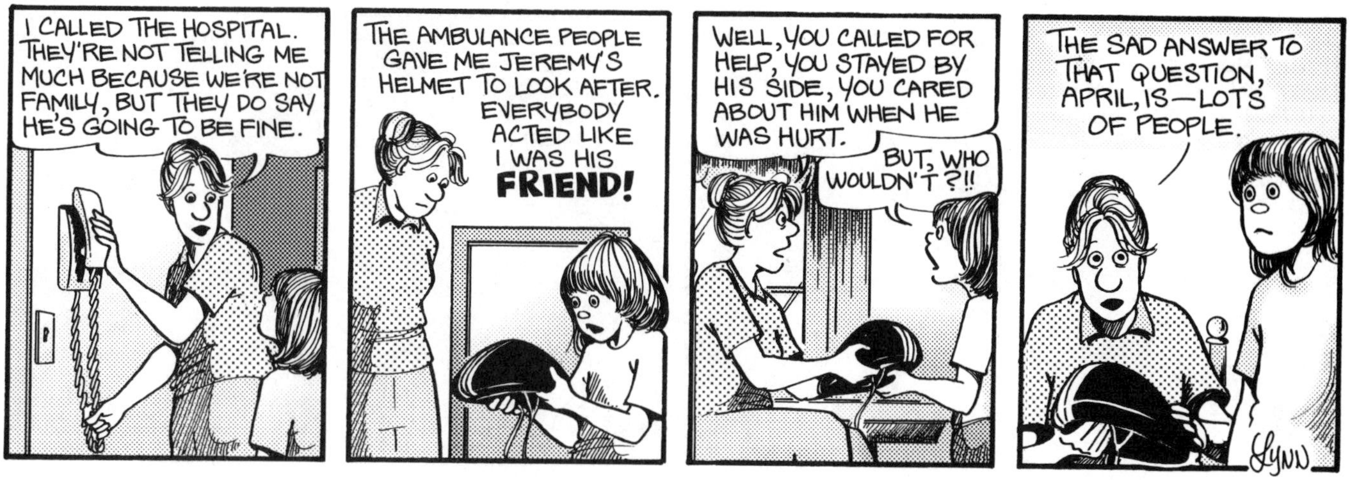
I CALLED THE HOSPITAL. THEY'RE NOT TELLING ME MUCH BECAUSE WE'RE NOT FAMILY, BUT THEY DO SAY HE'S GOING TO BE FINE.
THE AMBULANCE PEOPLE GAVE ME JEREMY'S HELMET TO LOOK AFTER.
EVERYBODY ACTED LIKE I WAS HIS **FRIEND!**
WELL, YOU CALLED FOR HELP, YOU STAYED BY HIS SIDE, YOU CARED ABOUT HIM WHEN HE WAS HURT.
BUT, WHO WOULDN'T?!!
THE SAD ANSWER TO THAT QUESTION, APRIL, IS—LOTS OF PEOPLE.
LYNN

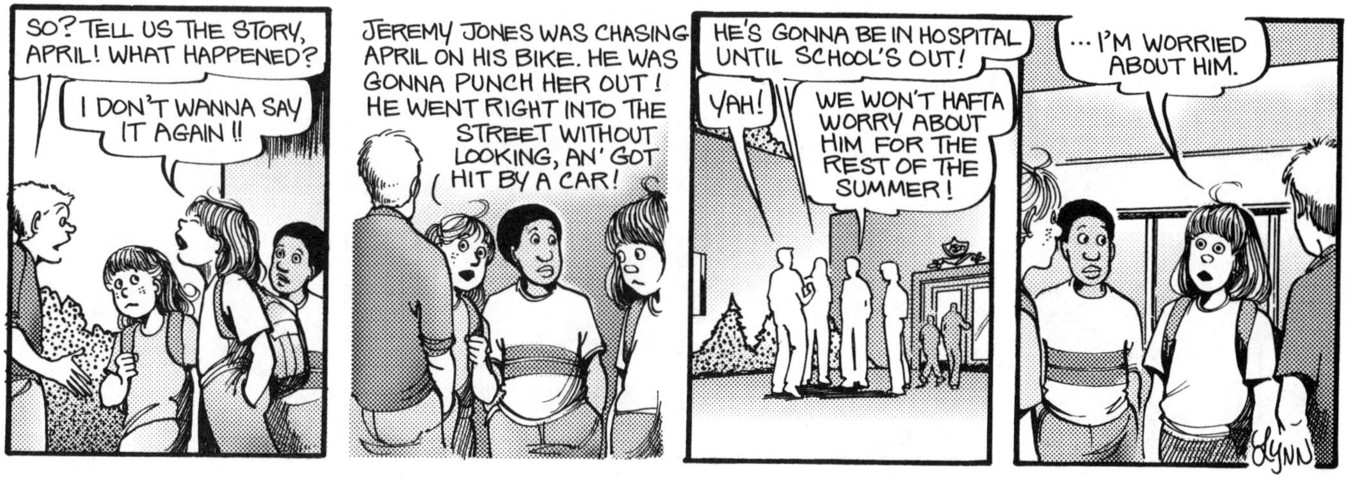
SO? TELL US THE STORY, APRIL! WHAT HAPPENED?
I DON'T WANNA SAY IT AGAIN !!
JEREMY JONES WAS CHASING APRIL ON HIS BIKE. HE WAS GONNA PUNCH HER OUT! HE WENT RIGHT INTO THE STREET WITHOUT LOOKING, AN' GOT HIT BY A CAR!
HE'S GONNA BE IN HOSPITAL UNTIL SCHOOL'S OUT!
YAH!
WE WON'T HAFTA WORRY ABOUT HIM FOR THE REST OF THE SUMMER!
...I'M WORRIED ABOUT HIM.
LYNN

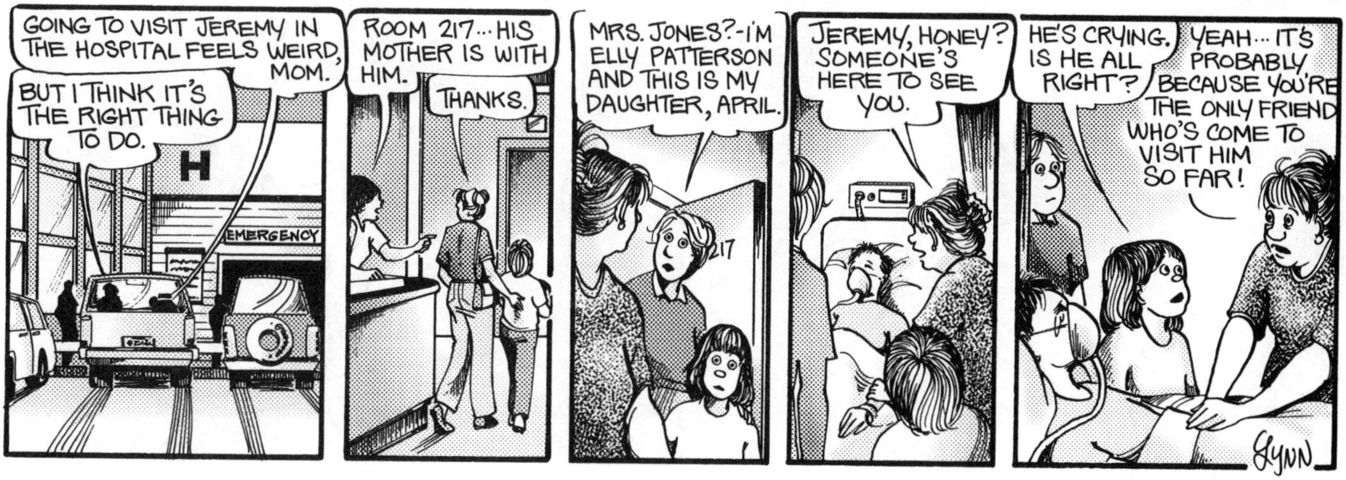
GOING TO VISIT JEREMY IN THE HOSPITAL FEELS WEIRD, MOM.
BUT I THINK IT'S THE RIGHT THING TO DO.
H
EMERGENCY
ROOM 217... HIS MOTHER IS WITH HIM.
THANKS.
MRS. JONES?-I'M ELLY PATTERSON AND THIS IS MY DAUGHTER, APRIL.
217
JEREMY, HONEY? SOMEONE'S HERE TO SEE YOU.
HE'S CRYING. IS HE ALL RIGHT?
YEAH... IT'S PROBABLY BECAUSE YOU'RE THE ONLY FRIEND WHO'S COME TO VISIT HIM SO FAR!
LYNN

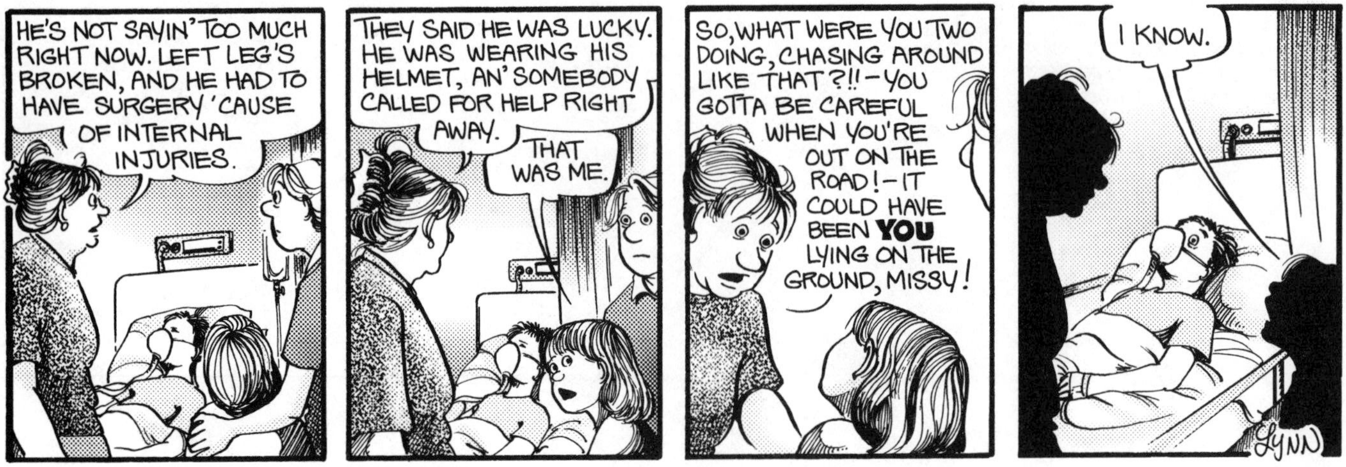
HE'S NOT SAYIN' TOO MUCH RIGHT NOW. LEFT LEG'S BROKEN, AND HE HAD TO HAVE SURGERY 'CAUSE OF INTERNAL INJURIES.
THEY SAID HE WAS LUCKY. HE WAS WEARING HIS HELMET, AN' SOMEBODY CALLED FOR HELP RIGHT AWAY.
THAT WAS ME.
SO, WHAT WERE YOU TWO DOING, CHASING AROUND LIKE THAT?!! – YOU GOTTA BE CAREFUL WHEN YOU'RE OUT ON THE ROAD! – IT COULD HAVE BEEN YOU LYING ON THE GROUND, MISSY!
I KNOW.
LYNN

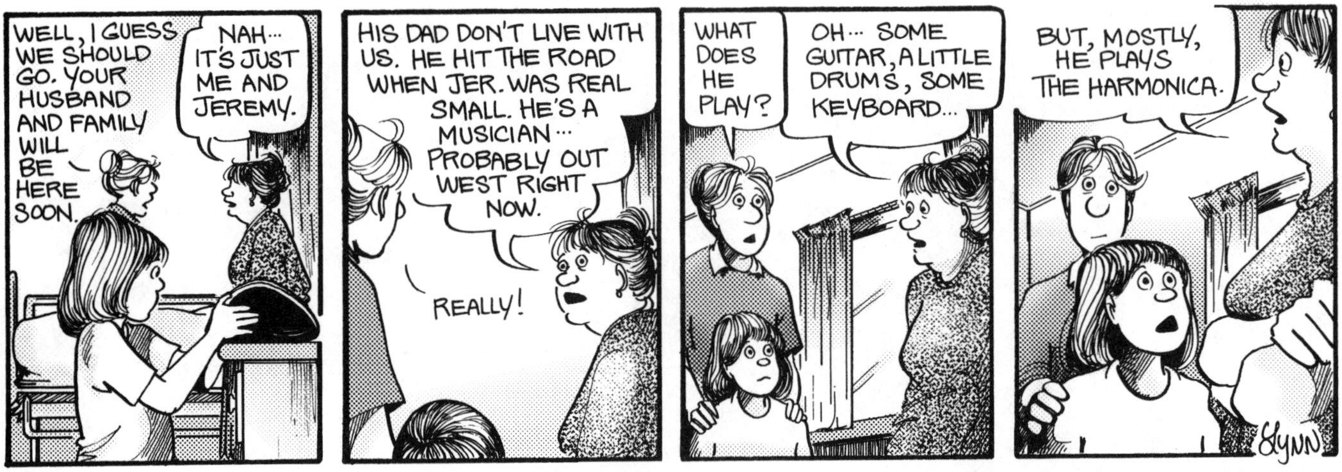
WELL, I GUESS WE SHOULD GO. YOUR HUSBAND AND FAMILY WILL BE HERE SOON.
NAH... IT'S JUST ME AND JEREMY.
HIS DAD DON'T LIVE WITH US. HE HIT THE ROAD WHEN JER. WAS REAL SMALL. HE'S A MUSICIAN... PROBABLY OUT WEST RIGHT NOW.
REALLY!
WHAT DOES HE PLAY?
OH... SOME GUITAR, A LITTLE DRUMS, SOME KEYBOARD...
BUT, MOSTLY, HE PLAYS THE HARMONICA.
LYNN

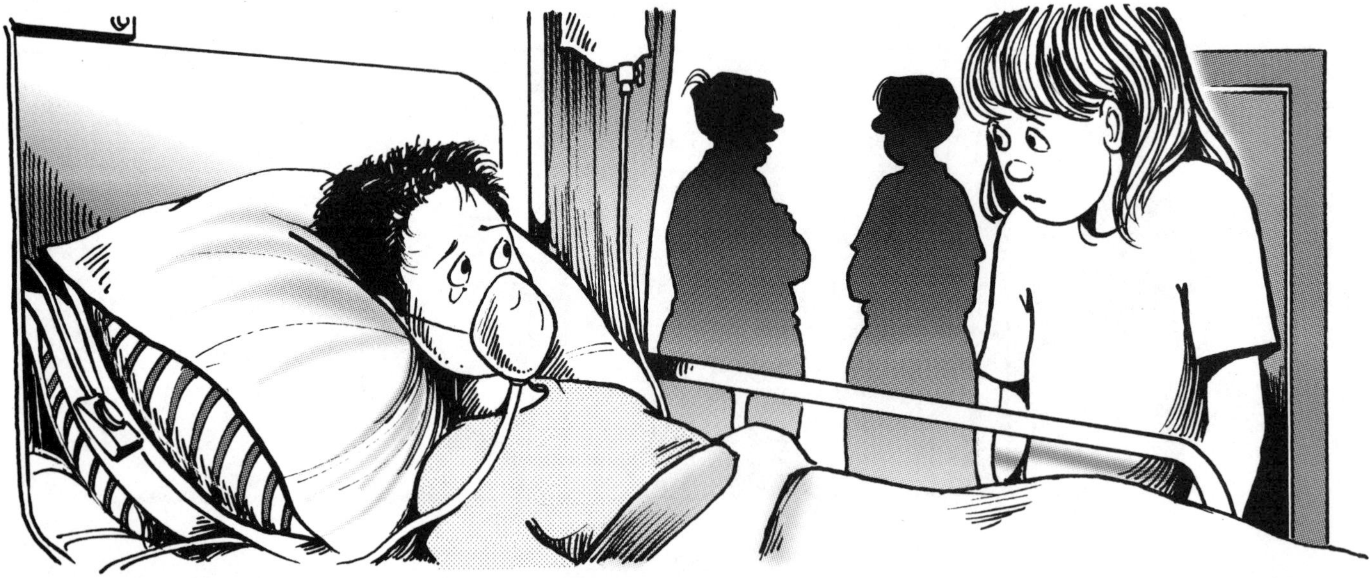

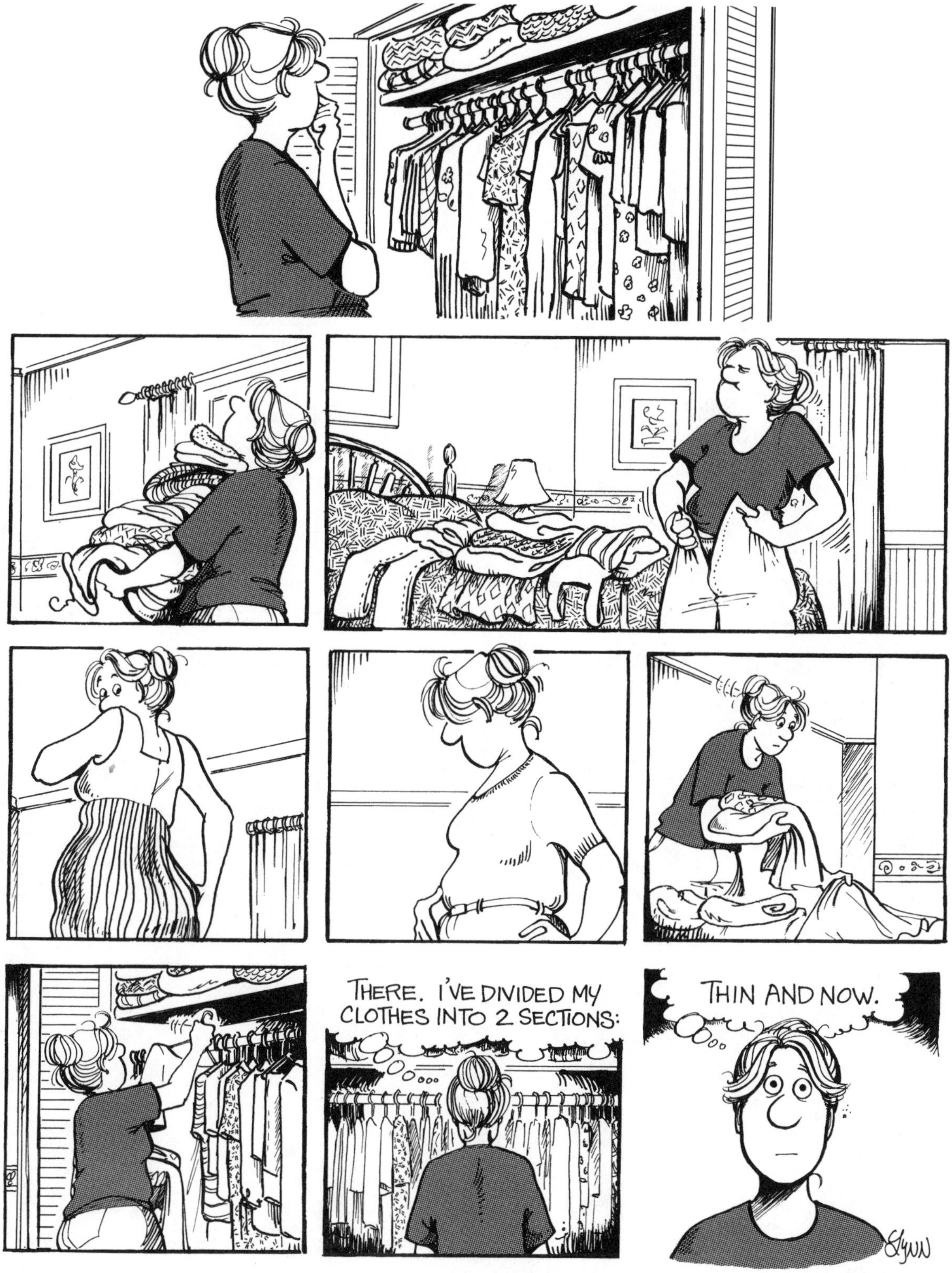
THERE. I'VE DIVIDED MY CLOTHES INTO 2 SECTIONS:
THIN AND NOW.

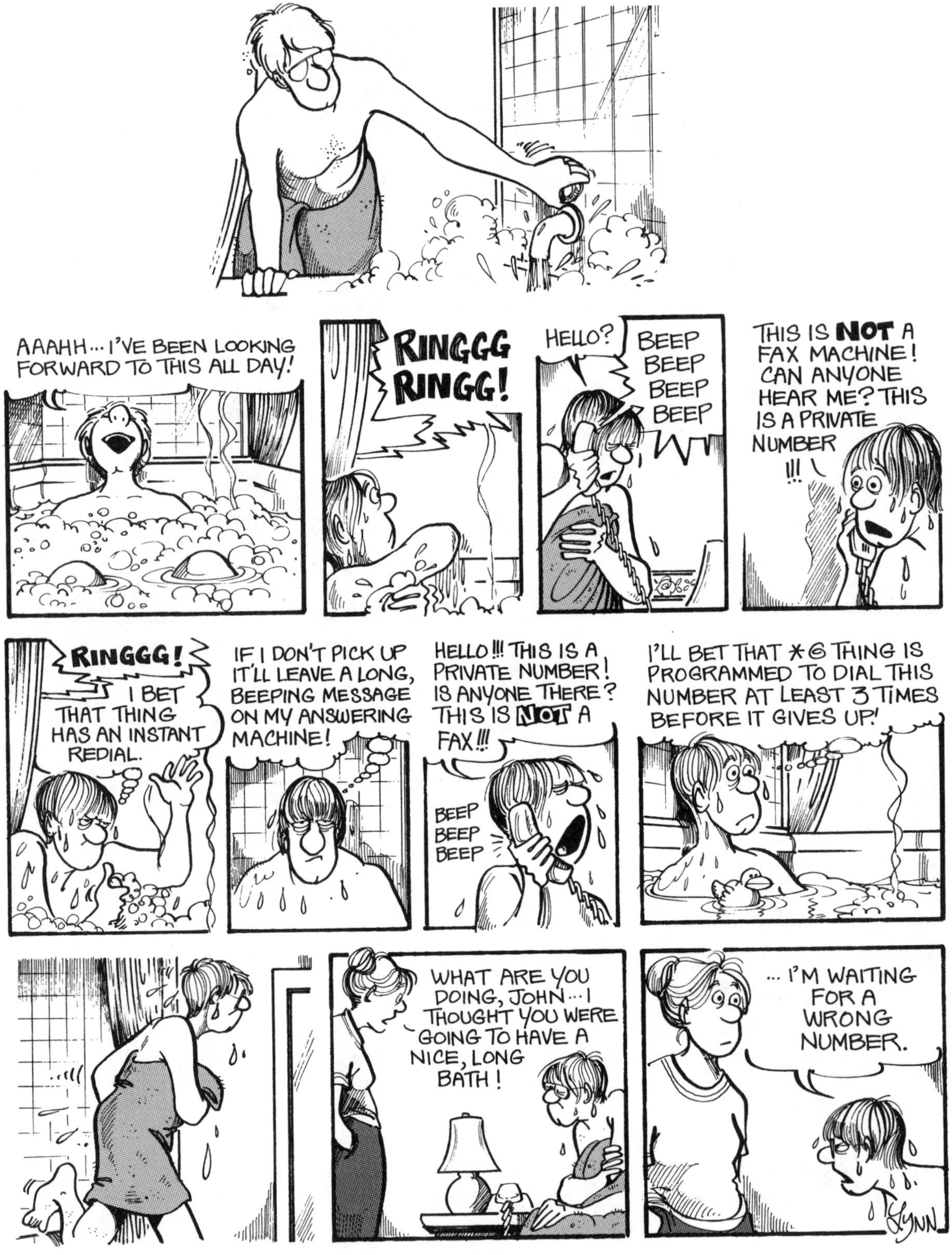
AAAHH... I'VE BEEN LOOKING FORWARD TO THIS ALL DAY!
RINGGG RINGG!
HELLO?
BEEP BEEP BEEP BEEP BEEP
THIS IS NOT A FAX MACHINE! CAN ANYONE HEAR ME? THIS IS A PRIVATE NUMBER !!!
RINGGG!
I BET THAT THING HAS AN INSTANT REDIAL.
IF I DON'T PICK UP IT'LL LEAVE A LONG, BEEPING MESSAGE ON MY ANSWERING MACHINE!
HELLO!!! THIS IS A PRIVATE NUMBER! IS ANYONE THERE? THIS IS NOT A FAX!!!
BEEP BEEP BEEP
I'LL BET THAT *6 THING IS PROGRAMMED TO DIAL THIS NUMBER AT LEAST 3 TIMES BEFORE IT GIVES UP!
WHAT ARE YOU DOING, JOHN... I THOUGHT YOU WERE GOING TO HAVE A NICE, LONG BATH!
... I'M WAITING FOR A WRONG NUMBER.
Lynn

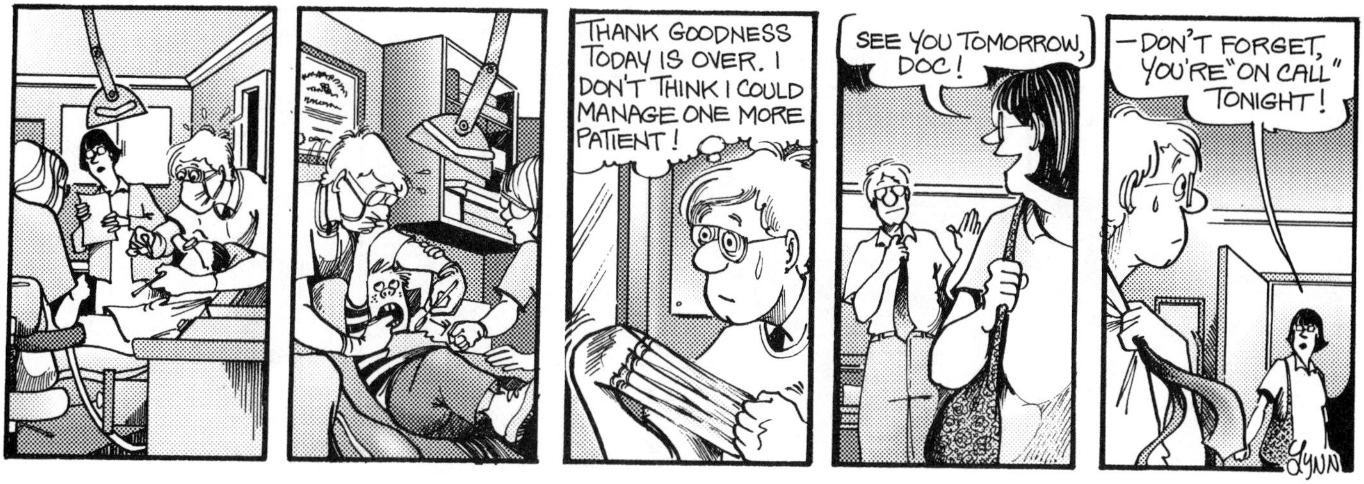
THANK GOODNESS TODAY IS OVER. I DON'T THINK I COULD MANAGE ONE MORE PATIENT!
SEE YOU TOMORROW, DOC!
—DON'T FORGET, YOU'RE "ON CALL" TONIGHT!
LYNN

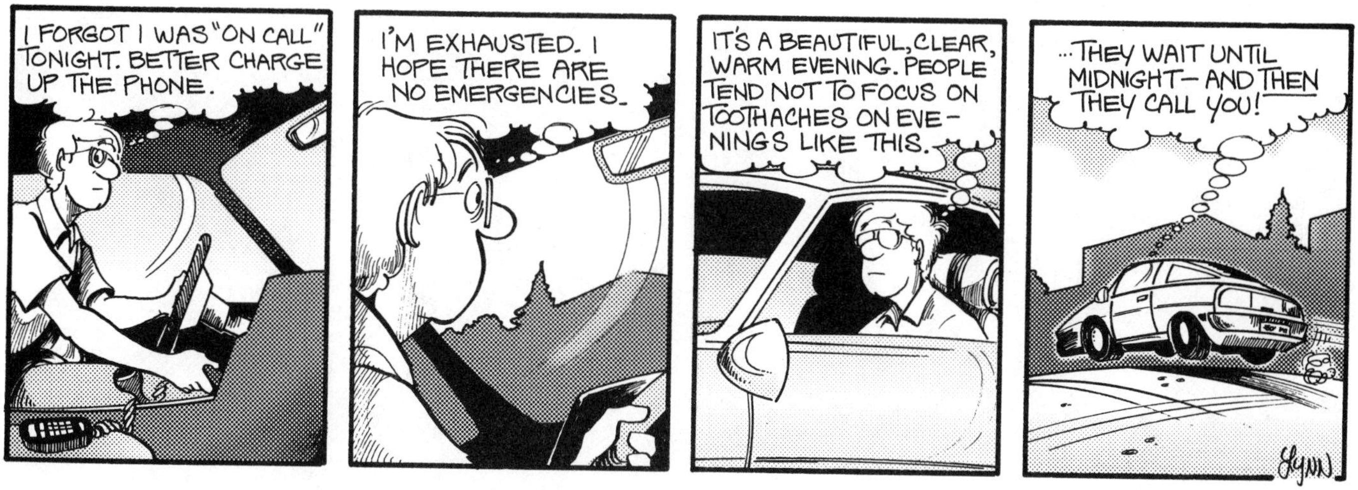
I FORGOT I WAS "ON CALL" TONIGHT. BETTER CHARGE UP THE PHONE.
I'M EXHAUSTED. I HOPE THERE ARE NO EMERGENCIES.
IT'S A BEAUTIFUL, CLEAR, WARM EVENING. PEOPLE TEND NOT TO FOCUS ON TOOTHACHES ON EVENINGS LIKE THIS.
...THEY WAIT UNTIL MIDNIGHT— AND THEN THEY CALL YOU!
LYNN

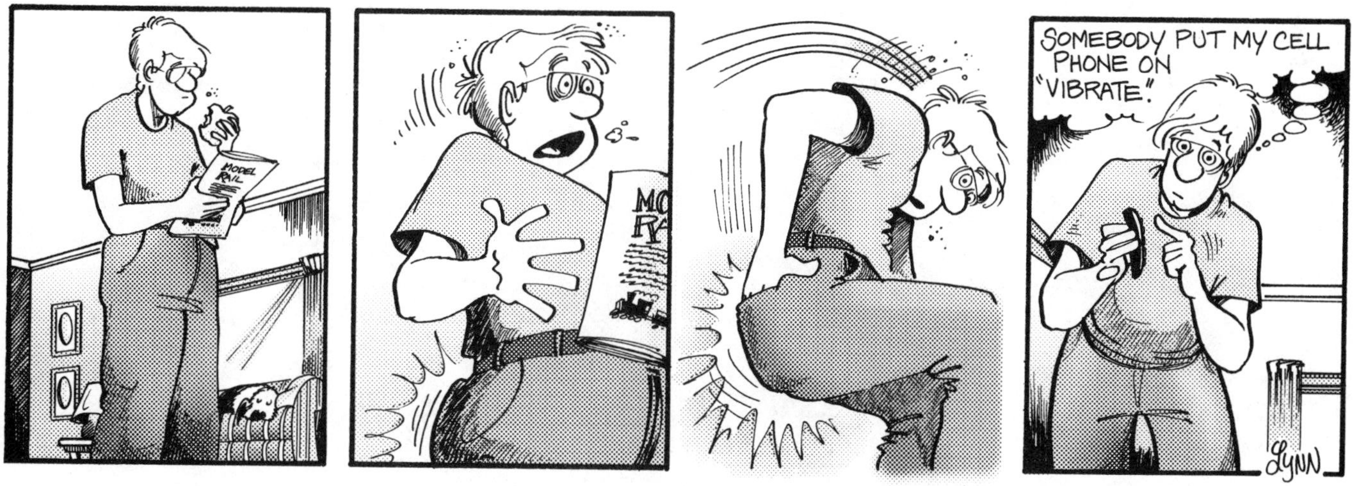
MODEL RAIL
SOMEBODY PUT MY CELL PHONE ON "VIBRATE."
LYNN

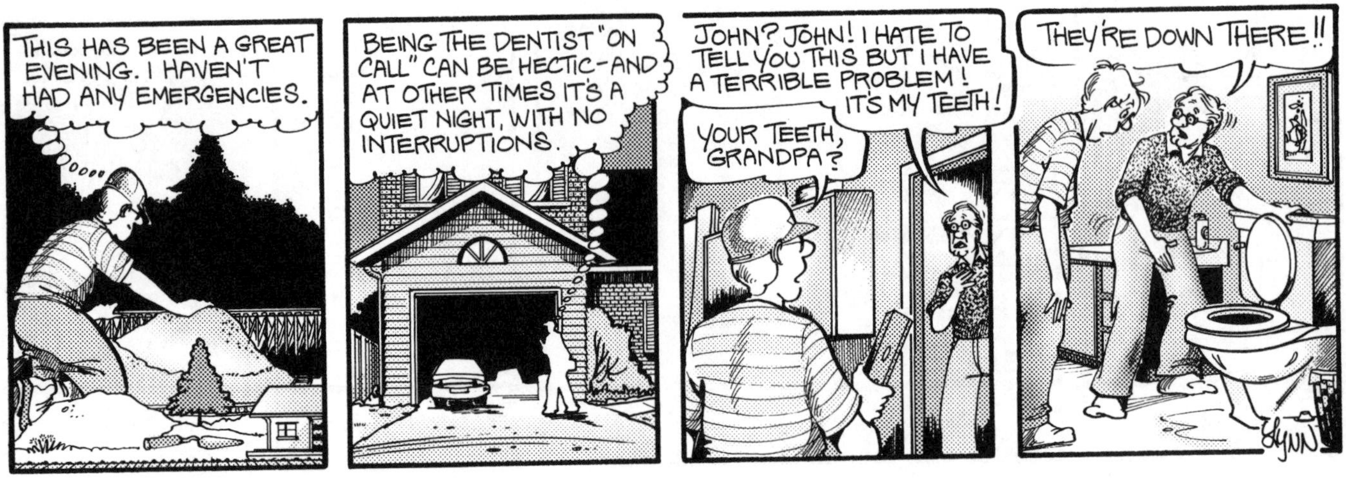
THIS HAS BEEN A GREAT EVENING. I HAVEN'T HAD ANY EMERGENCIES.
BEING THE DENTIST "ON CALL" CAN BE HECTIC - AND AT OTHER TIMES IT'S A QUIET NIGHT, WITH NO INTERRUPTIONS.
JOHN? JOHN! I HATE TO TELL YOU THIS BUT I HAVE A TERRIBLE PROBLEM!
IT'S MY TEETH!
YOUR TEETH, GRANDPA?
THEY'RE DOWN THERE!!
LYNN

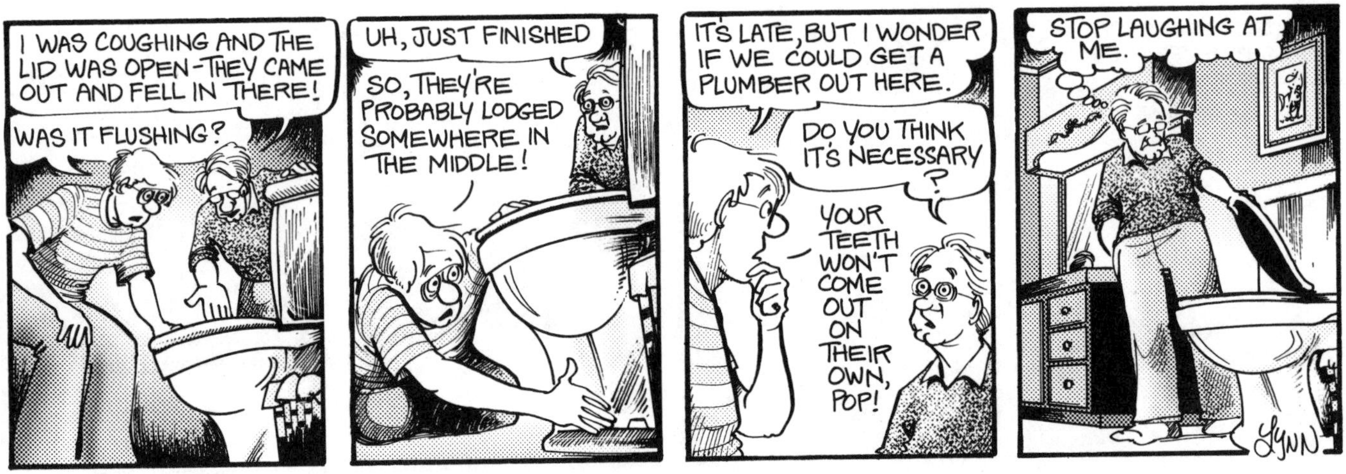
I WAS COUGHING AND THE LID WAS OPEN - THEY CAME OUT AND FELL IN THERE!
WAS IT FLUSHING?
UH, JUST FINISHED
SO, THEY'RE PROBABLY LODGED SOMEWHERE IN THE MIDDLE!
IT'S LATE, BUT I WONDER IF WE COULD GET A PLUMBER OUT HERE.
DO YOU THINK IT'S NECESSARY?
YOUR TEETH WON'T COME OUT ON THEIR OWN, POP!
STOP LAUGHING AT ME.
LYNN

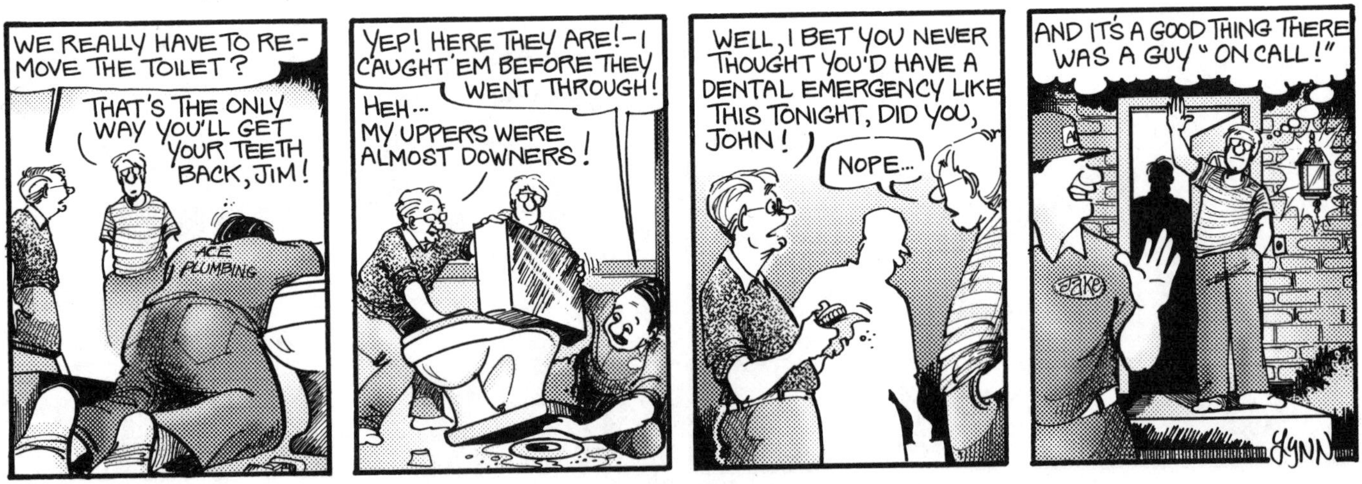
WE REALLY HAVE TO RE-MOVE THE TOILET?
THAT'S THE ONLY WAY YOU'LL GET YOUR TEETH BACK, JIM!
ACE PLUMBING
YEP! HERE THEY ARE! - I CAUGHT 'EM BEFORE THEY WENT THROUGH!
HEH... MY UPPERS WERE ALMOST DOWNERS!
WELL, I BET YOU NEVER THOUGHT YOU'D HAVE A DENTAL EMERGENCY LIKE THIS TONIGHT, DID YOU, JOHN!
NOPE...
AND IT'S A GOOD THING THERE WAS A GUY "ON CALL!"
JAKE
LYNN

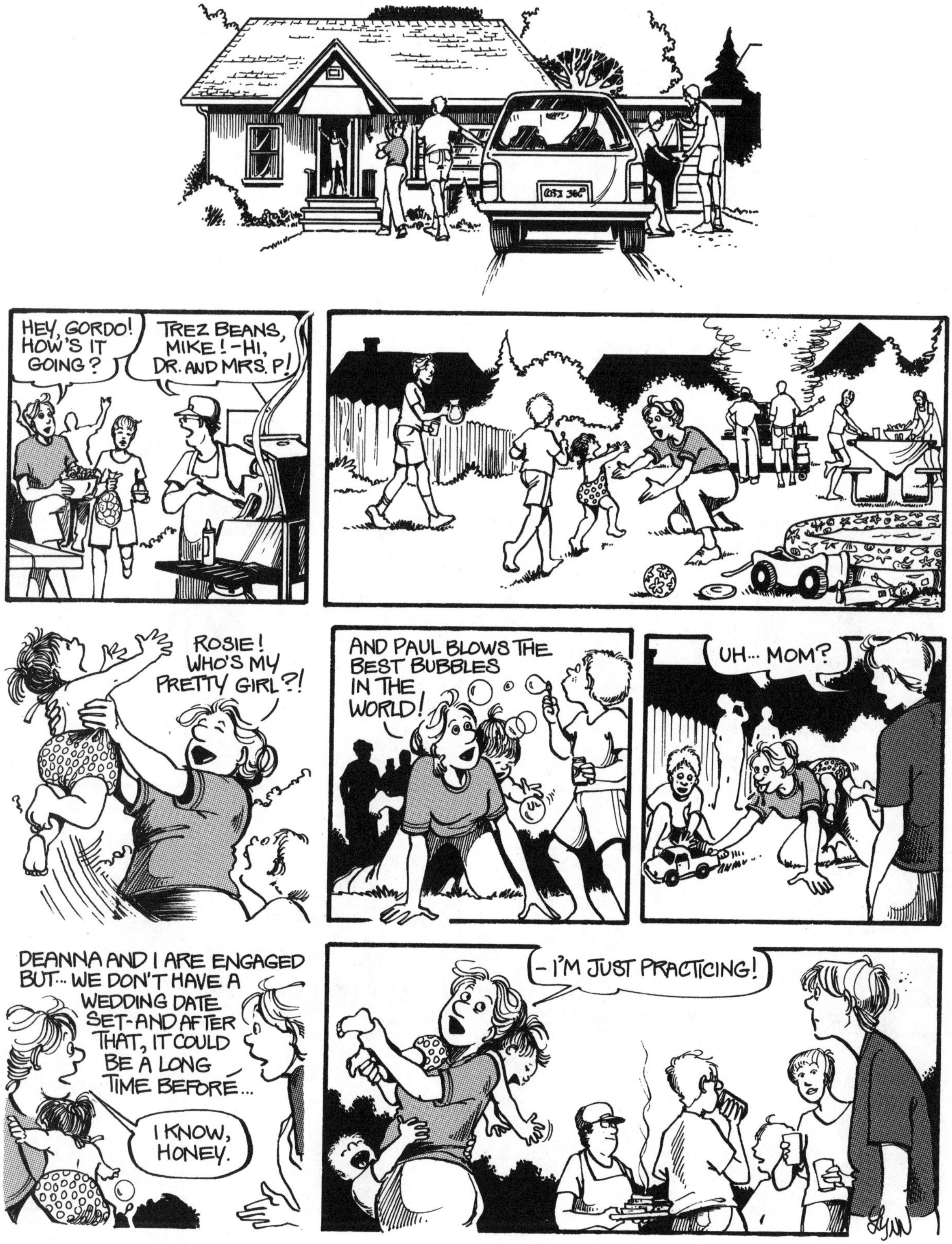
HEY, GORDO! HOW'S IT GOING?
TREZ BEANS, MIKE! -HI, DR. AND MRS. P!
ROSIE! WHO'S MY PRETTY GIRL?!
AND PAUL BLOWS THE BEST BUBBLES IN THE WORLD!
UH... MOM?
DEANNA AND I ARE ENGAGED BUT... WE DON'T HAVE A WEDDING DATE SET-AND AFTER THAT, IT COULD BE A LONG TIME BEFORE...
I KNOW, HONEY.
- I'M JUST PRACTICING!

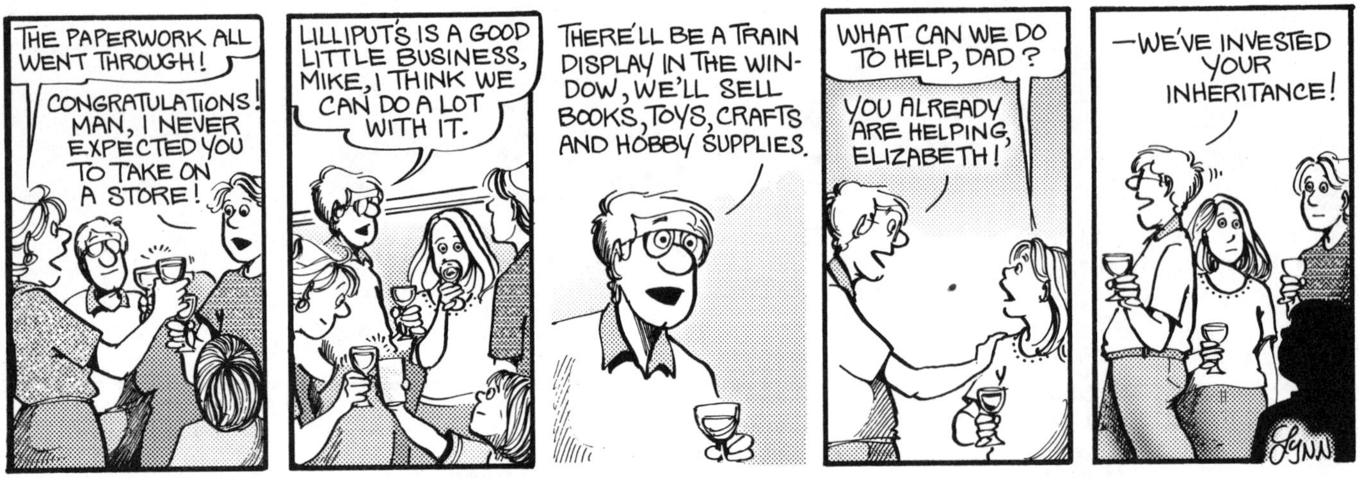
THE PAPERWORK ALL WENT THROUGH!
CONGRATULATIONS! MAN, I NEVER EXPECTED YOU TO TAKE ON A STORE!
LILLIPUT'S IS A GOOD LITTLE BUSINESS, MIKE, I THINK WE CAN DO A LOT WITH IT.
THERE'LL BE A TRAIN DISPLAY IN THE WINDOW, WE'LL SELL BOOKS, TOYS, CRAFTS AND HOBBY SUPPLIES.
WHAT CAN WE DO TO HELP, DAD?
YOU ALREADY ARE HELPING, ELIZABETH!
—WE'VE INVESTED YOUR INHERITANCE!
Lynn

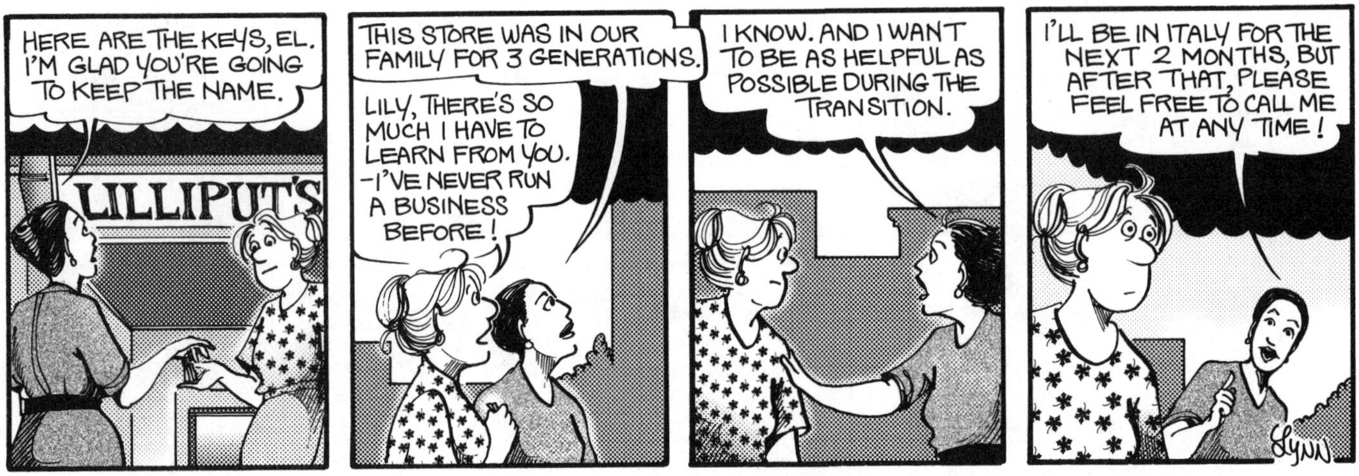
HERE ARE THE KEYS, EL. I'M GLAD YOU'RE GOING TO KEEP THE NAME.
LILLIPUT'S
THIS STORE WAS IN OUR FAMILY FOR 3 GENERATIONS.
LILY, THERE'S SO MUCH I HAVE TO LEARN FROM YOU. -I'VE NEVER RUN A BUSINESS BEFORE!
I KNOW. AND I WANT TO BE AS HELPFUL AS POSSIBLE DURING THE TRANSITION.
I'LL BE IN ITALY FOR THE NEXT 2 MONTHS, BUT AFTER THAT, PLEASE FEEL FREE TO CALL ME AT ANY TIME!
Lynn

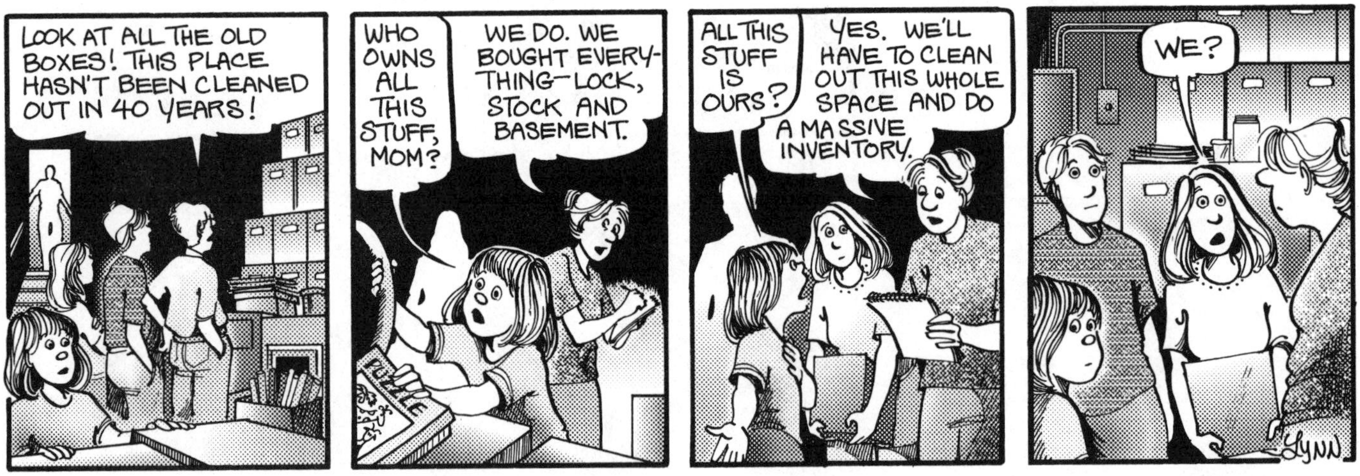
LOOK AT ALL THE OLD BOXES! THIS PLACE HASN'T BEEN CLEANED OUT IN 40 YEARS!
WHO OWNS ALL THIS STUFF, MOM?
WE DO. WE BOUGHT EVERYTHING—LOCK, STOCK AND BASEMENT.
PUZZLE
ALL THIS STUFF IS OURS?
YES. WE'LL HAVE TO CLEAN OUT THIS WHOLE SPACE AND DO A MASSIVE INVENTORY.
WE?
Lynn

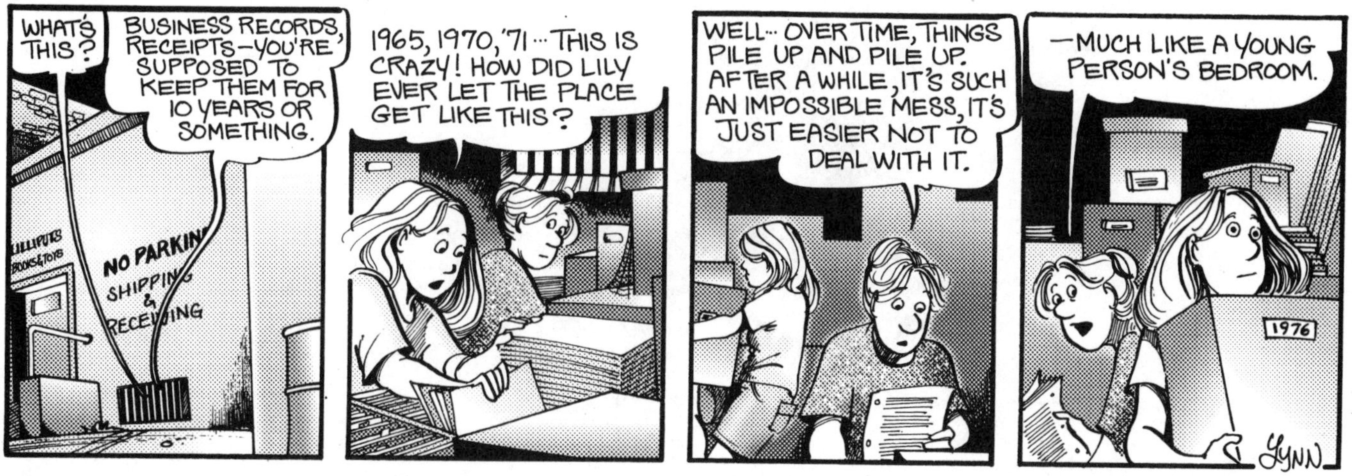
WHAT'S THIS?
BUSINESS RECORDS, RECEIPTS—YOU'RE SUPPOSED TO KEEP THEM FOR 10 YEARS OR SOMETHING.
1965, 1970, '71 ... THIS IS CRAZY! HOW DID LILY EVER LET THE PLACE GET LIKE THIS?
WELL ... OVER TIME, THINGS PILE UP AND PILE UP. AFTER A WHILE, IT'S SUCH AN IMPOSSIBLE MESS, IT'S JUST EASIER NOT TO DEAL WITH IT.
—MUCH LIKE A YOUNG PERSON'S BEDROOM.
1976
LYNN

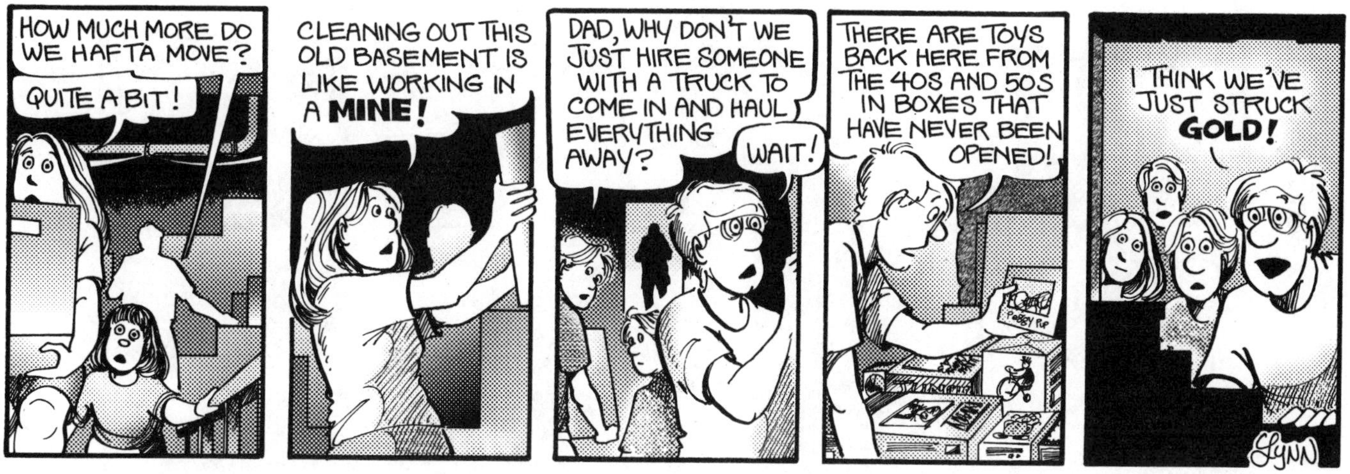
HOW MUCH MORE DO WE HAFTA MOVE?
QUITE A BIT!
CLEANING OUT THIS OLD BASEMENT IS LIKE WORKING IN A **MINE**!
DAD, WHY DON'T WE JUST HIRE SOMEONE WITH A TRUCK TO COME IN AND HAUL EVERYTHING AWAY?
WAIT!
THERE ARE TOYS BACK HERE FROM THE 40S AND 50S IN BOXES THAT HAVE NEVER BEEN OPENED!
I THINK WE'VE JUST STRUCK **GOLD**!
LYNN

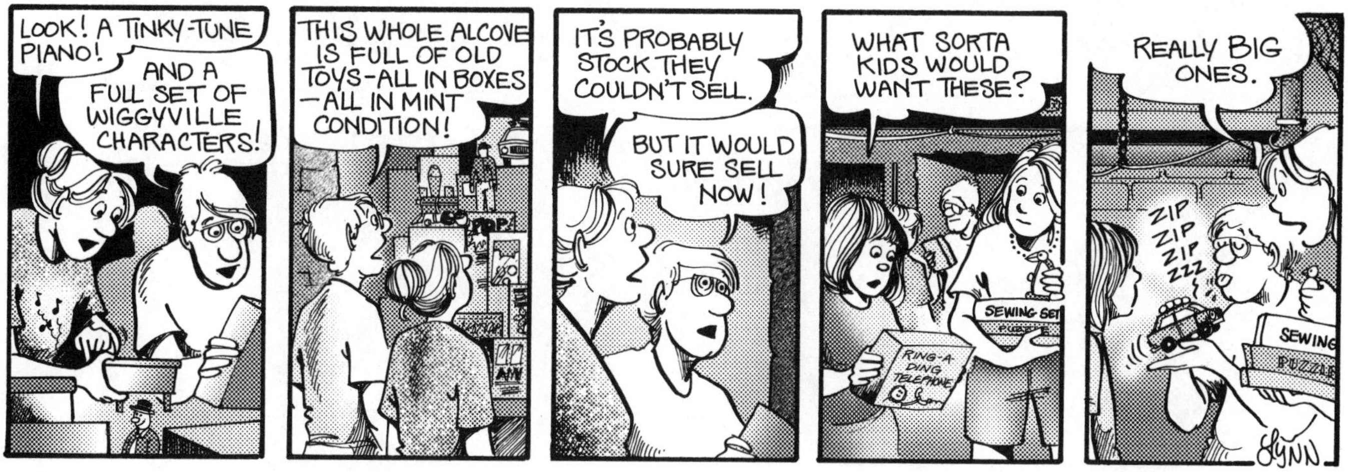
LOOK! A TINKY-TUNE PIANO!
AND A FULL SET OF WIGGYVILLE CHARACTERS!
THIS WHOLE ALCOVE IS FULL OF OLD TOYS—ALL IN BOXES —ALL IN MINT CONDITION!
IT'S PROBABLY STOCK THEY COULDN'T SELL.
BUT IT WOULD SURE SELL NOW!
WHAT SORTA KIDS WOULD WANT THESE?
SEWING SET
RING-A-DING TELEPHONE
REALLY BIG ONES.
ZIP
ZIP
ZIP
ZZZ
SEWING
PUZZLE
LYNN

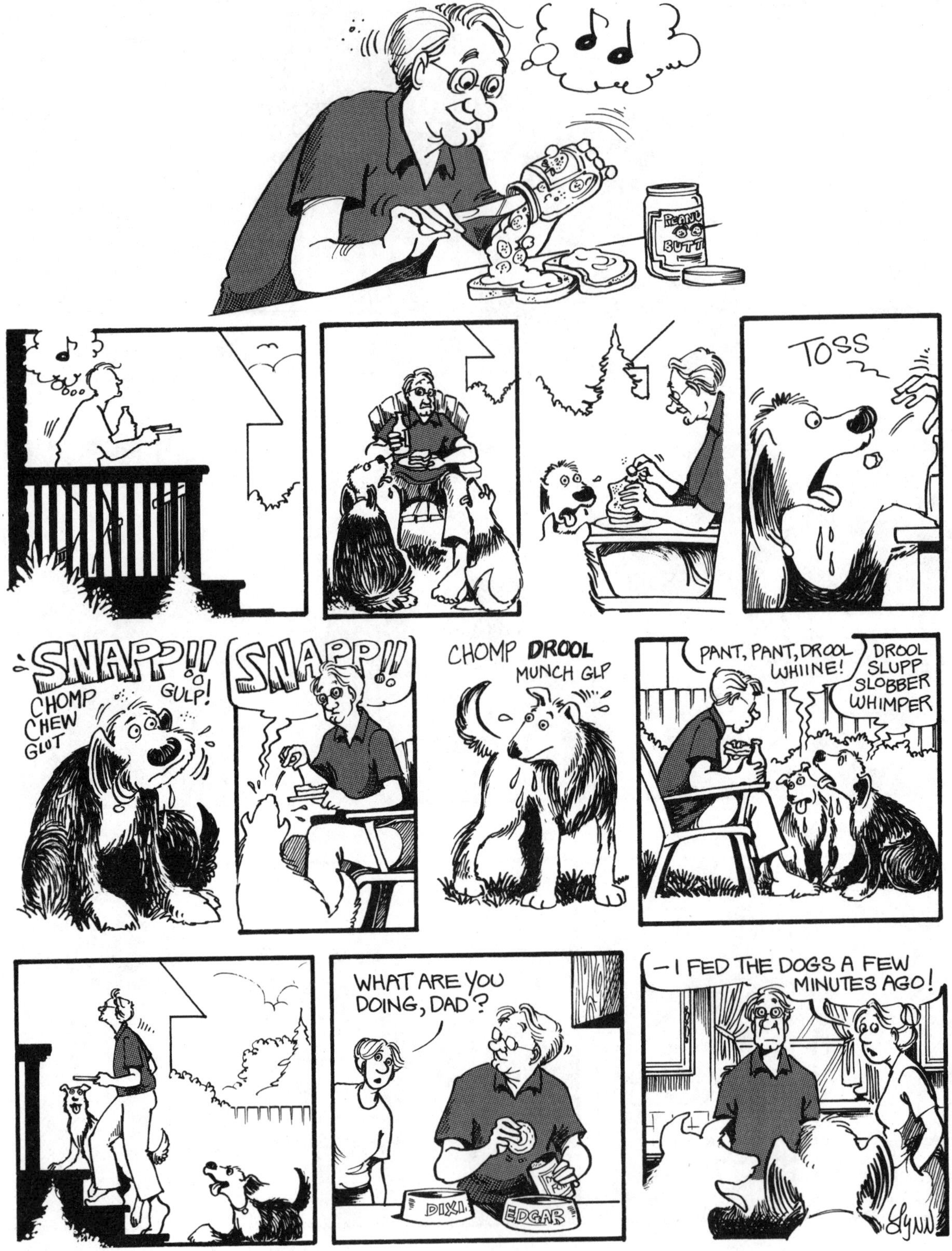
PEANUT BUTT
TOSS
SNAPP!!
CHOMP
CHEW
GLOT
GULP!
SNAPP!!
CHOMP DROOL
MUNCH GLP
PANT, PANT, DROOL
WHIINE!
DROOL
SLUPP
SLOBBER
WHIMPER
WHAT ARE YOU DOING, DAD?
DIXI
EDGAR
—I FED THE DOGS A FEW MINUTES AGO!
Lynn

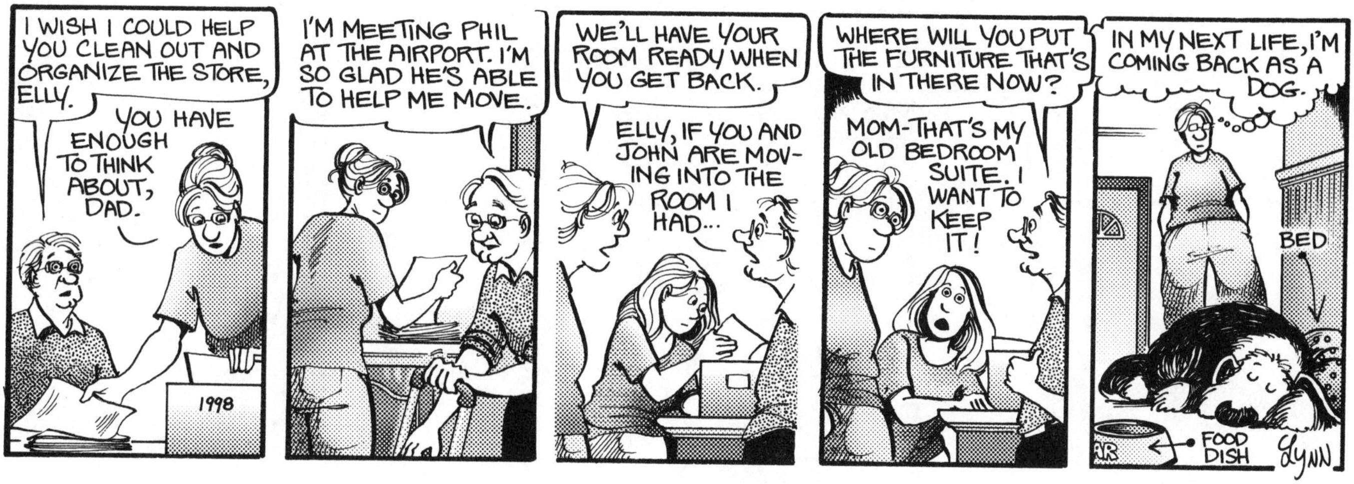
I WISH I COULD HELP YOU CLEAN OUT AND ORGANIZE THE STORE, ELLY.
YOU HAVE ENOUGH TO THINK ABOUT, DAD.
1998
I'M MEETING PHIL AT THE AIRPORT. I'M SO GLAD HE'S ABLE TO HELP ME MOVE.
WE'LL HAVE YOUR ROOM READY WHEN YOU GET BACK.
ELLY, IF YOU AND JOHN ARE MOVING INTO THE ROOM I HAD...
WHERE WILL YOU PUT THE FURNITURE THAT'S IN THERE NOW?
MOM-THAT'S MY OLD BEDROOM SUITE. I WANT TO KEEP IT!
IN MY NEXT LIFE, I'M COMING BACK AS A DOG.
BED
FOOD DISH
LYNN

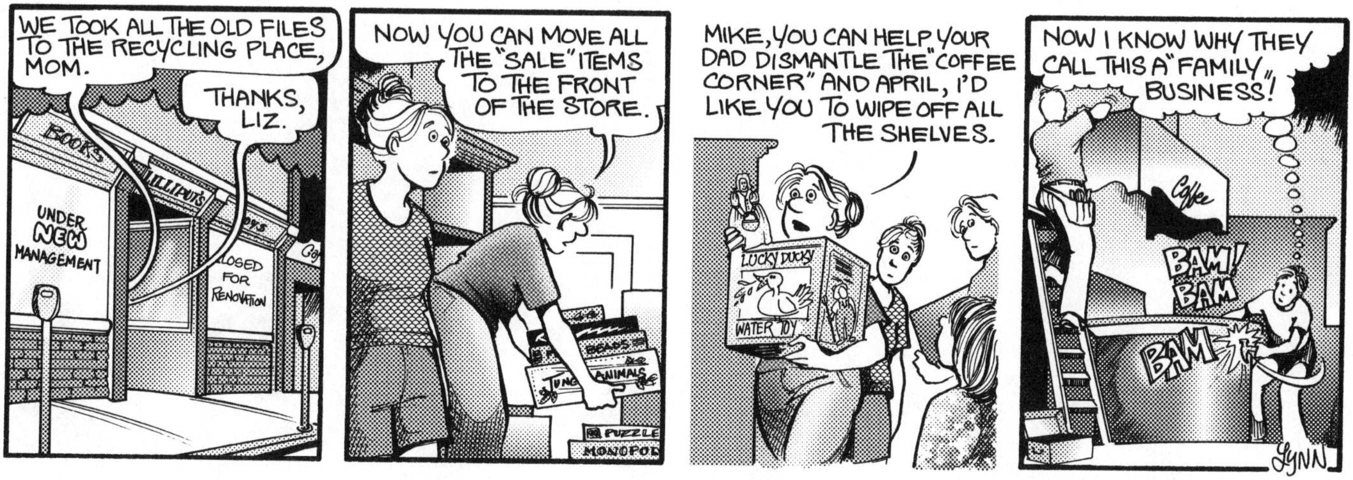
WE TOOK ALL THE OLD FILES TO THE RECYCLING PLACE, MOM.
THANKS, LIZ.
BOOKS
LILLIPUT'S
UNDER NEW MANAGEMENT
CLOSED FOR RENOVATION
NOW YOU CAN MOVE ALL THE "SALE" ITEMS TO THE FRONT OF THE STORE.
PUZZLE
MIKE, YOU CAN HELP YOUR DAD DISMANTLE THE "COFFEE CORNER" AND APRIL, I'D LIKE YOU TO WIPE OFF ALL THE SHELVES.
LUCKY DUCKY
WATER TOY
NOW I KNOW WHY THEY CALL THIS A "FAMILY" BUSINESS!
Coffee
BAM! BAM
BAM
LYNN

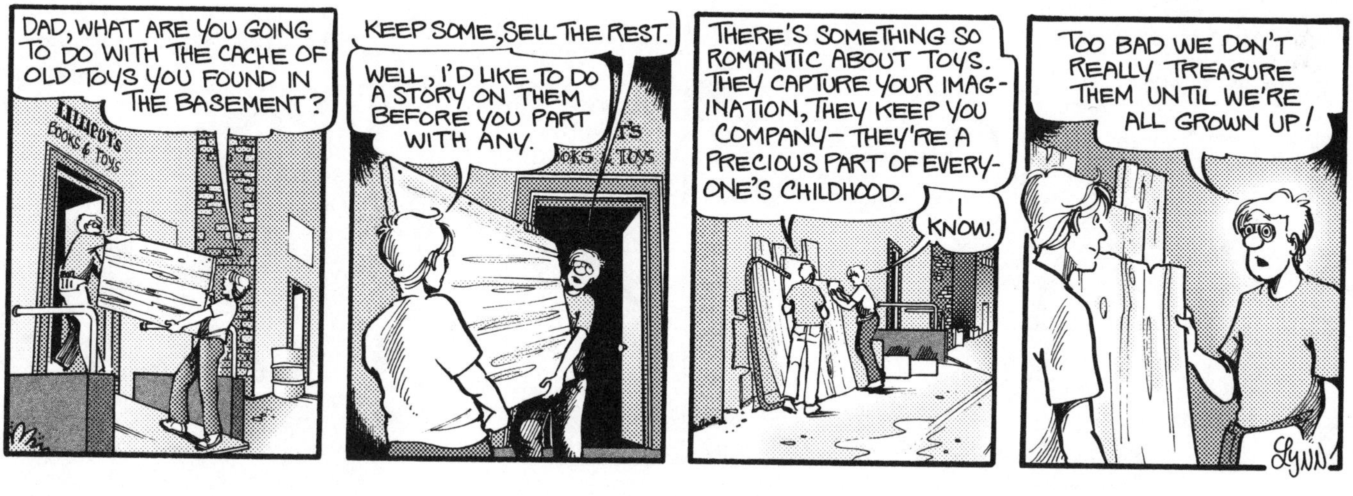
DAD, WHAT ARE YOU GOING TO DO WITH THE CACHE OF OLD TOYS YOU FOUND IN THE BASEMENT?
LILLIPUT'S BOOKS & TOYS
KEEP SOME, SELL THE REST.
WELL, I'D LIKE TO DO A STORY ON THEM BEFORE YOU PART WITH ANY.
THERE'S SOMETHING SO ROMANTIC ABOUT TOYS. THEY CAPTURE YOUR IMAGINATION, THEY KEEP YOU COMPANY– THEY'RE A PRECIOUS PART OF EVERYONE'S CHILDHOOD.
I KNOW.
TOO BAD WE DON'T REALLY TREASURE THEM UNTIL WE'RE ALL GROWN UP!
LYNN

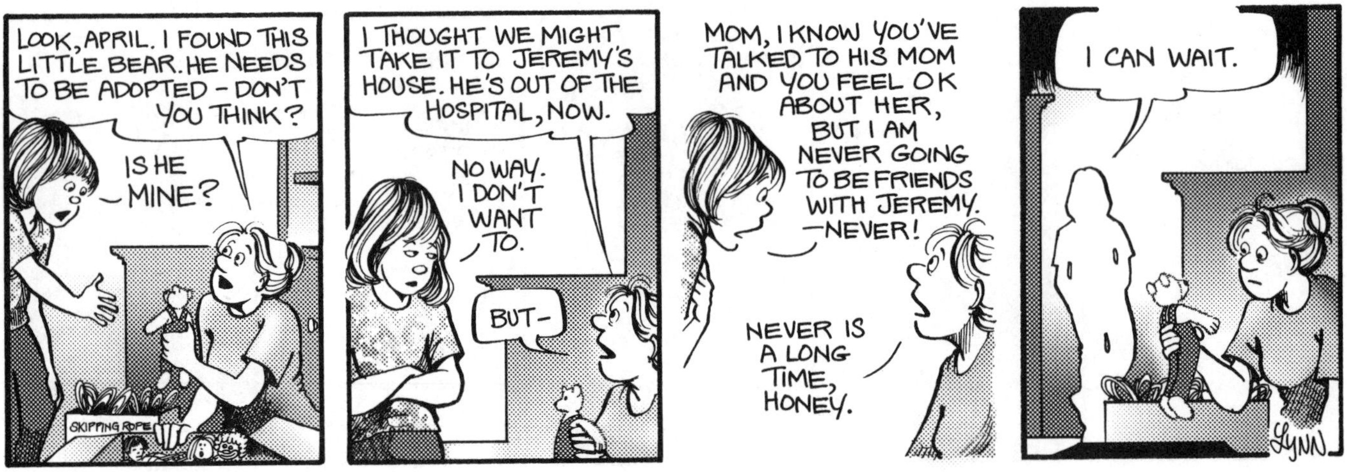
LOOK, APRIL. I FOUND THIS LITTLE BEAR. HE NEEDS TO BE ADOPTED - DON'T YOU THINK?
IS HE MINE?
I THOUGHT WE MIGHT TAKE IT TO JEREMY'S HOUSE. HE'S OUT OF THE HOSPITAL, NOW.
NO WAY. I DON'T WANT TO.
BUT-
MOM, I KNOW YOU'VE TALKED TO HIS MOM AND YOU FEEL OK ABOUT HER, BUT I AM NEVER GOING TO BE FRIENDS WITH JEREMY. —NEVER!
NEVER IS A LONG TIME, HONEY.
I CAN WAIT.
SKIPPING ROPE
LYNN

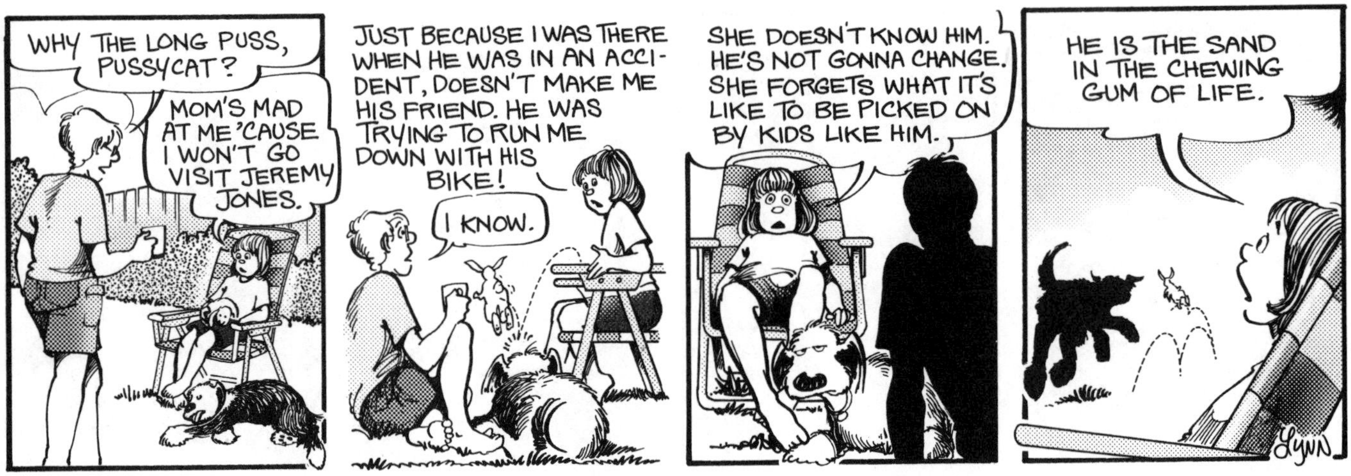
WHY THE LONG PUSS, PUSSYCAT?
MOM'S MAD AT ME 'CAUSE I WON'T GO VISIT JEREMY JONES.
JUST BECAUSE I WAS THERE WHEN HE WAS IN AN ACCIDENT, DOESN'T MAKE ME HIS FRIEND. HE WAS TRYING TO RUN ME DOWN WITH HIS BIKE!
I KNOW.
SHE DOESN'T KNOW HIM. HE'S NOT GONNA CHANGE. SHE FORGETS WHAT IT'S LIKE TO BE PICKED ON BY KIDS LIKE HIM.
HE IS THE SAND IN THE CHEWING GUM OF LIFE.
LYNN

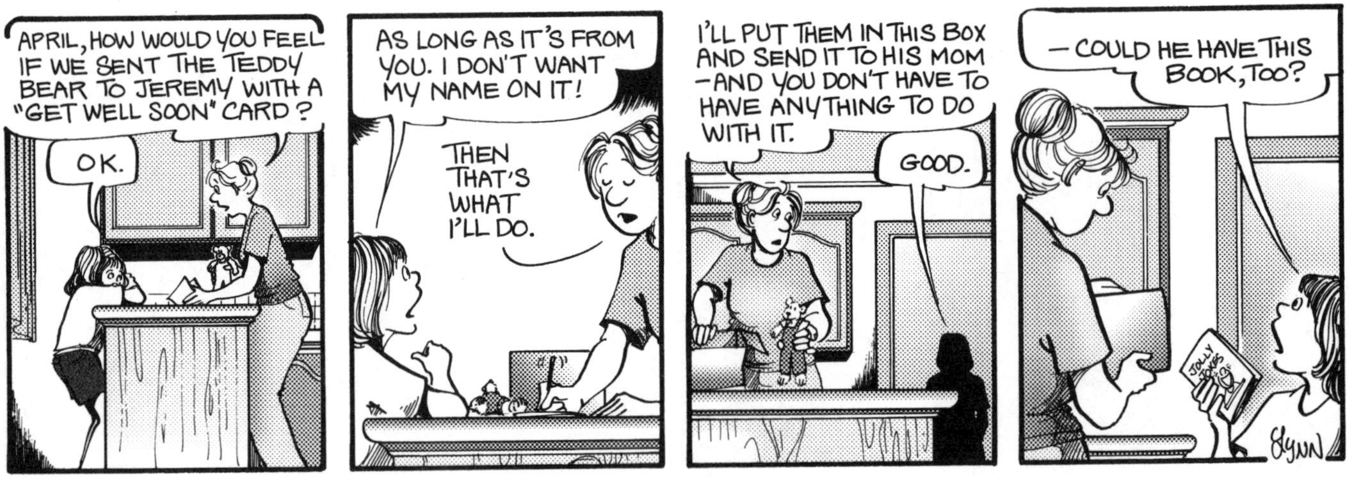
APRIL, HOW WOULD YOU FEEL IF WE SENT THE TEDDY BEAR TO JEREMY WITH A "GET WELL SOON" CARD?
OK.
AS LONG AS IT'S FROM YOU. I DON'T WANT MY NAME ON IT!
THEN THAT'S WHAT I'LL DO.
I'LL PUT THEM IN THIS BOX AND SEND IT TO HIS MOM —AND YOU DON'T HAVE TO HAVE ANYTHING TO DO WITH IT.
GOOD.
— COULD HE HAVE THIS BOOK, TOO?
LYNN

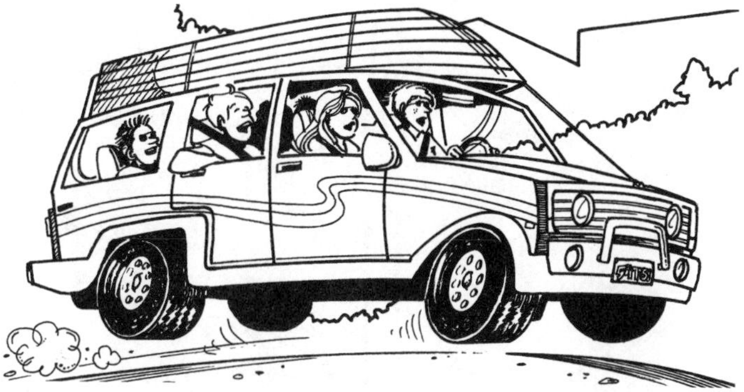

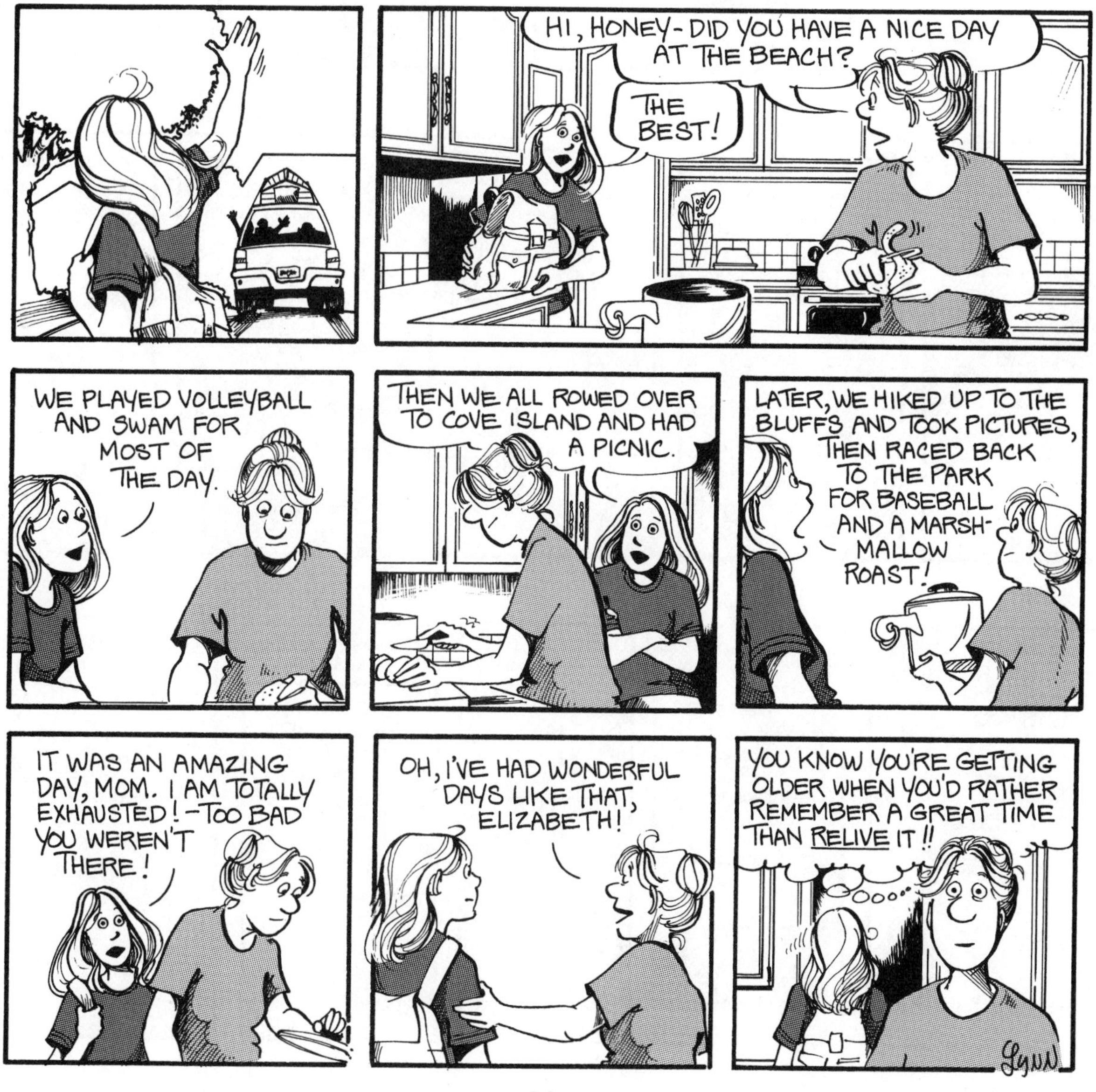
HI, HONEY- DID YOU HAVE A NICE DAY AT THE BEACH?
THE BEST!
WE PLAYED VOLLEYBALL AND SWAM FOR MOST OF THE DAY.
THEN WE ALL ROWED OVER TO COVE ISLAND AND HAD A PICNIC.
LATER, WE HIKED UP TO THE BLUFFS AND TOOK PICTURES, THEN RACED BACK TO THE PARK FOR BASEBALL AND A MARSH-MALLOW ROAST!
IT WAS AN AMAZING DAY, MOM. I AM TOTALLY EXHAUSTED! -TOO BAD YOU WEREN'T THERE!
OH, I'VE HAD WONDERFUL DAYS LIKE THAT, ELIZABETH!
YOU KNOW YOU'RE GETTING OLDER WHEN YOU'D RATHER REMEMBER A GREAT TIME THAN RELIVE IT!!
Lynn

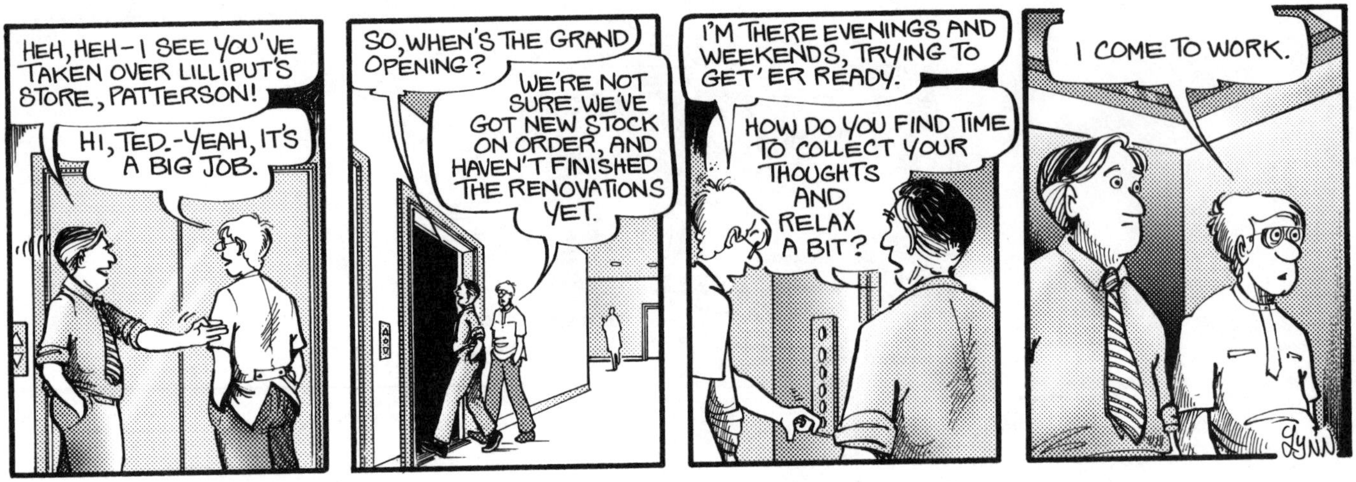
HEH, HEH - I SEE YOU'VE TAKEN OVER LILLIPUT'S STORE, PATTERSON!
HI, TED.-YEAH, IT'S A BIG JOB.
SO, WHEN'S THE GRAND OPENING?
WE'RE NOT SURE. WE'VE GOT NEW STOCK ON ORDER, AND HAVEN'T FINISHED THE RENOVATIONS YET.
I'M THERE EVENINGS AND WEEKENDS, TRYING TO GET'ER READY.
HOW DO YOU FIND TIME TO COLLECT YOUR THOUGHTS AND RELAX A BIT?
I COME TO WORK.
LYNN

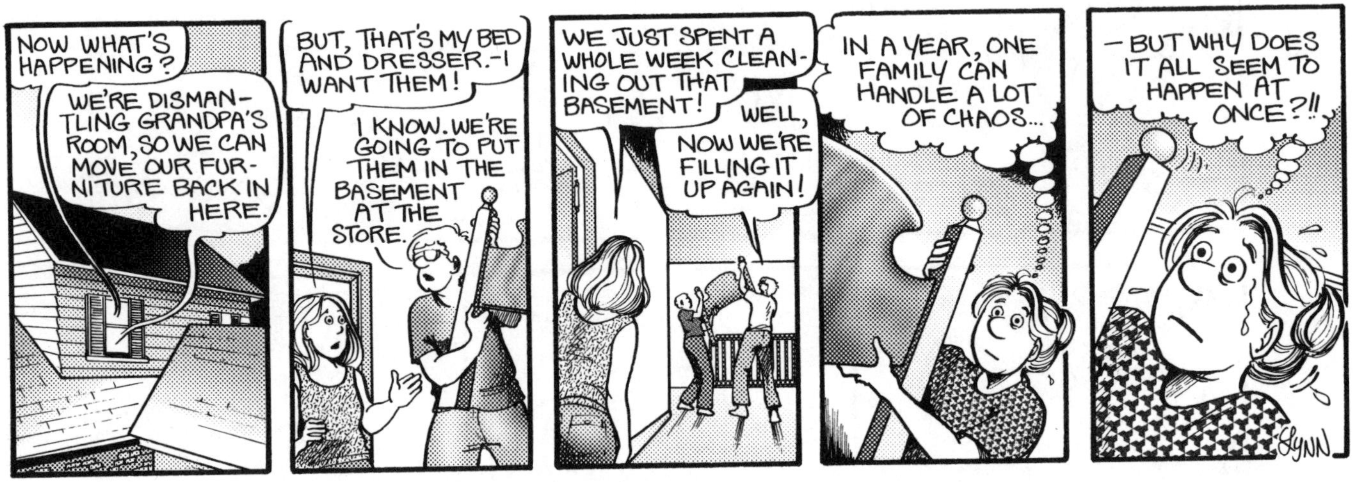
NOW WHAT'S HAPPENING?
WE'RE DISMANTLING GRANDPA'S ROOM, SO WE CAN MOVE OUR FURNITURE BACK IN HERE.
BUT, THAT'S MY BED AND DRESSER.-I WANT THEM!
I KNOW. WE'RE GOING TO PUT THEM IN THE BASEMENT AT THE STORE.
WE JUST SPENT A WHOLE WEEK CLEANING OUT THAT BASEMENT!
WELL, NOW WE'RE FILLING IT UP AGAIN!
IN A YEAR, ONE FAMILY CAN HANDLE A LOT OF CHAOS...
-BUT WHY DOES IT ALL SEEM TO HAPPEN AT ONCE?!!
LYNN

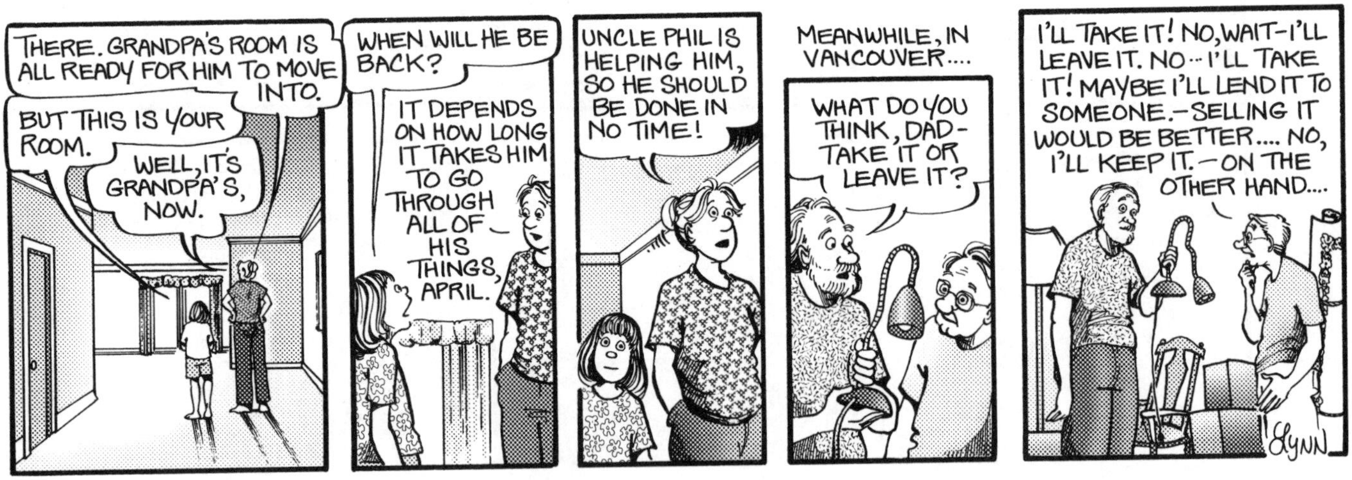
THERE. GRANDPA'S ROOM IS ALL READY FOR HIM TO MOVE INTO.
BUT THIS IS YOUR ROOM.
WELL, IT'S GRANDPA'S, NOW.
WHEN WILL HE BE BACK?
IT DEPENDS ON HOW LONG IT TAKES HIM TO GO THROUGH ALL OF HIS THINGS, APRIL.
UNCLE PHIL IS HELPING HIM, SO HE SHOULD BE DONE IN NO TIME!
MEANWHILE, IN VANCOUVER....
WHAT DO YOU THINK, DAD-TAKE IT OR LEAVE IT?
I'LL TAKE IT! NO, WAIT-I'LL LEAVE IT. NO...I'LL TAKE IT! MAYBE I'LL LEND IT TO SOMEONE.-SELLING IT WOULD BE BETTER.... NO, I'LL KEEP IT.-ON THE OTHER HAND....
LYNN

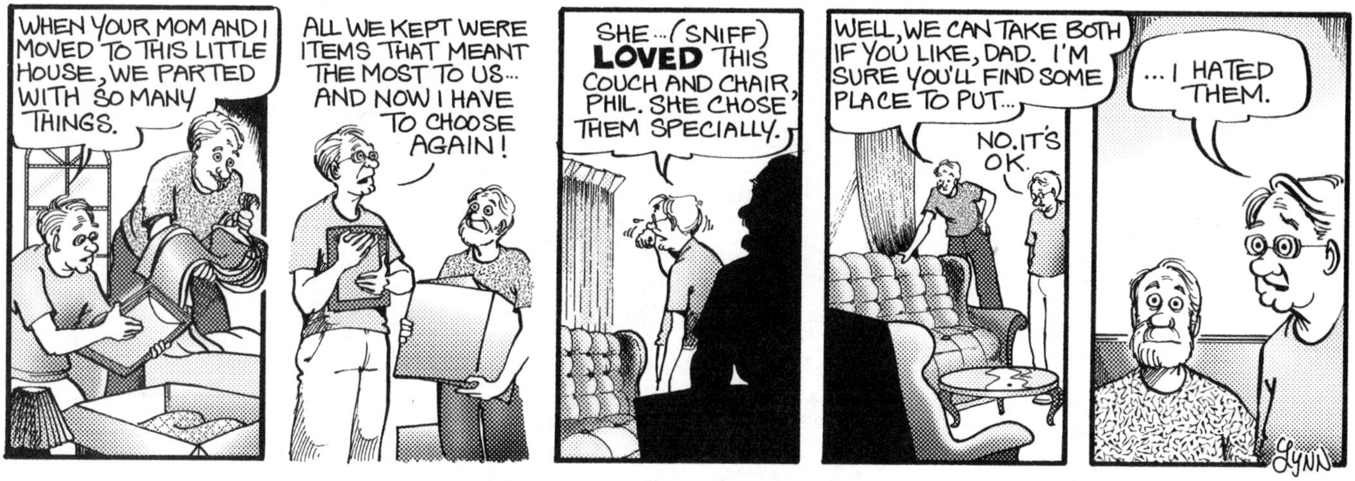
WHEN YOUR MOM AND I MOVED TO THIS LITTLE HOUSE, WE PARTED WITH SO MANY THINGS.
ALL WE KEPT WERE ITEMS THAT MEANT THE MOST TO US... AND NOW I HAVE TO CHOOSE AGAIN!
SHE...(SNIFF) LOVED THIS COUCH AND CHAIR, PHIL. SHE CHOSE THEM SPECIALLY.
WELL, WE CAN TAKE BOTH IF YOU LIKE, DAD. I'M SURE YOU'LL FIND SOME PLACE TO PUT...
NO. IT'S OK.
...I HATED THEM.
LYNN

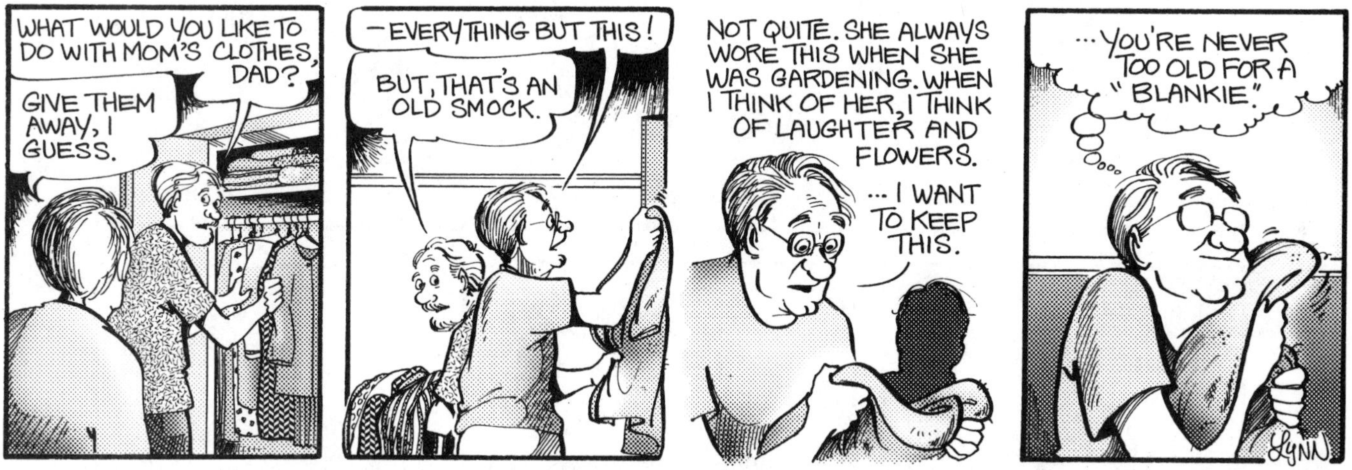
WHAT WOULD YOU LIKE TO DO WITH MOM'S CLOTHES, DAD?
GIVE THEM AWAY, I GUESS.
—EVERYTHING BUT THIS!
BUT, THAT'S AN OLD SMOCK.
NOT QUITE. SHE ALWAYS WORE THIS WHEN SHE WAS GARDENING. WHEN I THINK OF HER, I THINK OF LAUGHTER AND FLOWERS.
...I WANT TO KEEP THIS.
...YOU'RE NEVER TOO OLD FOR A "BLANKIE."
LYNN

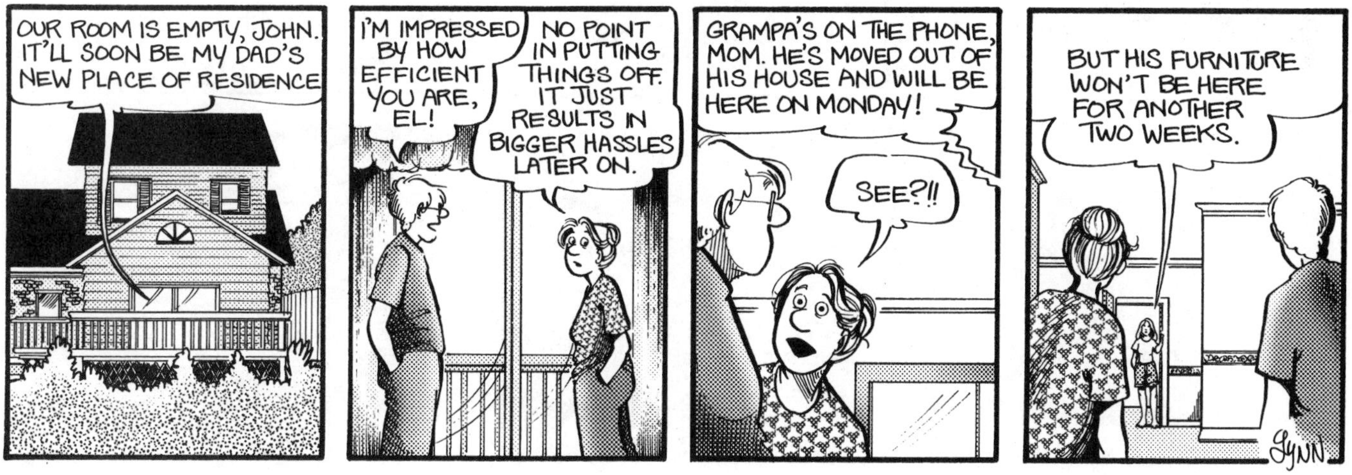
OUR ROOM IS EMPTY, JOHN. IT'LL SOON BE MY DAD'S NEW PLACE OF RESIDENCE
I'M IMPRESSED BY HOW EFFICIENT YOU ARE, EL!
NO POINT IN PUTTING THINGS OFF. IT JUST RESULTS IN BIGGER HASSLES LATER ON.
GRAMPA'S ON THE PHONE, MOM. HE'S MOVED OUT OF HIS HOUSE AND WILL BE HERE ON MONDAY!
SEE?!!
BUT HIS FURNITURE WON'T BE HERE FOR ANOTHER TWO WEEKS.
LYNN

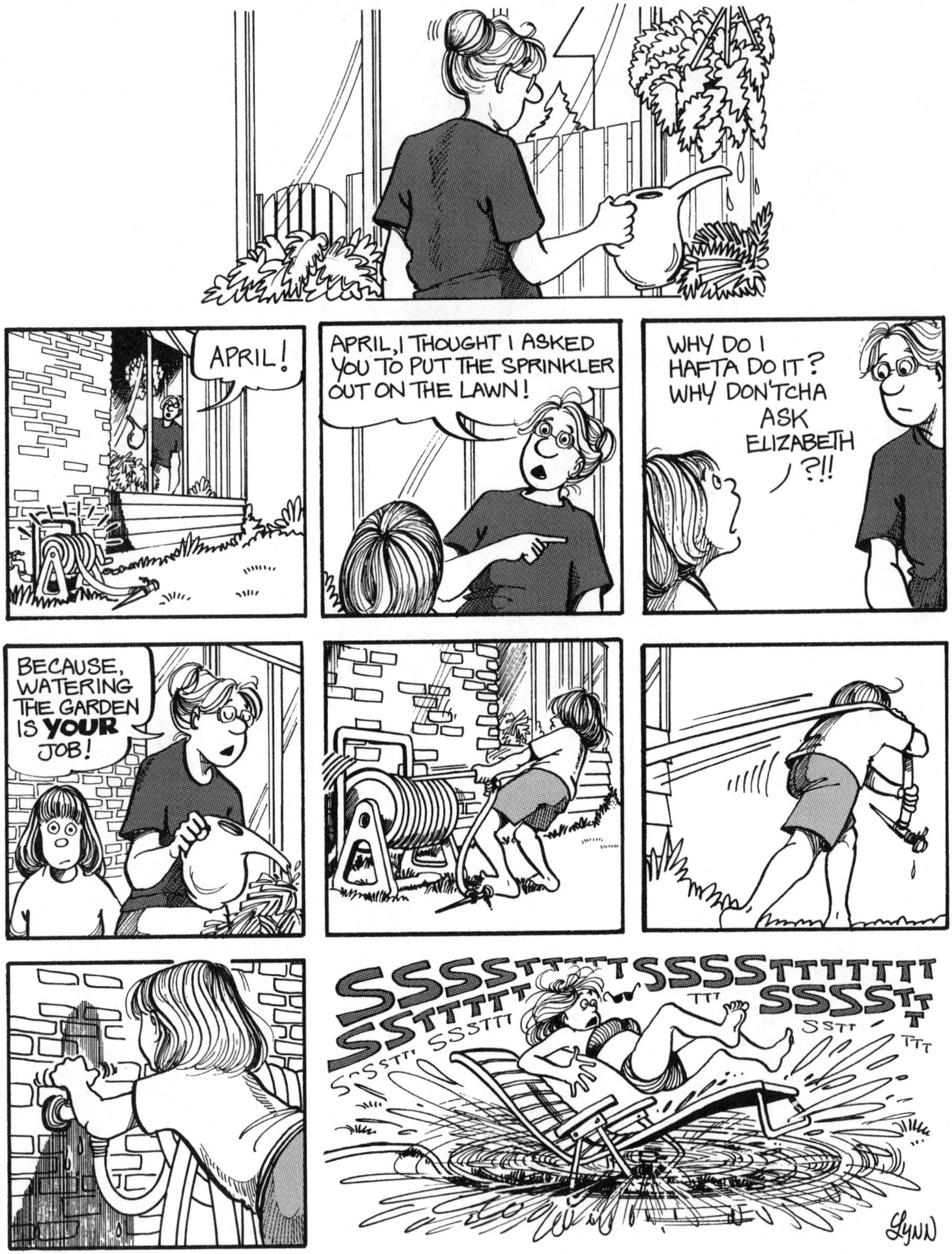

APRIL!
APRIL, I THOUGHT I ASKED YOU TO PUT THE SPRINKLER OUT ON THE LAWN!
WHY DO I HAFTA DO IT? WHY DON'TCHA ASK ELIZABETH ?!!
BECAUSE, WATERING THE GARDEN IS **YOUR** JOB!
SSSSTTTTTTSSSSSTTTTTTT
SSTTTTTT
SSSTTT
SSSTTT
TTT
SSSSTTT
SSTT
TTT
Lynn

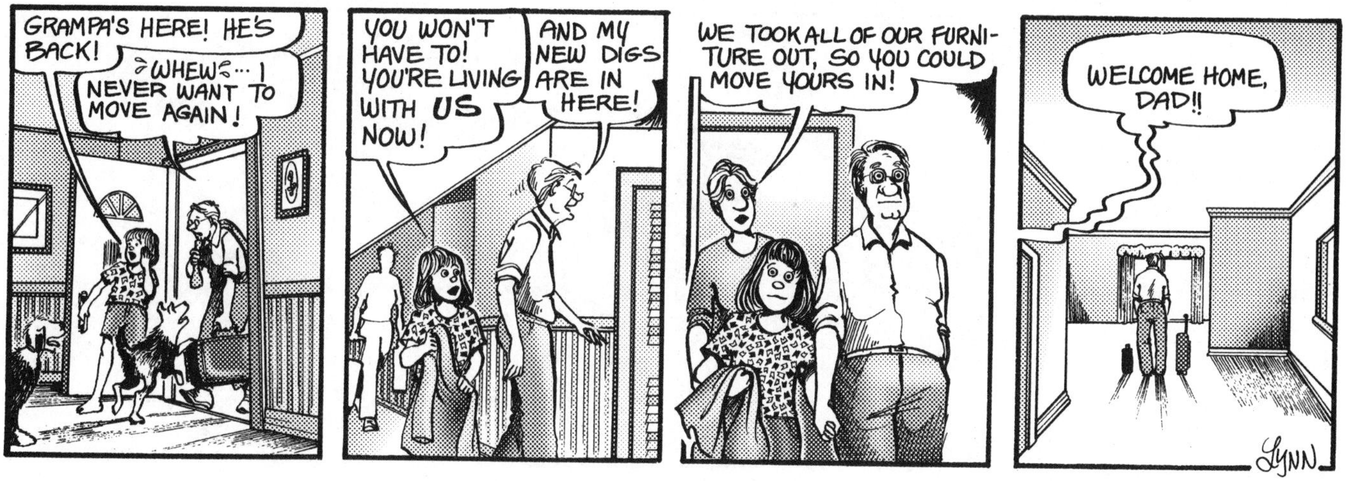
GRAMPA'S HERE! HE'S BACK!
≈WHEW≈... I NEVER WANT TO MOVE AGAIN!
YOU WON'T HAVE TO! YOU'RE LIVING WITH **US** NOW!
AND MY NEW DIGS ARE IN HERE!
WE TOOK ALL OF OUR FURNITURE OUT, SO YOU COULD MOVE YOURS IN!
WELCOME HOME, DAD!!
LYNN

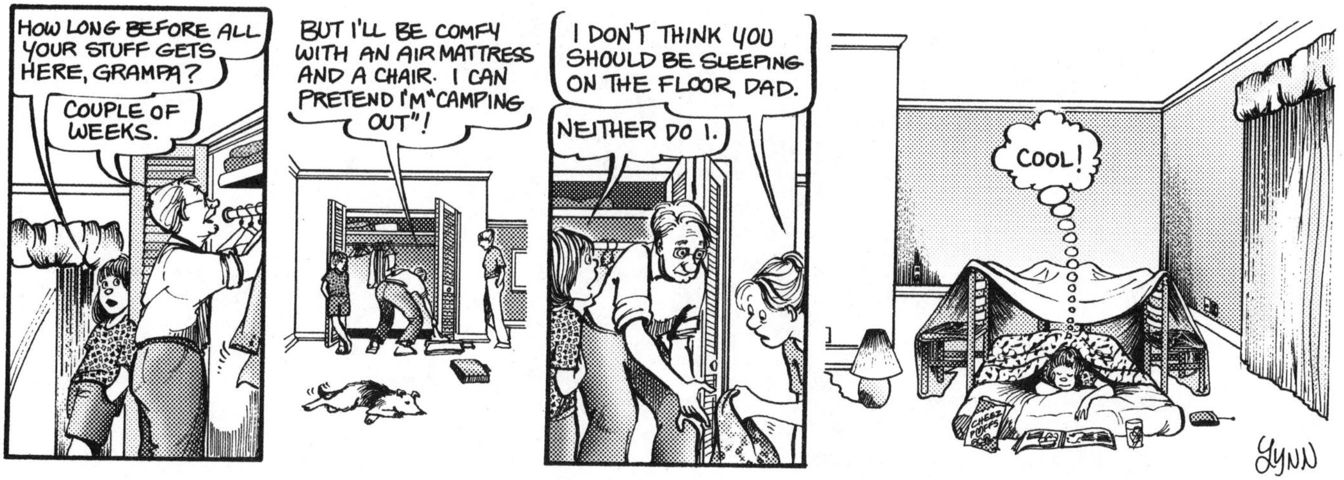
HOW LONG BEFORE ALL YOUR STUFF GETS HERE, GRAMPA?
COUPLE OF WEEKS.
BUT I'LL BE COMFY WITH AN AIR MATTRESS AND A CHAIR. I CAN PRETEND I'M "CAMPING OUT"!
I DON'T THINK YOU SHOULD BE SLEEPING ON THE FLOOR, DAD.
NEITHER DO I.
COOL!
LYNN

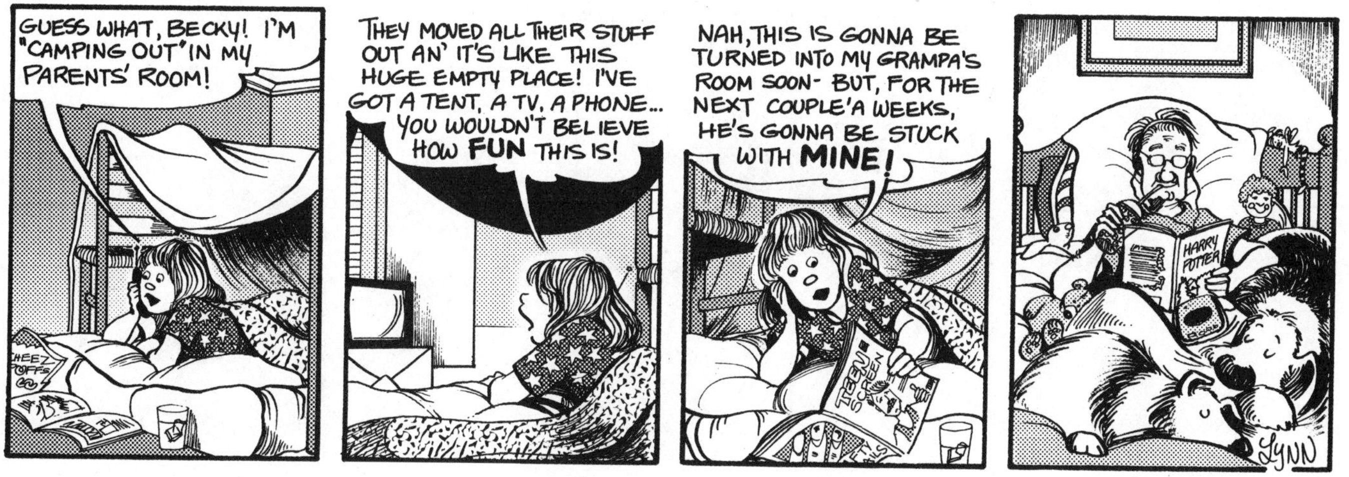
GUESS WHAT, BECKY! I'M "CAMPING OUT" IN MY PARENTS' ROOM!
THEY MOVED ALL THEIR STUFF OUT AN' IT'S LIKE THIS HUGE EMPTY PLACE! I'VE GOT A TENT, A TV, A PHONE... YOU WOULDN'T BELIEVE HOW **FUN** THIS IS!
NAH, THIS IS GONNA BE TURNED INTO MY GRAMPA'S ROOM SOON- BUT, FOR THE NEXT COUPLE'A WEEKS, HE'S GONNA BE STUCK WITH **MINE**!
HARRY POTTER
LYNN

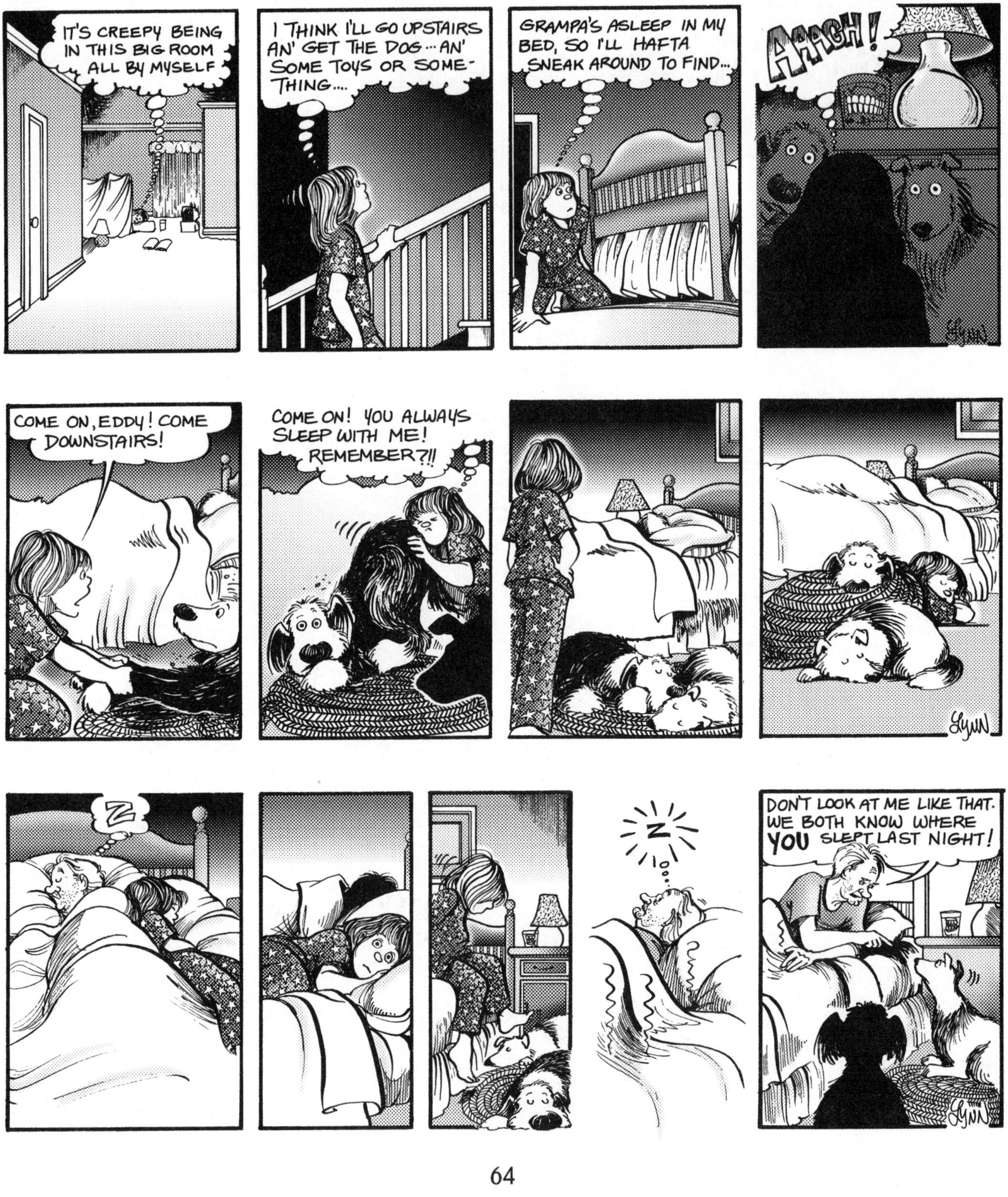
IT'S CREEPY BEING IN THIS BIG ROOM ALL BY MYSELF
I THINK I'LL GO UPSTAIRS AN' GET THE DOG... AN' SOME TOYS OR SOME-THING....
GRAMPA'S ASLEEP IN MY BED, SO I'LL HAFTA SNEAK AROUND TO FIND...
AAAGH!
LYNN
COME ON, EDDY! COME DOWNSTAIRS!
COME ON! YOU ALWAYS SLEEP WITH ME! REMEMBER?!!
LYNN
Z
Z
DON'T LOOK AT ME LIKE THAT. WE BOTH KNOW WHERE YOU SLEPT LAST NIGHT!
LYNN

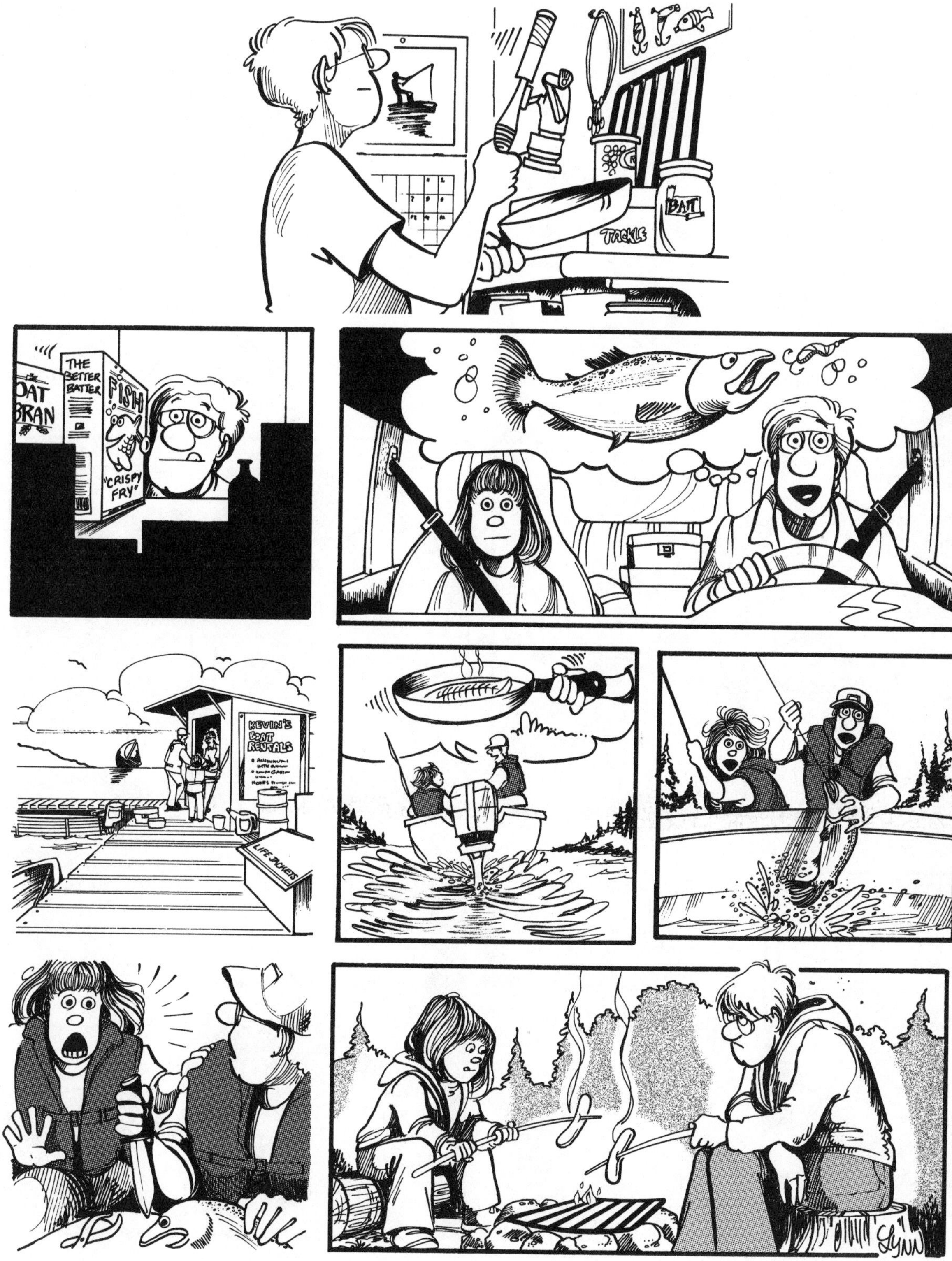
BAIT
TACKLE
BRAN
THE BETTER BATTER
FISH
"CRISPY FRY"
KEVIN'S BOAT RENTALS
LIFE JACKETS
LYNN

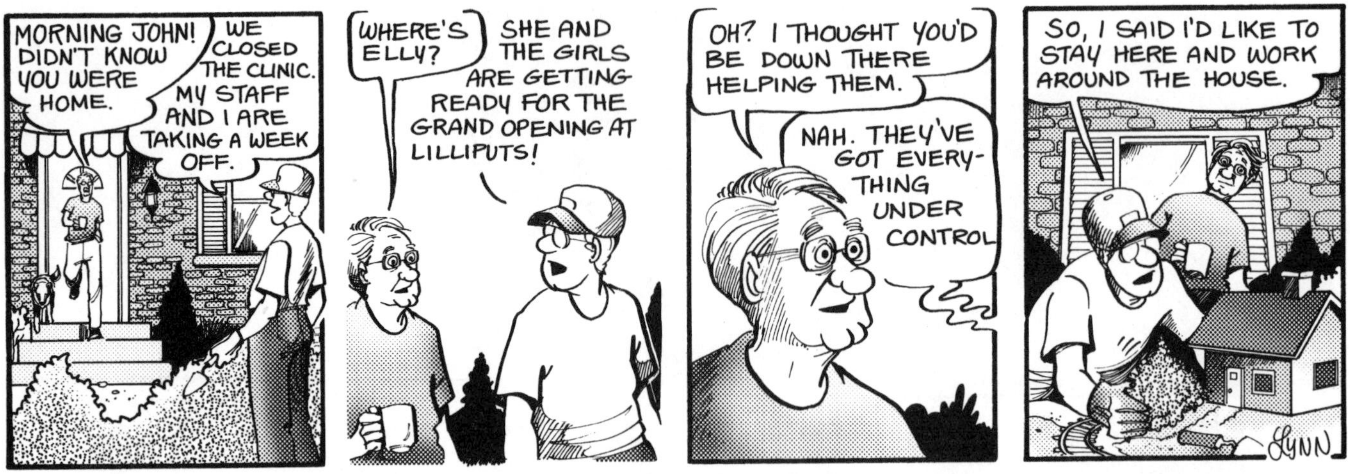
MORNING JOHN! DIDN'T KNOW YOU WERE HOME.
WE CLOSED THE CLINIC. MY STAFF AND I ARE TAKING A WEEK OFF.
WHERE'S ELLY?
SHE AND THE GIRLS ARE GETTING READY FOR THE GRAND OPENING AT LILLIPUTS!
OH? I THOUGHT YOU'D BE DOWN THERE HELPING THEM.
NAH. THEY'VE GOT EVERYTHING UNDER CONTROL
SO, I SAID I'D LIKE TO STAY HERE AND WORK AROUND THE HOUSE.
LYNN

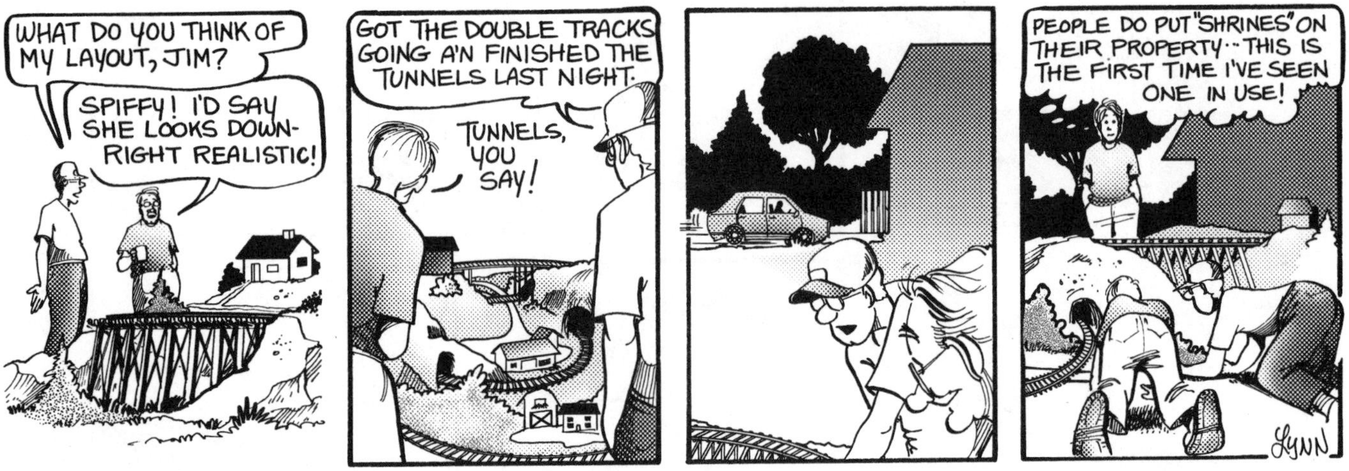
WHAT DO YOU THINK OF MY LAYOUT, JIM?
SPIFFY! I'D SAY SHE LOOKS DOWNRIGHT REALISTIC!
GOT THE DOUBLE TRACKS GOING A'N FINISHED THE TUNNELS LAST NIGHT.
TUNNELS, YOU SAY!
PEOPLE DO PUT "SHRINES" ON THEIR PROPERTY·· THIS IS THE FIRST TIME I'VE SEEN ONE IN USE!
LYNN

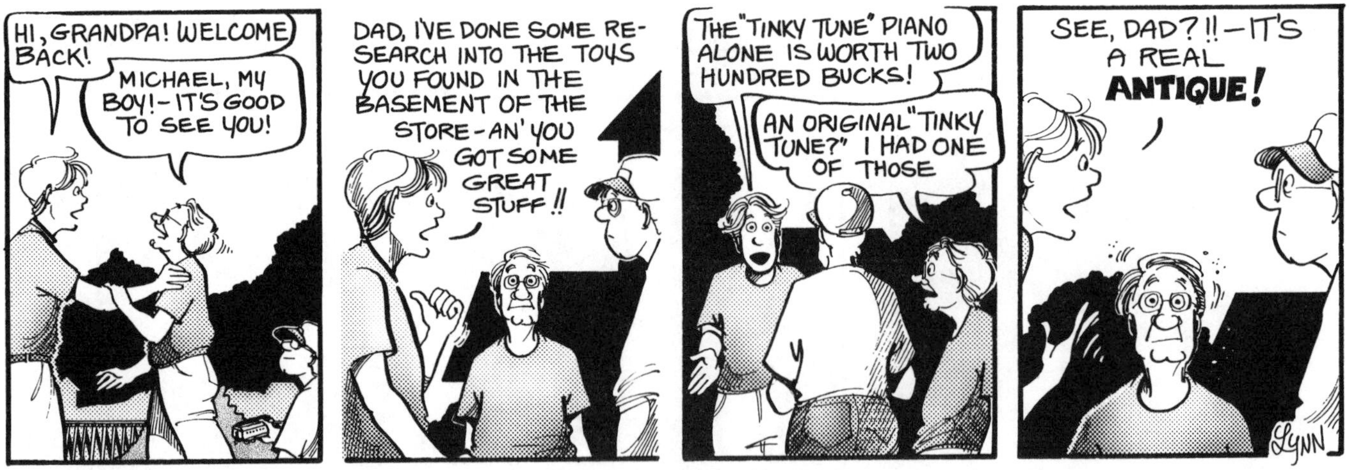
HI, GRANDPA! WELCOME BACK!
MICHAEL, MY BOY! - IT'S GOOD TO SEE YOU!
DAD, I'VE DONE SOME RESEARCH INTO THE TOYS YOU FOUND IN THE BASEMENT OF THE STORE - AN' YOU GOT SOME GREAT STUFF!!
THE "TINKY TUNE" PIANO ALONE IS WORTH TWO HUNDRED BUCKS!
AN ORIGINAL "TINKY TUNE?" I HAD ONE OF THOSE
SEE, DAD?!! - IT'S A REAL ANTIQUE!
LYNN

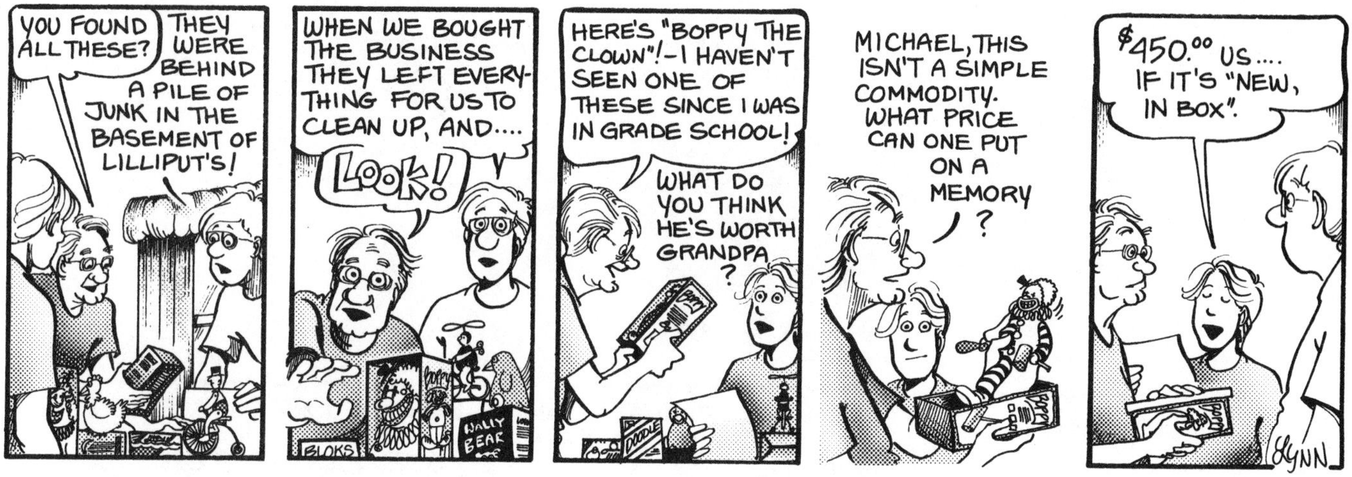
YOU FOUND ALL THESE?
THEY WERE BEHIND A PILE OF JUNK IN THE BASEMENT OF LILLIPUT'S!
WHEN WE BOUGHT THE BUSINESS THEY LEFT EVERYTHING FOR US TO CLEAN UP, AND....
LOOK!
BLOKS
WALLY BEAR
HERE'S "BOPPY THE CLOWN"! – I HAVEN'T SEEN ONE OF THESE SINCE I WAS IN GRADE SCHOOL!
WHAT DO YOU THINK HE'S WORTH GRANDPA ?
DOODLE
MICHAEL, THIS ISN'T A SIMPLE COMMODITY. WHAT PRICE CAN ONE PUT ON A MEMORY ?
$450.00 US.... IF IT'S "NEW, IN BOX".
LYNN

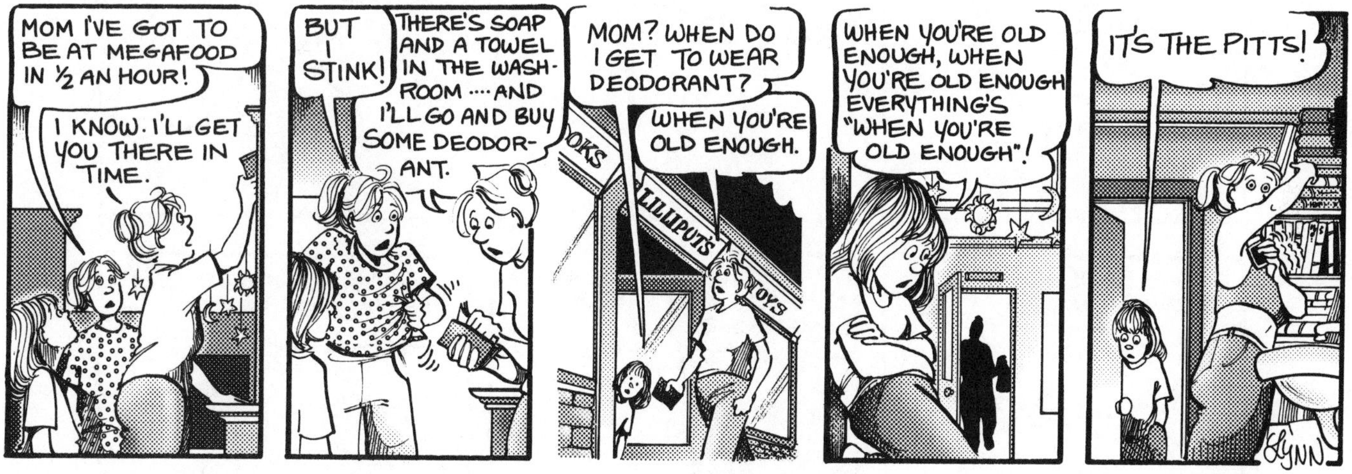
MOM I'VE GOT TO BE AT MEGAFOOD IN 1/2 AN HOUR!
I KNOW. I'LL GET YOU THERE IN TIME.
BUT I STINK!
THERE'S SOAP AND A TOWEL IN THE WASHROOM.... AND I'LL GO AND BUY SOME DEODORANT.
MOM? WHEN DO I GET TO WEAR DEODORANT?
WHEN YOU'RE OLD ENOUGH.
LILLIPUTS
WHEN YOU'RE OLD ENOUGH, WHEN YOU'RE OLD ENOUGH EVERYTHING'S "WHEN YOU'RE OLD ENOUGH"!
IT'S THE PITTS!
LYNN

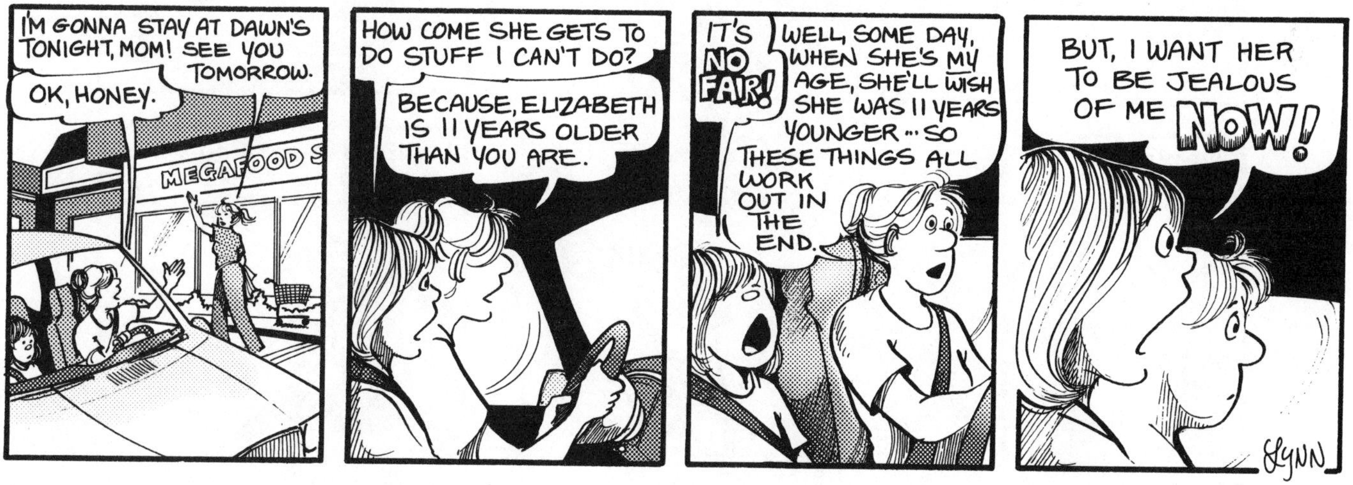
I'M GONNA STAY AT DAWN'S TONIGHT, MOM! SEE YOU TOMORROW.
OK, HONEY.
MEGAFOOD S
HOW COME SHE GETS TO DO STUFF I CAN'T DO?
BECAUSE, ELIZABETH IS 11 YEARS OLDER THAN YOU ARE.
IT'S NO FAIR!
WELL, SOME DAY, WHEN SHE'S MY AGE, SHE'LL WISH SHE WAS 11 YEARS YOUNGER... SO THESE THINGS ALL WORK OUT IN THE END.
BUT, I WANT HER TO BE JEALOUS OF ME NOW!
LYNN

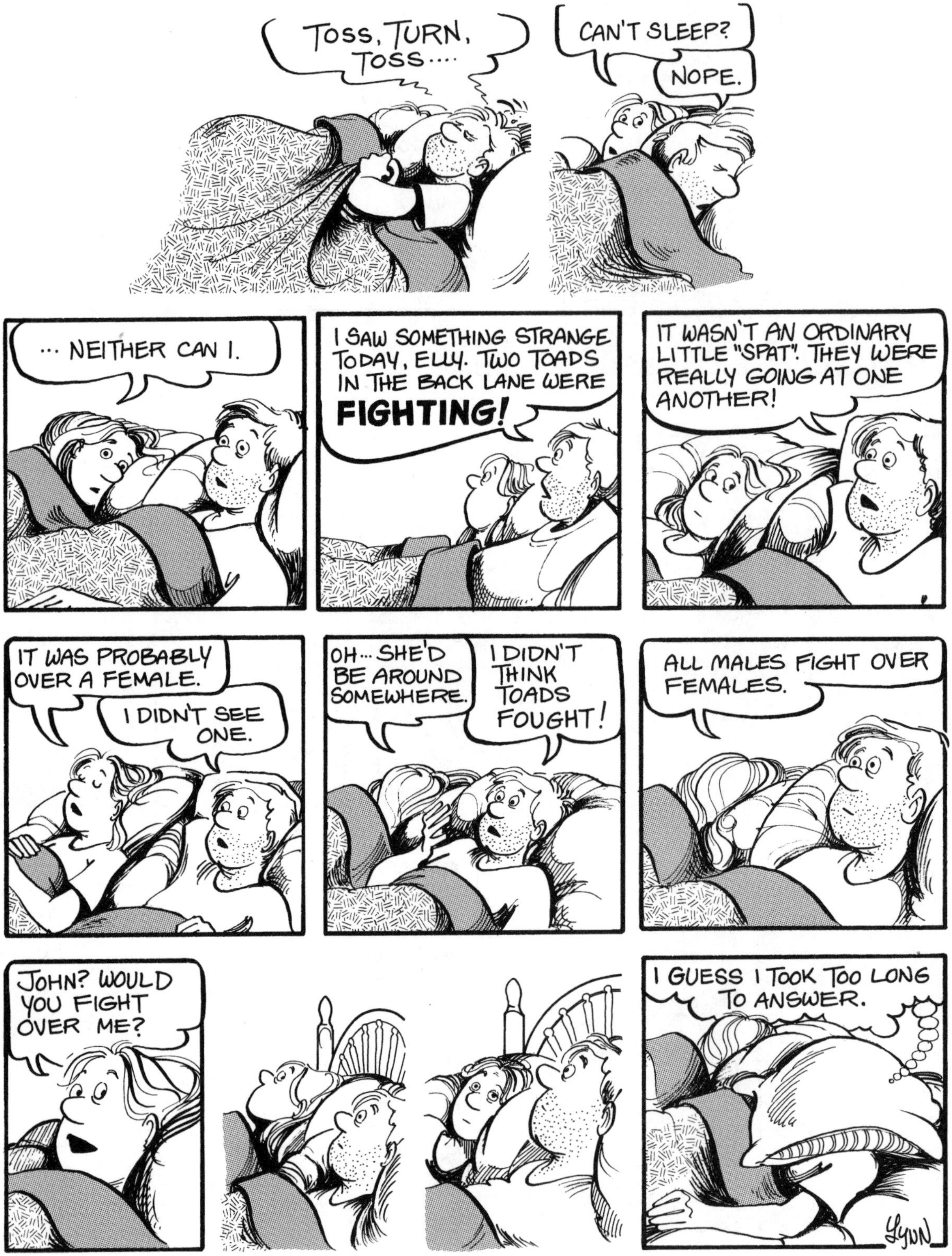
TOSS, TURN, TOSS....
CAN'T SLEEP?
NOPE.
... NEITHER CAN I.
I SAW SOMETHING STRANGE TODAY, ELLY. TWO TOADS IN THE BACK LANE WERE FIGHTING!
IT WASN'T AN ORDINARY LITTLE "SPAT". THEY WERE REALLY GOING AT ONE ANOTHER!
IT WAS PROBABLY OVER A FEMALE.
I DIDN'T SEE ONE.
OH... SHE'D BE AROUND SOMEWHERE.
I DIDN'T THINK TOADS FOUGHT!
ALL MALES FIGHT OVER FEMALES.
JOHN? WOULD YOU FIGHT OVER ME?
I GUESS I TOOK TOO LONG TO ANSWER.
LYNN

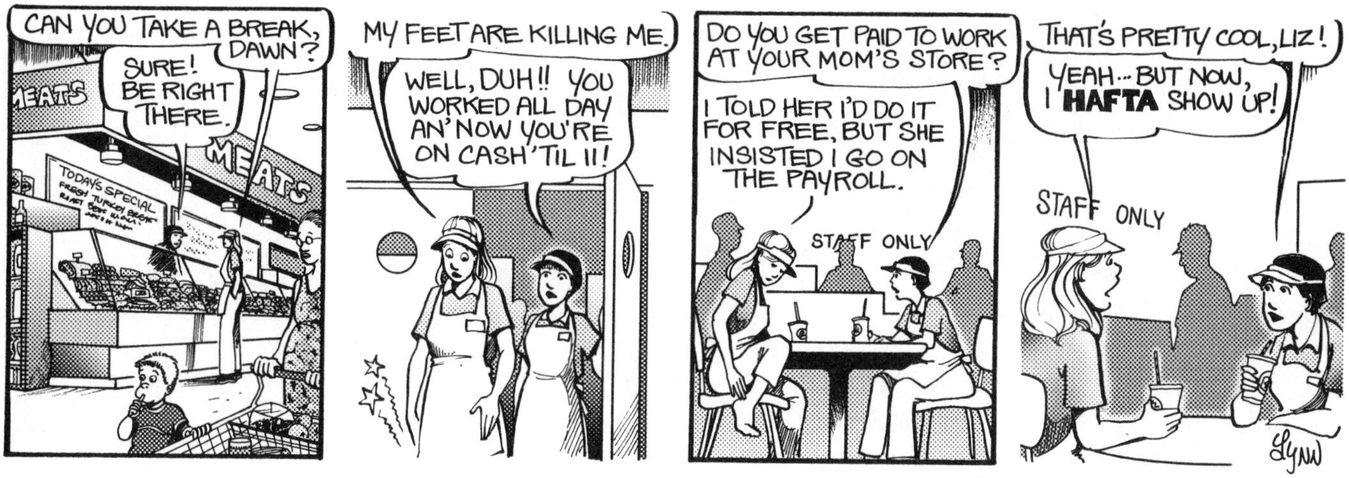
CAN YOU TAKE A BREAK, DAWN?
SURE! BE RIGHT THERE.
MEATS
MEATS
TODAY'S SPECIAL
MY FEET ARE KILLING ME.
WELL, DUH!! YOU WORKED ALL DAY AN' NOW YOU'RE ON CASH 'TIL 11!
DO YOU GET PAID TO WORK AT YOUR MOM'S STORE?
I TOLD HER I'D DO IT FOR FREE, BUT SHE INSISTED I GO ON THE PAYROLL.
STAFF ONLY
THAT'S PRETTY COOL, LIZ!
YEAH... BUT NOW, I HAFTA SHOW UP!
STAFF ONLY
LYNN

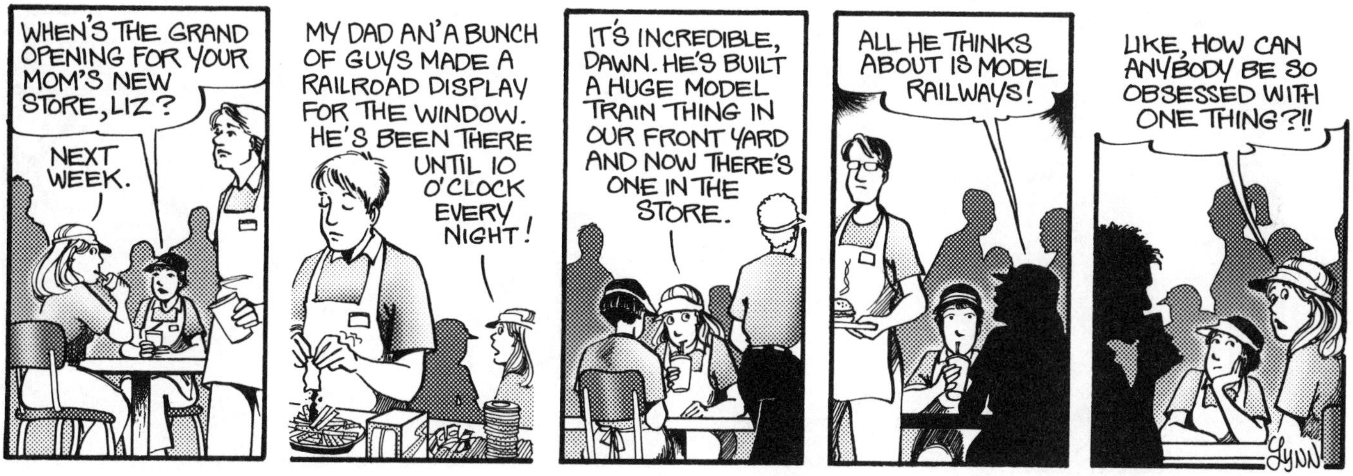
WHEN'S THE GRAND OPENING FOR YOUR MOM'S NEW STORE, LIZ?
NEXT WEEK.
MY DAD AN' A BUNCH OF GUYS MADE A RAILROAD DISPLAY FOR THE WINDOW. HE'S BEEN THERE UNTIL 10 O'CLOCK EVERY NIGHT!
IT'S INCREDIBLE, DAWN. HE'S BUILT A HUGE MODEL TRAIN THING IN OUR FRONT YARD AND NOW THERE'S ONE IN THE STORE.
ALL HE THINKS ABOUT IS MODEL RAILWAYS!
LIKE, HOW CAN ANYBODY BE SO OBSESSED WITH ONE THING?!!
LYNN

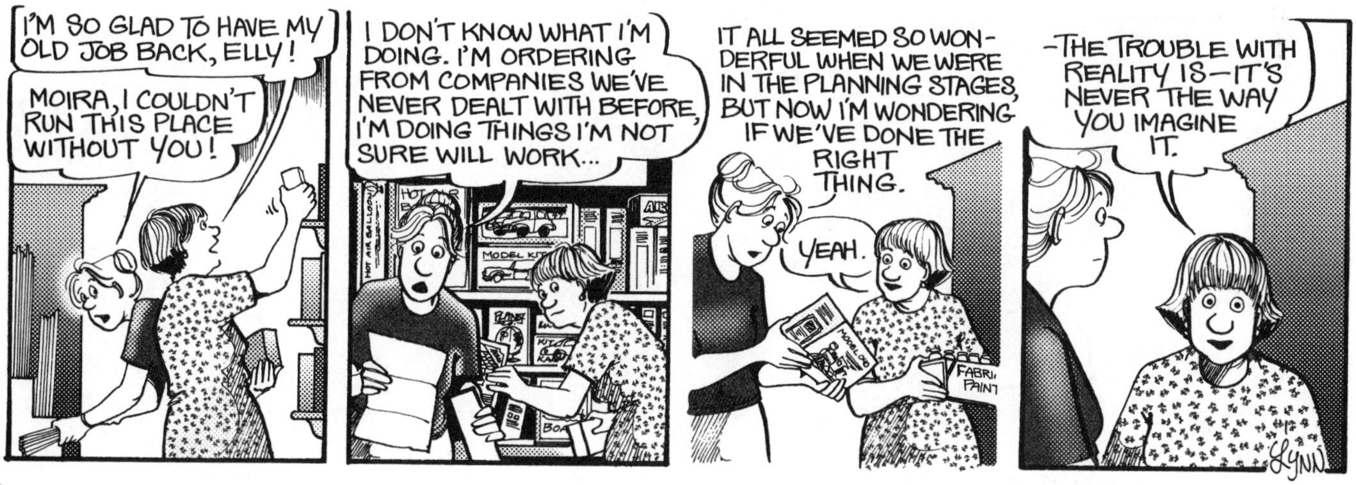
I'M SO GLAD TO HAVE MY OLD JOB BACK, ELLY!
MOIRA, I COULDN'T RUN THIS PLACE WITHOUT YOU!
I DON'T KNOW WHAT I'M DOING. I'M ORDERING FROM COMPANIES WE'VE NEVER DEALT WITH BEFORE, I'M DOING THINGS I'M NOT SURE WILL WORK...
HOT AIR BALLOON
MODEL KIT
IT ALL SEEMED SO WONDERFUL WHEN WE WERE IN THE PLANNING STAGES, BUT NOW I'M WONDERING IF WE'VE DONE THE RIGHT THING.
YEAH.
FABRIC PAINT
-THE TROUBLE WITH REALITY IS—IT'S NEVER THE WAY YOU IMAGINE IT.
LYNN

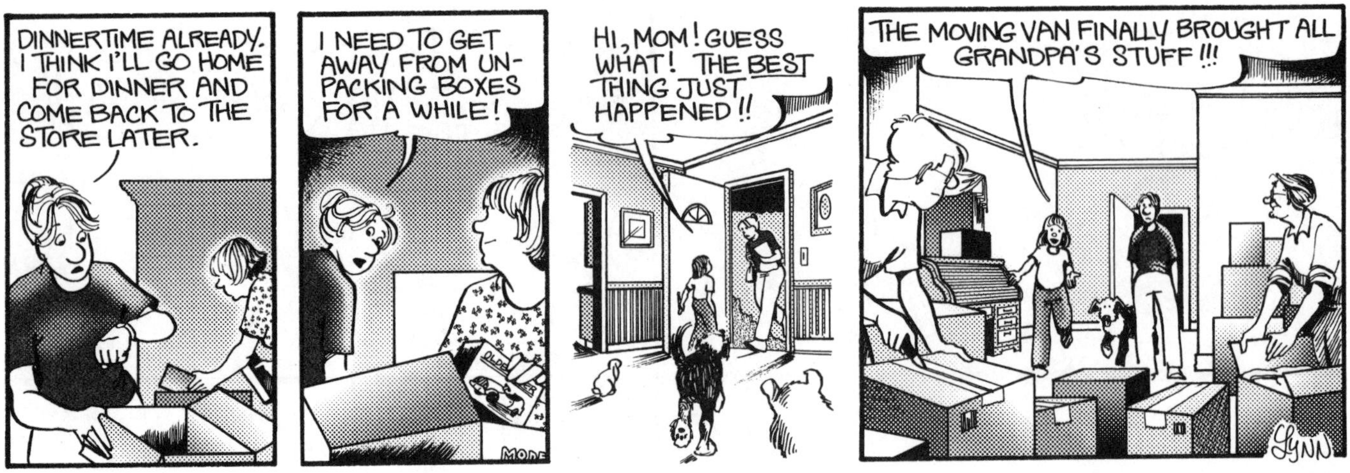
DINNERTIME ALREADY. I THINK I'LL GO HOME FOR DINNER AND COME BACK TO THE STORE LATER.
I NEED TO GET AWAY FROM UNPACKING BOXES FOR A WHILE!
HI, MOM! GUESS WHAT! THE BEST THING JUST HAPPENED!!
THE MOVING VAN FINALLY BROUGHT ALL GRANDPA'S STUFF!!!
LYNN

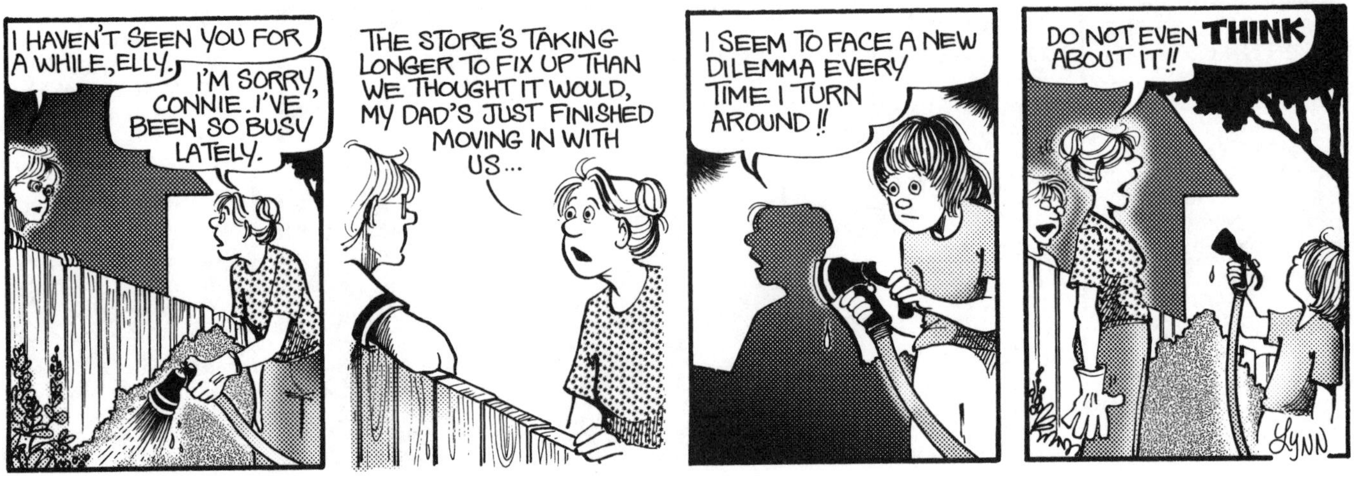
I HAVEN'T SEEN YOU FOR A WHILE, ELLY.
I'M SORRY, CONNIE. I'VE BEEN SO BUSY LATELY.
THE STORE'S TAKING LONGER TO FIX UP THAN WE THOUGHT IT WOULD, MY DAD'S JUST FINISHED MOVING IN WITH US...
I SEEM TO FACE A NEW DILEMMA EVERY TIME I TURN AROUND!!
DO NOT EVEN THINK ABOUT IT!!
LYNN

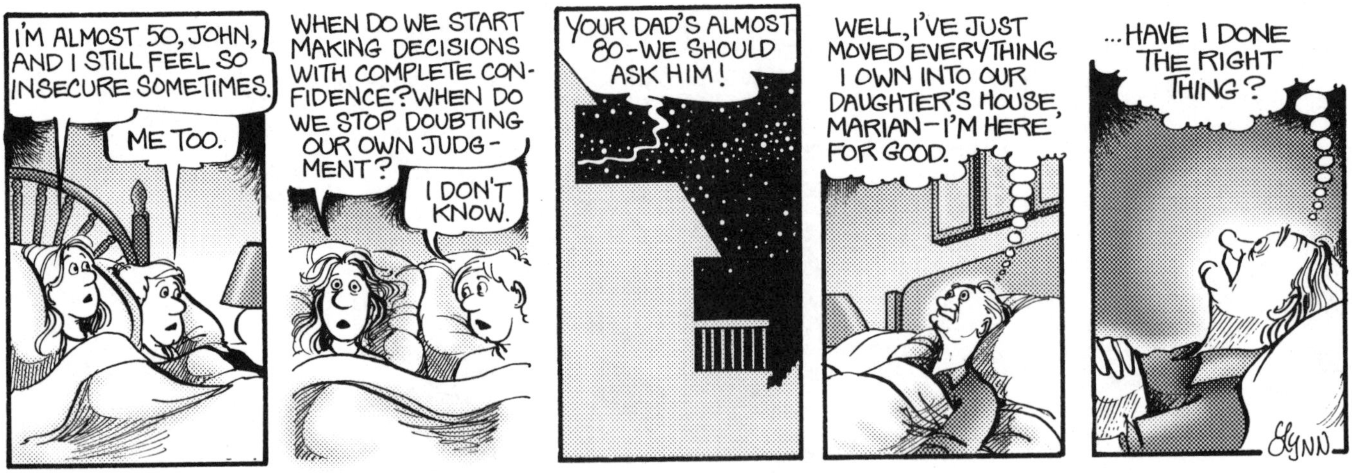
I'M ALMOST 50, JOHN, AND I STILL FEEL SO INSECURE SOMETIMES.
ME TOO.
WHEN DO WE START MAKING DECISIONS WITH COMPLETE CONFIDENCE? WHEN DO WE STOP DOUBTING OUR OWN JUDGMENT?
I DON'T KNOW.
YOUR DAD'S ALMOST 80-WE SHOULD ASK HIM!
WELL, I'VE JUST MOVED EVERYTHING I OWN INTO OUR DAUGHTER'S HOUSE, MARIAN-I'M HERE FOR GOOD.
...HAVE I DONE THE RIGHT THING?
LYNN

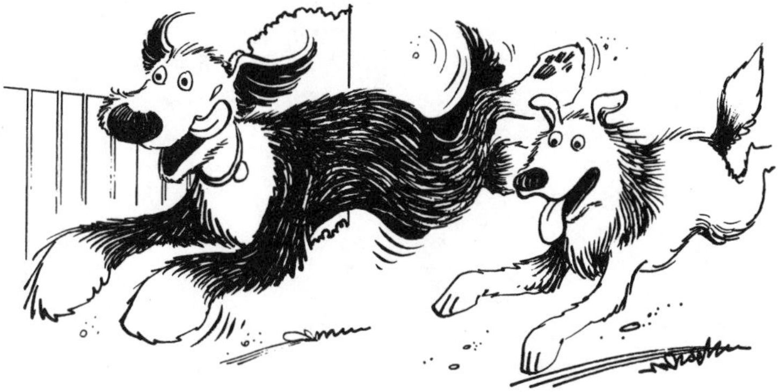

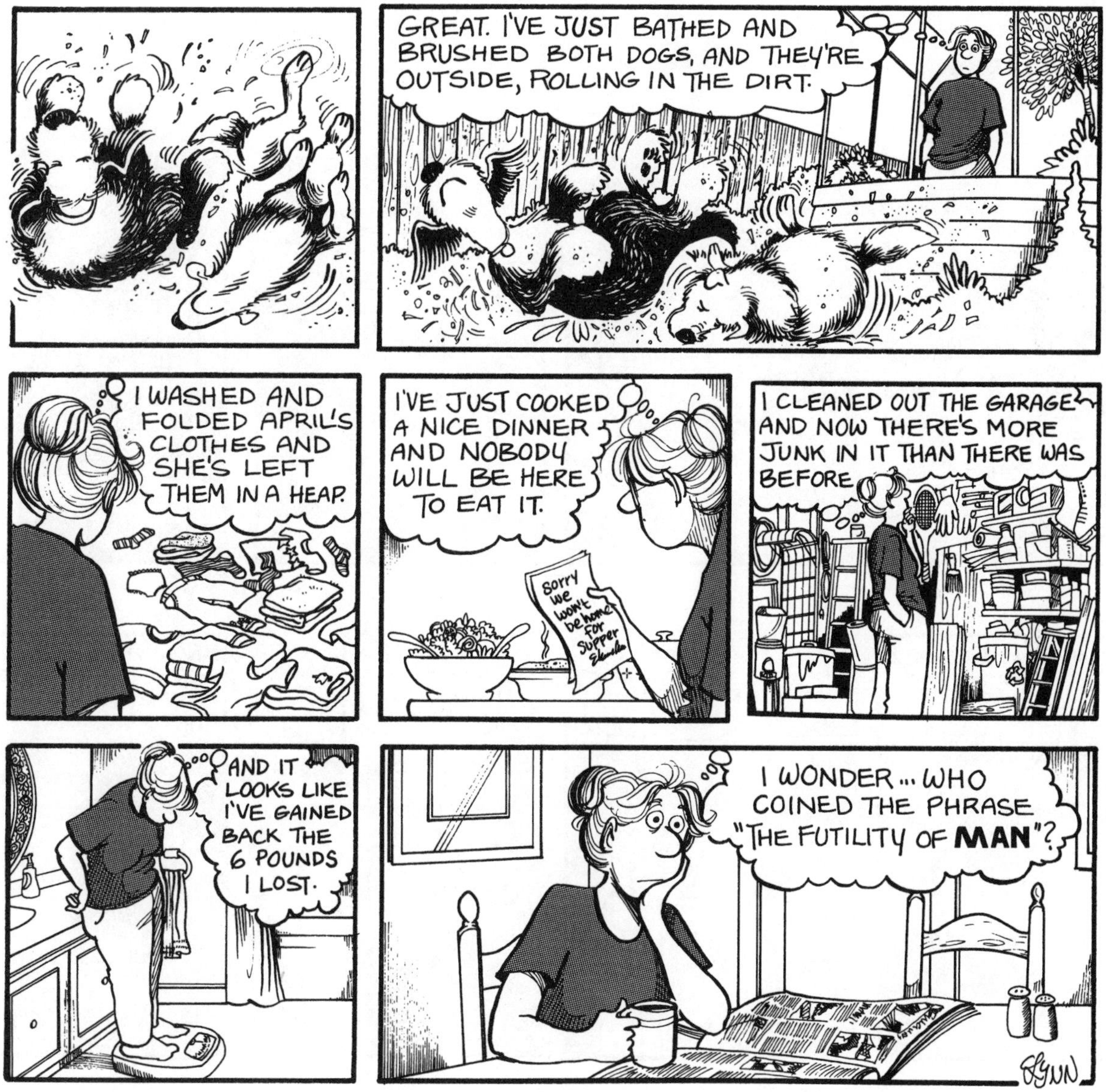
GREAT. I'VE JUST BATHED AND BRUSHED BOTH DOGS, AND THEY'RE OUTSIDE, ROLLING IN THE DIRT.
I WASHED AND FOLDED APRIL'S CLOTHES AND SHE'S LEFT THEM IN A HEAP.
I'VE JUST COOKED A NICE DINNER AND NOBODY WILL BE HERE TO EAT IT.
Sorry we won't be home for supper
I CLEANED OUT THE GARAGE AND NOW THERE'S MORE JUNK IN IT THAN THERE WAS BEFORE.
AND IT LOOKS LIKE I'VE GAINED BACK THE 6 POUNDS I LOST.
I WONDER... WHO COINED THE PHRASE "THE FUTILITY OF **MAN**"?

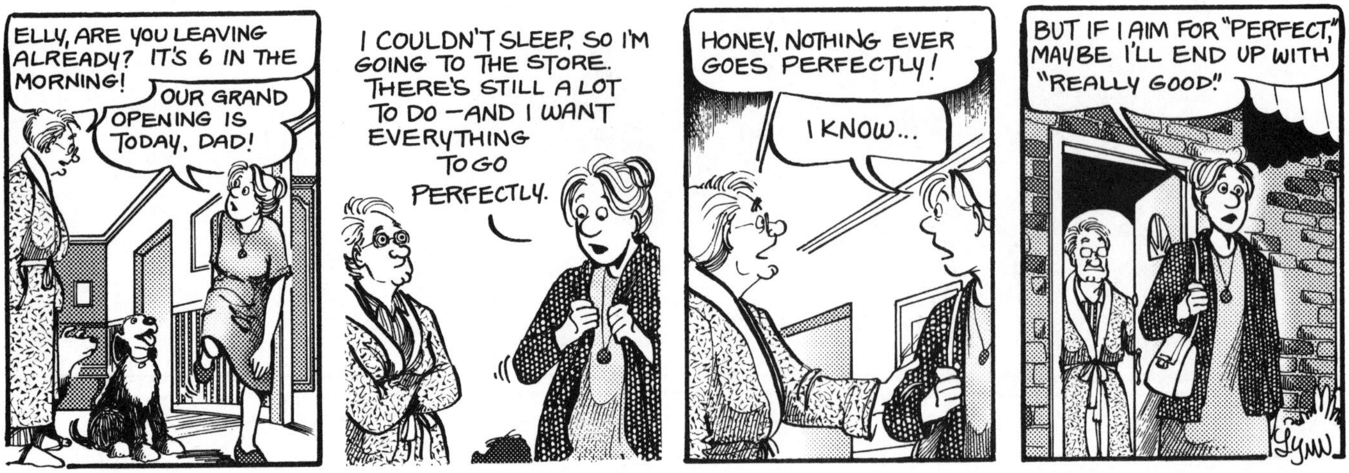
ELLY, ARE YOU LEAVING ALREADY? IT'S 6 IN THE MORNING!
OUR GRAND OPENING IS TODAY, DAD!
I COULDN'T SLEEP, SO I'M GOING TO THE STORE. THERE'S STILL A LOT TO DO — AND I WANT EVERYTHING TO GO PERFECTLY.
HONEY, NOTHING EVER GOES PERFECTLY!
I KNOW...
BUT IF I AIM FOR "PERFECT," MAYBE I'LL END UP WITH "REALLY GOOD."

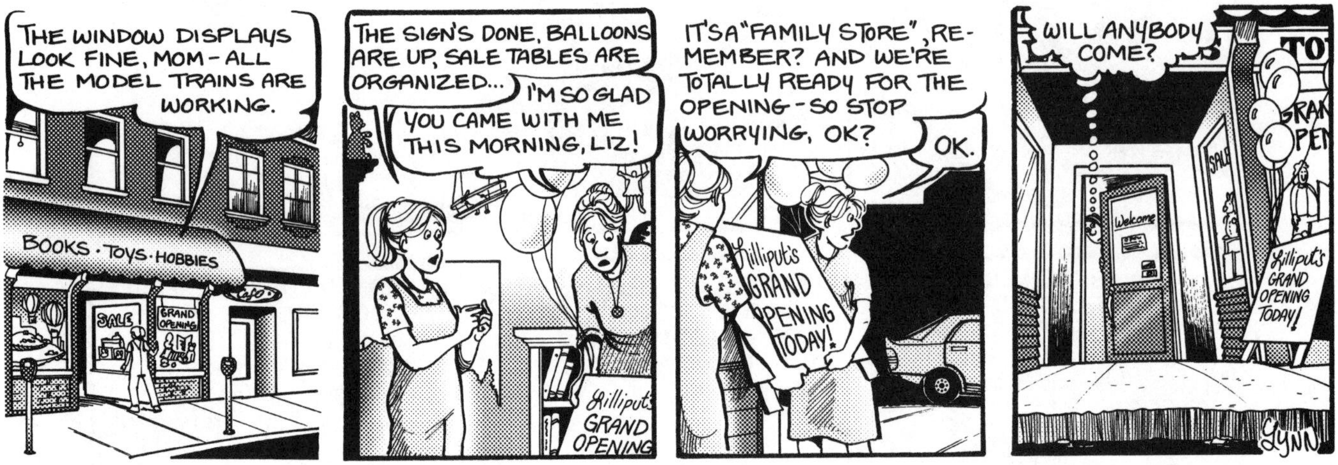
THE WINDOW DISPLAYS LOOK FINE, MOM - ALL THE MODEL TRAINS ARE WORKING.
BOOKS · TOYS · HOBBIES
SALE
GRAND OPENING
THE SIGN'S DONE, BALLOONS ARE UP, SALE TABLES ARE ORGANIZED...
I'M SO GLAD YOU CAME WITH ME THIS MORNING, LIZ!
Lilliput's GRAND OPENING
IT'S A "FAMILY STORE", REMEMBER? AND WE'RE TOTALLY READY FOR THE OPENING - SO STOP WORRYING, OK?
OK.
Lilliput's GRAND OPENING TODAY!
WILL ANYBODY COME?
Welcome
Lilliput's GRAND OPENING TODAY!

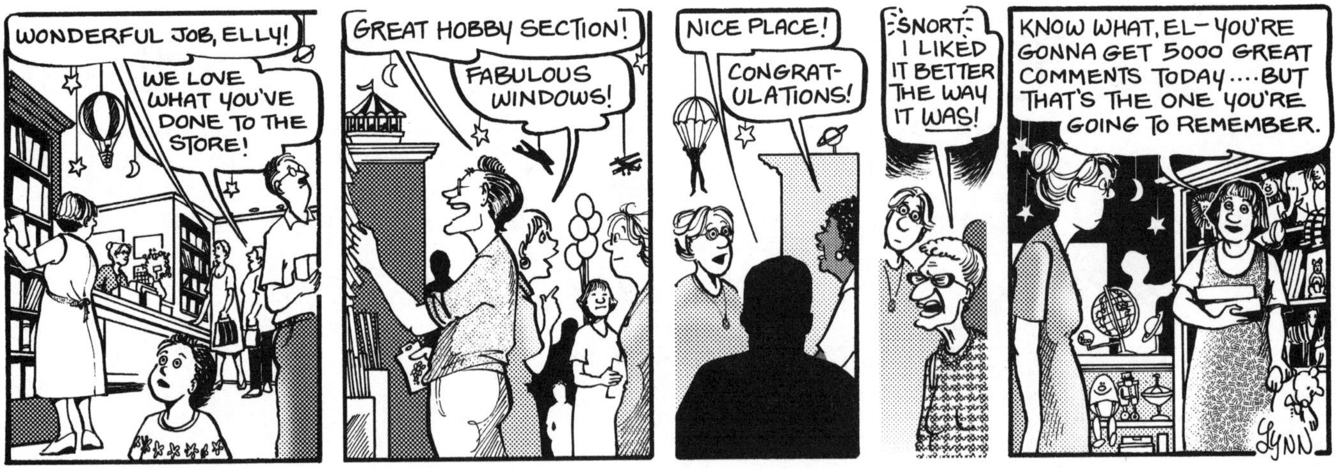
WONDERFUL JOB, ELLY!
WE LOVE WHAT YOU'VE DONE TO THE STORE!
GREAT HOBBY SECTION!
FABULOUS WINDOWS!
NICE PLACE!
CONGRATULATIONS!
SNORT. I LIKED IT BETTER THE WAY IT WAS!
KNOW WHAT, EL- YOU'RE GONNA GET 5000 GREAT COMMENTS TODAY....BUT THAT'S THE ONE YOU'RE GOING TO REMEMBER.

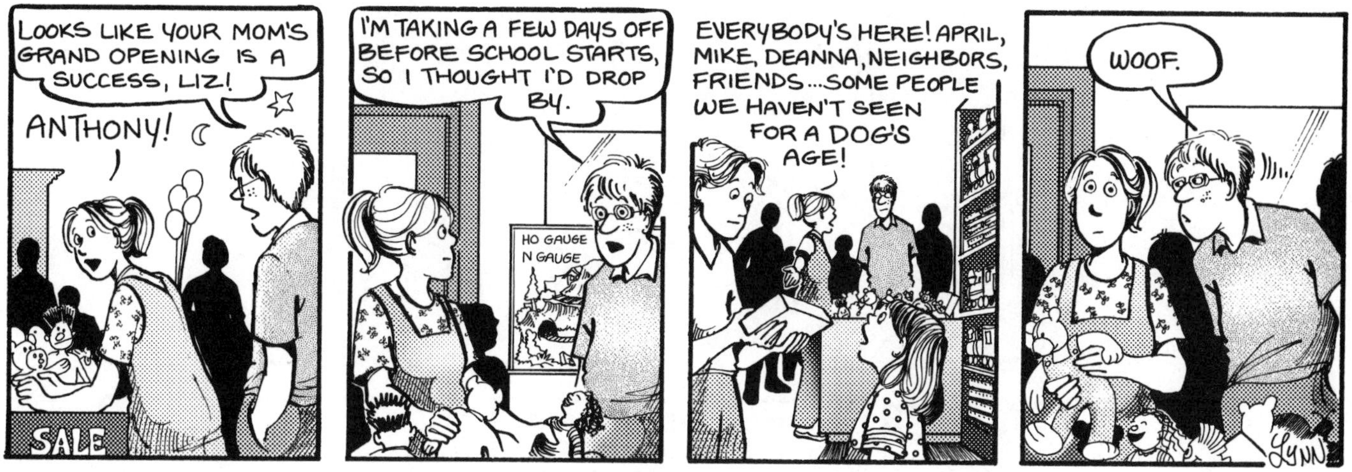
LOOKS LIKE YOUR MOM'S GRAND OPENING IS A SUCCESS, LIZ!
ANTHONY!
SALE
I'M TAKING A FEW DAYS OFF BEFORE SCHOOL STARTS, SO I THOUGHT I'D DROP BY.
HO GAUGE
N GAUGE
EVERYBODY'S HERE! APRIL, MIKE, DEANNA, NEIGHBORS, FRIENDS...SOME PEOPLE WE HAVEN'T SEEN FOR A DOG'S AGE!
WOOF.
LYNN

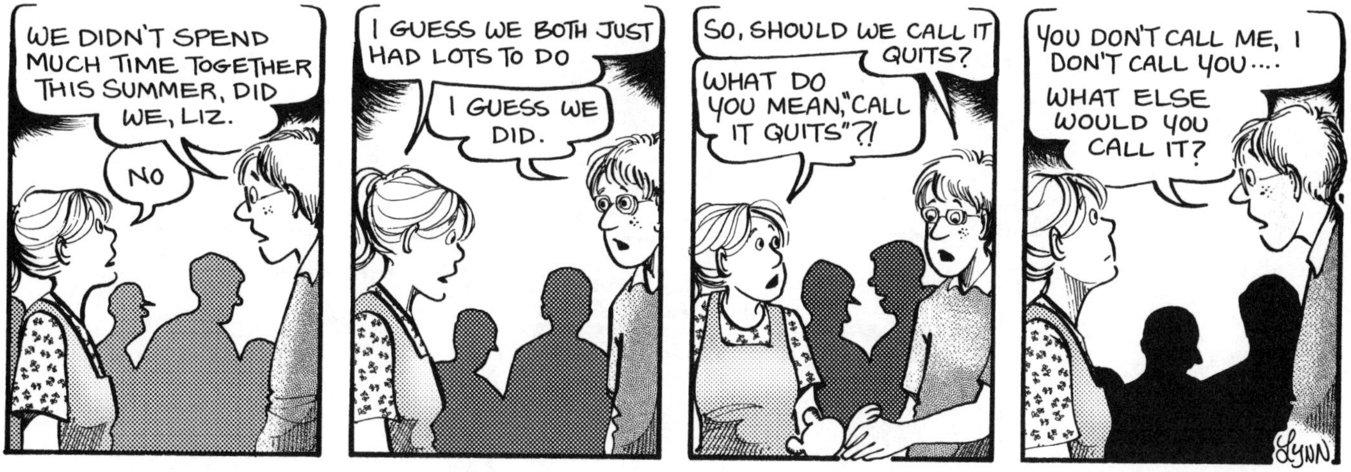
WE DIDN'T SPEND MUCH TIME TOGETHER THIS SUMMER, DID WE, LIZ.
NO
I GUESS WE BOTH JUST HAD LOTS TO DO
I GUESS WE DID.
SO, SHOULD WE CALL IT QUITS?
WHAT DO YOU MEAN, "CALL IT QUITS"?!
YOU DON'T CALL ME, I DON'T CALL YOU....
WHAT ELSE WOULD YOU CALL IT?
LYNN

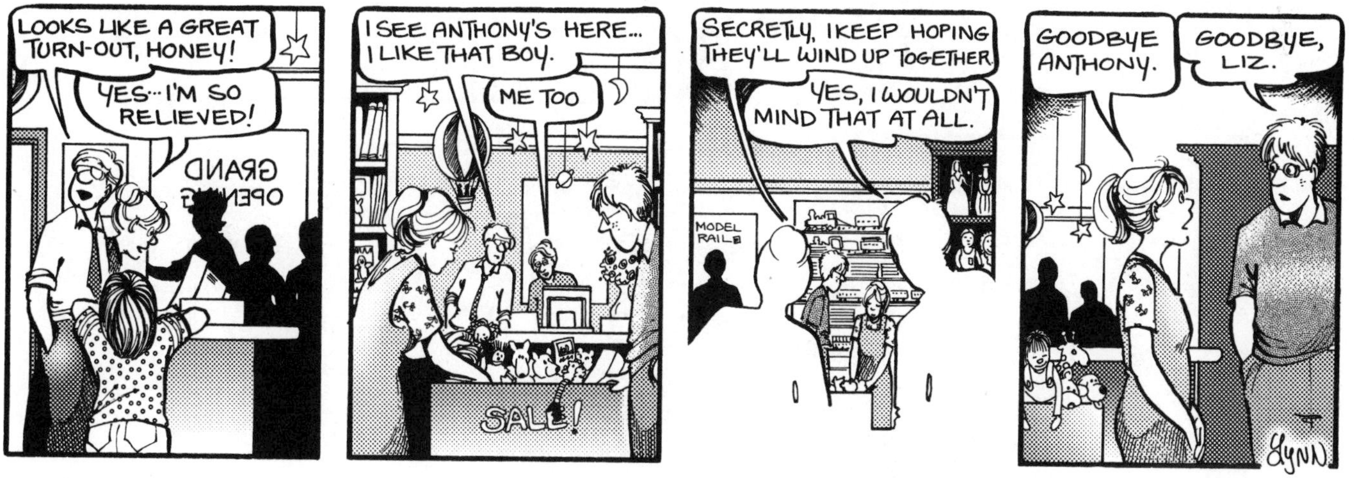
LOOKS LIKE A GREAT TURN-OUT, HONEY!
YES.. I'M SO RELIEVED!
I SEE ANTHONY'S HERE... I LIKE THAT BOY.
ME TOO
SALE!
SECRETLY, I KEEP HOPING THEY'LL WIND UP TOGETHER
YES, I WOULDN'T MIND THAT AT ALL.
MODEL RAIL
GOODBYE ANTHONY.
GOODBYE, LIZ.
LYNN

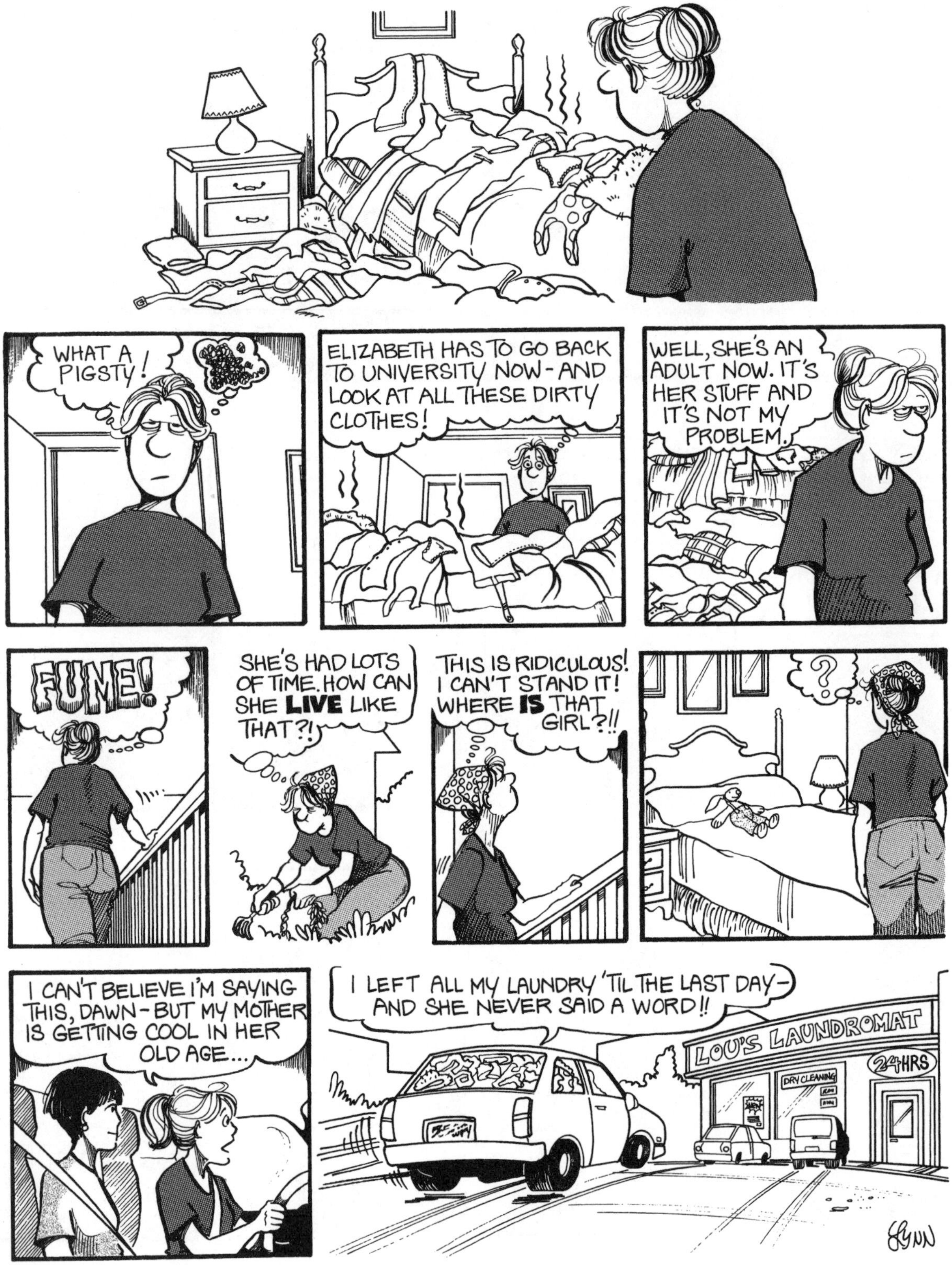
WHAT A PIGSTY!
ELIZABETH HAS TO GO BACK TO UNIVERSITY NOW - AND LOOK AT ALL THESE DIRTY CLOTHES!
WELL, SHE'S AN ADULT NOW. IT'S HER STUFF AND IT'S NOT MY PROBLEM.
FUME!
SHE'S HAD LOTS OF TIME. HOW CAN SHE LIVE LIKE THAT?!
THIS IS RIDICULOUS! I CAN'T STAND IT! WHERE IS THAT GIRL?!!
?
I CAN'T BELIEVE I'M SAYING THIS, DAWN - BUT MY MOTHER IS GETTING COOL IN HER OLD AGE...
I LEFT ALL MY LAUNDRY 'TIL THE LAST DAY - AND SHE NEVER SAID A WORD!!
LOU'S LAUNDROMAT
24HRS
DRY CLEANING
LYNN

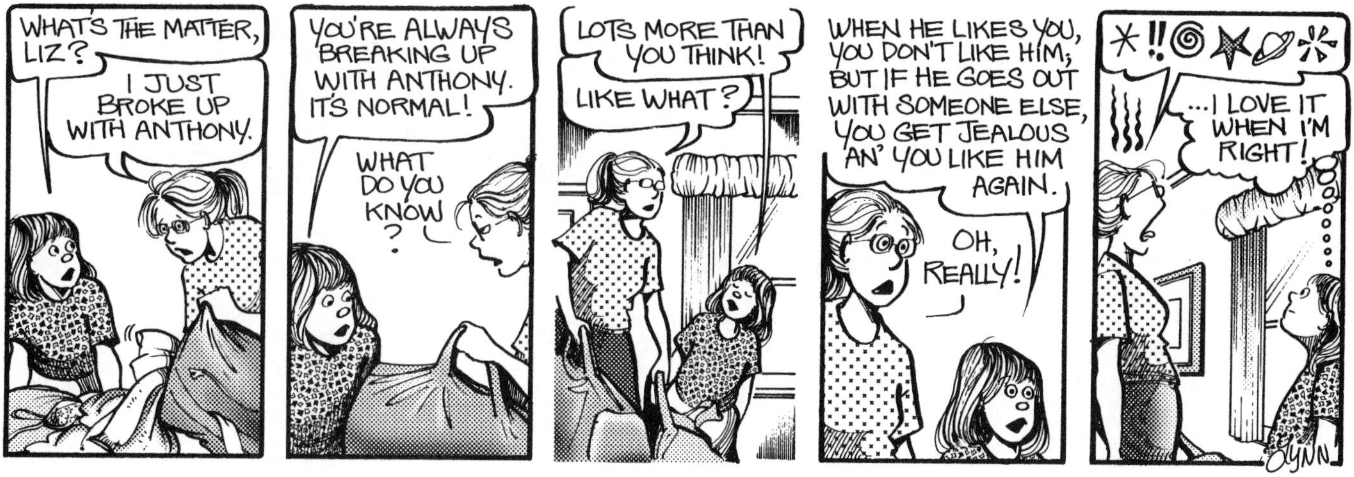
WHAT'S THE MATTER, LIZ?
I JUST BROKE UP WITH ANTHONY.
YOU'RE ALWAYS BREAKING UP WITH ANTHONY. IT'S NORMAL!
WHAT DO YOU KNOW?
LOTS MORE THAN YOU THINK!
LIKE WHAT?
WHEN HE LIKES YOU, YOU DON'T LIKE HIM; BUT IF HE GOES OUT WITH SOMEONE ELSE, YOU GET JEALOUS AN' YOU LIKE HIM AGAIN.
OH, REALLY!
*!!
...I LOVE IT WHEN I'M RIGHT!
LYNN

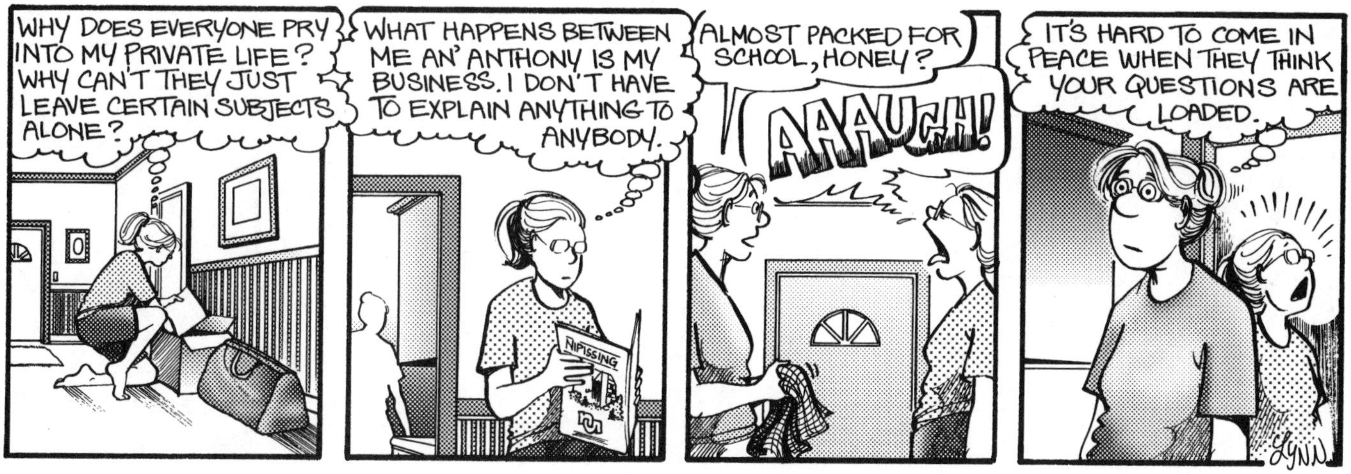
WHY DOES EVERYONE PRY INTO MY PRIVATE LIFE? WHY CAN'T THEY JUST LEAVE CERTAIN SUBJECTS ALONE?
WHAT HAPPENS BETWEEN ME AN' ANTHONY IS MY BUSINESS. I DON'T HAVE TO EXPLAIN ANYTHING TO ANYBODY.
NIPISSING
ALMOST PACKED FOR SCHOOL, HONEY?
AAAUGH!
IT'S HARD TO COME IN PEACE WHEN THEY THINK YOUR QUESTIONS ARE LOADED.
LYNN

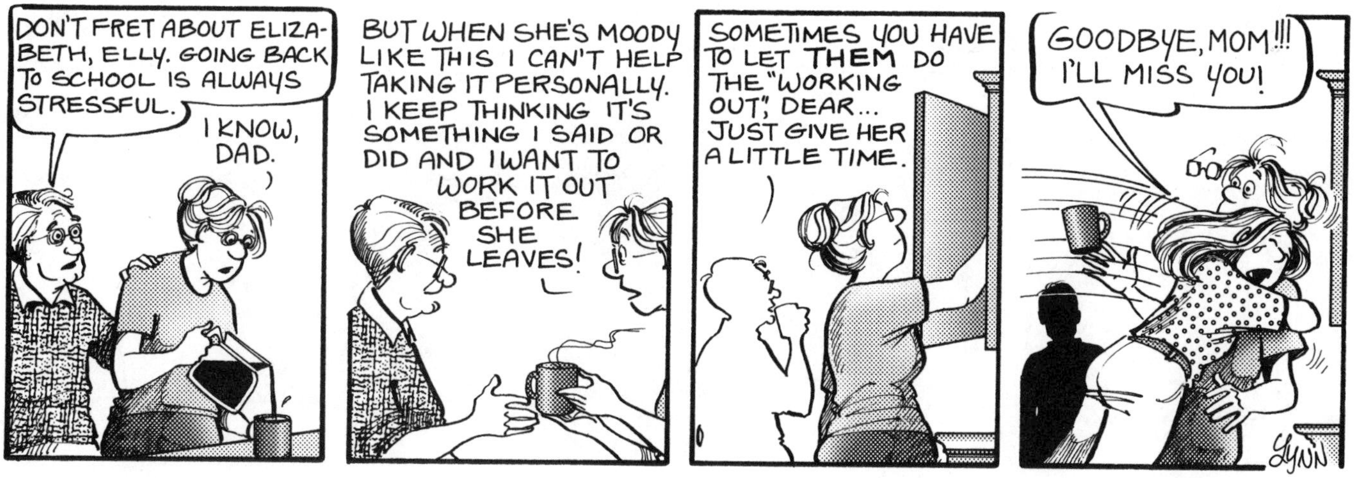
DON'T FRET ABOUT ELIZABETH, ELLY. GOING BACK TO SCHOOL IS ALWAYS STRESSFUL.
I KNOW, DAD.
BUT WHEN SHE'S MOODY LIKE THIS I CAN'T HELP TAKING IT PERSONALLY. I KEEP THINKING IT'S SOMETHING I SAID OR DID AND I WANT TO WORK IT OUT BEFORE SHE LEAVES!
SOMETIMES YOU HAVE TO LET THEM DO THE "WORKING OUT," DEAR... JUST GIVE HER A LITTLE TIME.
GOODBYE, MOM!!! I'LL MISS YOU!
LYNN

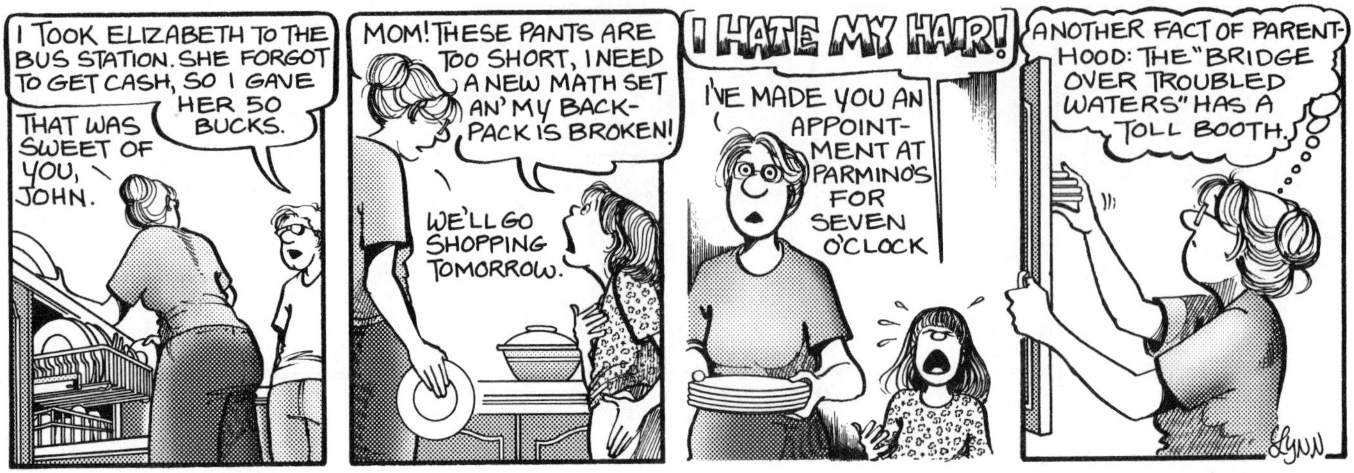
I TOOK ELIZABETH TO THE BUS STATION. SHE FORGOT TO GET CASH, SO I GAVE HER 50 BUCKS.
THAT WAS SWEET OF YOU, JOHN.
MOM! THESE PANTS ARE TOO SHORT, I NEED A NEW MATH SET AN' MY BACK-PACK IS BROKEN!
WE'LL GO SHOPPING TOMORROW.
I HATE MY HAIR!
I'VE MADE YOU AN APPOINT-MENT AT PARMINO'S FOR SEVEN O'CLOCK
ANOTHER FACT OF PARENT-HOOD: THE "BRIDGE OVER TROUBLED WATERS" HAS A TOLL BOOTH.

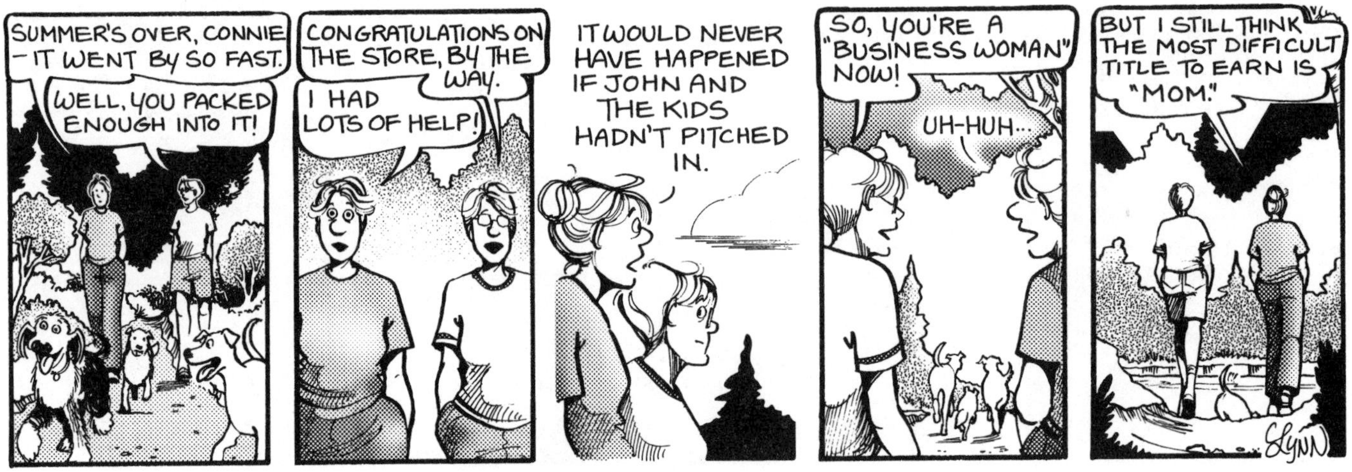
SUMMER'S OVER, CONNIE - IT WENT BY SO FAST.
WELL, YOU PACKED ENOUGH INTO IT!
CONGRATULATIONS ON THE STORE, BY THE WAY.
I HAD LOTS OF HELP!
IT WOULD NEVER HAVE HAPPENED IF JOHN AND THE KIDS HADN'T PITCHED IN.
SO, YOU'RE A "BUSINESS WOMAN" NOW!
UH-HUH...
BUT I STILL THINK THE MOST DIFFICULT TITLE TO EARN IS "MOM."

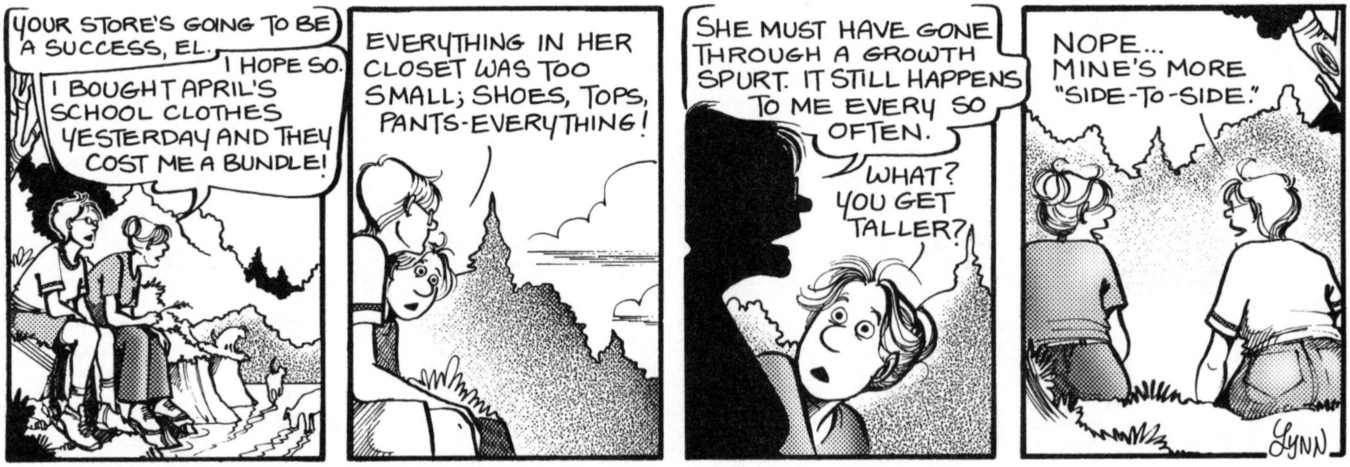
YOUR STORE'S GOING TO BE A SUCCESS, EL.
I HOPE SO.
I BOUGHT APRIL'S SCHOOL CLOTHES YESTERDAY AND THEY COST ME A BUNDLE!
EVERYTHING IN HER CLOSET WAS TOO SMALL; SHOES, TOPS, PANTS-EVERYTHING!
SHE MUST HAVE GONE THROUGH A GROWTH SPURT. IT STILL HAPPENS TO ME EVERY SO OFTEN.
WHAT? YOU GET TALLER?
NOPE... MINE'S MORE "SIDE-TO-SIDE."

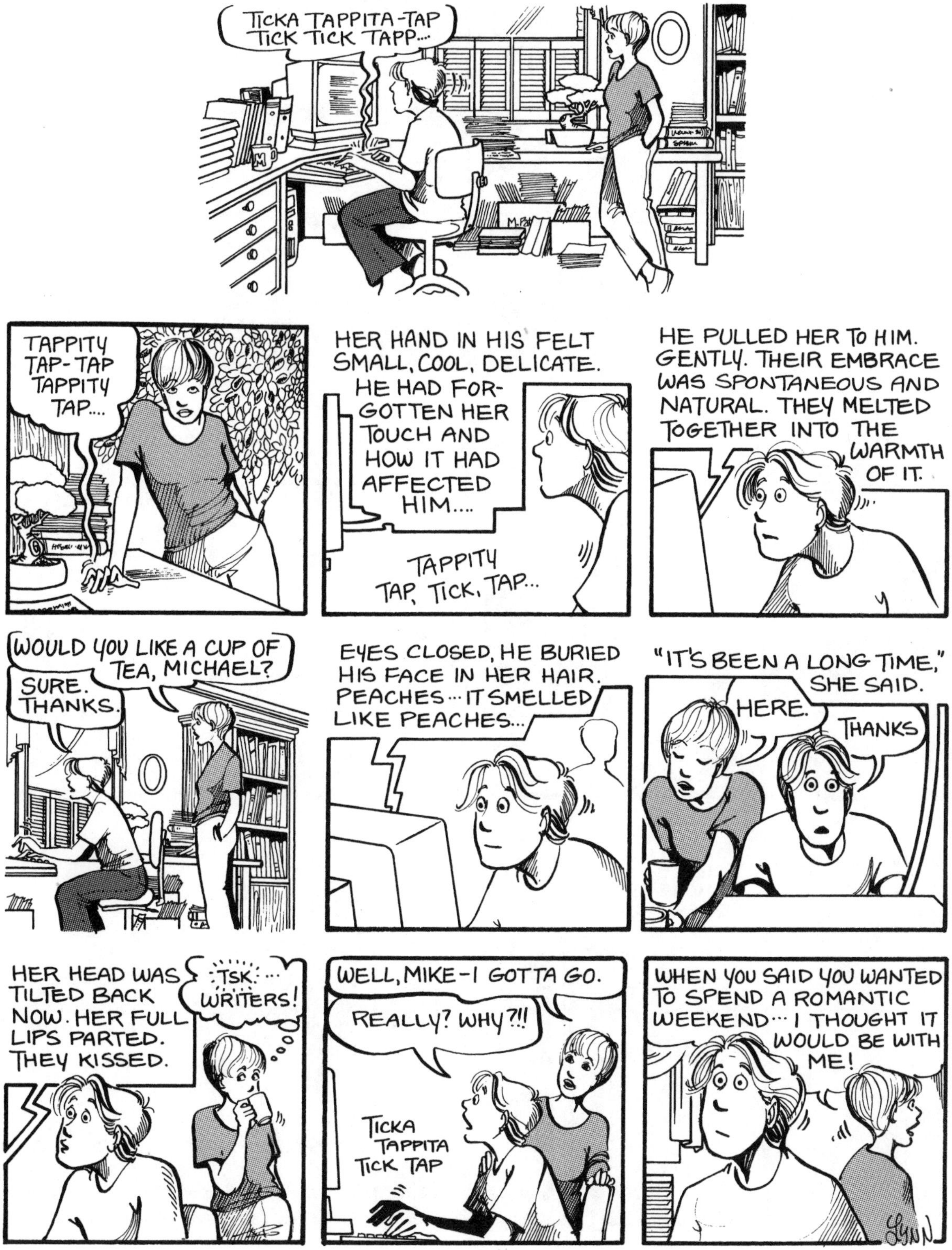
TICKA TAPPITA-TAP TICK TICK TAPP....
TAPPITY TAP-TAP TAPPITY TAP....
HER HAND IN HIS FELT SMALL, COOL, DELICATE.
HE HAD FORGOTTEN HER TOUCH AND HOW IT HAD AFFECTED HIM....
TAPPITY TAP, TICK, TAP...
HE PULLED HER TO HIM. GENTLY. THEIR EMBRACE WAS SPONTANEOUS AND NATURAL. THEY MELTED TOGETHER INTO THE WARMTH OF IT.
WOULD YOU LIKE A CUP OF TEA, MICHAEL?
SURE. THANKS.
EYES CLOSED, HE BURIED HIS FACE IN HER HAIR. PEACHES... IT SMELLED LIKE PEACHES...
"IT'S BEEN A LONG TIME," SHE SAID.
HERE.
THANKS
HER HEAD WAS TILTED BACK NOW. HER FULL LIPS PARTED. THEY KISSED.
TSK... WRITERS!
WELL, MIKE - I GOTTA GO.
REALLY? WHY?!!
TICKA TAPPITA TICK TAP
WHEN YOU SAID YOU WANTED TO SPEND A ROMANTIC WEEKEND... I THOUGHT IT WOULD BE WITH ME!
LYNN

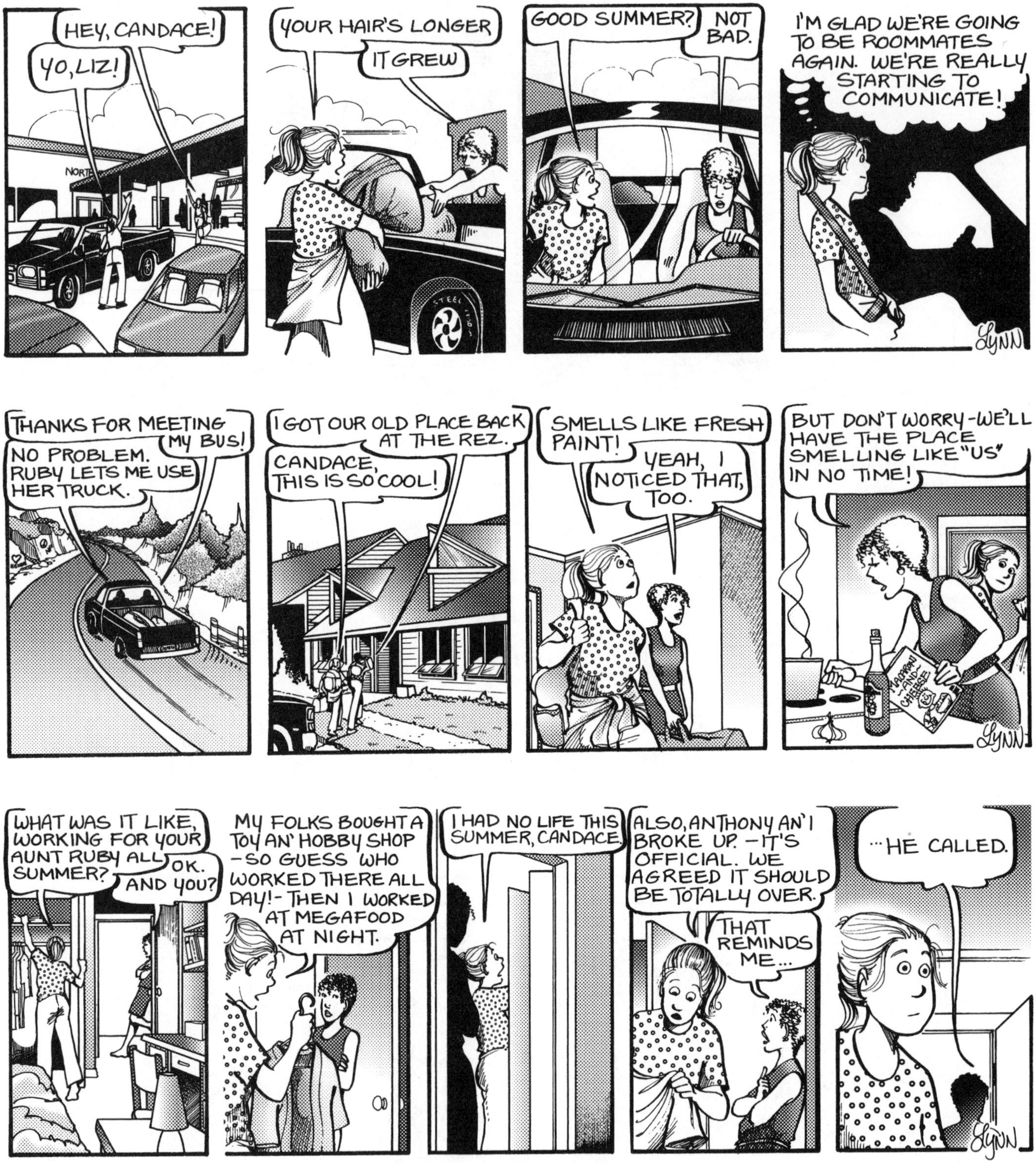
HEY, CANDACE!
YO, LIZ!
YOUR HAIR'S LONGER
IT GREW
GOOD SUMMER?
NOT BAD.
I'M GLAD WE'RE GOING TO BE ROOMMATES AGAIN. WE'RE REALLY STARTING TO COMMUNICATE!
THANKS FOR MEETING MY BUS!
NO PROBLEM. RUBY LETS ME USE HER TRUCK.
I GOT OUR OLD PLACE BACK AT THE REZ.
CANDACE, THIS IS SO COOL!
SMELLS LIKE FRESH PAINT!
YEAH, I NOTICED THAT, TOO.
BUT DON'T WORRY–WE'LL HAVE THE PLACE SMELLING LIKE "US" IN NO TIME!
MACARONI AND CHEESE
WHAT WAS IT LIKE, WORKING FOR YOUR AUNT RUBY ALL SUMMER?
OK. AND YOU?
MY FOLKS BOUGHT A TOY AN' HOBBY SHOP –SO GUESS WHO WORKED THERE ALL DAY!– THEN I WORKED AT MEGAFOOD AT NIGHT.
I HAD NO LIFE THIS SUMMER, CANDACE.
ALSO, ANTHONY AN' I BROKE UP. –IT'S OFFICIAL. WE AGREED IT SHOULD BE TOTALLY OVER.
THAT REMINDS ME...
...HE CALLED.

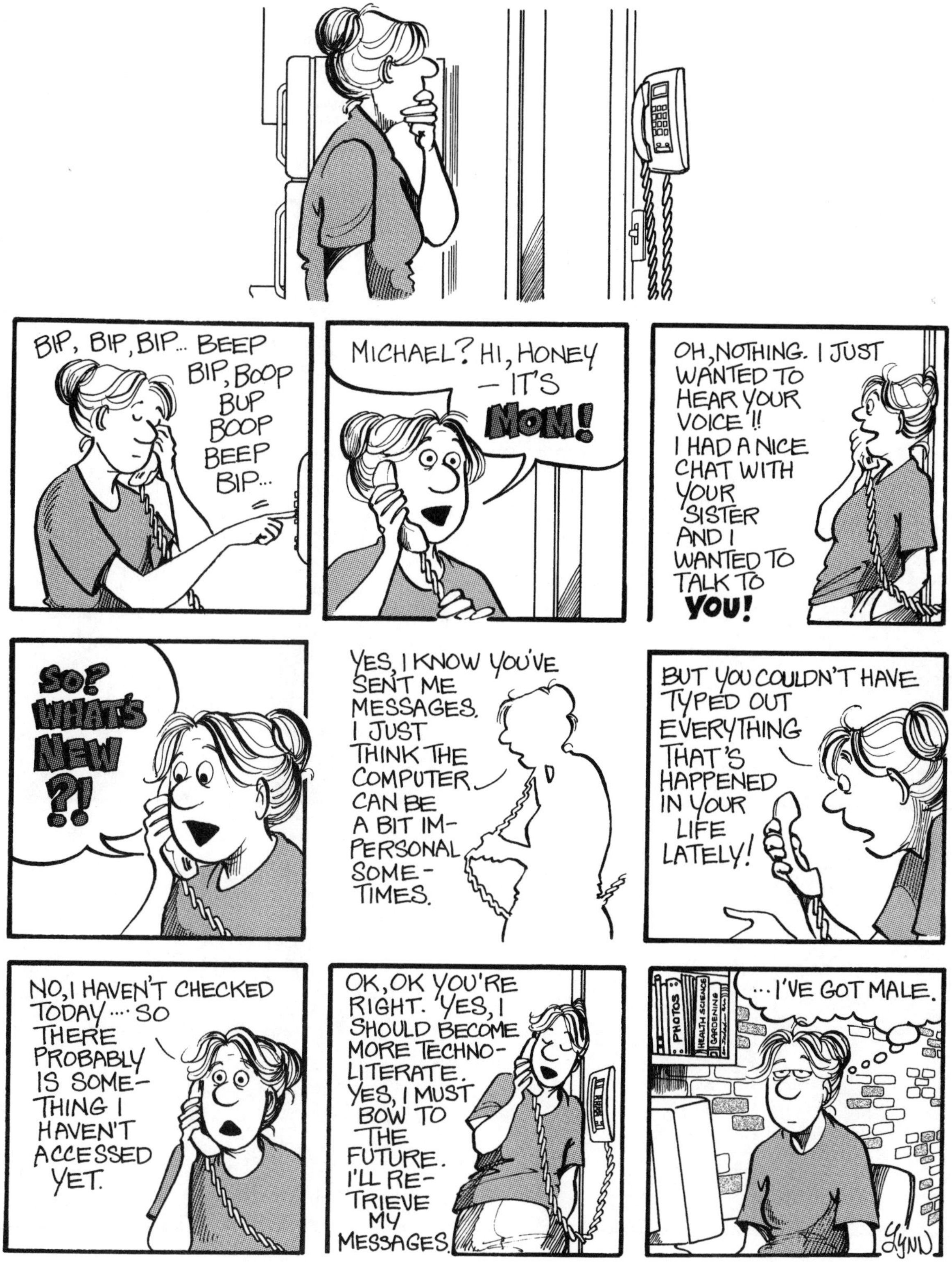

BIP, BIP, BIP... BEEP BIP, BOOP BUP BOOP BEEP BIP...
MICHAEL? HI, HONEY — IT'S MOM!
OH, NOTHING. I JUST WANTED TO HEAR YOUR VOICE!! I HAD A NICE CHAT WITH YOUR SISTER AND I WANTED TO TALK TO YOU!
SO? WHAT'S NEW?!
YES, I KNOW YOU'VE SENT ME MESSAGES. I JUST THINK THE COMPUTER CAN BE A BIT IM-PERSONAL SOME-TIMES.
BUT YOU COULDN'T HAVE TYPED OUT EVERYTHING THAT'S HAPPENED IN YOUR LIFE LATELY!
NO, I HAVEN'T CHECKED TODAY.... SO THERE PROBABLY IS SOME-THING I HAVEN'T ACCESSED YET.
OK, OK YOU'RE RIGHT. YES, I SHOULD BECOME MORE TECHNO-LITERATE. YES, I MUST BOW TO THE FUTURE. I'LL RE-TRIEVE MY MESSAGES.
PHOTOS
HEALTH SCIENCE
GARDENING
...I'VE GOT MALE.
LYNN

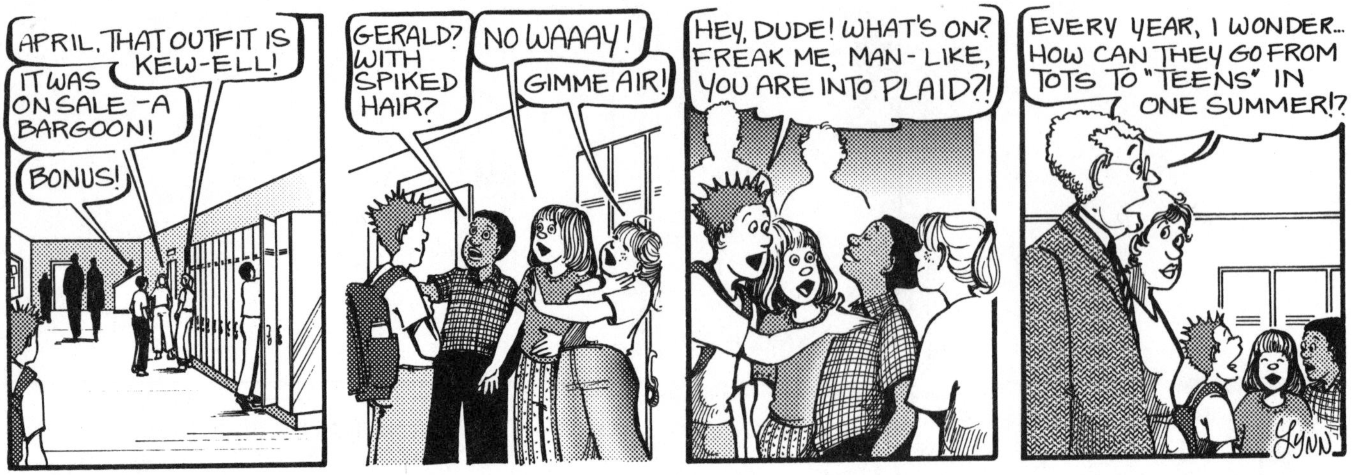
APRIL, THAT OUTFIT IS KEW-ELL!
IT WAS ON SALE - A BARGOON!
BONUS!
GERALD? WITH SPIKED HAIR?
NO WAAAY!
GIMME AIR!
HEY, DUDE! WHAT'S ON? FREAK ME, MAN - LIKE, YOU ARE INTO PLAID?!
EVERY YEAR, I WONDER... HOW CAN THEY GO FROM TOTS TO "TEENS" IN ONE SUMMER!?
LYNN

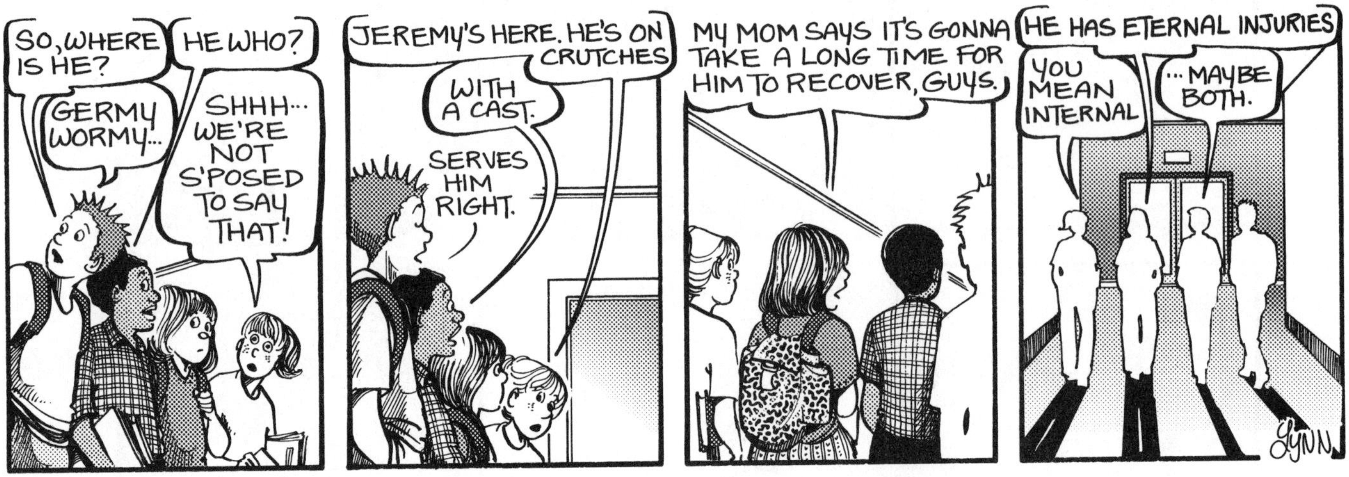
SO, WHERE IS HE?
HE WHO?
GERMY WORMY...
SHHH... WE'RE NOT S'POSED TO SAY THAT!
JEREMY'S HERE. HE'S ON CRUTCHES
WITH A CAST.
SERVES HIM RIGHT.
MY MOM SAYS IT'S GONNA TAKE A LONG TIME FOR HIM TO RECOVER, GUYS.
HE HAS ETERNAL INJURIES
YOU MEAN INTERNAL
...MAYBE BOTH.
LYNN

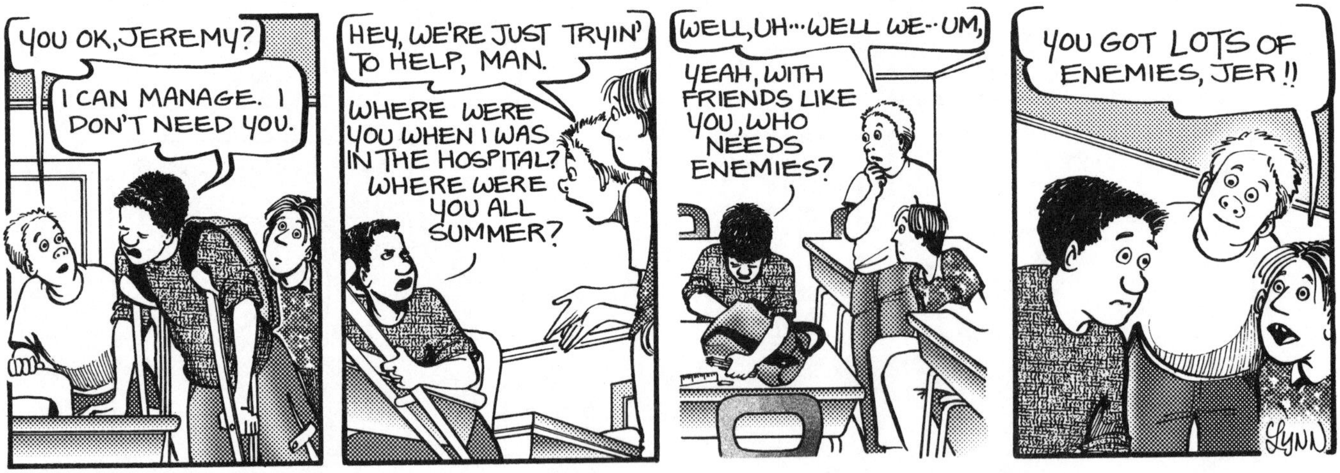
YOU OK, JEREMY?
I CAN MANAGE. I DON'T NEED YOU.
HEY, WE'RE JUST TRYIN' TO HELP, MAN.
WHERE WERE YOU WHEN I WAS IN THE HOSPITAL? WHERE WERE YOU ALL SUMMER?
WELL, UH... WELL WE... UM,
YEAH, WITH FRIENDS LIKE YOU, WHO NEEDS ENEMIES?
YOU GOT LOTS OF ENEMIES, JER!!
LYNN

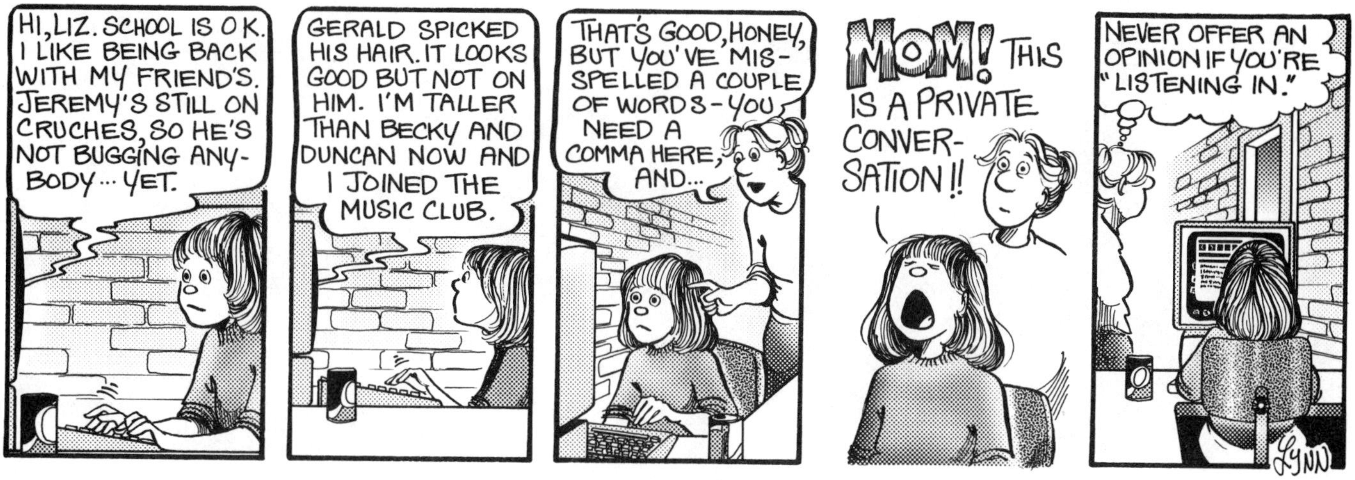
HI, LIZ. SCHOOL IS O K. I LIKE BEING BACK WITH MY FRIEND'S. JEREMY'S STILL ON CRUCHES, SO HE'S NOT BUGGING ANY-BODY... YET.
GERALD SPICKED HIS HAIR. IT LOOKS GOOD BUT NOT ON HIM. I'M TALLER THAN BECKY AND DUNCAN NOW AND I JOINED THE MUSIC CLUB.
THAT'S GOOD, HONEY, BUT YOU'VE MIS-SPELLED A COUPLE OF WORDS - YOU NEED A COMMA HERE, AND...
MOM! THIS IS A PRIVATE CONVER-SATION!!
NEVER OFFER AN OPINION IF YOU'RE "LISTENING IN."
LYNN

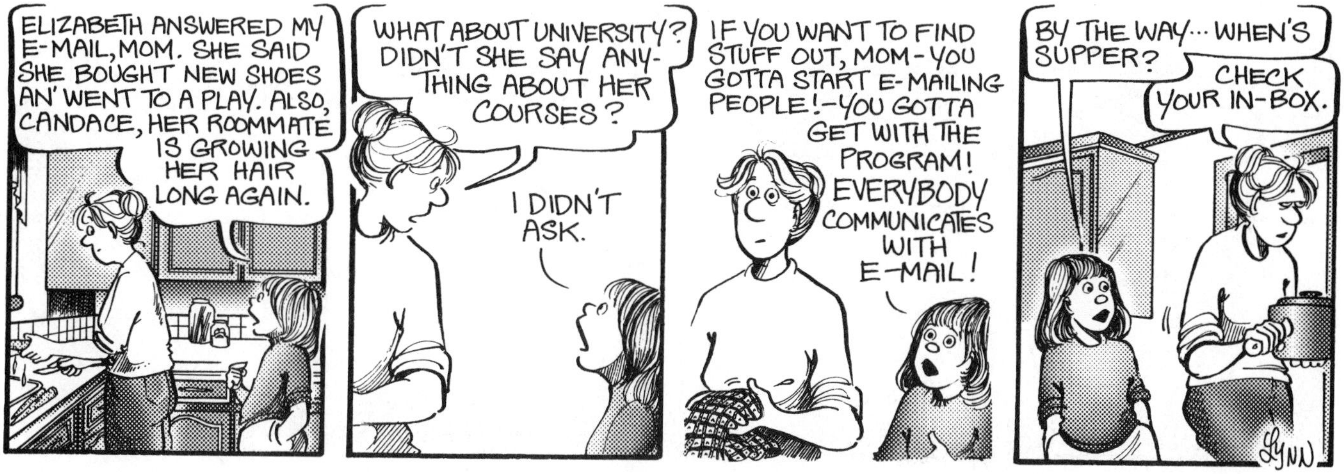
ELIZABETH ANSWERED MY E-MAIL, MOM. SHE SAID SHE BOUGHT NEW SHOES AN' WENT TO A PLAY. ALSO, CANDACE, HER ROOMMATE IS GROWING HER HAIR LONG AGAIN.
WHAT ABOUT UNIVERSITY? DIDN'T SHE SAY ANY-THING ABOUT HER COURSES?
I DIDN'T ASK.
IF YOU WANT TO FIND STUFF OUT, MOM - YOU GOTTA START E-MAILING PEOPLE! - YOU GOTTA GET WITH THE PROGRAM! EVERYBODY COMMUNICATES WITH E-MAIL!
BY THE WAY... WHEN'S SUPPER?
CHECK YOUR IN-BOX.
LYNN

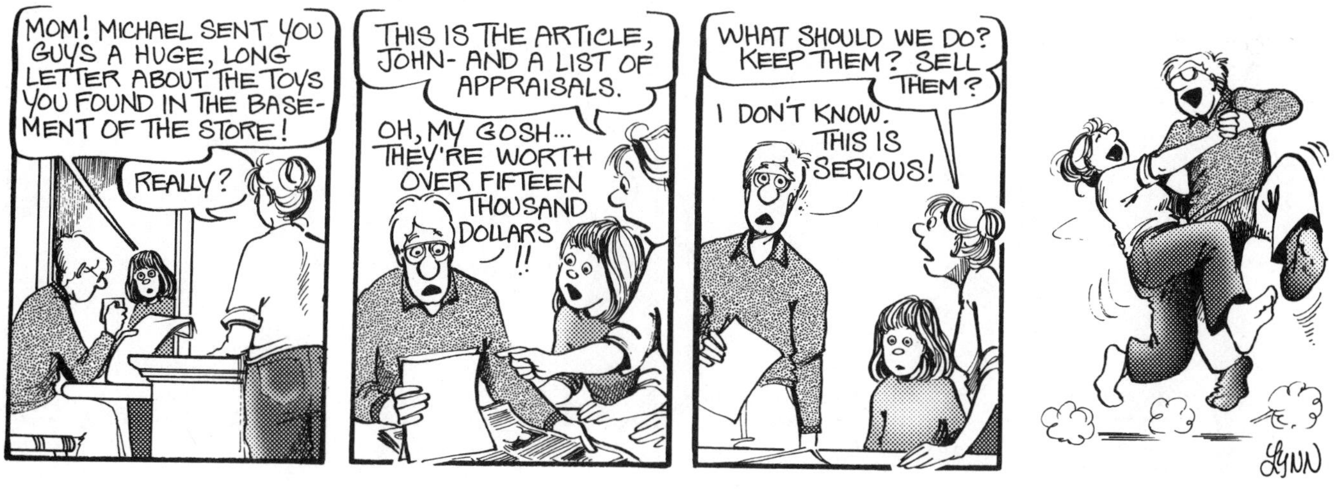
MOM! MICHAEL SENT YOU GUYS A HUGE, LONG LETTER ABOUT THE TOYS YOU FOUND IN THE BASE-MENT OF THE STORE!
REALLY?
THIS IS THE ARTICLE, JOHN - AND A LIST OF APPRAISALS.
OH, MY GOSH... THEY'RE WORTH OVER FIFTEEN THOUSAND DOLLARS!!
WHAT SHOULD WE DO? KEEP THEM? SELL THEM?
I DON'T KNOW. THIS IS SERIOUS!
LYNN

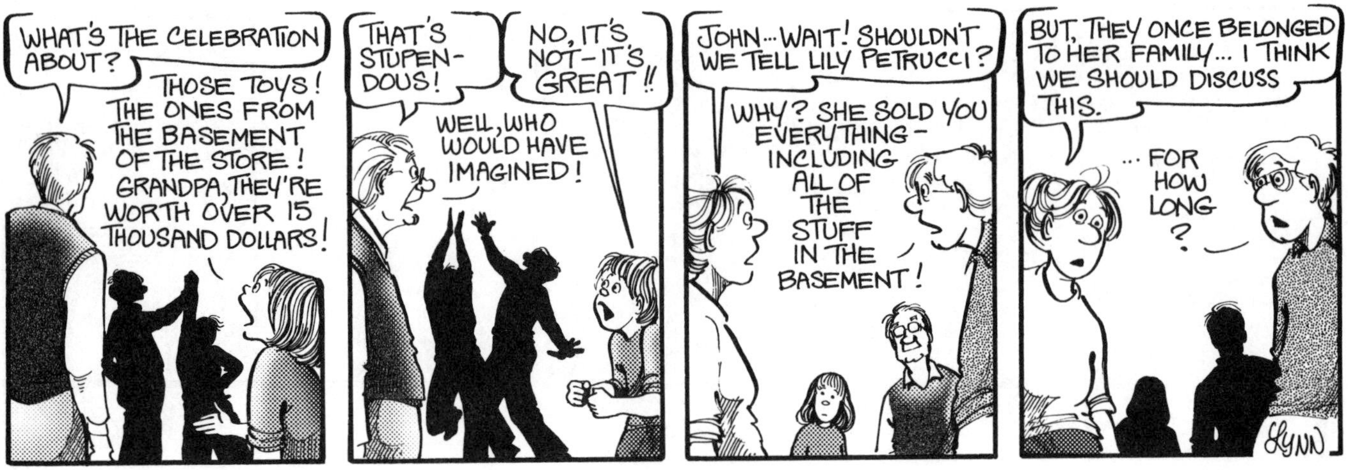
WHAT'S THE CELEBRATION ABOUT?
THOSE TOYS! THE ONES FROM THE BASEMENT OF THE STORE! GRANDPA, THEY'RE WORTH OVER 15 THOUSAND DOLLARS!
THAT'S STUPENDOUS!
NO, IT'S NOT - IT'S GREAT!!
WELL, WHO WOULD HAVE IMAGINED!
JOHN... WAIT! SHOULDN'T WE TELL LILY PETRUCCI?
WHY? SHE SOLD YOU EVERYTHING - INCLUDING ALL OF THE STUFF IN THE BASEMENT!
BUT, THEY ONCE BELONGED TO HER FAMILY... I THINK WE SHOULD DISCUSS THIS.
...FOR HOW LONG?
LYNN

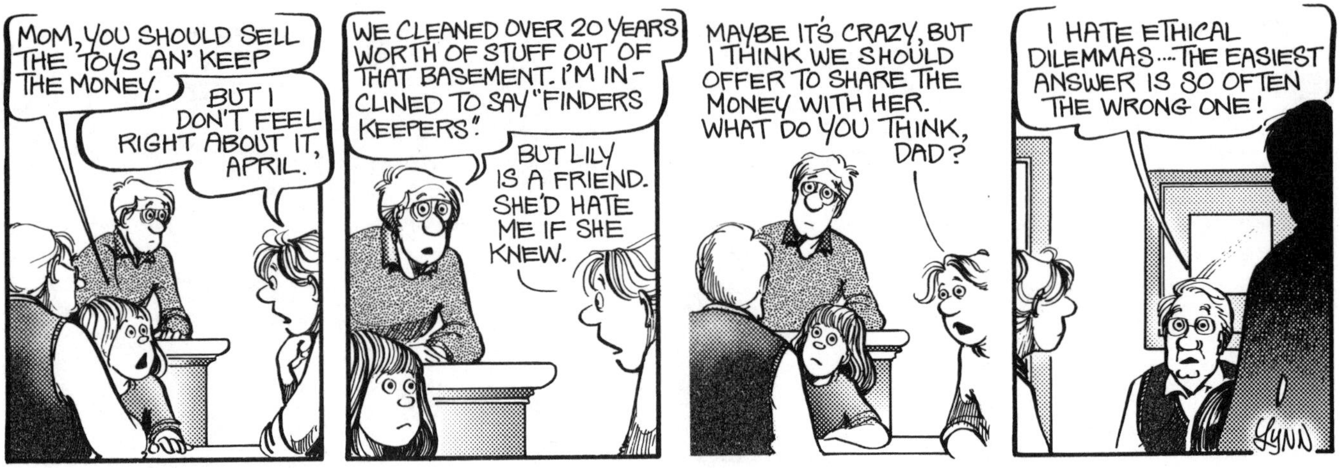
MOM, YOU SHOULD SELL THE TOYS AN' KEEP THE MONEY.
BUT I DON'T FEEL RIGHT ABOUT IT, APRIL.
WE CLEANED OVER 20 YEARS WORTH OF STUFF OUT OF THAT BASEMENT. I'M INCLINED TO SAY "FINDERS KEEPERS."
BUT LILY IS A FRIEND. SHE'D HATE ME IF SHE KNEW.
MAYBE IT'S CRAZY, BUT I THINK WE SHOULD OFFER TO SHARE THE MONEY WITH HER. WHAT DO YOU THINK, DAD?
I HATE ETHICAL DILEMMAS... THE EASIEST ANSWER IS SO OFTEN THE WRONG ONE!
LYNN

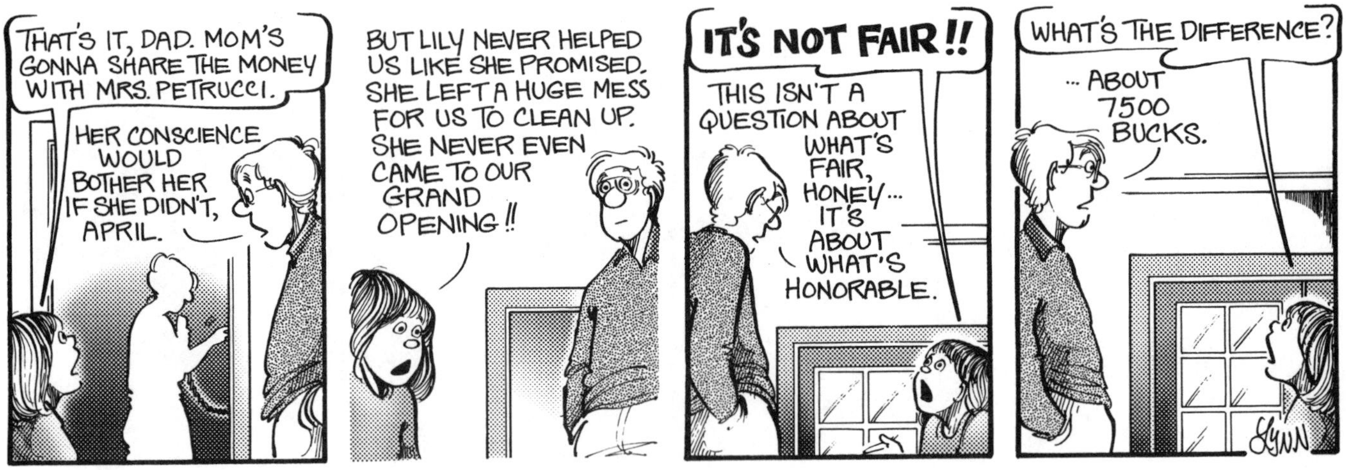
THAT'S IT, DAD. MOM'S GONNA SHARE THE MONEY WITH MRS. PETRUCCI.
HER CONSCIENCE WOULD BOTHER HER IF SHE DIDN'T, APRIL.
BUT LILY NEVER HELPED US LIKE SHE PROMISED. SHE LEFT A HUGE MESS FOR US TO CLEAN UP. SHE NEVER EVEN CAME TO OUR GRAND OPENING!!
IT'S NOT FAIR!!
THIS ISN'T A QUESTION ABOUT WHAT'S FAIR, HONEY... IT'S ABOUT WHAT'S HONORABLE.
WHAT'S THE DIFFERENCE?
...ABOUT 7500 BUCKS.
LYNN

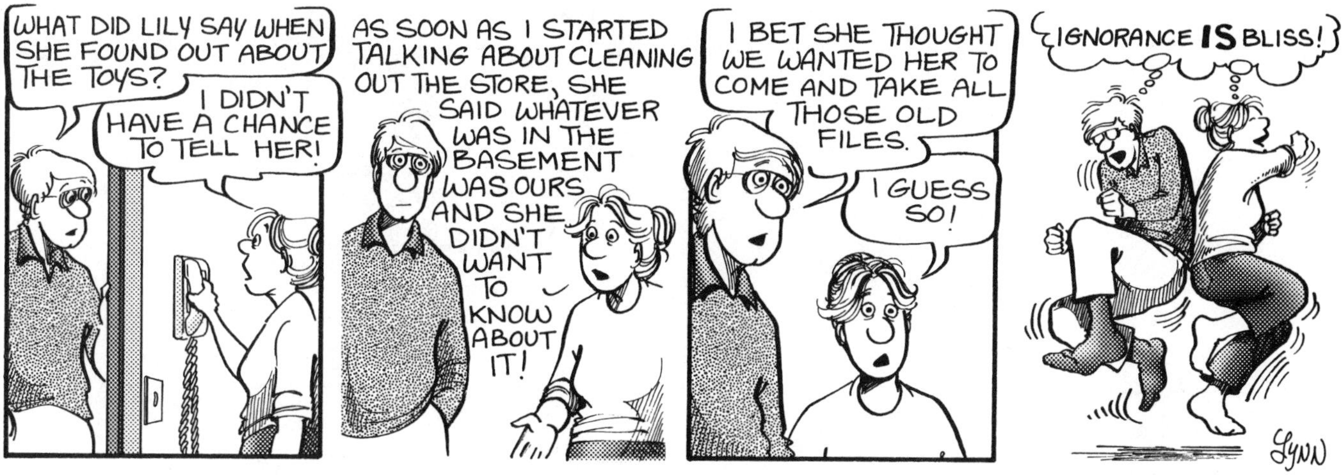
WHAT DID LILY SAY WHEN SHE FOUND OUT ABOUT THE TOYS?
I DIDN'T HAVE A CHANCE TO TELL HER!
AS SOON AS I STARTED TALKING ABOUT CLEANING OUT THE STORE, SHE SAID WHATEVER WAS IN THE BASEMENT WAS OURS AND SHE DIDN'T WANT TO KNOW ABOUT IT!
I BET SHE THOUGHT WE WANTED HER TO COME AND TAKE ALL THOSE OLD FILES.
I GUESS SO!
IGNORANCE IS BLISS!
Lynn

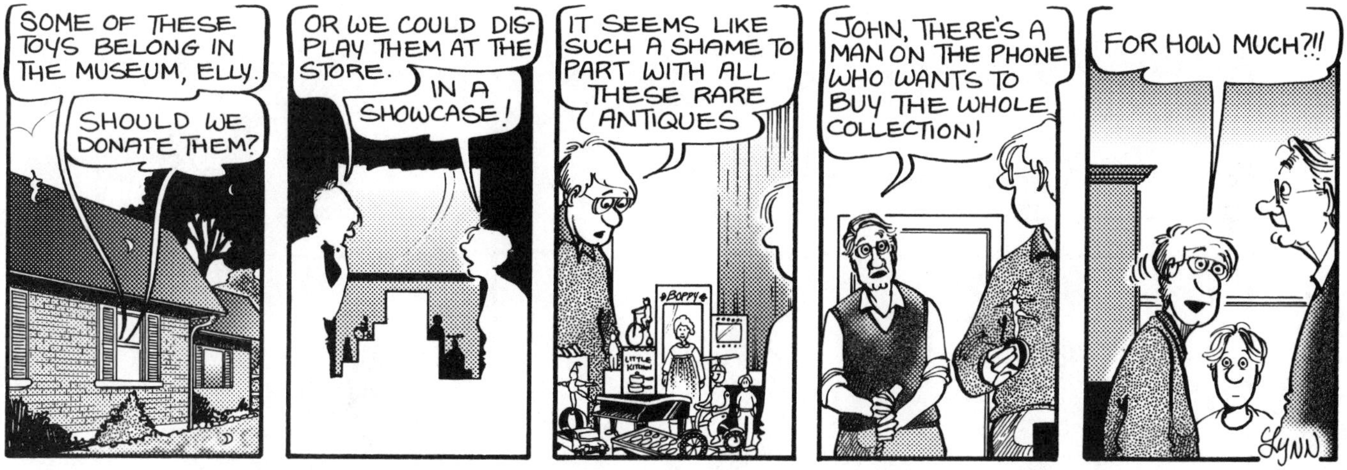
SOME OF THESE TOYS BELONG IN THE MUSEUM, ELLY.
SHOULD WE DONATE THEM?
OR WE COULD DISPLAY THEM AT THE STORE.
IN A SHOWCASE!
IT SEEMS LIKE SUCH A SHAME TO PART WITH ALL THESE RARE ANTIQUES
JOHN, THERE'S A MAN ON THE PHONE WHO WANTS TO BUY THE WHOLE COLLECTION!
FOR HOW MUCH?!!
Lynn

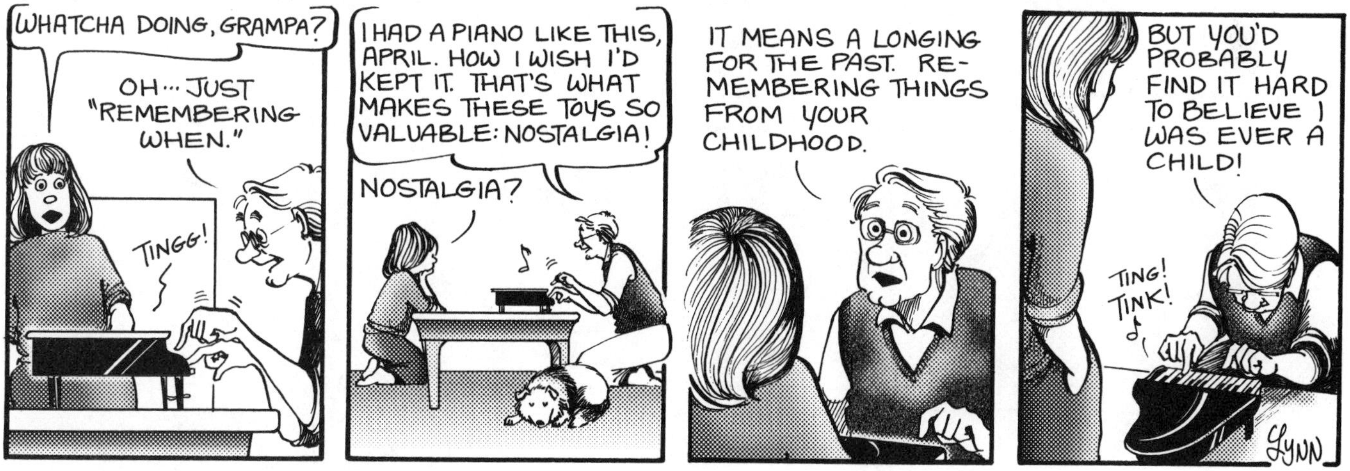
WHATCHA DOING, GRAMPA?
OH... JUST "REMEMBERING WHEN."
TINGG!
I HAD A PIANO LIKE THIS, APRIL. HOW I WISH I'D KEPT IT. THAT'S WHAT MAKES THESE TOYS SO VALUABLE: NOSTALGIA!
NOSTALGIA?
IT MEANS A LONGING FOR THE PAST. REMEMBERING THINGS FROM YOUR CHILDHOOD.
BUT YOU'D PROBABLY FIND IT HARD TO BELIEVE I WAS EVER A CHILD!
TING! TINK!
Lynn

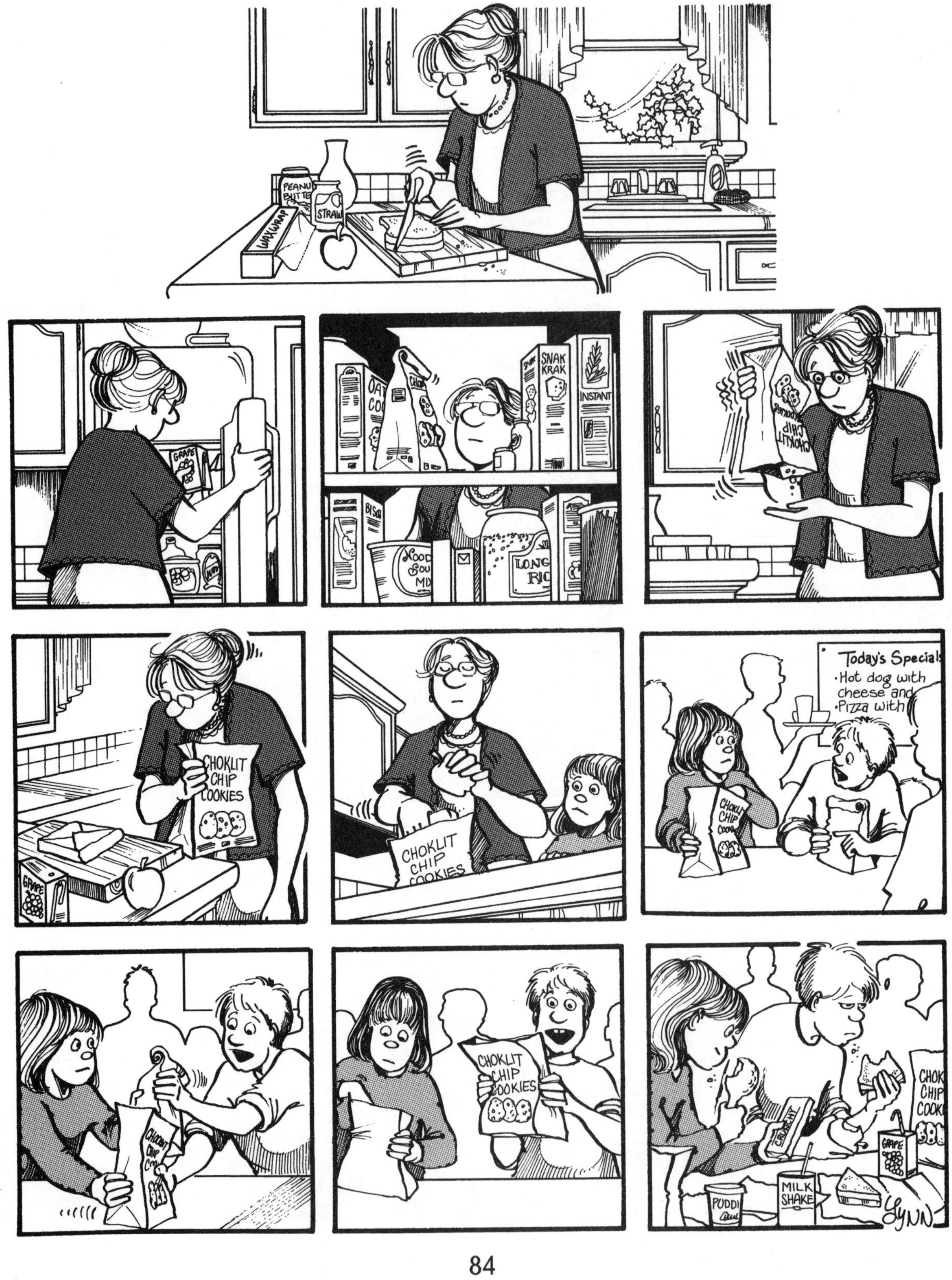
WAXWRAP
STRAW
GRAPE
SNAK KRAK
INSTANT
CHOKLIT CHIP COOKIES
Today's Specials
·Hot dog with cheese and
·Pizza with
CHOKLIT CHIP COOKIES
MILK SHAKE
GRAPE
Lynn

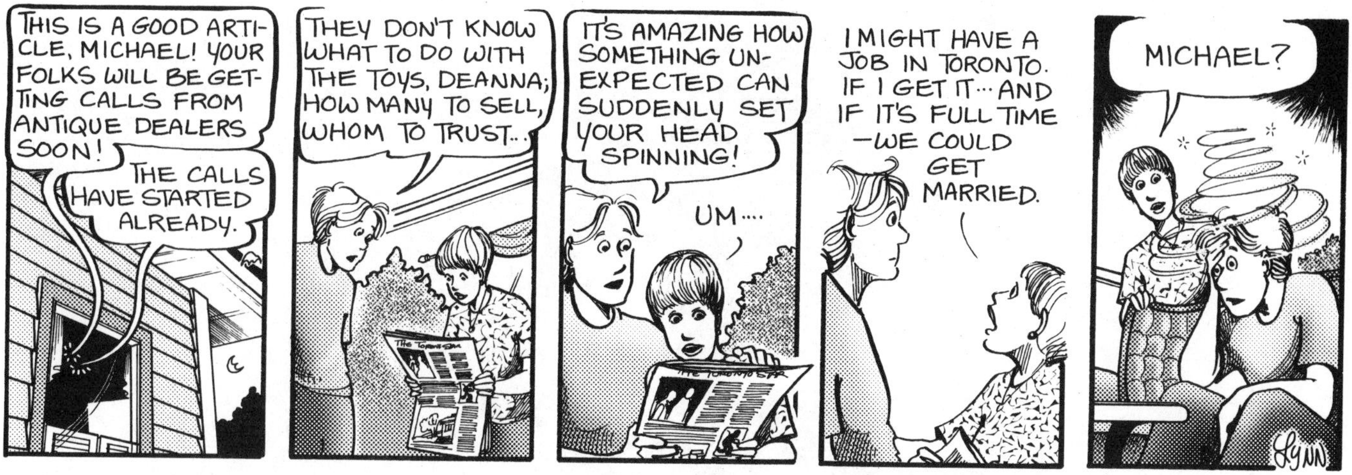
THIS IS A GOOD ARTICLE, MICHAEL! YOUR FOLKS WILL BE GETTING CALLS FROM ANTIQUE DEALERS SOON!
THE CALLS HAVE STARTED ALREADY.
THEY DON'T KNOW WHAT TO DO WITH THE TOYS, DEANNA; HOW MANY TO SELL, WHOM TO TRUST...
IT'S AMAZING HOW SOMETHING UNEXPECTED CAN SUDDENLY SET YOUR HEAD SPINNING!
UM....
I MIGHT HAVE A JOB IN TORONTO. IF I GET IT... AND IF IT'S FULL TIME —WE COULD GET MARRIED.
MICHAEL?
LYNN

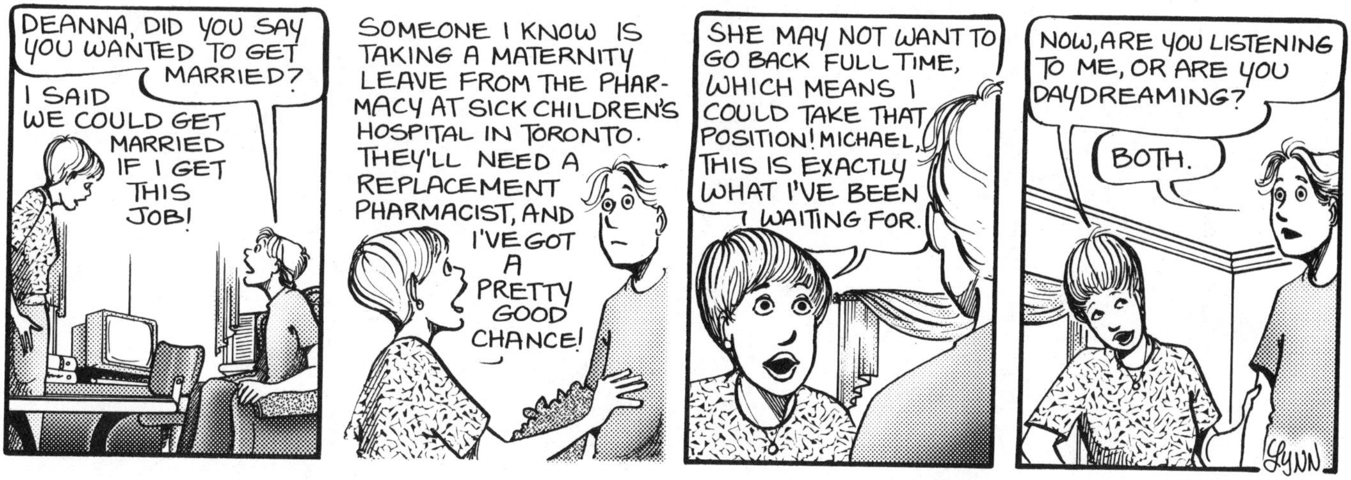
DEANNA, DID YOU SAY YOU WANTED TO GET MARRIED?
I SAID WE COULD GET MARRIED IF I GET THIS JOB!
SOMEONE I KNOW IS TAKING A MATERNITY LEAVE FROM THE PHARMACY AT SICK CHILDREN'S HOSPITAL IN TORONTO. THEY'LL NEED A REPLACEMENT PHARMACIST, AND I'VE GOT A PRETTY GOOD CHANCE!
SHE MAY NOT WANT TO GO BACK FULL TIME, WHICH MEANS I COULD TAKE THAT POSITION! MICHAEL, THIS IS EXACTLY WHAT I'VE BEEN WAITING FOR.
NOW, ARE YOU LISTENING TO ME, OR ARE YOU DAYDREAMING?
BOTH.
LYNN

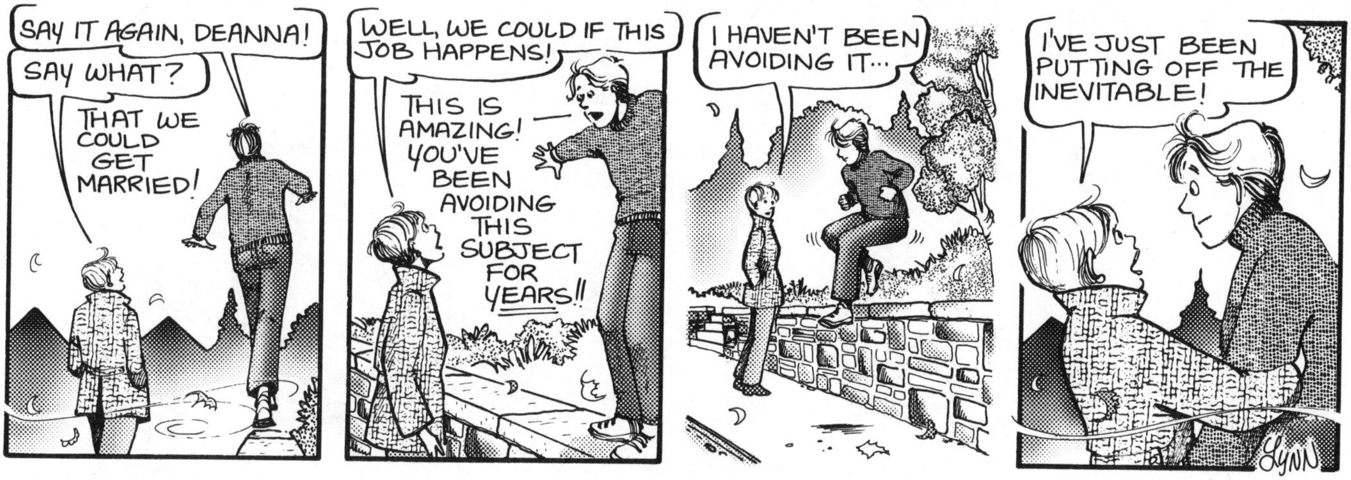
SAY IT AGAIN, DEANNA!
SAY WHAT?
THAT WE COULD GET MARRIED!
WELL, WE COULD IF THIS JOB HAPPENS!
THIS IS AMAZING! YOU'VE BEEN AVOIDING THIS SUBJECT FOR YEARS!!
I HAVEN'T BEEN AVOIDING IT...
I'VE JUST BEEN PUTTING OFF THE INEVITABLE!
LYNN

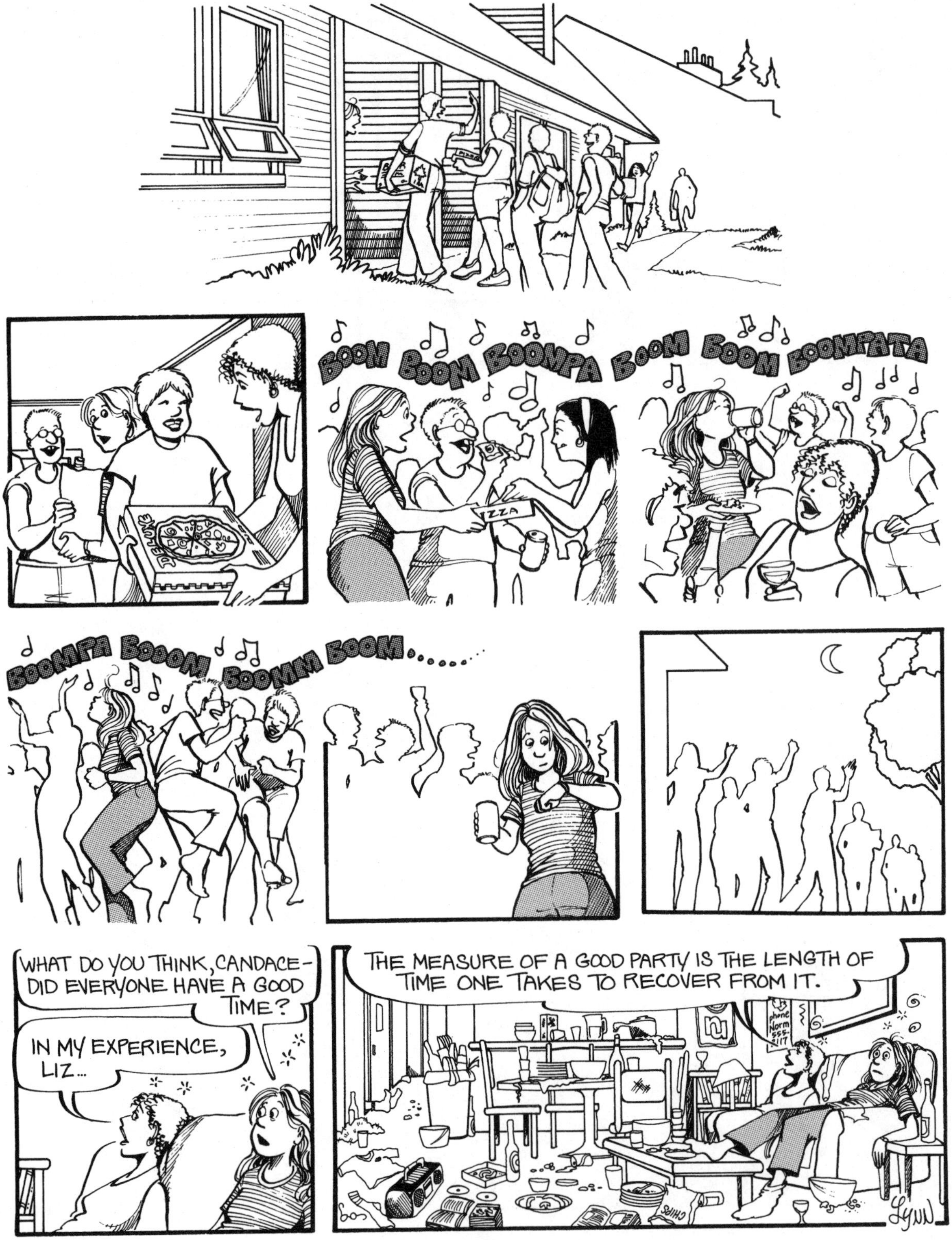
BOOM BOOM BOOMPA BOOM BOOM BOOMPATA
DELUXE
BOOMPA BOOOM BOOMM BOOM......
WHAT DO YOU THINK, CANDACE- DID EVERYONE HAVE A GOOD TIME?
IN MY EXPERIENCE, LIZ...
THE MEASURE OF A GOOD PARTY IS THE LENGTH OF TIME ONE TAKES TO RECOVER FROM IT.
Lynn

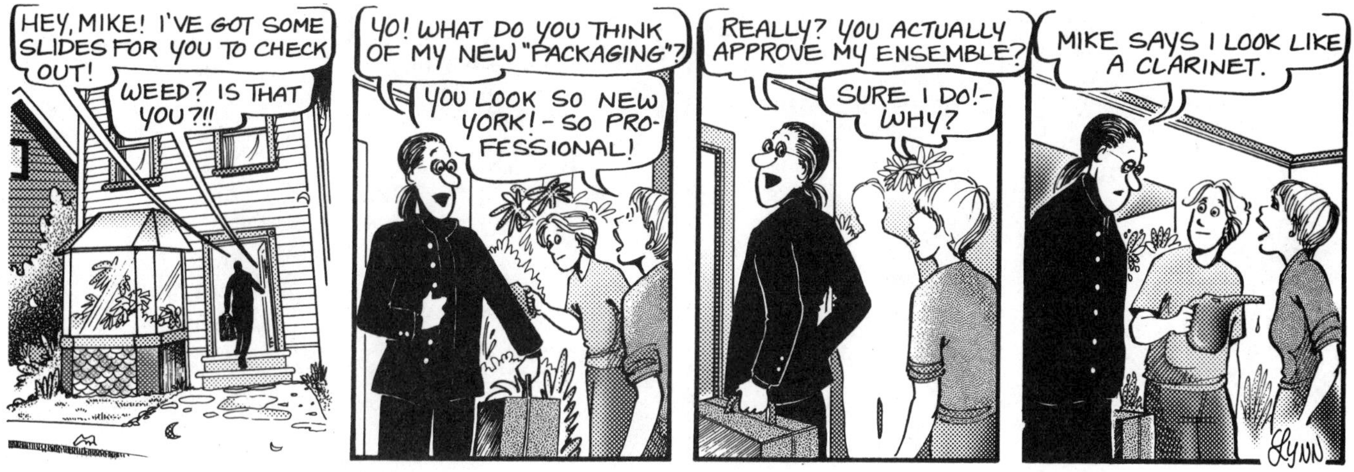
HEY, MIKE! I'VE GOT SOME SLIDES FOR YOU TO CHECK OUT!
WEED? IS THAT YOU?!!
YO! WHAT DO YOU THINK OF MY NEW "PACKAGING"?
YOU LOOK SO NEW YORK! - SO PROFESSIONAL!
REALLY? YOU ACTUALLY APPROVE MY ENSEMBLE?
SURE I DO!- WHY?
MIKE SAYS I LOOK LIKE A CLARINET.
LYNN

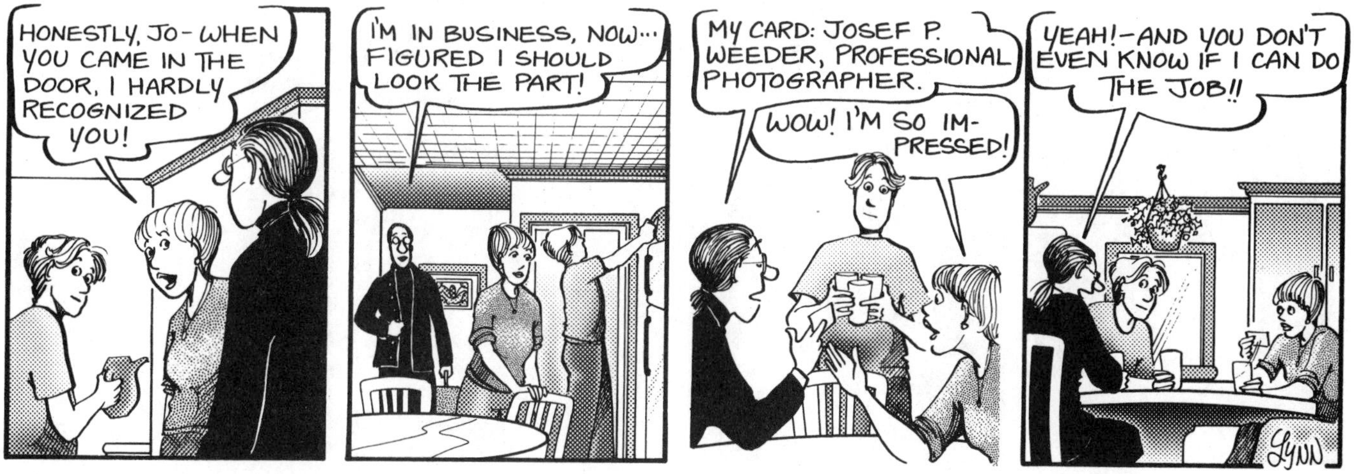
HONESTLY, JO- WHEN YOU CAME IN THE DOOR, I HARDLY RECOGNIZED YOU!
I'M IN BUSINESS, NOW... FIGURED I SHOULD LOOK THE PART!
MY CARD: JOSEF P. WEEDER, PROFESSIONAL PHOTOGRAPHER.
WOW! I'M SO IMPRESSED!
YEAH!-AND YOU DON'T EVEN KNOW IF I CAN DO THE JOB!!
LYNN

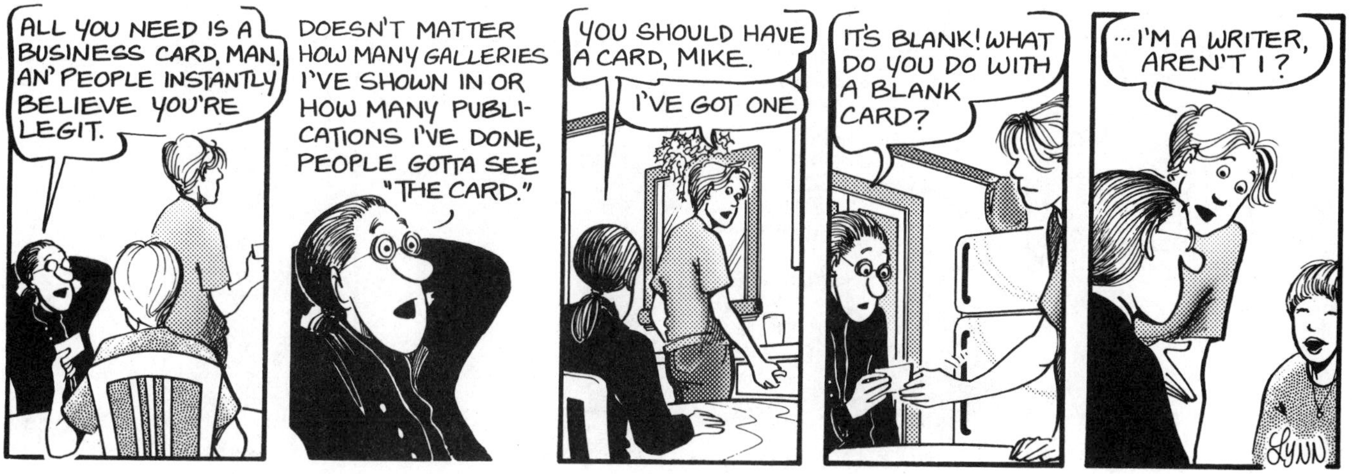
ALL YOU NEED IS A BUSINESS CARD, MAN, AN' PEOPLE INSTANTLY BELIEVE YOU'RE LEGIT.
DOESN'T MATTER HOW MANY GALLERIES I'VE SHOWN IN OR HOW MANY PUBLICATIONS I'VE DONE, PEOPLE GOTTA SEE "THE CARD."
YOU SHOULD HAVE A CARD, MIKE.
I'VE GOT ONE
IT'S BLANK! WHAT DO YOU DO WITH A BLANK CARD?
... I'M A WRITER, AREN'T I?
LYNN

Panel 1: I LIKE YOUR HAIR, JOSEF.
MERCY! — I WANTED A STYLE THAT SAID I WAS CONFIDENT AND IN CONTROL.

Panel 2: AND THE NEW GLASSES?
CLEAR, UNTINTED LENSES SAY "THIS GUY IS DIRECT AND HONEST."

Panel 3: AND WHAT'S THE FASHION STATEMENT BEHIND THE TOTALLY BLACK "LOOK"?

Panel 4: ...HIDES THE DIRT.

Panel 5: SO, BESIDES ME... WHAT'S CHANGED AROUND HERE?

Panel 6: I MIGHT HAVE A JOB IN TORONTO!
THAT MEANS WE COULD GET MARRIED, WEED-O!

Panel 7: ISN'T THAT INCREDIBLE NEWS?!
I DUNNO...

Panel 8: WOULD I BE INVITED AS A FRIEND OR A PHOTOGRAPHER?

Panel 9: SEE, THE PROBLEM WITH BEING A PROFESSIONAL PHOTOGRAPHER IS THAT FRIENDS ALWAYS WANT YOU TO TAKE THEIR WEDDING PHOTOS!

Panel 10: SO, YOU END UP TAKING ORDERS, STRUGGLING WITH KIDS, ORGANIZING RELATIVES, GETTING THOSE "CANDID" SHOTS OF THE HAPPY COUPLE — AND WORKING...
WHILE EVERYONE ELSE PARTIES ON!!!

Panel 11: SO, WHO DO YOU SUGGEST WE ASK, WEED?
ME....

Panel 12: .....I'D WANT YOU TO HAVE THE BEST.

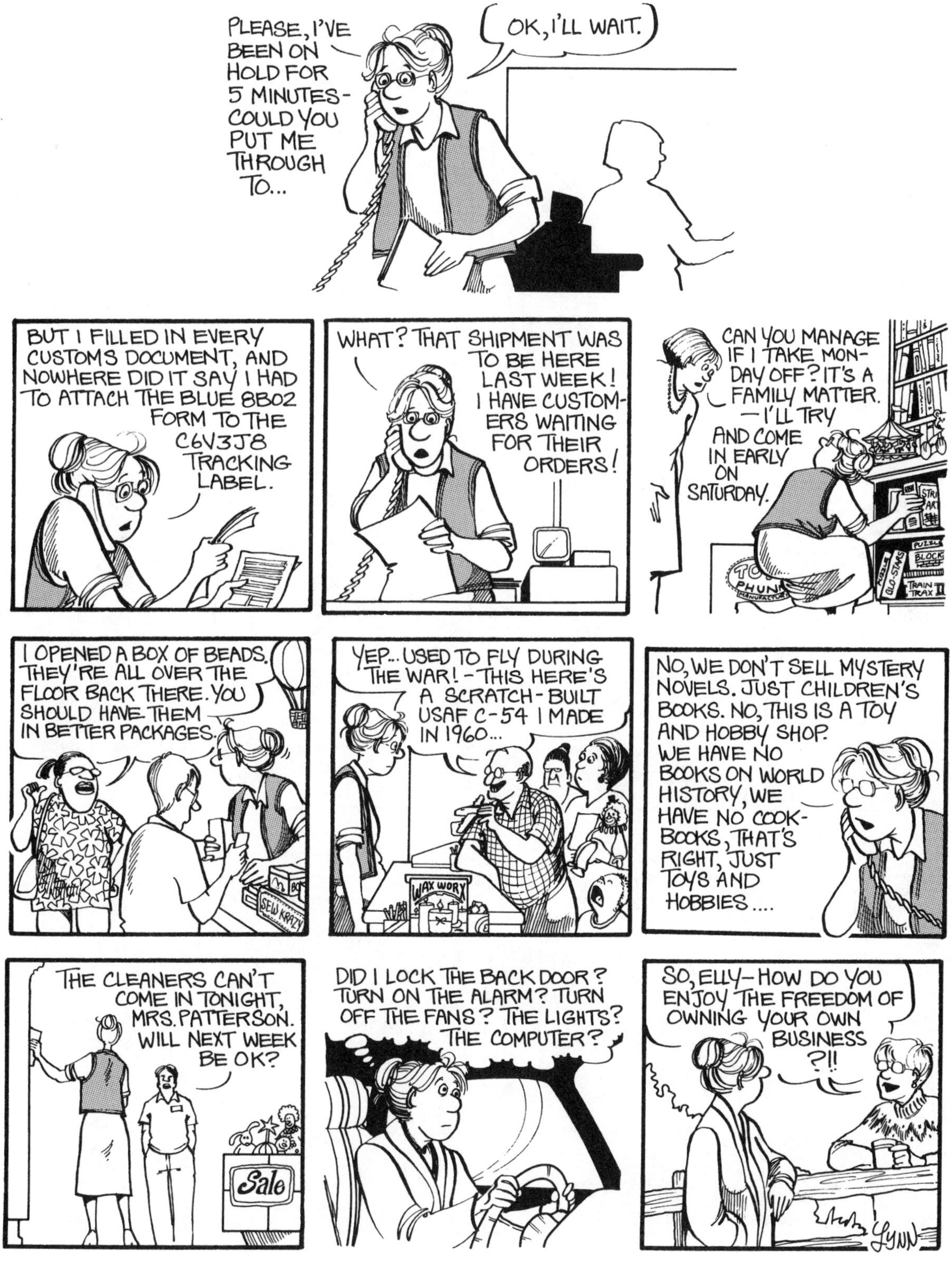
PLEASE, I'VE BEEN ON HOLD FOR 5 MINUTES- COULD YOU PUT ME THROUGH TO...
OK, I'LL WAIT.
BUT I FILLED IN EVERY CUSTOMS DOCUMENT, AND NOWHERE DID IT SAY I HAD TO ATTACH THE BLUE 8B02 FORM TO THE C6V3J8 TRACKING LABEL.
WHAT? THAT SHIPMENT WAS TO BE HERE LAST WEEK! I HAVE CUSTOMERS WAITING FOR THEIR ORDERS!
CAN YOU MANAGE IF I TAKE MONDAY OFF? IT'S A FAMILY MATTER.
—I'LL TRY AND COME IN EARLY ON SATURDAY.
I OPENED A BOX OF BEADS. THEY'RE ALL OVER THE FLOOR BACK THERE. YOU SHOULD HAVE THEM IN BETTER PACKAGES.
SEW KRAZY
YEP... USED TO FLY DURING THE WAR! - THIS HERE'S A SCRATCH-BUILT USAF C-54 I MADE IN 1960...
WAX WORX
NO, WE DON'T SELL MYSTERY NOVELS. JUST CHILDREN'S BOOKS. NO, THIS IS A TOY AND HOBBY SHOP. WE HAVE NO BOOKS ON WORLD HISTORY, WE HAVE NO COOKBOOKS, THAT'S RIGHT, JUST TOYS AND HOBBIES....
THE CLEANERS CAN'T COME IN TONIGHT, MRS. PATTERSON. WILL NEXT WEEK BE OK?
Sale
DID I LOCK THE BACK DOOR? TURN ON THE ALARM? TURN OFF THE FANS? THE LIGHTS? THE COMPUTER?
SO, ELLY—HOW DO YOU ENJOY THE FREEDOM OF OWNING YOUR OWN BUSINESS ?!!
LYNN

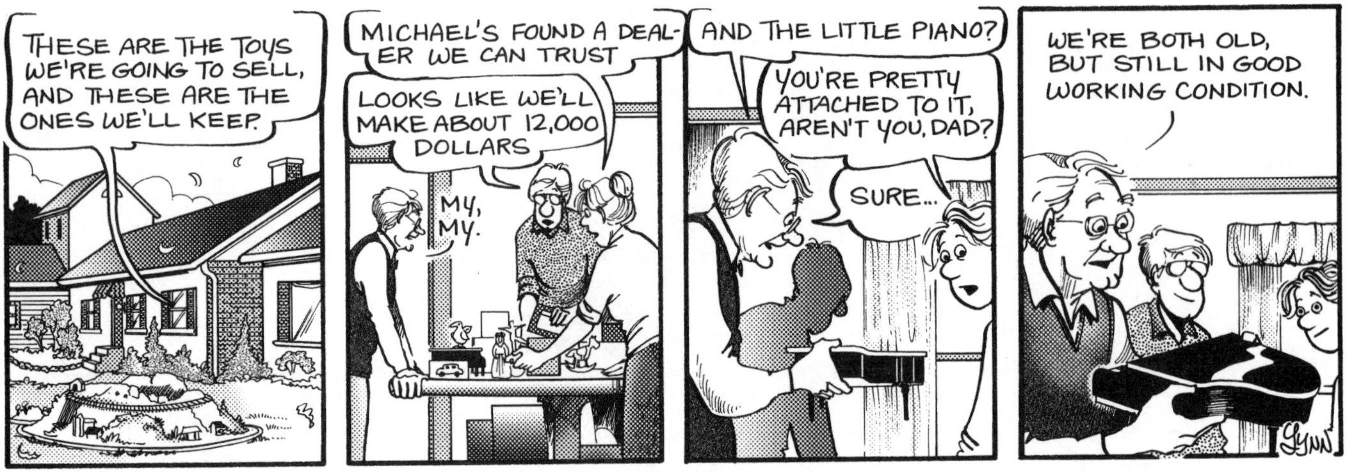
THESE ARE THE TOYS WE'RE GOING TO SELL, AND THESE ARE THE ONES WE'LL KEEP.
MICHAEL'S FOUND A DEAL-ER WE CAN TRUST
LOOKS LIKE WE'LL MAKE ABOUT 12,000 DOLLARS
MY, MY.
AND THE LITTLE PIANO?
YOU'RE PRETTY ATTACHED TO IT, AREN'T YOU, DAD?
SURE...
WE'RE BOTH OLD, BUT STILL IN GOOD WORKING CONDITION.
LYNN

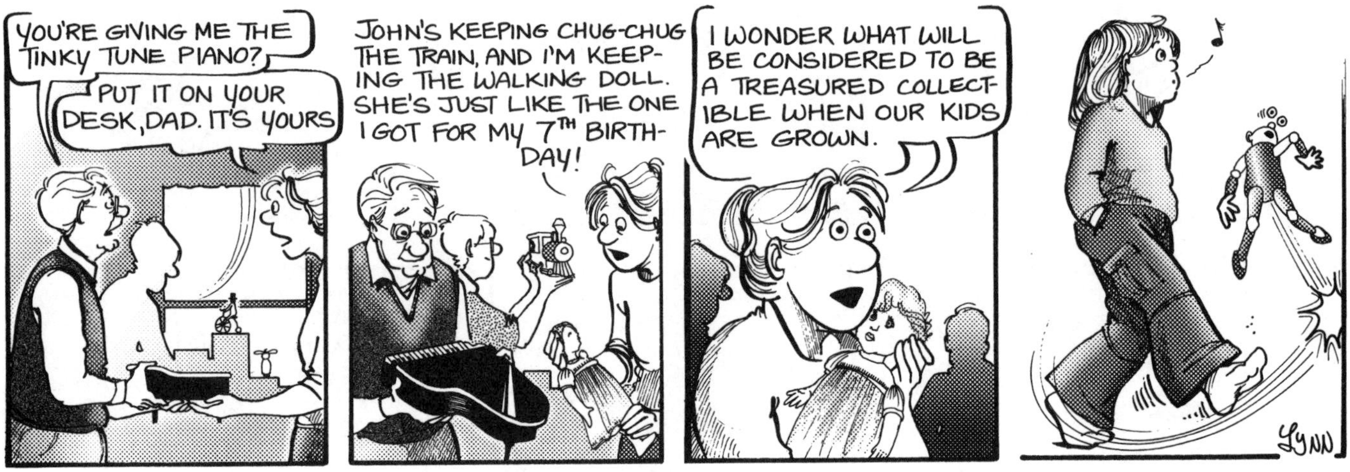
YOU'RE GIVING ME THE TINKY TUNE PIANO?
PUT IT ON YOUR DESK, DAD. IT'S YOURS
JOHN'S KEEPING CHUG-CHUG THE TRAIN, AND I'M KEEP-ING THE WALKING DOLL. SHE'S JUST LIKE THE ONE I GOT FOR MY 7TH BIRTH-DAY!
I WONDER WHAT WILL BE CONSIDERED TO BE A TREASURED COLLECT-IBLE WHEN OUR KIDS ARE GROWN.
LYNN

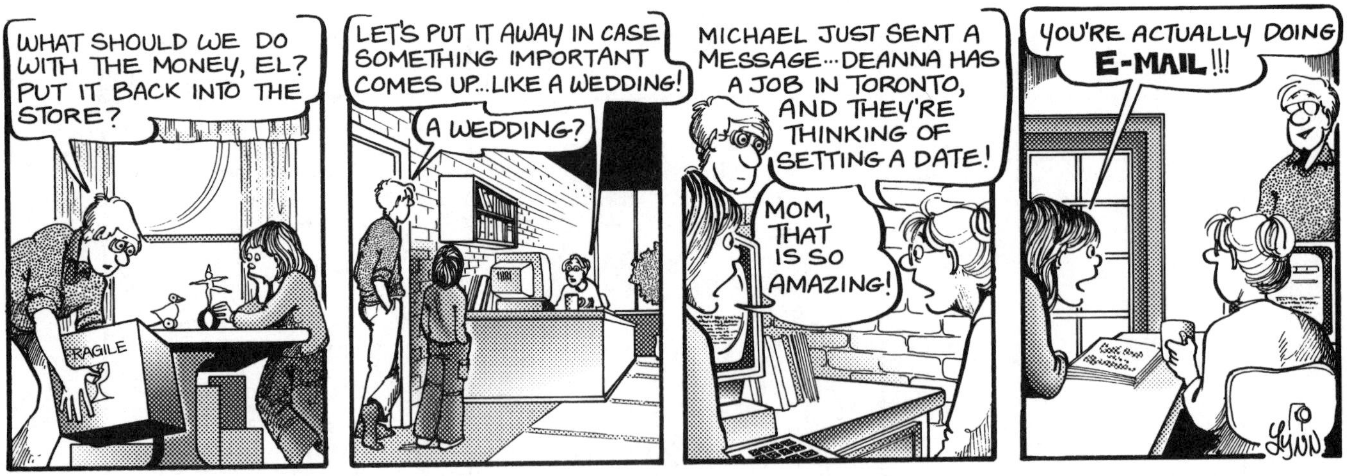
WHAT SHOULD WE DO WITH THE MONEY, EL? PUT IT BACK INTO THE STORE?
FRAGILE
LET'S PUT IT AWAY IN CASE SOMETHING IMPORTANT COMES UP...LIKE A WEDDING!
A WEDDING?
MICHAEL JUST SENT A MESSAGE...DEANNA HAS A JOB IN TORONTO, AND THEY'RE THINKING OF SETTING A DATE!
MOM, THAT IS SO AMAZING!
YOU'RE ACTUALLY DOING E-MAIL!!!
LYNN

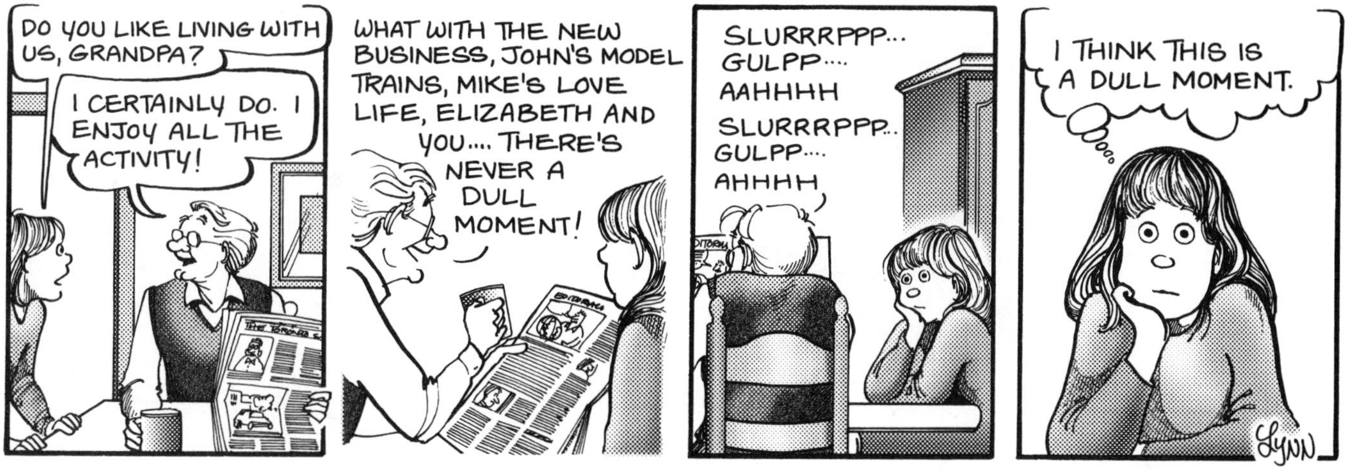
DO YOU LIKE LIVING WITH US, GRANDPA?
I CERTAINLY DO. I ENJOY ALL THE ACTIVITY!
WHAT WITH THE NEW BUSINESS, JOHN'S MODEL TRAINS, MIKE'S LOVE LIFE, ELIZABETH AND YOU.... THERE'S NEVER A DULL MOMENT!
SLURRRPPP... GULPP.... AAHHHH
SLURRRPPP... GULPP.... AHHHH
I THINK THIS IS A DULL MOMENT.
LYNN

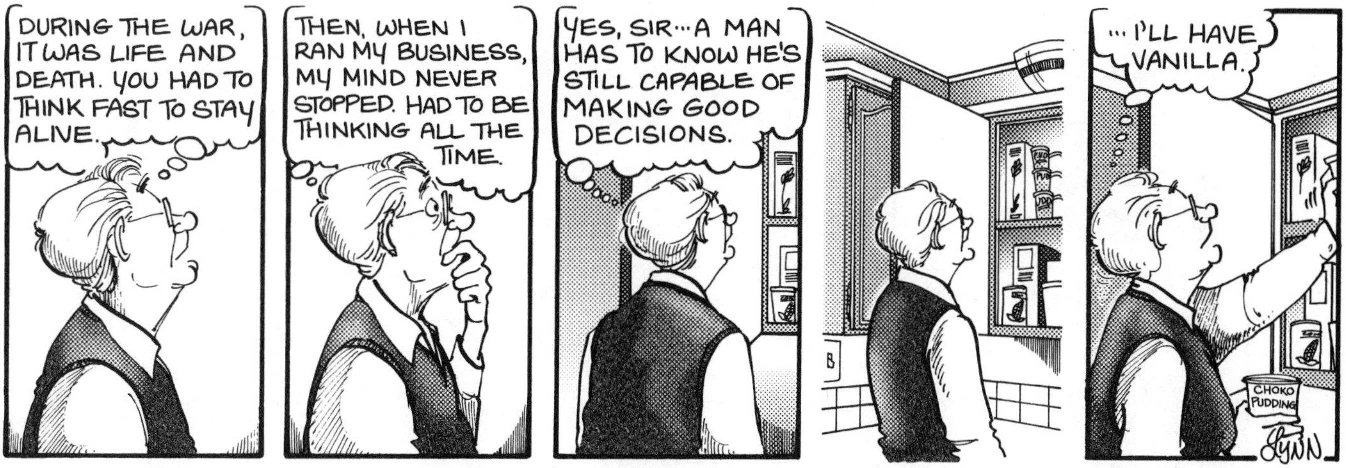
DURING THE WAR, IT WAS LIFE AND DEATH. YOU HAD TO THINK FAST TO STAY ALIVE.
THEN, WHEN I RAN MY BUSINESS, MY MIND NEVER STOPPED. HAD TO BE THINKING ALL THE TIME.
YES, SIR... A MAN HAS TO KNOW HE'S STILL CAPABLE OF MAKING GOOD DECISIONS.
... I'LL HAVE VANILLA.
CHOKO PUDDING
LYNN

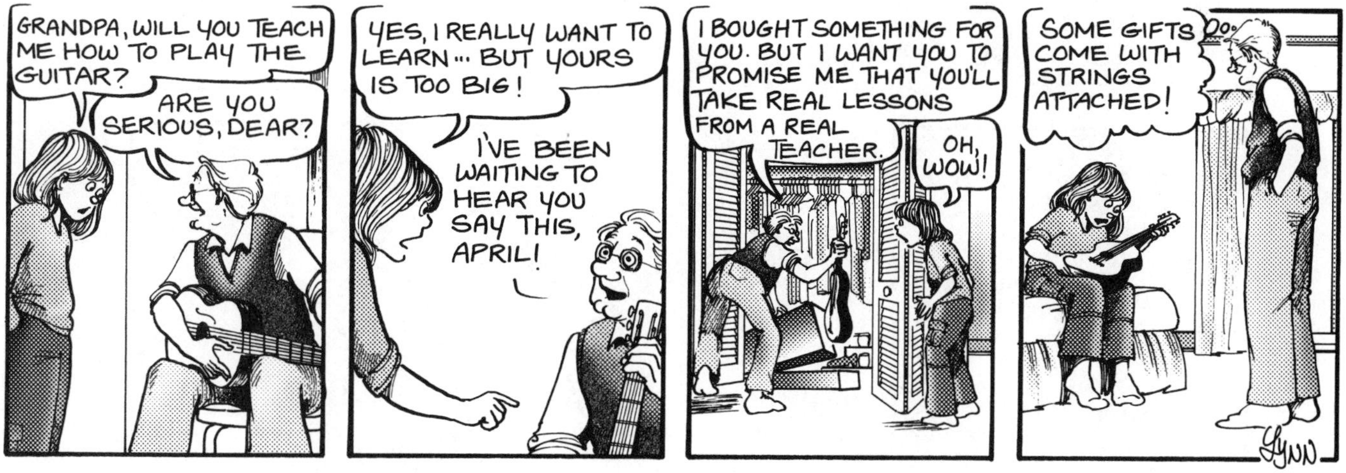
GRANDPA, WILL YOU TEACH ME HOW TO PLAY THE GUITAR?
ARE YOU SERIOUS, DEAR?
YES, I REALLY WANT TO LEARN... BUT YOURS IS TOO BIG!
I'VE BEEN WAITING TO HEAR YOU SAY THIS, APRIL!
I BOUGHT SOMETHING FOR YOU. BUT I WANT YOU TO PROMISE ME THAT YOU'LL TAKE REAL LESSONS FROM A REAL TEACHER.
OH, WOW!
SOME GIFTS COME WITH STRINGS ATTACHED!
LYNN

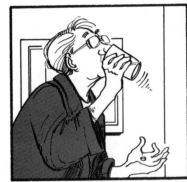

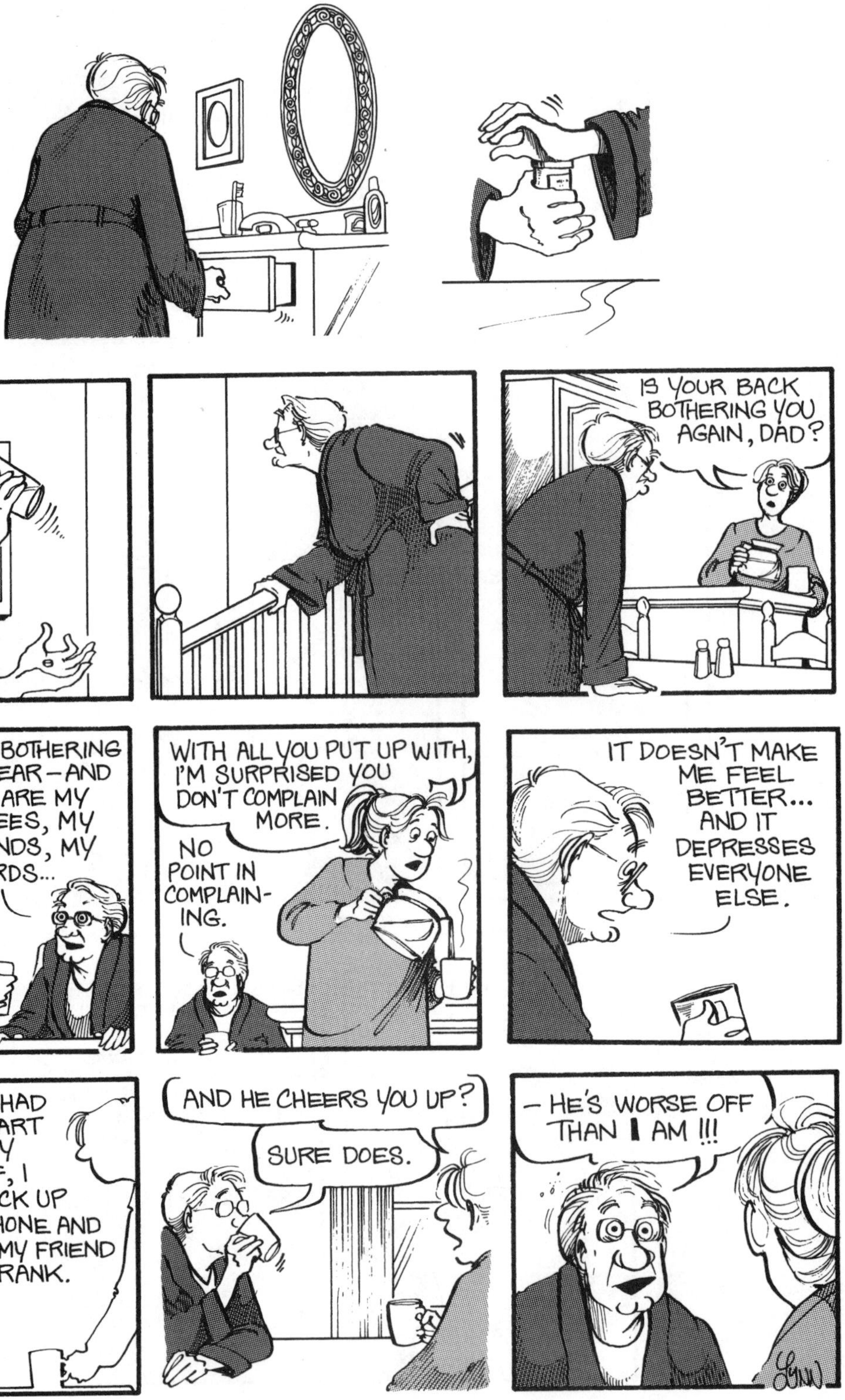
IS YOUR BACK BOTHERING YOU AGAIN, DAD?
OH, IT'S ALWAYS BOTHERING ME, DEAR — AND SO ARE MY KNEES, MY HANDS, MY INNARDS...
WITH ALL YOU PUT UP WITH, I'M SURPRISED YOU DON'T COMPLAIN MORE.
NO POINT IN COMPLAINING.
IT DOESN'T MAKE ME FEEL BETTER... AND IT DEPRESSES EVERYONE ELSE.
SO, WHEN I'VE HAD ENOUGH AND START FEELING SORRY FOR MYSELF, I JUST PICK UP THE PHONE AND CALL MY FRIEND FRANK.
AND HE CHEERS YOU UP?
SURE DOES.
— HE'S WORSE OFF THAN I AM !!!
LYNN

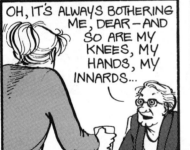

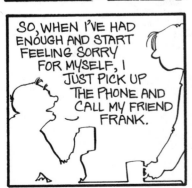

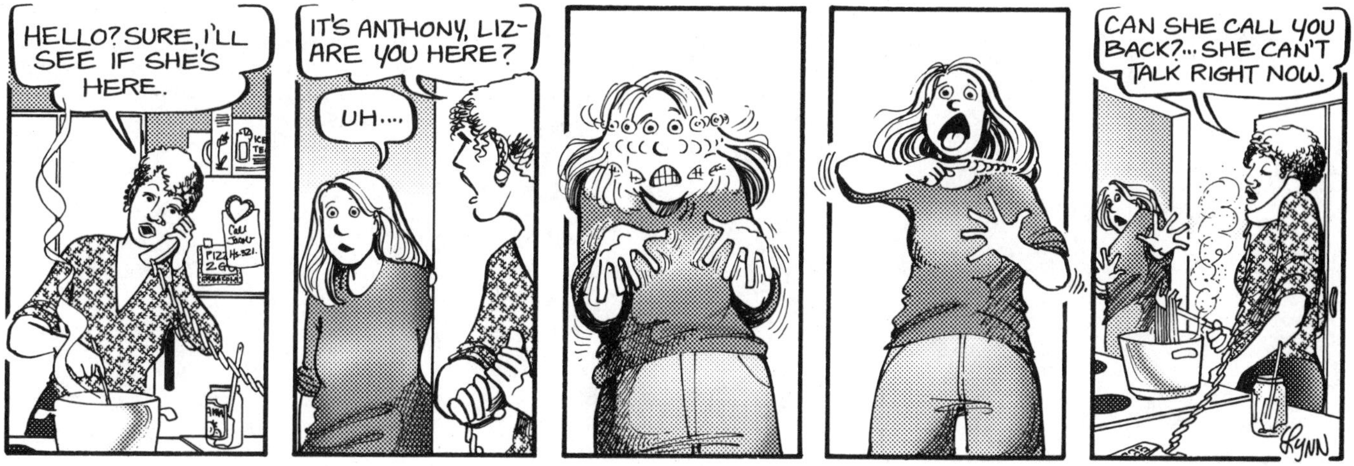
HELLO? SURE, I'LL SEE IF SHE'S HERE.
IT'S ANTHONY, LIZ- ARE YOU HERE?
UH....
CAN SHE CALL YOU BACK?... SHE CAN'T TALK RIGHT NOW.
LYNN

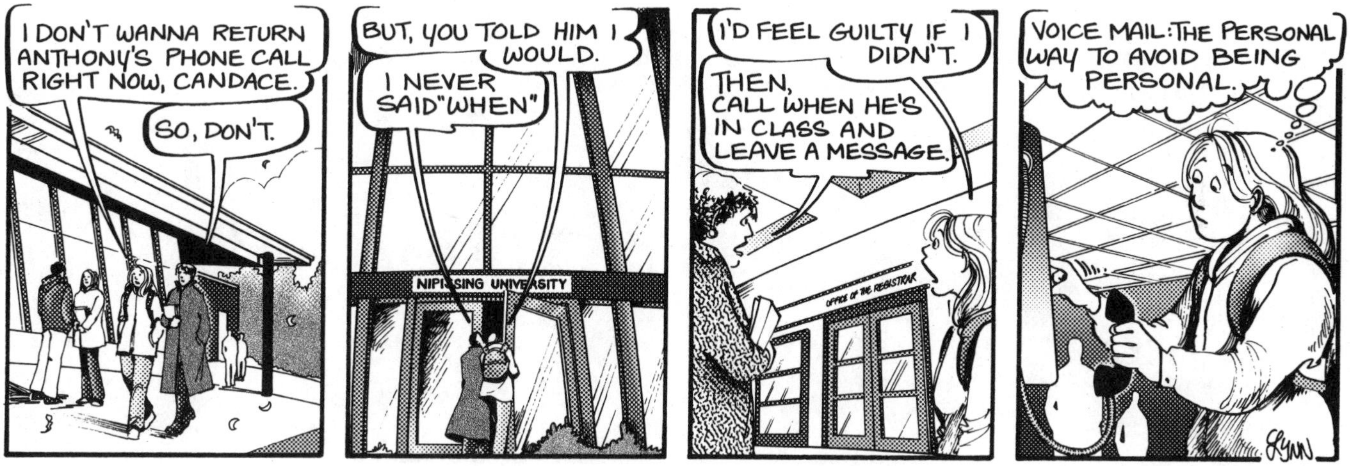
I DON'T WANNA RETURN ANTHONY'S PHONE CALL RIGHT NOW, CANDACE.
SO, DON'T.
BUT, YOU TOLD HIM I WOULD.
I NEVER SAID "WHEN"
NIPISSING UNIVERSITY
I'D FEEL GUILTY IF I DIDN'T.
THEN, CALL WHEN HE'S IN CLASS AND LEAVE A MESSAGE.
OFFICE OF THE REGISTRAR
VOICE MAIL: THE PERSONAL WAY TO AVOID BEING PERSONAL.
LYNN

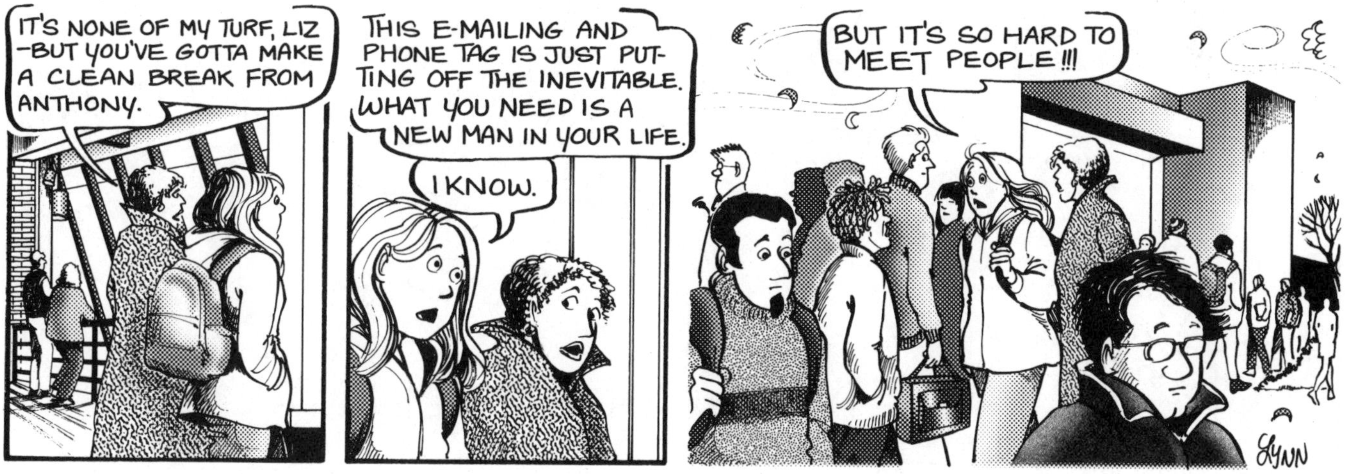
IT'S NONE OF MY TURF, LIZ -BUT YOU'VE GOTTA MAKE A CLEAN BREAK FROM ANTHONY.
THIS E-MAILING AND PHONE TAG IS JUST PUTTING OFF THE INEVITABLE. WHAT YOU NEED IS A NEW MAN IN YOUR LIFE.
I KNOW.
BUT IT'S SO HARD TO MEET PEOPLE!!!
LYNN

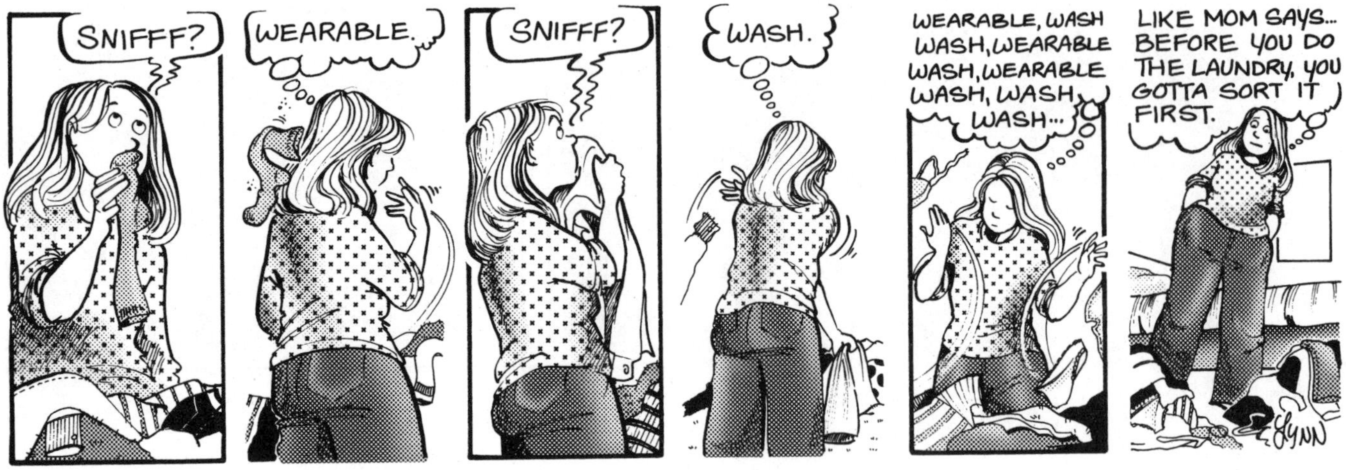
SNIFFF?
WEARABLE.
SNIFFF?
WASH.
WEARABLE, WASH WASH, WEARABLE WASH, WEARABLE WASH, WASH, WASH...
LIKE MOM SAYS... BEFORE YOU DO THE LAUNDRY, YOU GOTTA SORT IT FIRST.
LYNN

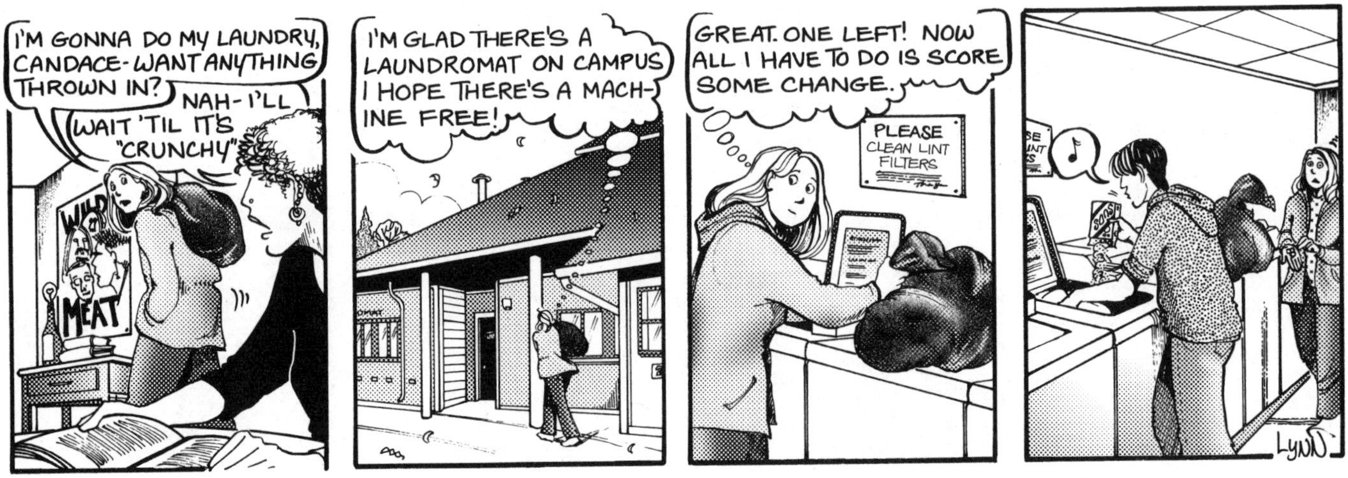
I'M GONNA DO MY LAUNDRY, CANDACE- WANT ANYTHING THROWN IN?
NAH- I'LL WAIT 'TIL IT'S "CRUNCHY"
MEAT
I'M GLAD THERE'S A LAUNDROMAT ON CAMPUS. I HOPE THERE'S A MACHINE FREE!
GREAT. ONE LEFT! NOW ALL I HAVE TO DO IS SCORE SOME CHANGE.
PLEASE CLEAN LINT FILTERS
LYNN

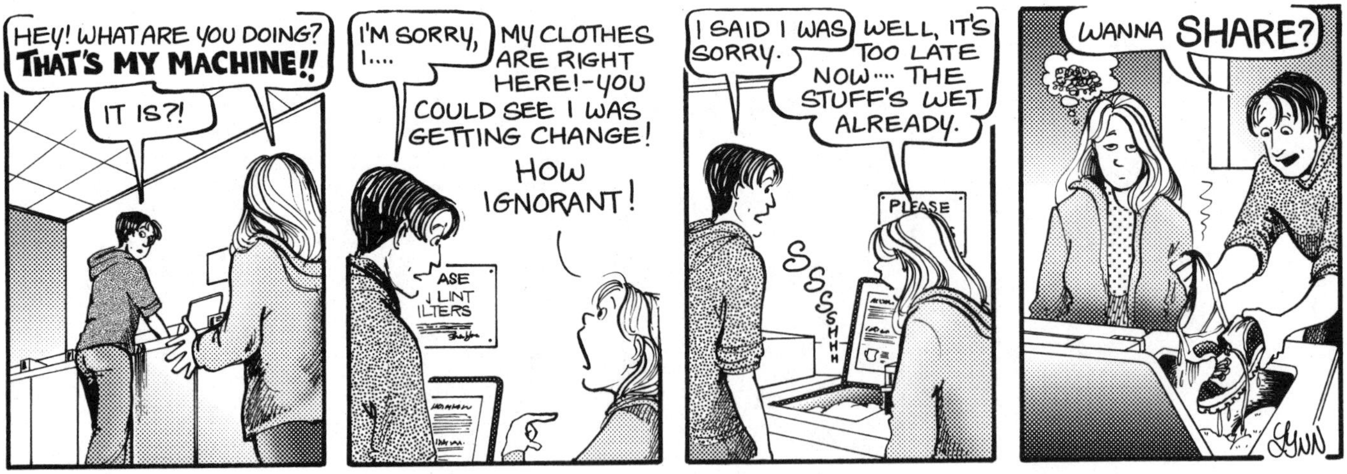
HEY! WHAT ARE YOU DOING? THAT'S MY MACHINE!!
IT IS?!
I'M SORRY, I....
MY CLOTHES ARE RIGHT HERE!-YOU COULD SEE I WAS GETTING CHANGE!
HOW IGNORANT!
I SAID I WAS SORRY.
WELL, IT'S TOO LATE NOW.... THE STUFF'S WET ALREADY.
PLEASE
SSSSHHH
WANNA SHARE?
LYNN

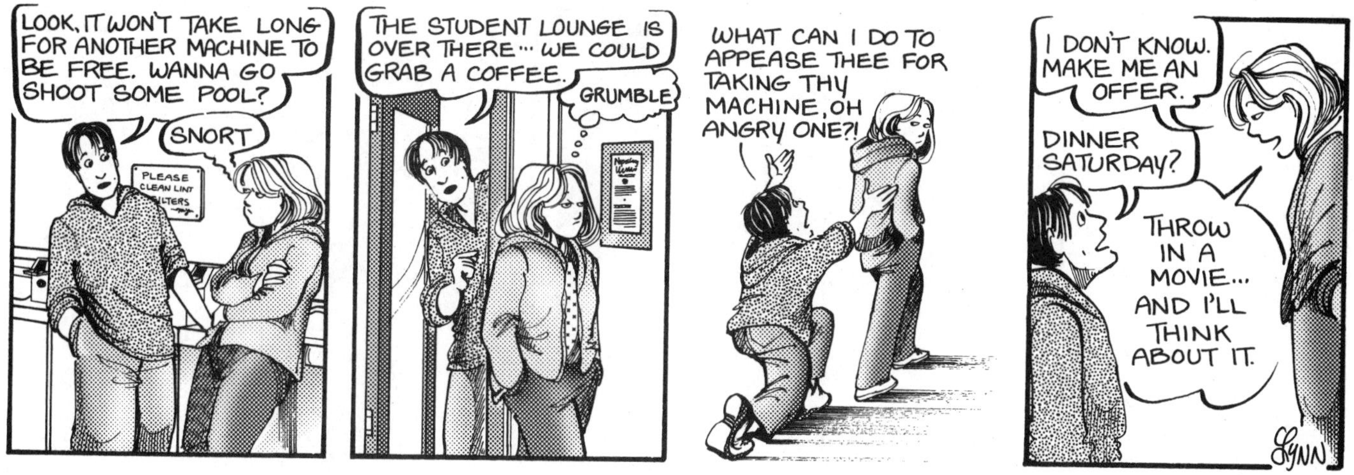
LOOK, IT WON'T TAKE LONG FOR ANOTHER MACHINE TO BE FREE. WANNA GO SHOOT SOME POOL?
SNORT
PLEASE CLEAN LINT
THE STUDENT LOUNGE IS OVER THERE··· WE COULD GRAB A COFFEE.
GRUMBLE
WHAT CAN I DO TO APPEASE THEE FOR TAKING THY MACHINE, OH ANGRY ONE?!
I DON'T KNOW. MAKE ME AN OFFER.
DINNER SATURDAY?
THROW IN A MOVIE... AND I'LL THINK ABOUT IT.
LYNN

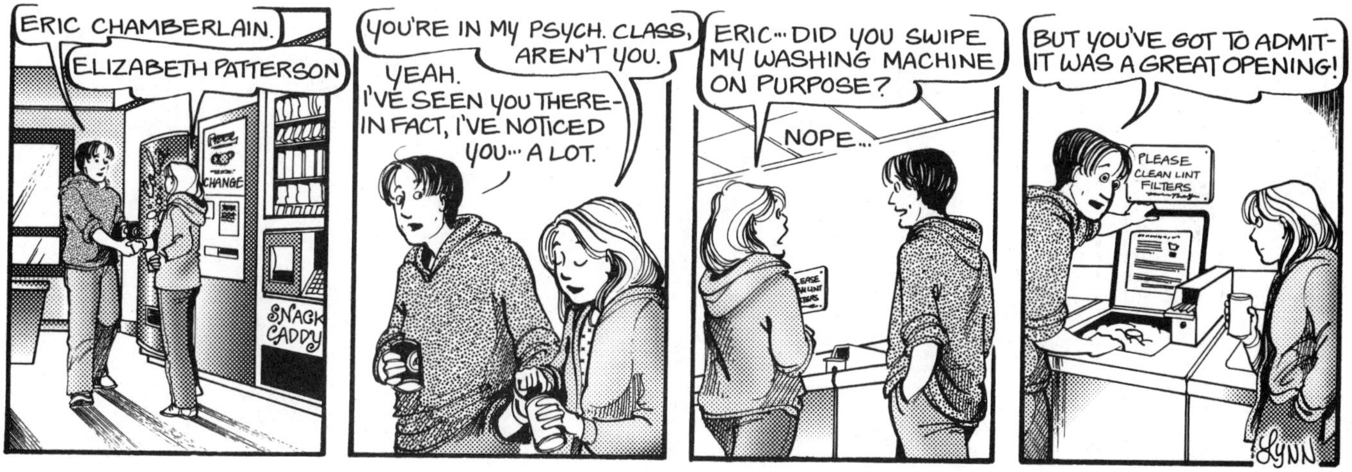
ERIC CHAMBERLAIN.
ELIZABETH PATTERSON
CHANGE
SNACK CADDY
YOU'RE IN MY PSYCH. CLASS, AREN'T YOU.
YEAH. I'VE SEEN YOU THERE- IN FACT, I'VE NOTICED YOU··· A LOT.
ERIC··· DID YOU SWIPE MY WASHING MACHINE ON PURPOSE?
NOPE...
BUT YOU'VE GOT TO ADMIT- IT WAS A GREAT OPENING!
PLEASE CLEAN LINT FILTERS
LYNN

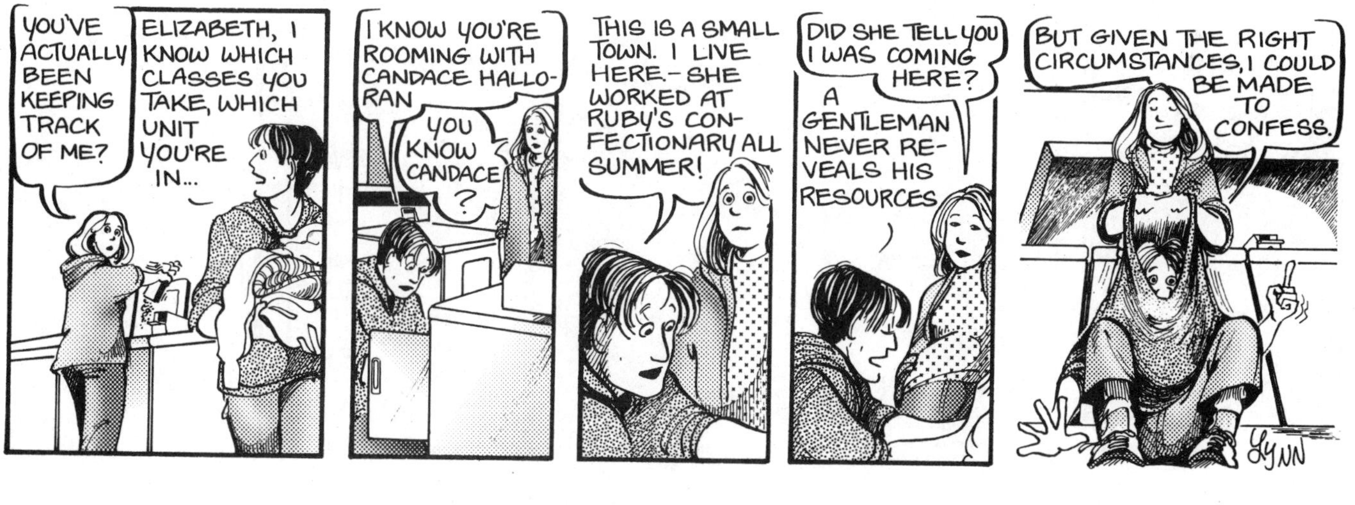
YOU'VE ACTUALLY BEEN KEEPING TRACK OF ME?
ELIZABETH, I KNOW WHICH CLASSES YOU TAKE, WHICH UNIT YOU'RE IN...
I KNOW YOU'RE ROOMING WITH CANDACE HALLO-RAN
YOU KNOW CANDACE?
THIS IS A SMALL TOWN. I LIVE HERE.- SHE WORKED AT RUBY'S CON-FECTIONARY ALL SUMMER!
DID SHE TELL YOU I WAS COMING HERE?
A GENTLEMAN NEVER RE-VEALS HIS RESOURCES
BUT GIVEN THE RIGHT CIRCUMSTANCES, I COULD BE MADE TO CONFESS.
LYNN

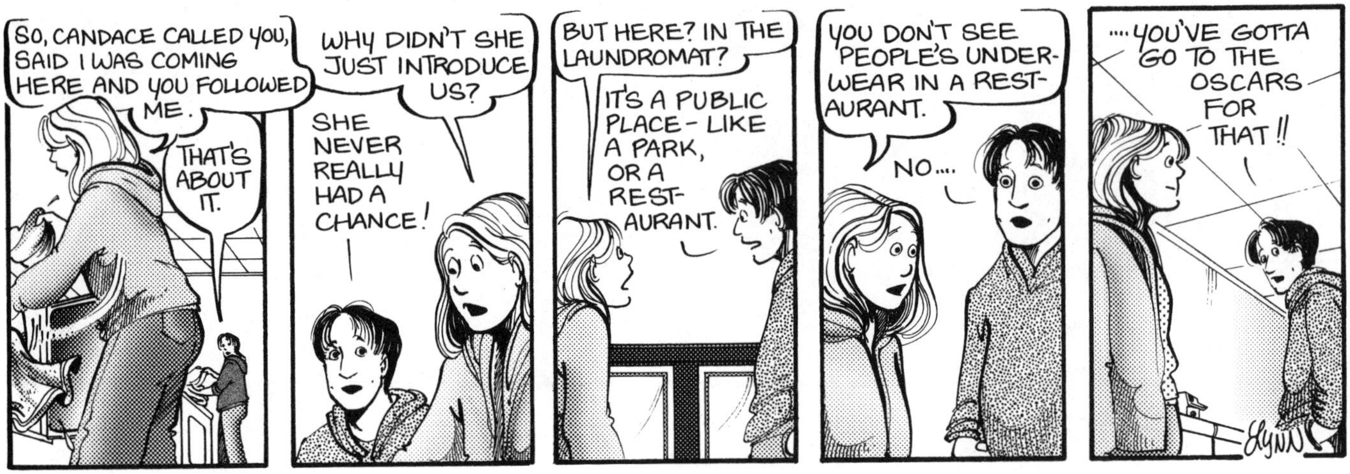
SO, CANDACE CALLED YOU, SAID I WAS COMING HERE AND YOU FOLLOWED ME.
THAT'S ABOUT IT.
WHY DIDN'T SHE JUST INTRODUCE US?
SHE NEVER REALLY HAD A CHANCE!
BUT HERE? IN THE LAUNDROMAT?
IT'S A PUBLIC PLACE - LIKE A PARK, OR A RESTAURANT.
YOU DON'T SEE PEOPLE'S UNDERWEAR IN A RESTAURANT.
NO....
....YOU'VE GOTTA GO TO THE OSCARS FOR THAT!!
LYNN

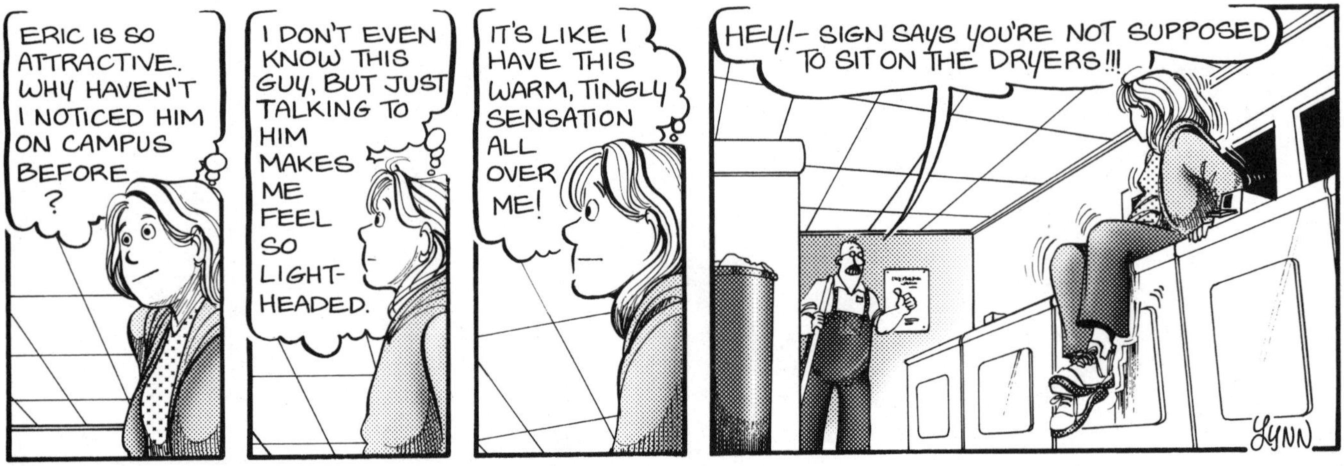
ERIC IS SO ATTRACTIVE. WHY HAVEN'T I NOTICED HIM ON CAMPUS BEFORE?
I DON'T EVEN KNOW THIS GUY, BUT JUST TALKING TO HIM MAKES ME FEEL SO LIGHT-HEADED.
IT'S LIKE I HAVE THIS WARM, TINGLY SENSATION ALL OVER ME!
HEY!- SIGN SAYS YOU'RE NOT SUPPOSED TO SIT ON THE DRYERS!!!
LYNN

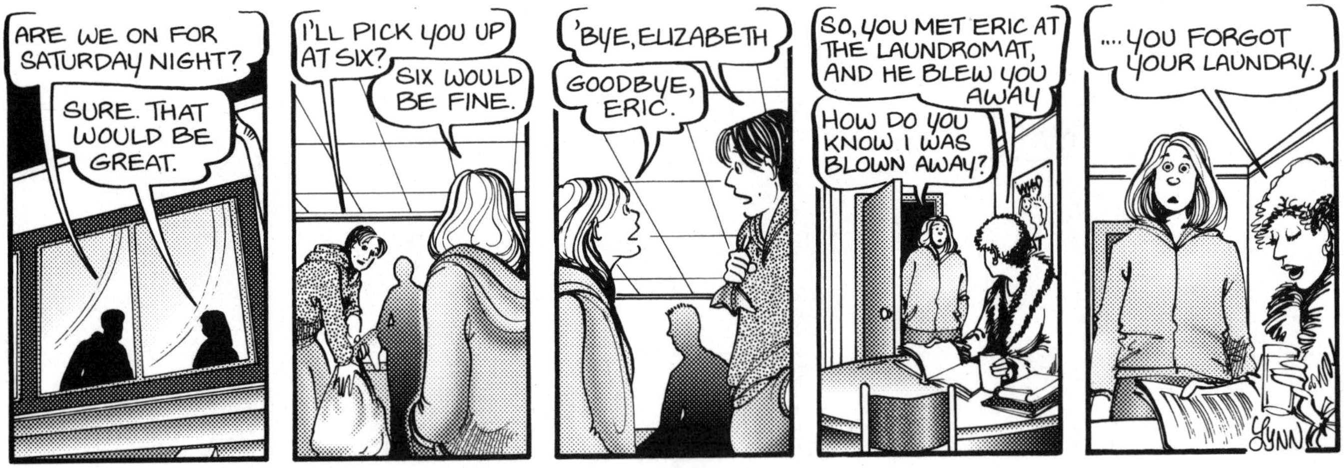
ARE WE ON FOR SATURDAY NIGHT?
SURE. THAT WOULD BE GREAT.
I'LL PICK YOU UP AT SIX?
SIX WOULD BE FINE.
'BYE, ELIZABETH
GOODBYE, ERIC.
SO, YOU MET ERIC AT THE LAUNDROMAT, AND HE BLEW YOU AWAY
HOW DO YOU KNOW I WAS BLOWN AWAY?
....YOU FORGOT YOUR LAUNDRY.
LYNN

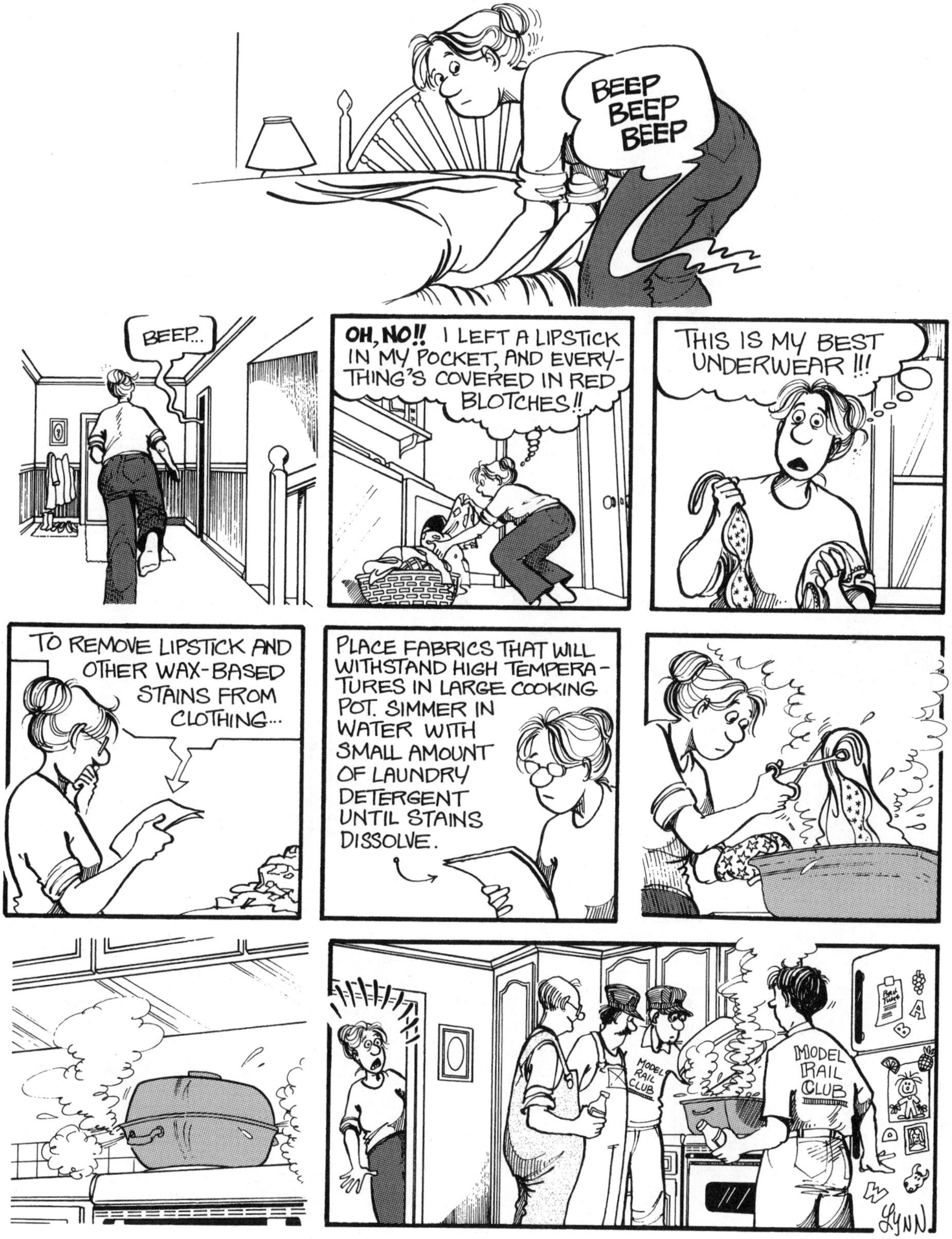
BEEP BEEP BEEP
BEEP...
OH, NO!! I LEFT A LIPSTICK IN MY POCKET, AND EVERYTHING'S COVERED IN RED BLOTCHES!!
THIS IS MY BEST UNDERWEAR!!!
TO REMOVE LIPSTICK AND OTHER WAX-BASED STAINS FROM CLOTHING...
PLACE FABRICS THAT WILL WITHSTAND HIGH TEMPERATURES IN LARGE COOKING POT. SIMMER IN WATER WITH SMALL AMOUNT OF LAUNDRY DETERGENT UNTIL STAINS DISSOLVE.
MODEL RAIL CLUB
MODEL RAIL CLUB
LYNN

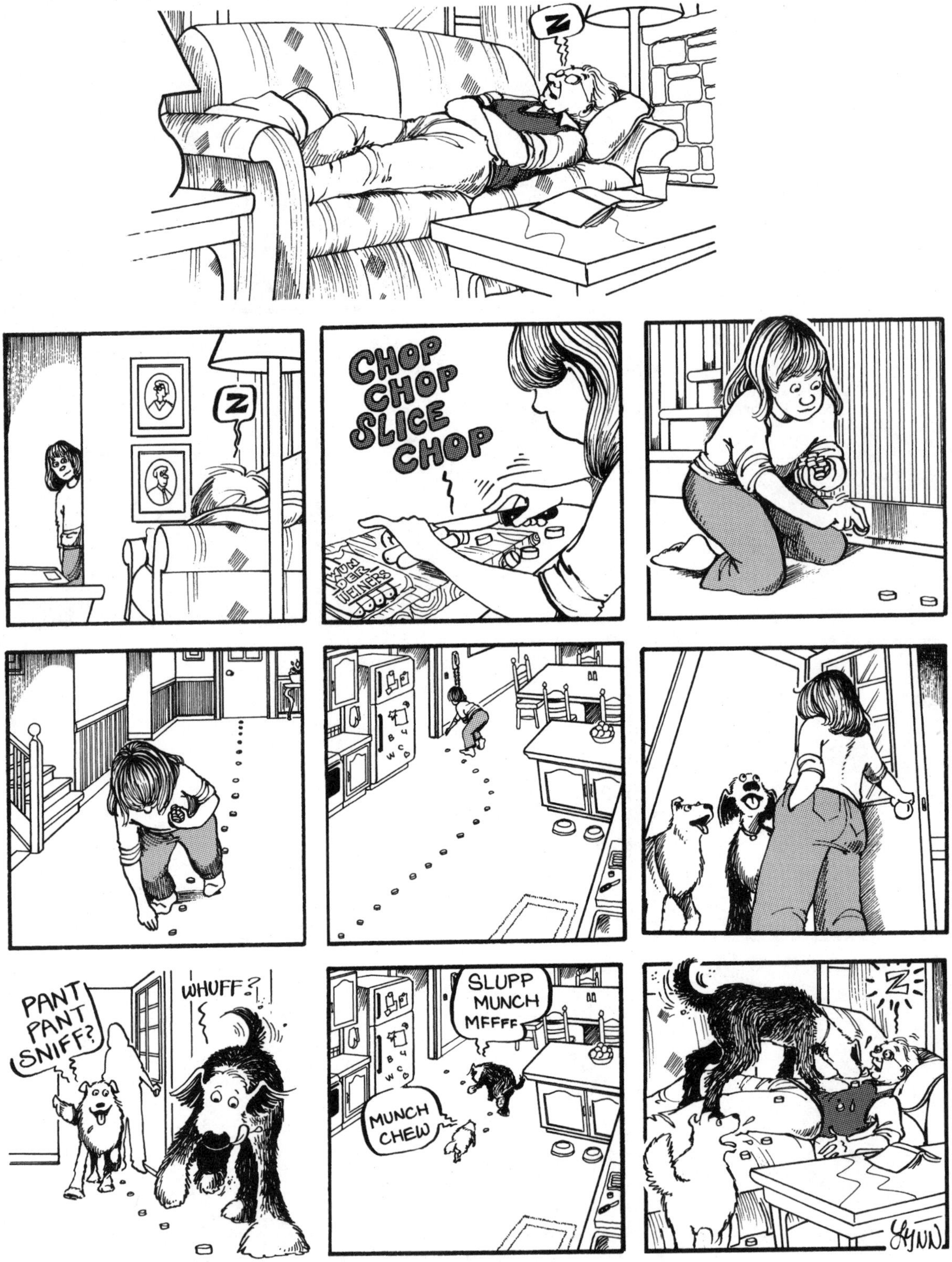
Z
Z
CHOP
CHOP
SLICE
CHOP
PANT
PANT
SNIFF?
WHUFF?
SLUPP
MUNCH
MFFFF
MUNCH
CHEW
Z

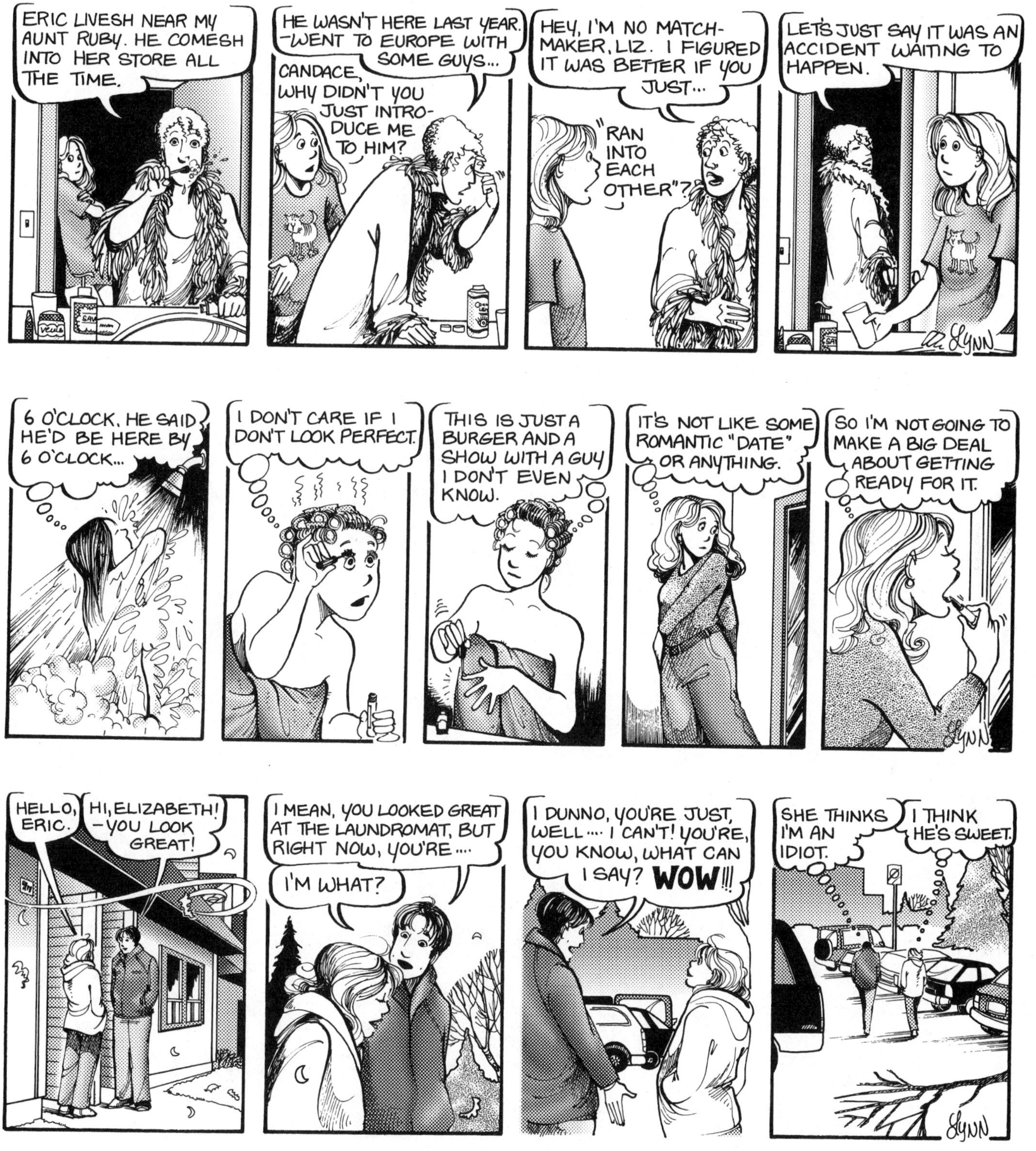
ERIC LIVESH NEAR MY AUNT RUBY. HE COMESH INTO HER STORE ALL THE TIME.
HE WASN'T HERE LAST YEAR. –WENT TO EUROPE WITH SOME GUYS...
CANDACE, WHY DIDN'T YOU JUST INTRODUCE ME TO HIM?
HEY, I'M NO MATCH-MAKER, LIZ. I FIGURED IT WAS BETTER IF YOU JUST...
"RAN INTO EACH OTHER"?
LET'S JUST SAY IT WAS AN ACCIDENT WAITING TO HAPPEN.
LYNN
6 O'CLOCK. HE SAID HE'D BE HERE BY 6 O'CLOCK...
I DON'T CARE IF I DON'T LOOK PERFECT.
THIS IS JUST A BURGER AND A SHOW WITH A GUY I DON'T EVEN KNOW.
IT'S NOT LIKE SOME ROMANTIC "DATE" OR ANYTHING.
SO I'M NOT GOING TO MAKE A BIG DEAL ABOUT GETTING READY FOR IT.
LYNN
HELLO, ERIC.
HI, ELIZABETH! –YOU LOOK GREAT!
I MEAN, YOU LOOKED GREAT AT THE LAUNDROMAT, BUT RIGHT NOW, YOU'RE....
I'M WHAT?
I DUNNO, YOU'RE JUST, WELL.... I CAN'T! YOU'RE, YOU KNOW, WHAT CAN I SAY? WOW!!!
SHE THINKS I'M AN IDIOT.
I THINK HE'S SWEET.
LYNN

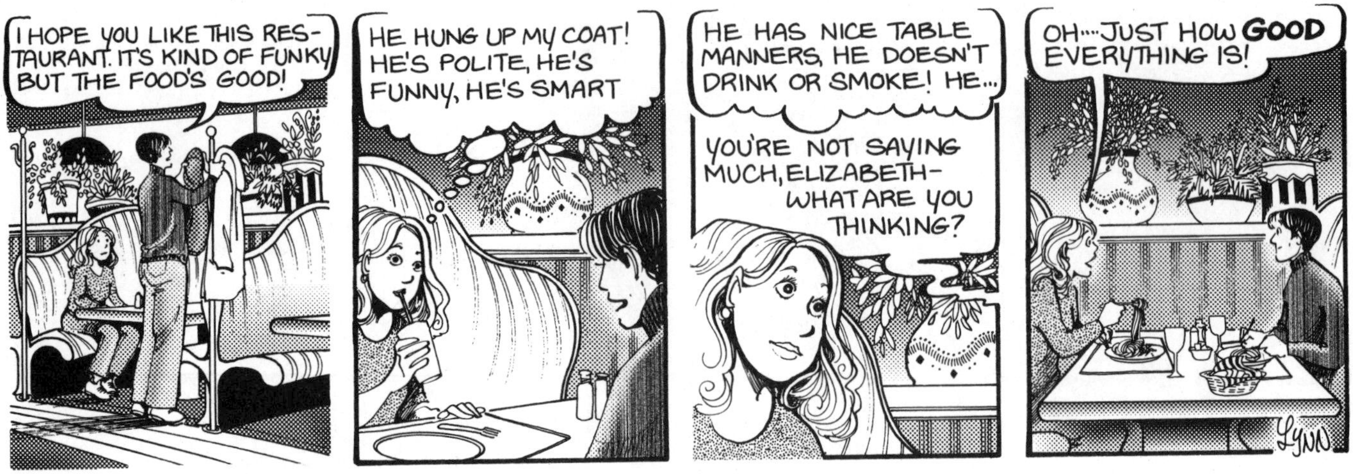
I HOPE YOU LIKE THIS RESTAURANT. IT'S KIND OF FUNKY BUT THE FOOD'S GOOD!
HE HUNG UP MY COAT! HE'S POLITE, HE'S FUNNY, HE'S SMART
HE HAS NICE TABLE MANNERS, HE DOESN'T DRINK OR SMOKE! HE...
YOU'RE NOT SAYING MUCH, ELIZABETH - WHAT ARE YOU THINKING?
OH.... JUST HOW GOOD EVERYTHING IS!
LYNN

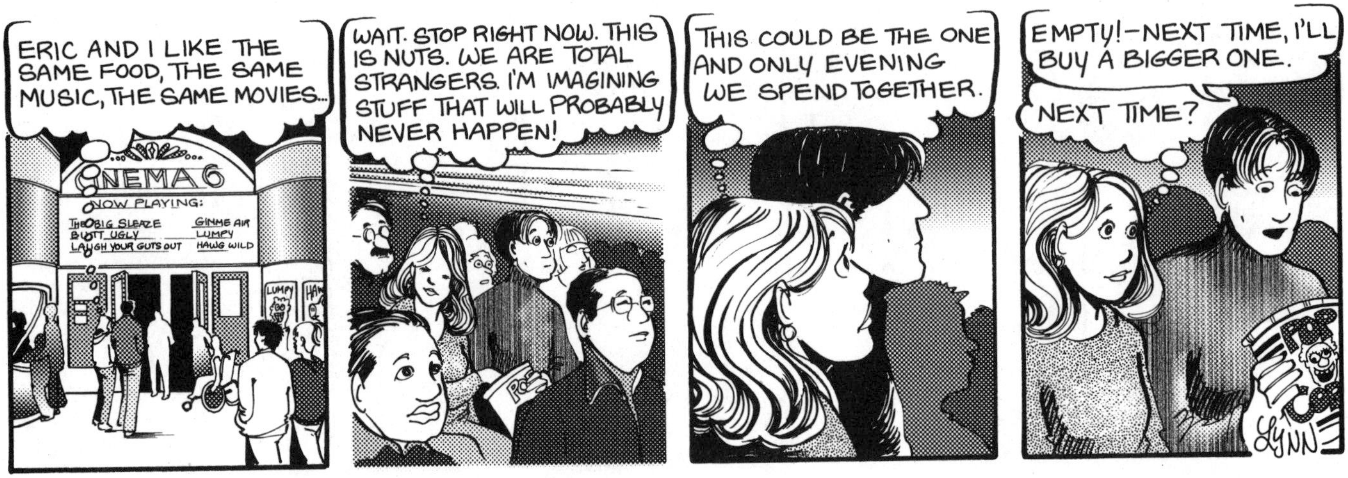
ERIC AND I LIKE THE SAME FOOD, THE SAME MUSIC, THE SAME MOVIES...
CINEMA 6
NOW PLAYING:
THE BIG SLEAZE
BUTT UGLY
LAUGH YOUR GUTS OUT
GIMME AIR
LUMPY
HAWG WILD
WAIT. STOP RIGHT NOW. THIS IS NUTS. WE ARE TOTAL STRANGERS. I'M IMAGINING STUFF THAT WILL PROBABLY NEVER HAPPEN!
THIS COULD BE THE ONE AND ONLY EVENING WE SPEND TOGETHER.
EMPTY! - NEXT TIME, I'LL BUY A BIGGER ONE.
NEXT TIME?
LYNN

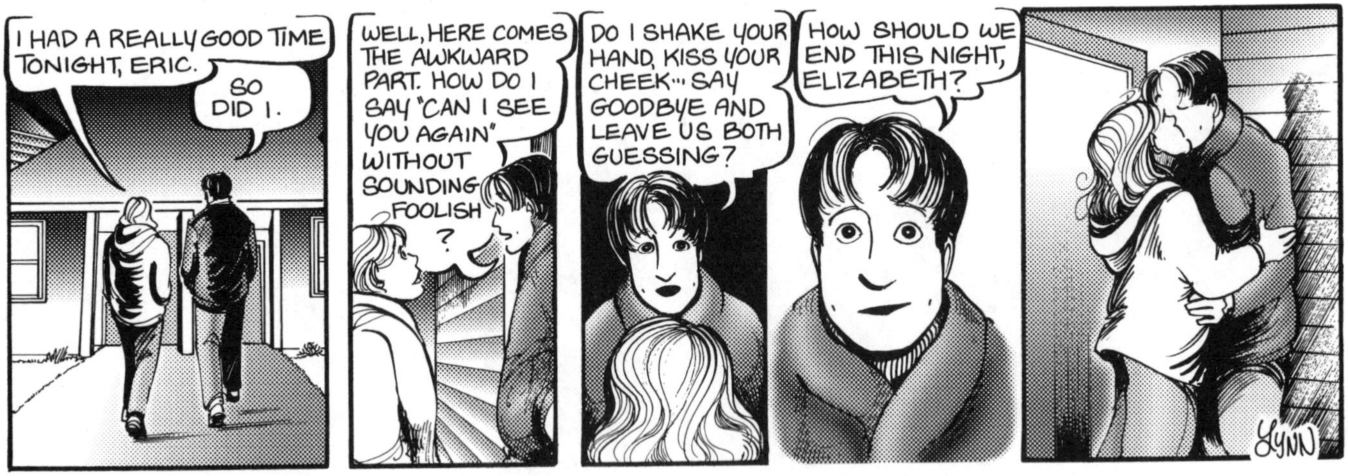
I HAD A REALLY GOOD TIME TONIGHT, ERIC.
SO DID I.
WELL, HERE COMES THE AWKWARD PART. HOW DO I SAY "CAN I SEE YOU AGAIN" WITHOUT SOUNDING FOOLISH?
DO I SHAKE YOUR HAND, KISS YOUR CHEEK... SAY GOODBYE AND LEAVE US BOTH GUESSING?
HOW SHOULD WE END THIS NIGHT, ELIZABETH?
LYNN

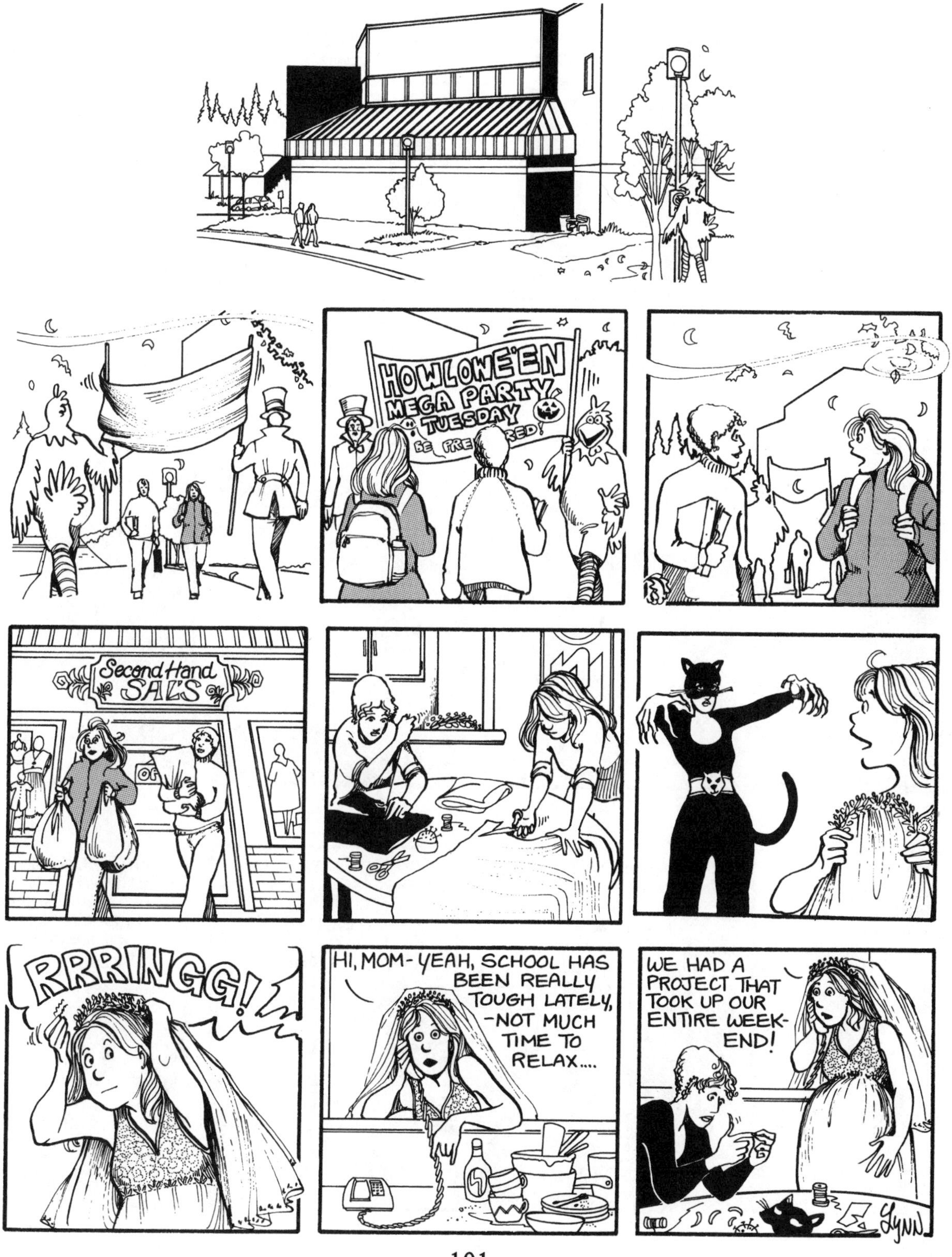
HOWLOWE'EN
MEGA PARTY
TUESDAY
Second Hand SAL'S
RRRINGG!
HI, MOM- YEAH, SCHOOL HAS BEEN REALLY TOUGH LATELY, -NOT MUCH TIME TO RELAX....
WE HAD A PROJECT THAT TOOK UP OUR ENTIRE WEEK-END!
LYNN

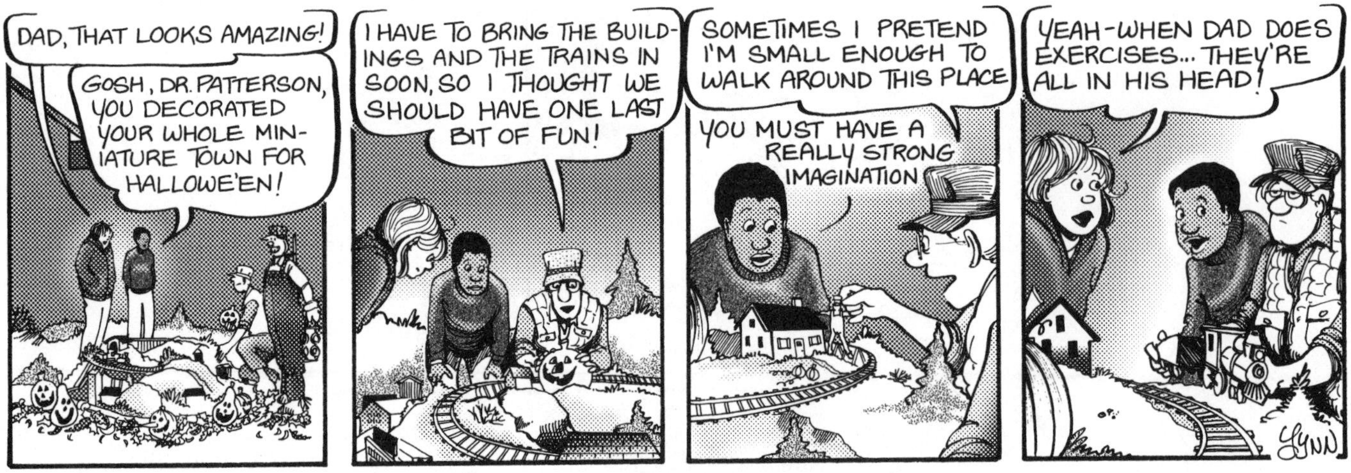
DAD, THAT LOOKS AMAZING!
GOSH, DR. PATTERSON, YOU DECORATED YOUR WHOLE MINIATURE TOWN FOR HALLOWE'EN!
I HAVE TO BRING THE BUILDINGS AND THE TRAINS IN SOON, SO I THOUGHT WE SHOULD HAVE ONE LAST BIT OF FUN!
SOMETIMES I PRETEND I'M SMALL ENOUGH TO WALK AROUND THIS PLACE
YOU MUST HAVE A REALLY STRONG IMAGINATION
YEAH-WHEN DAD DOES EXERCISES... THEY'RE ALL IN HIS HEAD!
LYNN

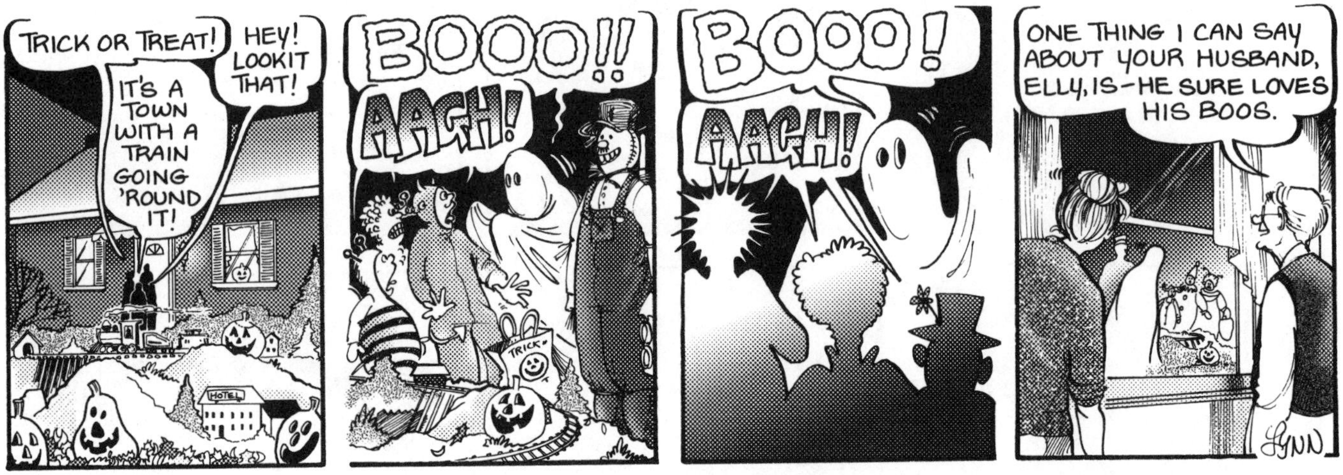
TRICK OR TREAT!
HEY! LOOKIT THAT!
IT'S A TOWN WITH A TRAIN GOING 'ROUND IT!
HOTEL
BOOO!!
AAGH!
TRICK
BOOO!
AAGH!
ONE THING I CAN SAY ABOUT YOUR HUSBAND, ELLY, IS-HE SURE LOVES HIS BOOS.
LYNN

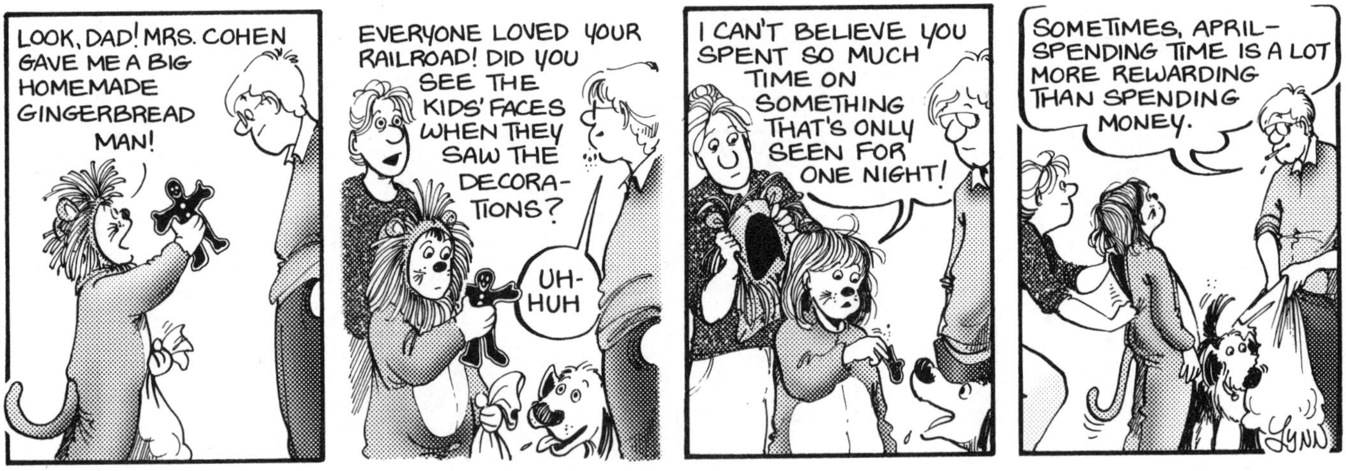
LOOK, DAD! MRS. COHEN GAVE ME A BIG HOMEMADE GINGERBREAD MAN!
EVERYONE LOVED YOUR RAILROAD! DID YOU SEE THE KIDS' FACES WHEN THEY SAW THE DECORATIONS?
UH-HUH
I CAN'T BELIEVE YOU SPENT SO MUCH TIME ON SOMETHING THAT'S ONLY SEEN FOR ONE NIGHT!
SOMETIMES, APRIL-SPENDING TIME IS A LOT MORE REWARDING THAN SPENDING MONEY.
LYNN

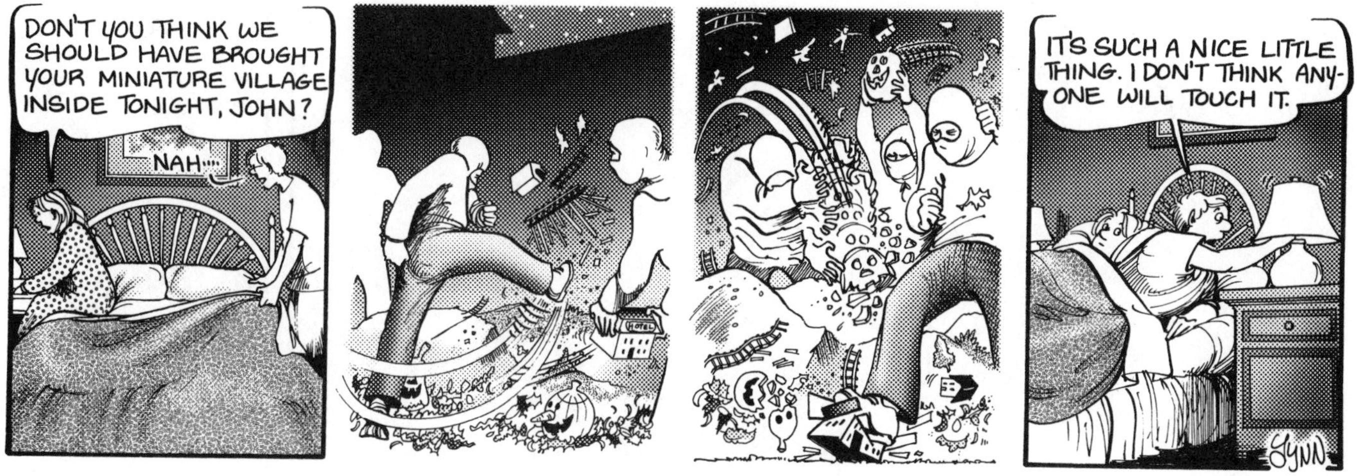
DON'T YOU THINK WE SHOULD HAVE BROUGHT YOUR MINIATURE VILLAGE INSIDE TONIGHT, JOHN?
NAH....
HOTEL
IT'S SUCH A NICE LITTLE THING. I DON'T THINK ANY-ONE WILL TOUCH IT.
LYNN

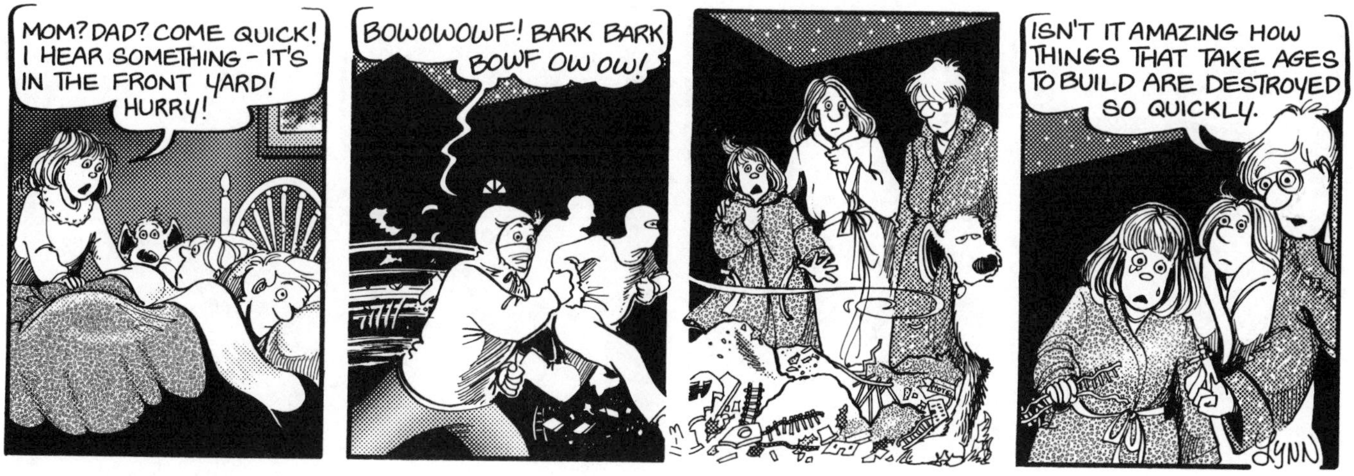
MOM? DAD? COME QUICK! I HEAR SOMETHING - IT'S IN THE FRONT YARD! HURRY!
BOWOWOWF! BARK BARK BOWF OW OW!
ISN'T IT AMAZING HOW THINGS THAT TAKE AGES TO BUILD ARE DESTROYED SO QUICKLY.
LYNN

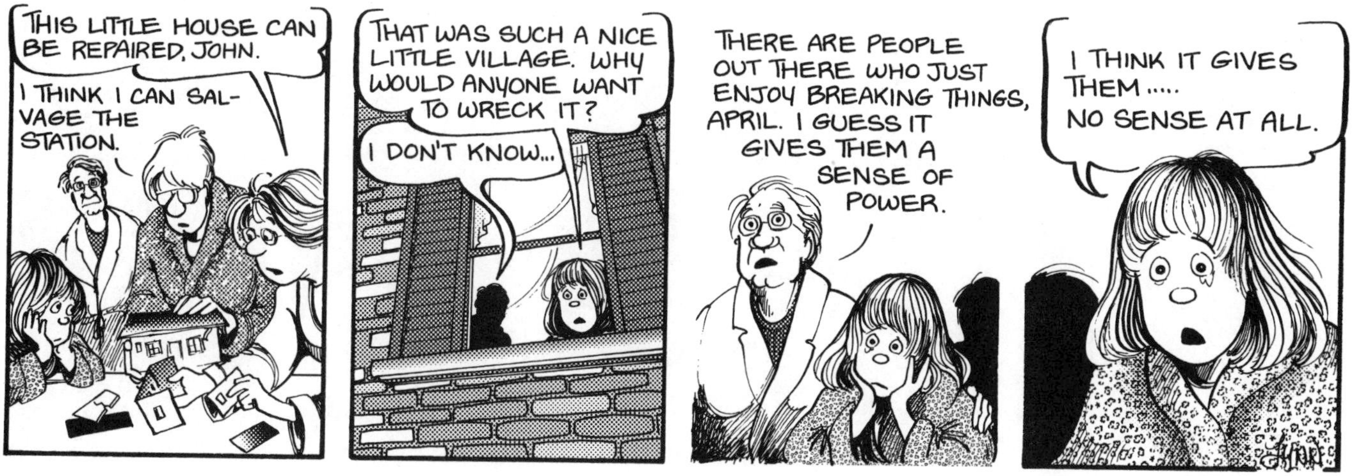
THIS LITTLE HOUSE CAN BE REPAIRED, JOHN.
I THINK I CAN SAL-VAGE THE STATION.
THAT WAS SUCH A NICE LITTLE VILLAGE. WHY WOULD ANYONE WANT TO WRECK IT?
I DON'T KNOW...
THERE ARE PEOPLE OUT THERE WHO JUST ENJOY BREAKING THINGS, APRIL. I GUESS IT GIVES THEM A SENSE OF POWER.
I THINK IT GIVES THEM .....
NO SENSE AT ALL.

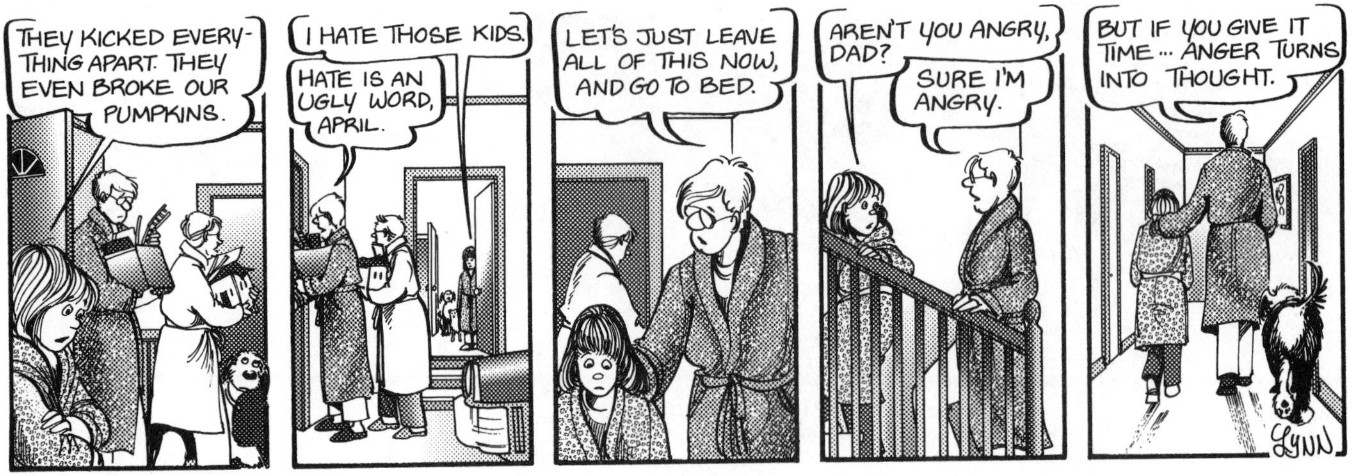
THEY KICKED EVERYTHING APART. THEY EVEN BROKE OUR PUMPKINS.
I HATE THOSE KIDS.
HATE IS AN UGLY WORD, APRIL.
LET'S JUST LEAVE ALL OF THIS NOW, AND GO TO BED.
AREN'T YOU ANGRY, DAD?
SURE I'M ANGRY.
BUT IF YOU GIVE IT TIME... ANGER TURNS INTO THOUGHT.
LYNN

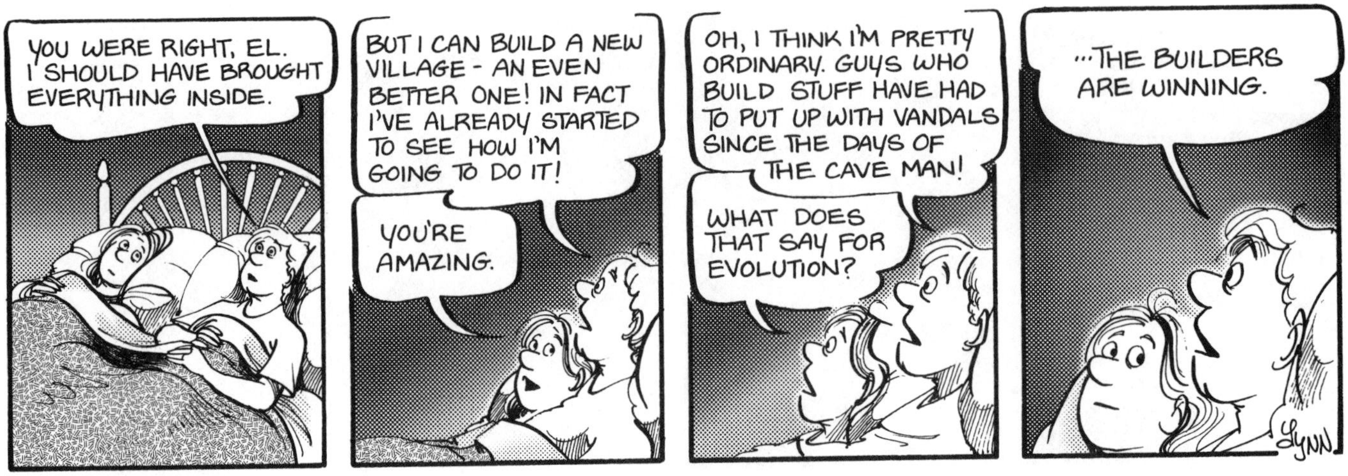
YOU WERE RIGHT, EL. I SHOULD HAVE BROUGHT EVERYTHING INSIDE.
BUT I CAN BUILD A NEW VILLAGE - AN EVEN BETTER ONE! IN FACT I'VE ALREADY STARTED TO SEE HOW I'M GOING TO DO IT!
YOU'RE AMAZING.
OH, I THINK I'M PRETTY ORDINARY. GUYS WHO BUILD STUFF HAVE HAD TO PUT UP WITH VANDALS SINCE THE DAYS OF THE CAVE MAN!
WHAT DOES THAT SAY FOR EVOLUTION?
...THE BUILDERS ARE WINNING.
LYNN

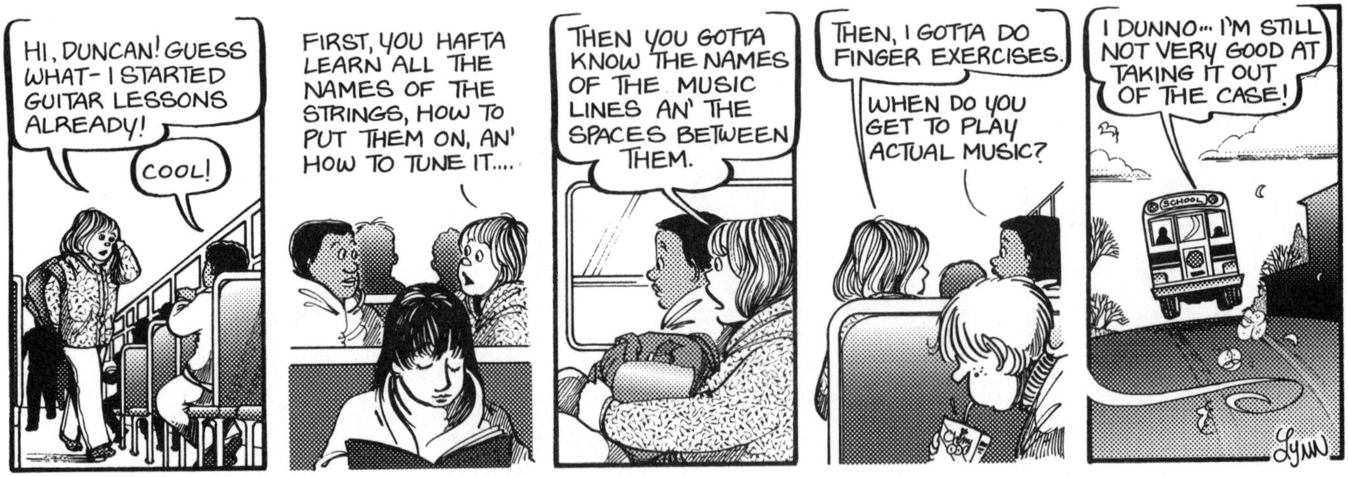
HI, DUNCAN! GUESS WHAT- I STARTED GUITAR LESSONS ALREADY!
COOL!
FIRST, YOU HAFTA LEARN ALL THE NAMES OF THE STRINGS, HOW TO PUT THEM ON, AN' HOW TO TUNE IT....
THEN YOU GOTTA KNOW THE NAMES OF THE MUSIC LINES AN' THE SPACES BETWEEN THEM.
THEN, I GOTTA DO FINGER EXERCISES.
WHEN DO YOU GET TO PLAY ACTUAL MUSIC?
I DUNNO... I'M STILL NOT VERY GOOD AT TAKING IT OUT OF THE CASE!
SCHOOL
LYNN

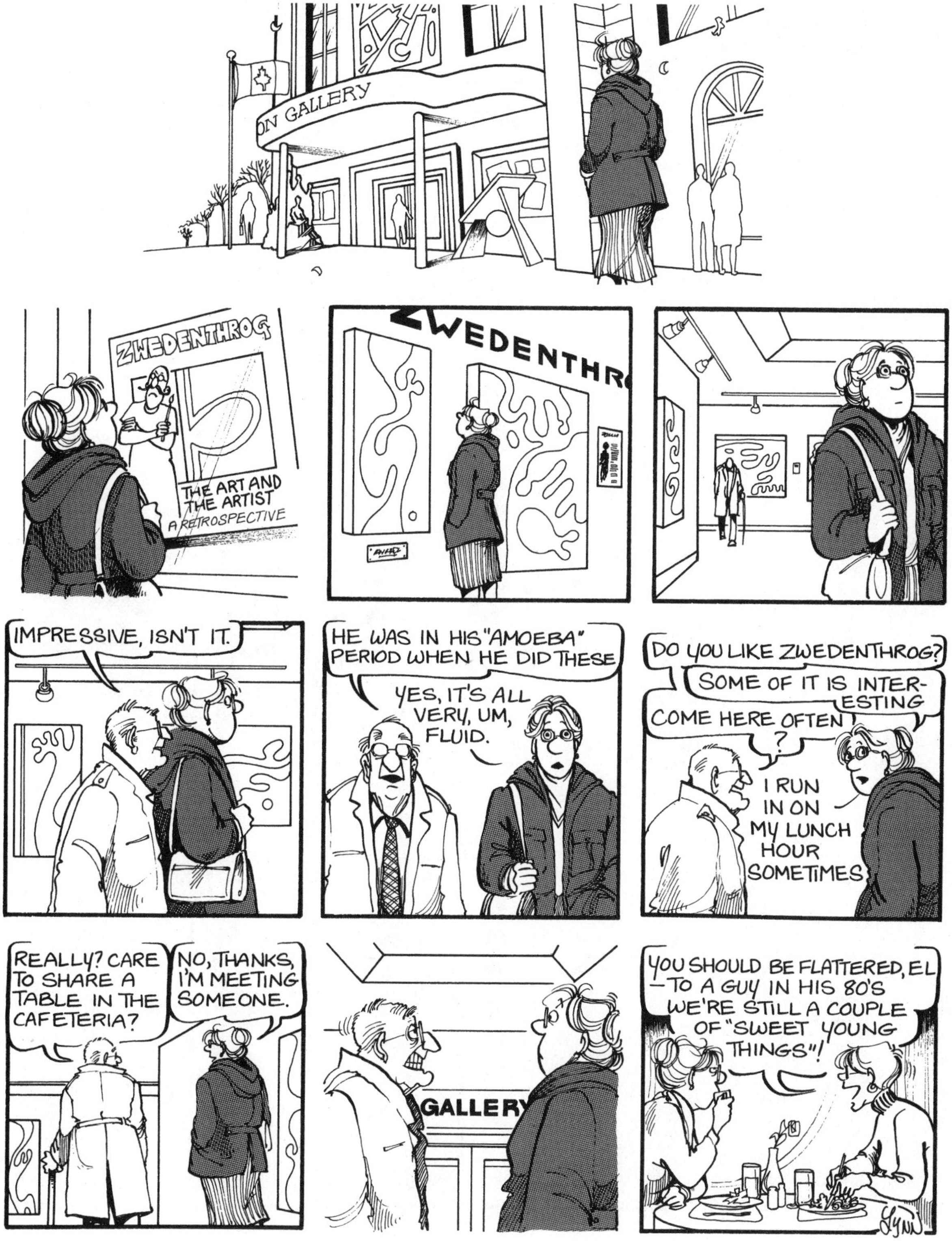

ON GALLERY
ZWEDENTHROG
THE ART AND THE ARTIST
A RETROSPECTIVE
IMPRESSIVE, ISN'T IT.
HE WAS IN HIS "AMOEBA" PERIOD WHEN HE DID THESE
YES, IT'S ALL VERY, UM, FLUID.
DO YOU LIKE ZWEDENTHROG?
SOME OF IT IS INTERESTING
COME HERE OFTEN?
I RUN IN ON MY LUNCH HOUR SOMETIMES
REALLY? CARE TO SHARE A TABLE IN THE CAFETERIA?
NO, THANKS, I'M MEETING SOMEONE.
GALLERY
YOU SHOULD BE FLATTERED, EL — TO A GUY IN HIS 80'S WE'RE STILL A COUPLE OF "SWEET YOUNG THINGS"!

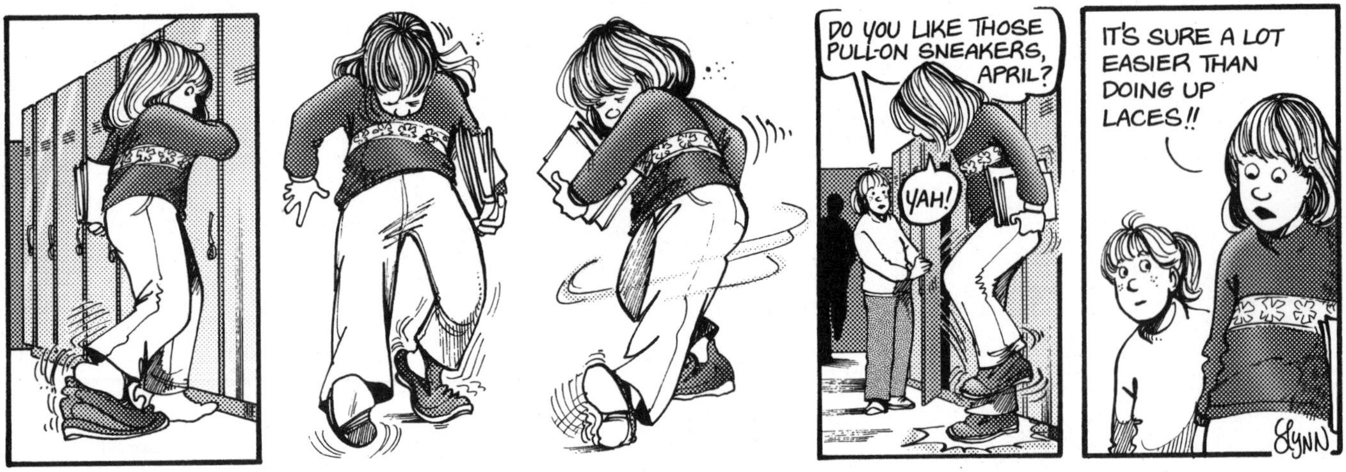
DO YOU LIKE THOSE PULL-ON SNEAKERS, APRIL?
YAH!
IT'S SURE A LOT EASIER THAN DOING UP LACES!!
LYNN

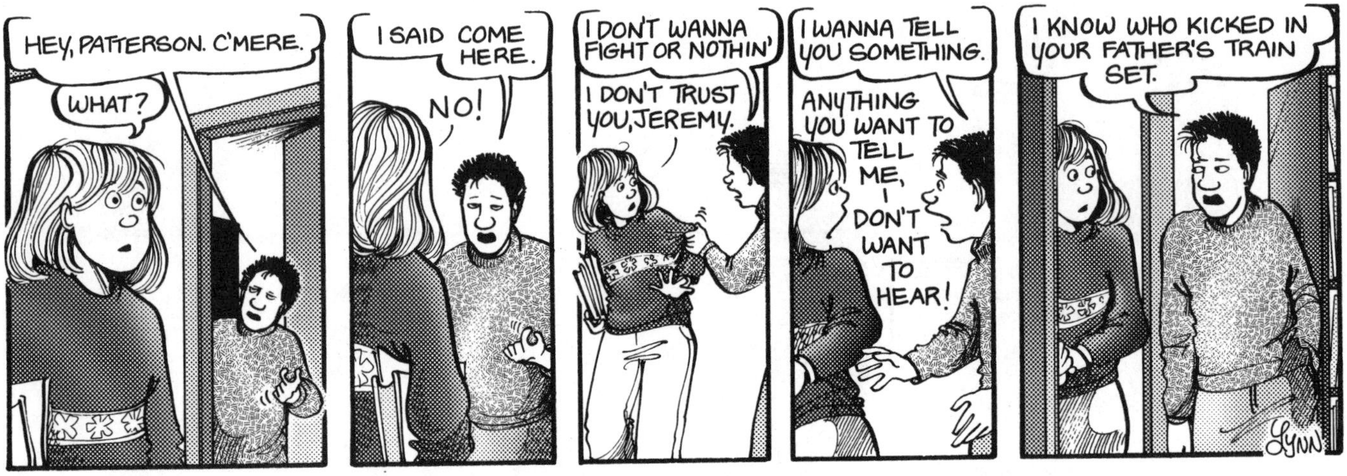
HEY, PATTERSON. C'MERE.
WHAT?
I SAID COME HERE.
NO!
I DON'T WANNA FIGHT OR NOTHIN'
I DON'T TRUST YOU, JEREMY.
I WANNA TELL YOU SOMETHING.
ANYTHING YOU WANT TO TELL ME, I DON'T WANT TO HEAR!
I KNOW WHO KICKED IN YOUR FATHER'S TRAIN SET.
LYNN

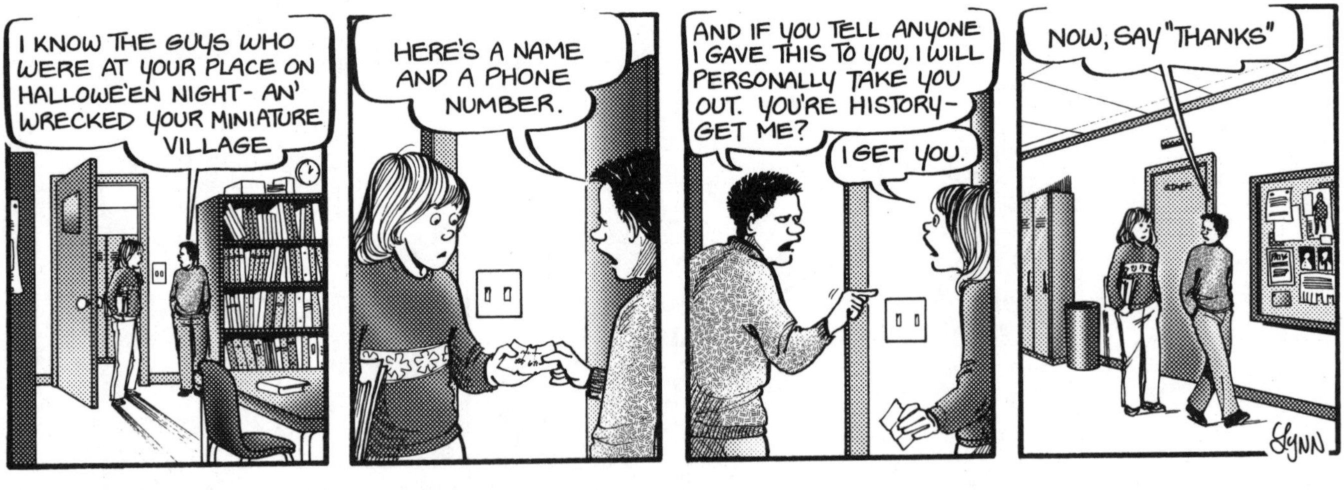
I KNOW THE GUYS WHO WERE AT YOUR PLACE ON HALLOWE'EN NIGHT- AN' WRECKED YOUR MINIATURE VILLAGE
HERE'S A NAME AND A PHONE NUMBER.
AND IF YOU TELL ANYONE I GAVE THIS TO YOU, I WILL PERSONALLY TAKE YOU OUT. YOU'RE HISTORY- GET ME?
I GET YOU.
NOW, SAY "THANKS"
LYNN

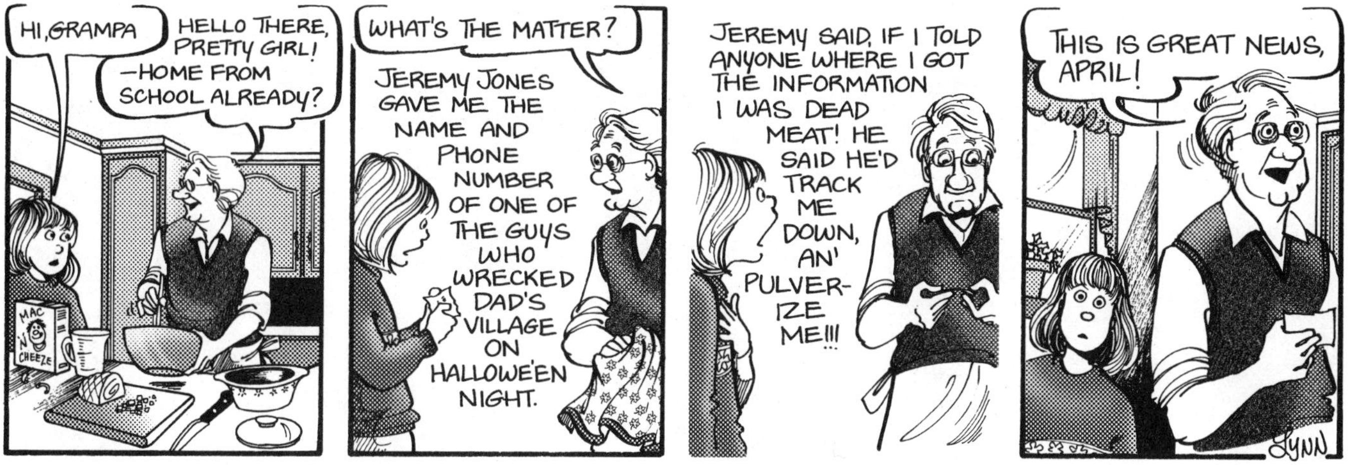
HI, GRAMPA
HELLO THERE, PRETTY GIRL! —HOME FROM SCHOOL ALREADY?
MAC 'N' CHEEZE
WHAT'S THE MATTER?
JEREMY JONES GAVE ME THE NAME AND PHONE NUMBER OF ONE OF THE GUYS WHO WRECKED DAD'S VILLAGE ON HALLOWE'EN NIGHT.
JEREMY SAID, IF I TOLD ANYONE WHERE I GOT THE INFORMATION I WAS DEAD MEAT! HE SAID HE'D TRACK ME DOWN, AN' PULVERIZE ME!!!
THIS IS GREAT NEWS, APRIL!
LYNN

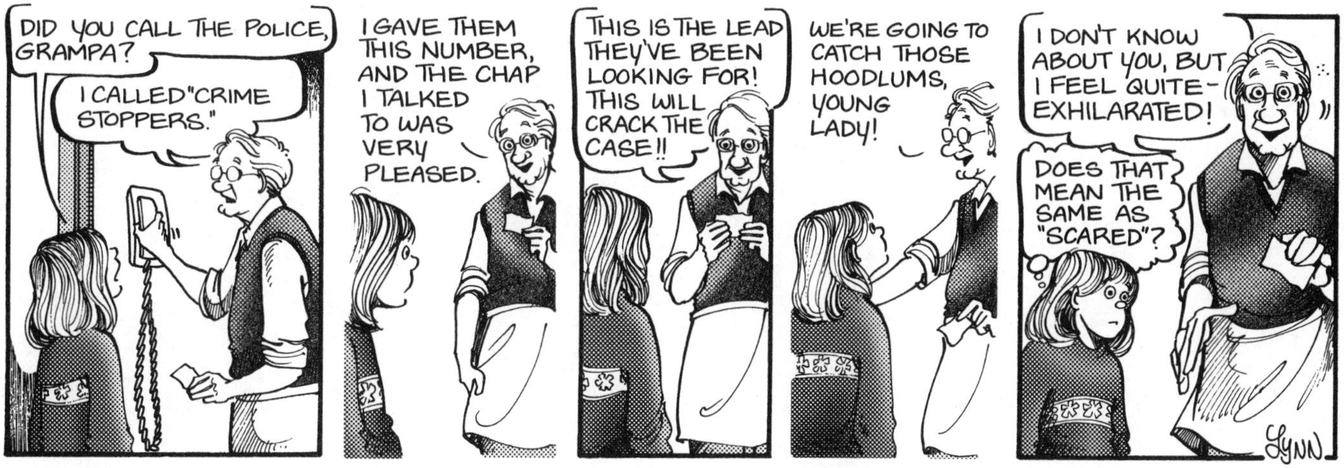
DID YOU CALL THE POLICE, GRAMPA?
I CALLED "CRIME STOPPERS."
I GAVE THEM THIS NUMBER, AND THE CHAP I TALKED TO WAS VERY PLEASED.
THIS IS THE LEAD THEY'VE BEEN LOOKING FOR! THIS WILL CRACK THE CASE!!
WE'RE GOING TO CATCH THOSE HOODLUMS, YOUNG LADY!
I DON'T KNOW ABOUT YOU, BUT I FEEL QUITE-EXHILARATED!
DOES THAT MEAN THE SAME AS "SCARED"?
LYNN

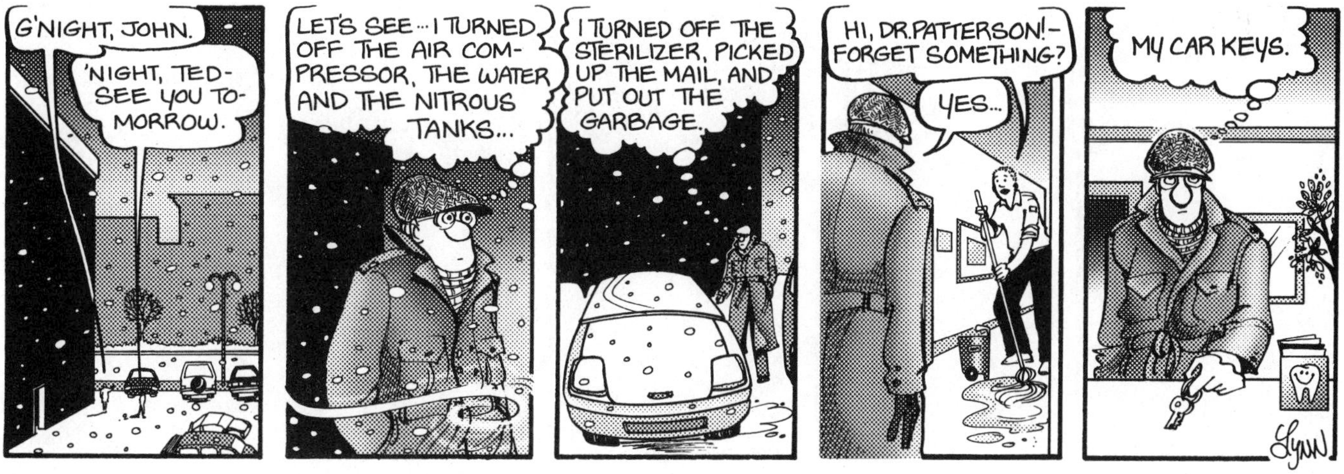
G'NIGHT, JOHN.
'NIGHT, TED- SEE YOU TOMORROW.
LET'S SEE... I TURNED OFF THE AIR COMPRESSOR, THE WATER AND THE NITROUS TANKS...
I TURNED OFF THE STERILIZER, PICKED UP THE MAIL, AND PUT OUT THE GARBAGE.
HI, DR. PATTERSON! —FORGET SOMETHING?
YES...
MY CAR KEYS.
LYNN

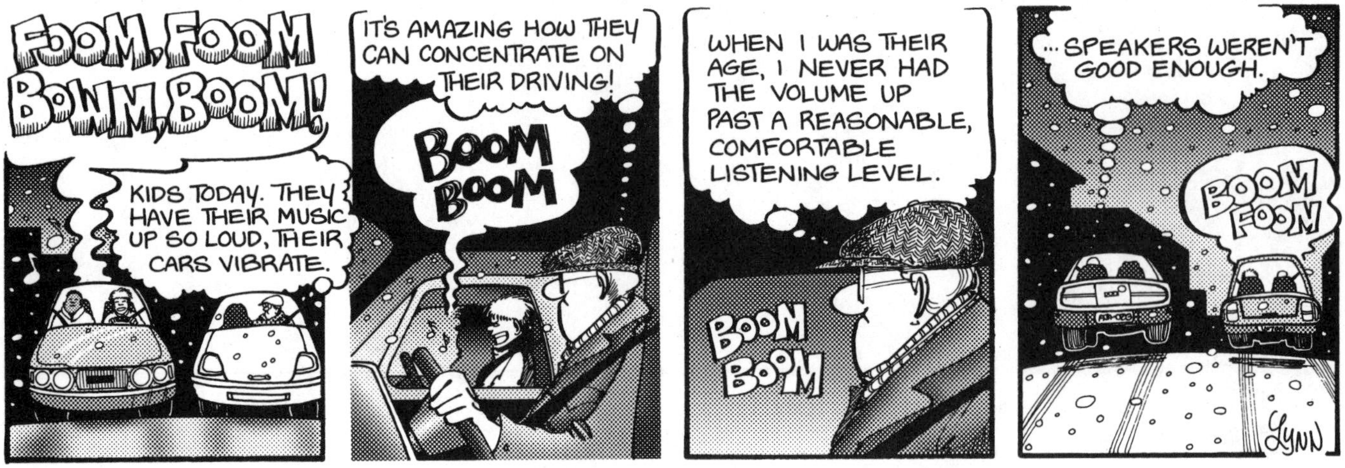
FOOM, FOOM BOWM, BOOM!
KIDS TODAY. THEY HAVE THEIR MUSIC UP SO LOUD, THEIR CARS VIBRATE.
IT'S AMAZING HOW THEY CAN CONCENTRATE ON THEIR DRIVING!
BOOM BOOM
WHEN I WAS THEIR AGE, I NEVER HAD THE VOLUME UP PAST A REASONABLE, COMFORTABLE LISTENING LEVEL.
BOOM BOOM
...SPEAKERS WEREN'T GOOD ENOUGH.
BOOM FOON
LYNN

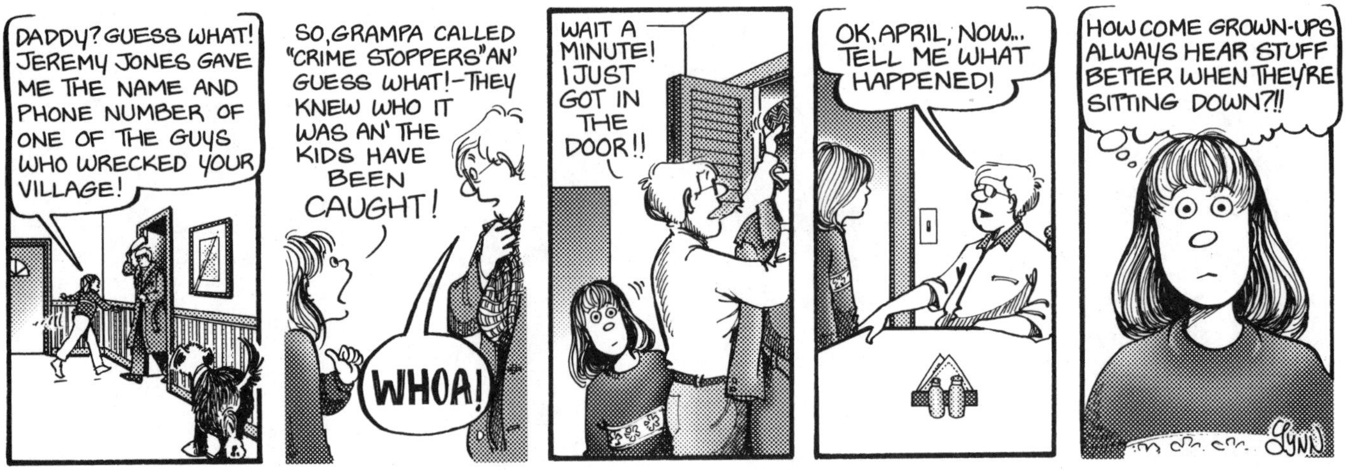
DADDY? GUESS WHAT! JEREMY JONES GAVE ME THE NAME AND PHONE NUMBER OF ONE OF THE GUYS WHO WRECKED YOUR VILLAGE!
SO, GRAMPA CALLED "CRIME STOPPERS" AN' GUESS WHAT! —THEY KNEW WHO IT WAS AN' THE KIDS HAVE BEEN CAUGHT!
WHOA!
WAIT A MINUTE! I JUST GOT IN THE DOOR!!
OK, APRIL, NOW... TELL ME WHAT HAPPENED!
HOW COME GROWN-UPS ALWAYS HEAR STUFF BETTER WHEN THEY'RE SITTING DOWN?!!
LYNN

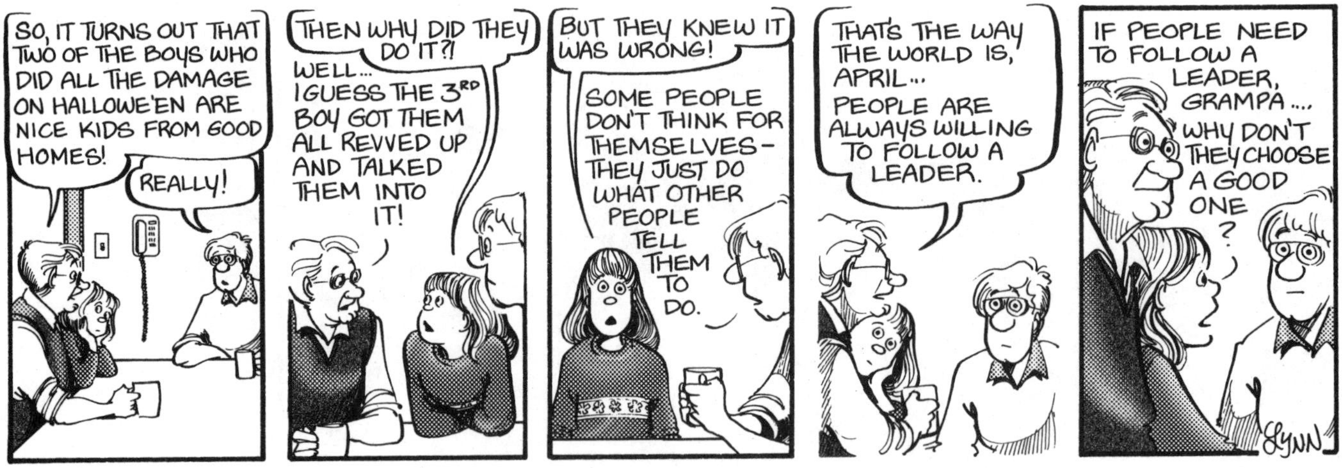
SO, IT TURNS OUT THAT TWO OF THE BOYS WHO DID ALL THE DAMAGE ON HALLOWE'EN ARE NICE KIDS FROM GOOD HOMES!
REALLY!
THEN WHY DID THEY DO IT?!
WELL... I GUESS THE 3RD BOY GOT THEM ALL REVVED UP AND TALKED THEM INTO IT!
BUT THEY KNEW IT WAS WRONG!
SOME PEOPLE DON'T THINK FOR THEMSELVES - THEY JUST DO WHAT OTHER PEOPLE TELL THEM TO DO.
THAT'S THE WAY THE WORLD IS, APRIL... PEOPLE ARE ALWAYS WILLING TO FOLLOW A LEADER.
IF PEOPLE NEED TO FOLLOW A LEADER, GRAMPA.... WHY DON'T THEY CHOOSE A GOOD ONE?
LYNN

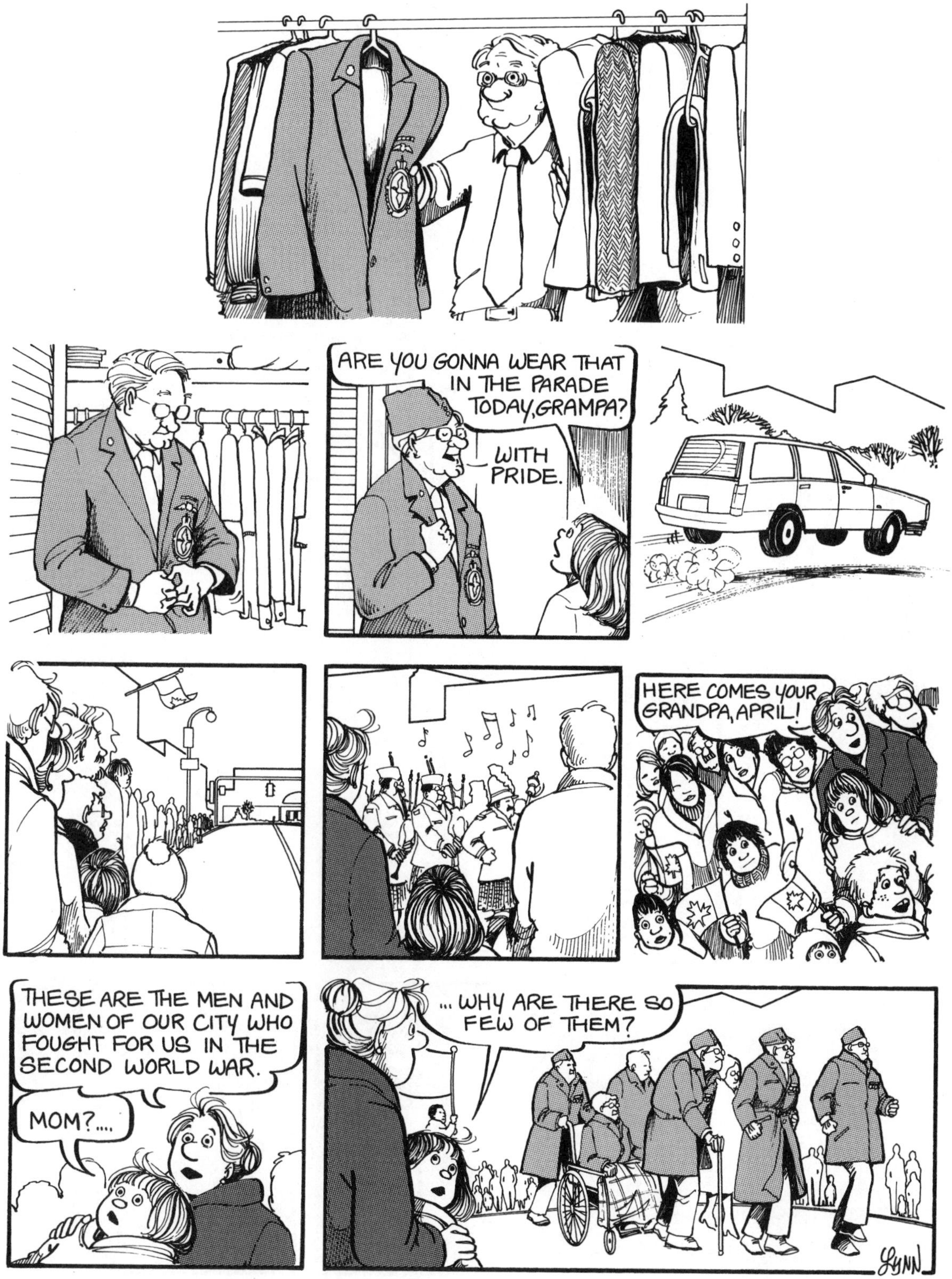
ARE YOU GONNA WEAR THAT IN THE PARADE TODAY, GRAMPA?
WITH PRIDE.
HERE COMES YOUR GRANDPA, APRIL!
THESE ARE THE MEN AND WOMEN OF OUR CITY WHO FOUGHT FOR US IN THE SECOND WORLD WAR.
MOM?....
... WHY ARE THERE SO FEW OF THEM?
LYNN

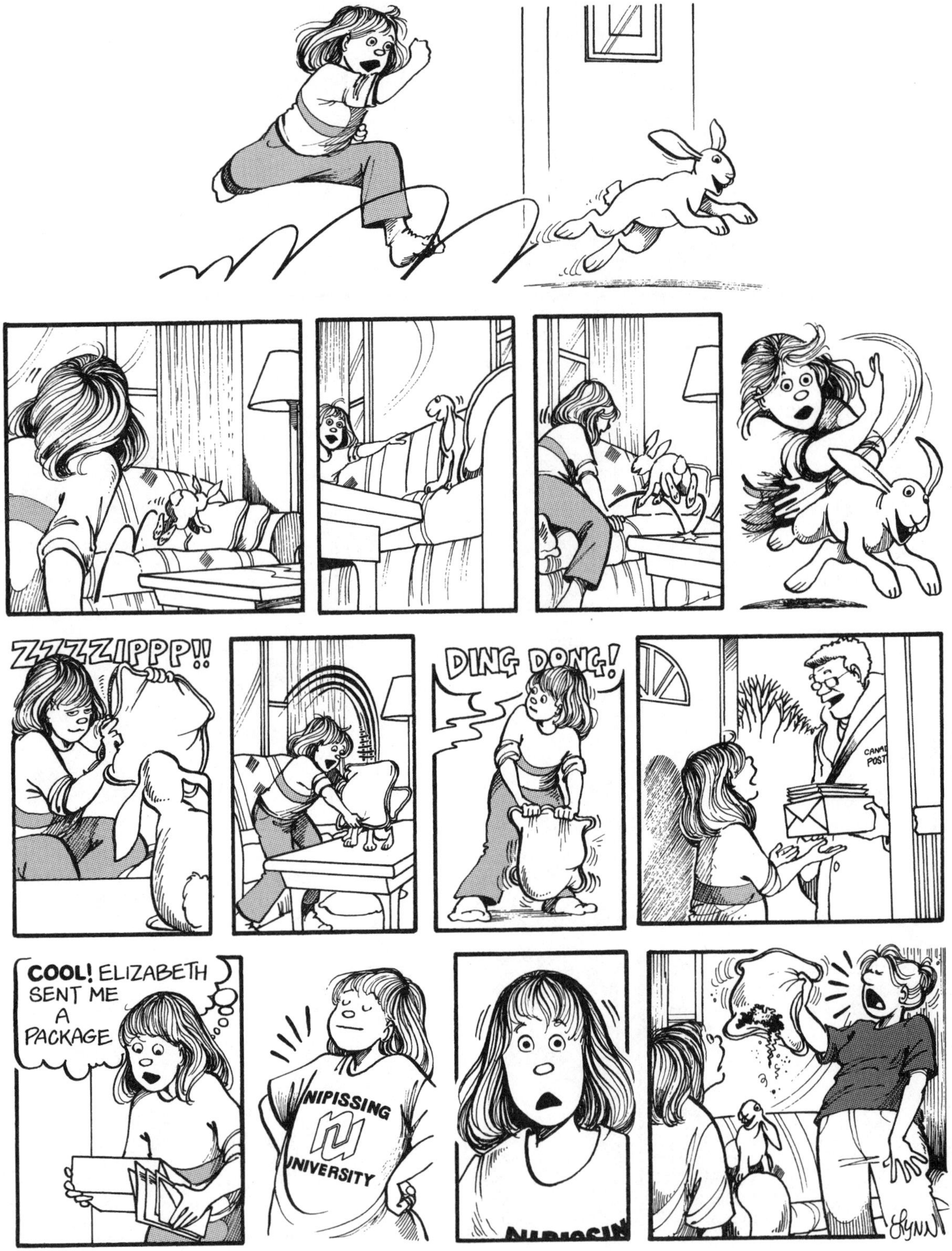
ZZZZIPPP!!
DING DONG!
CANADA POST
COOL! ELIZABETH SENT ME A PACKAGE
NIPISSING UNIVERSITY
NIPISSIN
LYNN

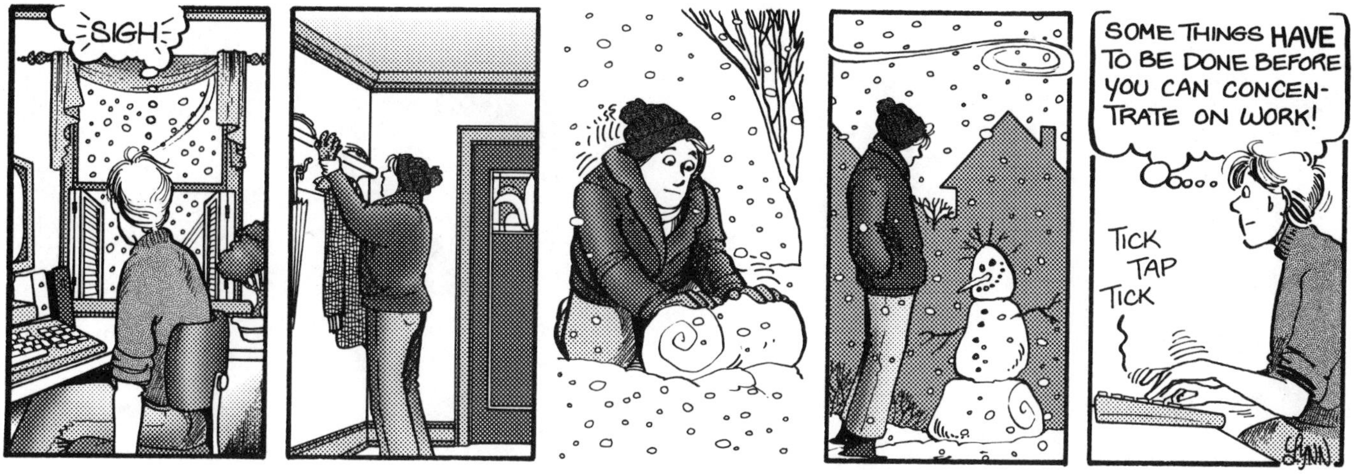
SIGH
SOME THINGS HAVE TO BE DONE BEFORE YOU CAN CONCENTRATE ON WORK!
TICK TAP TICK
LYNN

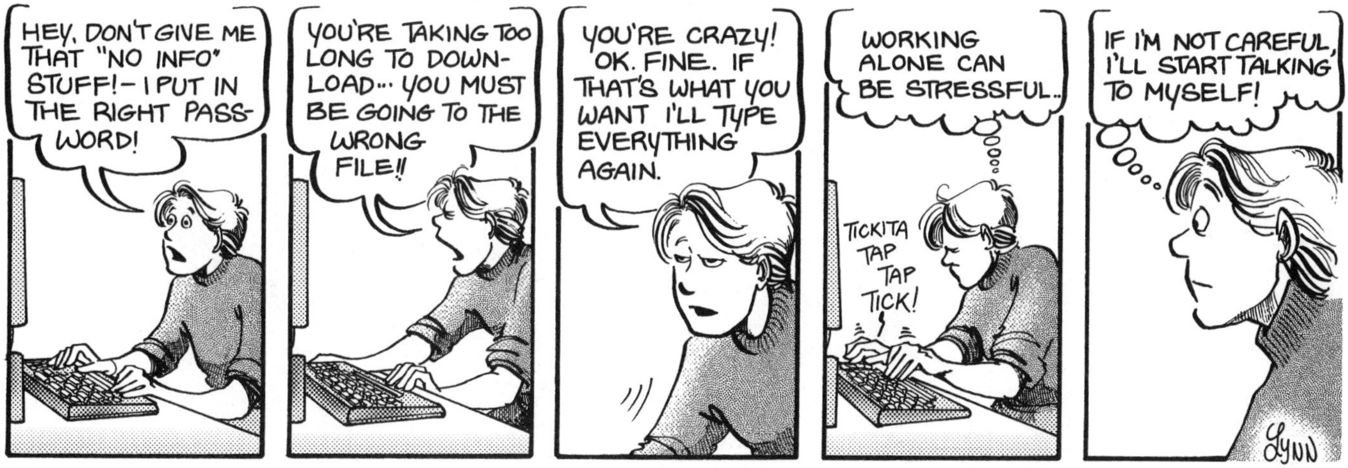
HEY, DON'T GIVE ME THAT "NO INFO" STUFF!– I PUT IN THE RIGHT PASSWORD!
YOU'RE TAKING TOO LONG TO DOWNLOAD... YOU MUST BE GOING TO THE WRONG FILE!!
YOU'RE CRAZY! OK. FINE. IF THAT'S WHAT YOU WANT I'LL TYPE EVERYTHING AGAIN.
WORKING ALONE CAN BE STRESSFUL..
TICKITA TAP TAP TICK!
IF I'M NOT CAREFUL, I'LL START TALKING TO MYSELF!
LYNN

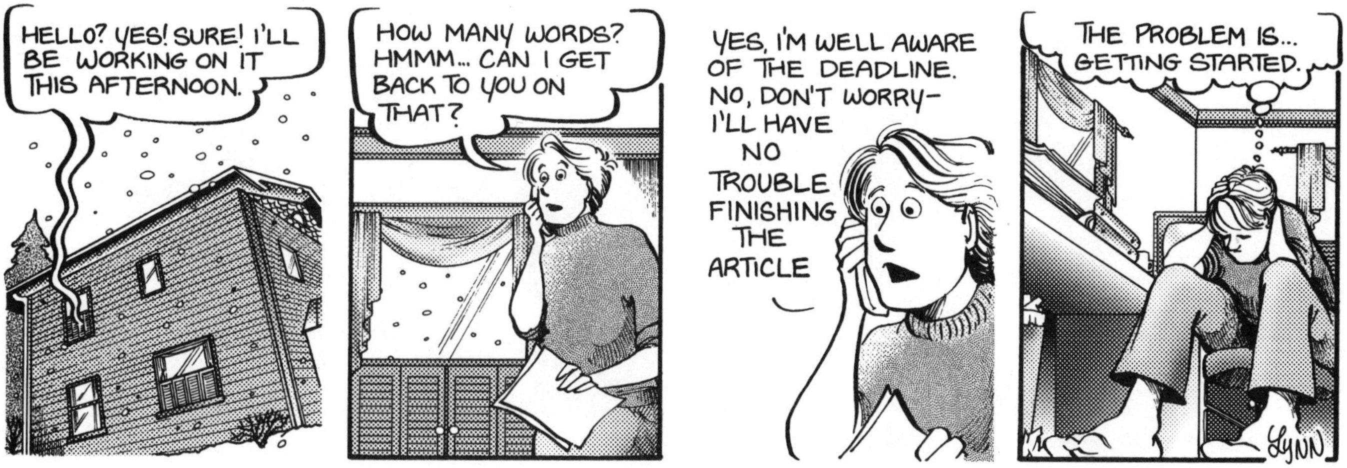
HELLO? YES! SURE! I'LL BE WORKING ON IT THIS AFTERNOON.
HOW MANY WORDS? HMMM... CAN I GET BACK TO YOU ON THAT?
YES, I'M WELL AWARE OF THE DEADLINE. NO, DON'T WORRY– I'LL HAVE NO TROUBLE FINISHING THE ARTICLE
THE PROBLEM IS... GETTING STARTED.
LYNN

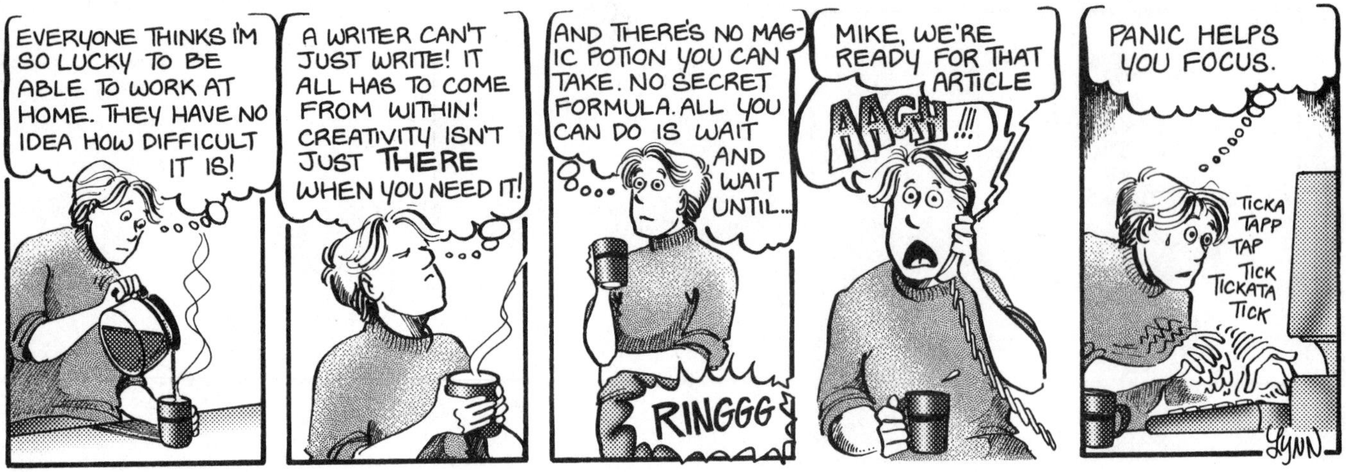
EVERYONE THINKS I'M SO LUCKY TO BE ABLE TO WORK AT HOME. THEY HAVE NO IDEA HOW DIFFICULT IT IS!
A WRITER CAN'T JUST WRITE! IT ALL HAS TO COME FROM WITHIN! CREATIVITY ISN'T JUST THERE WHEN YOU NEED IT!
AND THERE'S NO MAGIC POTION YOU CAN TAKE. NO SECRET FORMULA. ALL YOU CAN DO IS WAIT AND WAIT UNTIL...
RINGGG
MIKE, WE'RE READY FOR THAT ARTICLE
AAGH!!!
PANIC HELPS YOU FOCUS.
TICKA TAPP TAP TICK TICKATA TICK
LYNN

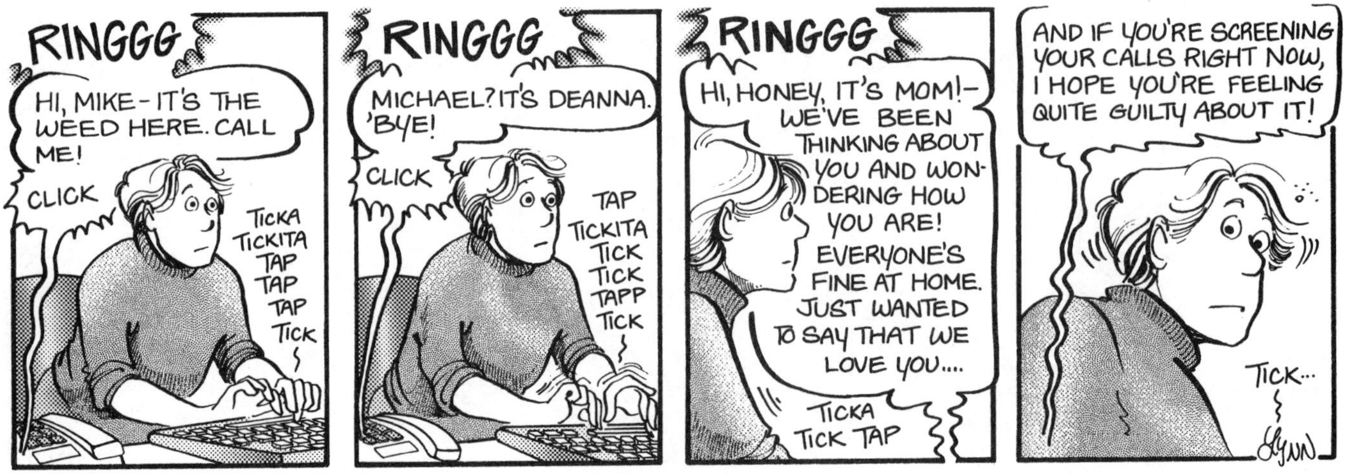
RINGGG
HI, MIKE - IT'S THE WEED HERE. CALL ME!
CLICK
TICKA TICKITA TAP TAP TAP TICK
RINGGG
MICHAEL? IT'S DEANNA. 'BYE!
CLICK
TAP TICKITA TICK TICK TAPP TICK
RINGGG
HI, HONEY, IT'S MOM! - WE'VE BEEN THINKING ABOUT YOU AND WONDERING HOW YOU ARE! EVERYONE'S FINE AT HOME. JUST WANTED TO SAY THAT WE LOVE YOU....
TICKA TICK TAP
AND IF YOU'RE SCREENING YOUR CALLS RIGHT NOW, I HOPE YOU'RE FEELING QUITE GUILTY ABOUT IT!
TICK...
LYNN

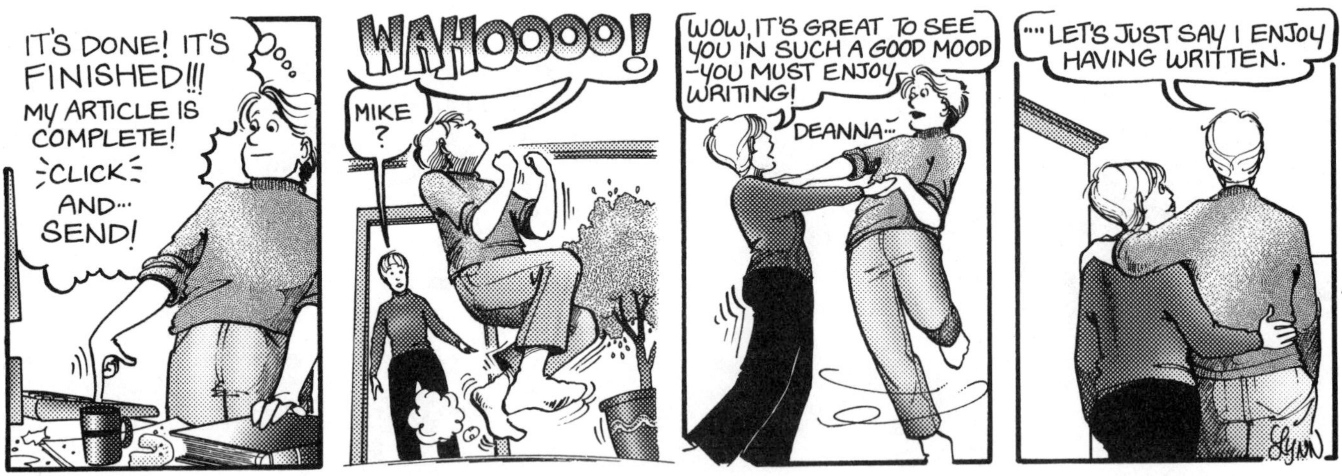
IT'S DONE! IT'S FINISHED!!! MY ARTICLE IS COMPLETE!
CLICK
AND... SEND!
WAHOOOOO!
MIKE ?
WOW, IT'S GREAT TO SEE YOU IN SUCH A GOOD MOOD -YOU MUST ENJOY WRITING!
DEANNA...
...LET'S JUST SAY I ENJOY HAVING WRITTEN.
LYNN

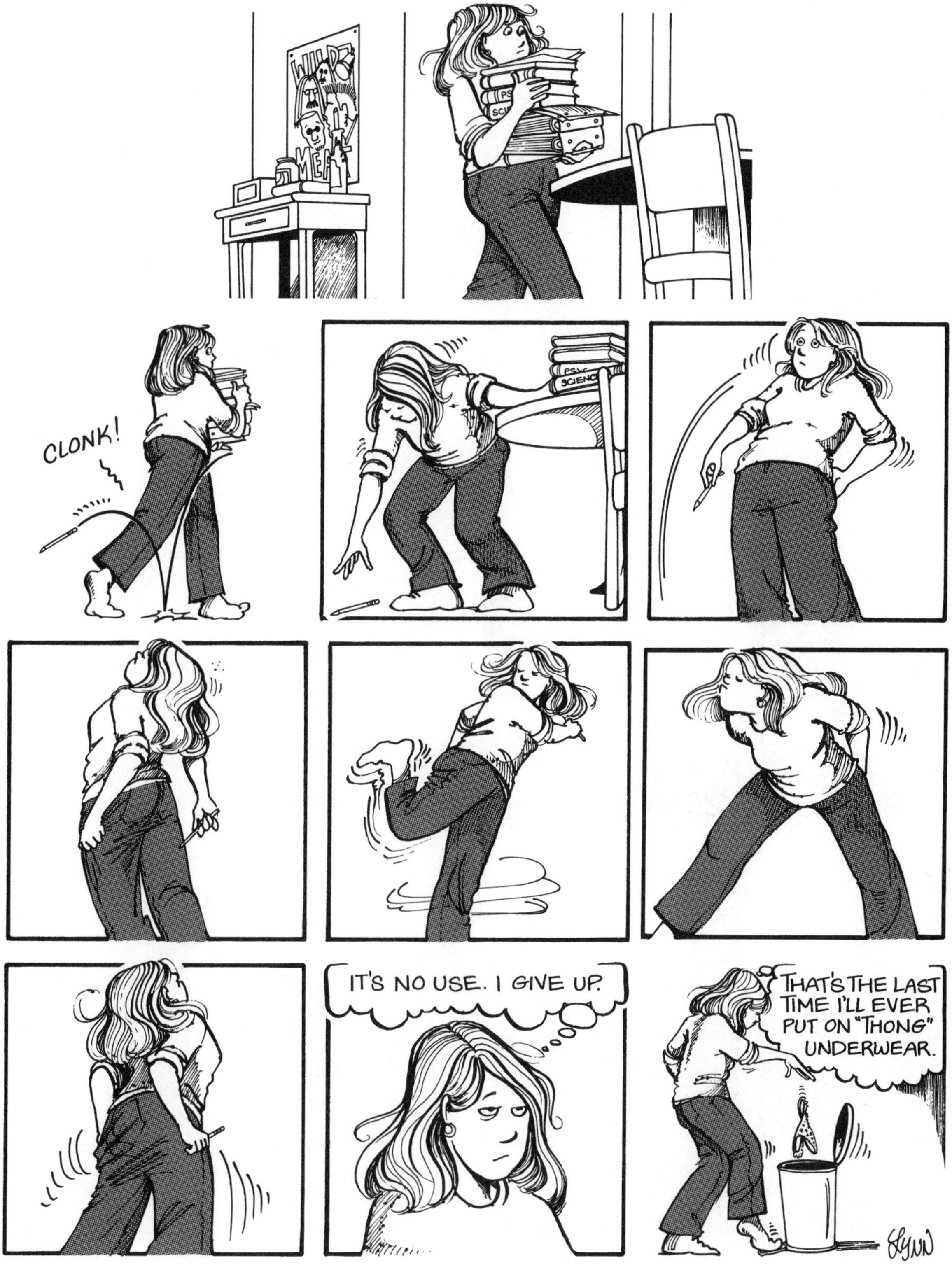
CLONK!
IT'S NO USE. I GIVE UP.
THAT'S THE LAST TIME I'LL EVER PUT ON "THONG" UNDERWEAR.
LYNN

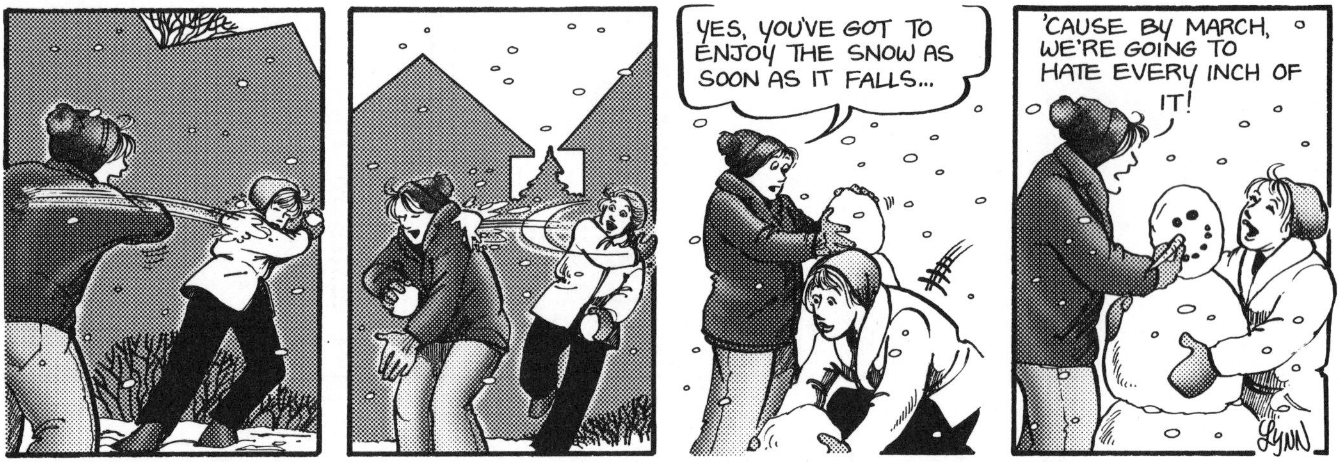
YES, YOU'VE GOT TO ENJOY THE SNOW AS SOON AS IT FALLS...
'CAUSE BY MARCH, WE'RE GOING TO HATE EVERY INCH OF IT!
LYNN

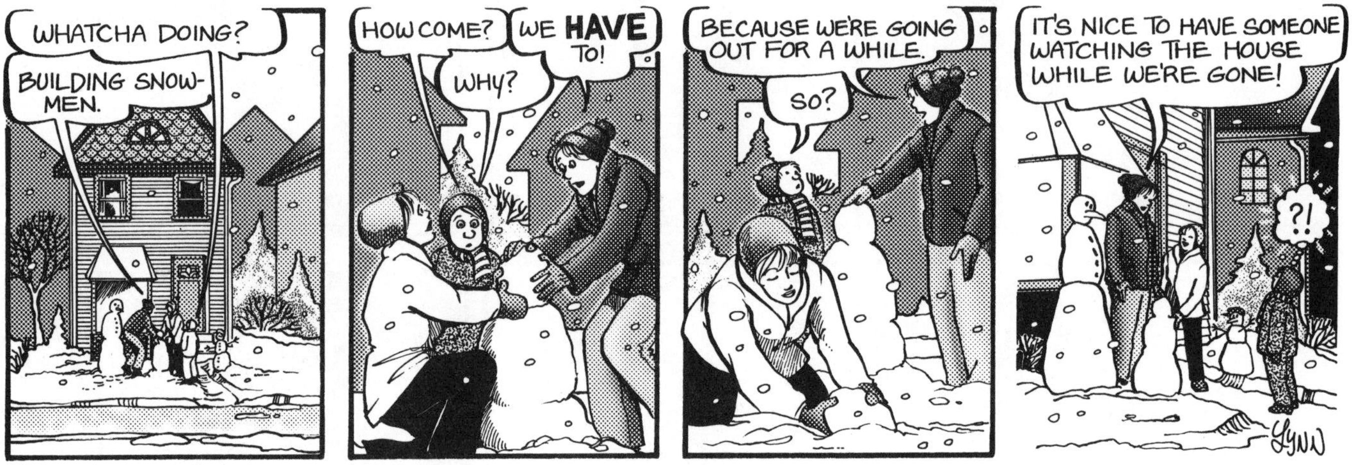
WHATCHA DOING?
BUILDING SNOW-MEN.
HOW COME?
WHY?
WE **HAVE** TO!
BECAUSE WE'RE GOING OUT FOR A WHILE.
SO?
IT'S NICE TO HAVE SOMEONE WATCHING THE HOUSE WHILE WE'RE GONE!
?!
LYNN

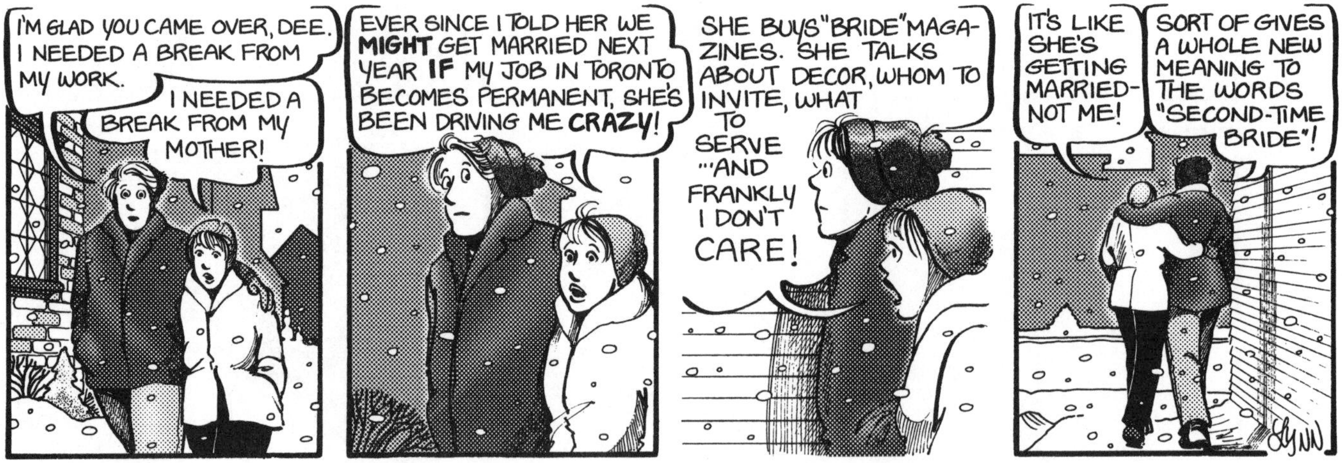
I'M GLAD YOU CAME OVER, DEE. I NEEDED A BREAK FROM MY WORK.
I NEEDED A BREAK FROM MY MOTHER!
EVER SINCE I TOLD HER WE **MIGHT** GET MARRIED NEXT YEAR **IF** MY JOB IN TORONTO BECOMES PERMANENT, SHE'S BEEN DRIVING ME **CRAZY**!
SHE BUYS "BRIDE" MAGA-ZINES. SHE TALKS ABOUT DECOR, WHOM TO INVITE, WHAT TO SERVE ...AND FRANKLY I DON'T CARE!
IT'S LIKE SHE'S GETTING MARRIED- NOT ME!
SORT OF GIVES A WHOLE NEW MEANING TO THE WORDS "SECOND-TIME BRIDE"!
LYNN

Panel 1: MY MOTHER WANTS A DESIGNER TO MAKE MY WEDDING DRESS—BUT I DON'T WANT ANYTHING FANCY.

Panel 2: SHE WANTS ROSES AND LACE AND A HARPIST. SHE WANTS A SIT-DOWN DINNER—SHE'S GOING TO TURN A SIMPLE CEREMONY INTO AN EXTRAVAGANT BALL.

Panel 3: MY SISTER WARNED ME THIS WOULD HAPPEN. SHE TOLD ME NOT TO TELL MOM ANYTHING UNTIL WE HAD OUR PLANS ALREADY LAID OUT!

Panel 4: THEN WHY DID YOU TELL HER?

WE WERE WASHING THE DISHES AND IT LEAKED OUT

Panel 5: WOW. YOUR MOM WANTS YOU TO WEAR A REAL ONE-OF-A-KIND DESIGNER GOWN!

I'D PREFER SOMETHING OFF THE RACK.

Panel 6: I WANT A DRESS I CAN WEAR AGAIN. I'D EVEN GO SECOND-HAND!—WHAT'S WRONG WITH WEARING A SECOND-HAND WEDDING DRESS?

HMM...

Panel 7: SOME PEOPLE SAY IT'S BAD LUCK!

Panel 8: I'D THINK ONE SHOULD BE MORE CONCERNED ABOUT BAD LUCK IN ONE'S CHOICE OF HUSBANDS, THAN IN ONE'S CHOICE OF DRESS!

Panel 9: MY SISTER AND HER HUSBAND WENT DOWN TO THE COURTHOUSE AND GOT MARRIED ON A HOLIDAY WEEKEND. IT WAS A SURPRISE TO EVERYONE.

Panel 10: MOM THREW A PARTY FOR THEM LATER... BUT IT WASN'T THE SAME.

Panel 11: MAYBE YOUR MOM WANTS YOU TO HAVE SOMETHING SHE NEVER HAD.

YES, WHEN SHE AND DAD WERE MARRIED, THEY HAD NOTHING.

Panel 12: SO, NOW SHE GETS TO PLAN AND BUY AND DECORATE AND ORGANIZE TO HER HEART'S CONTENT!

BUT MICHAEL—WE'RE TALKING ABOUT **OUR** WEDDING!!

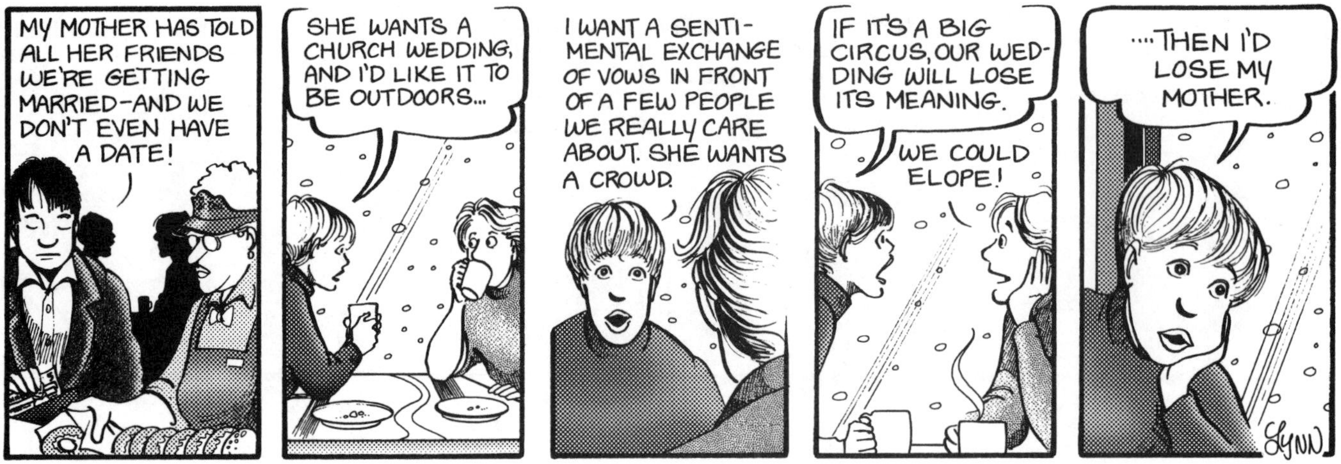
MY MOTHER HAS TOLD ALL HER FRIENDS WE'RE GETTING MARRIED-AND WE DON'T EVEN HAVE A DATE!
SHE WANTS A CHURCH WEDDING, AND I'D LIKE IT TO BE OUTDOORS...
I WANT A SENTIMENTAL EXCHANGE OF VOWS IN FRONT OF A FEW PEOPLE WE REALLY CARE ABOUT. SHE WANTS A CROWD.
IF IT'S A BIG CIRCUS, OUR WEDDING WILL LOSE ITS MEANING.
WE COULD ELOPE!
....THEN I'D LOSE MY MOTHER.
LYNN

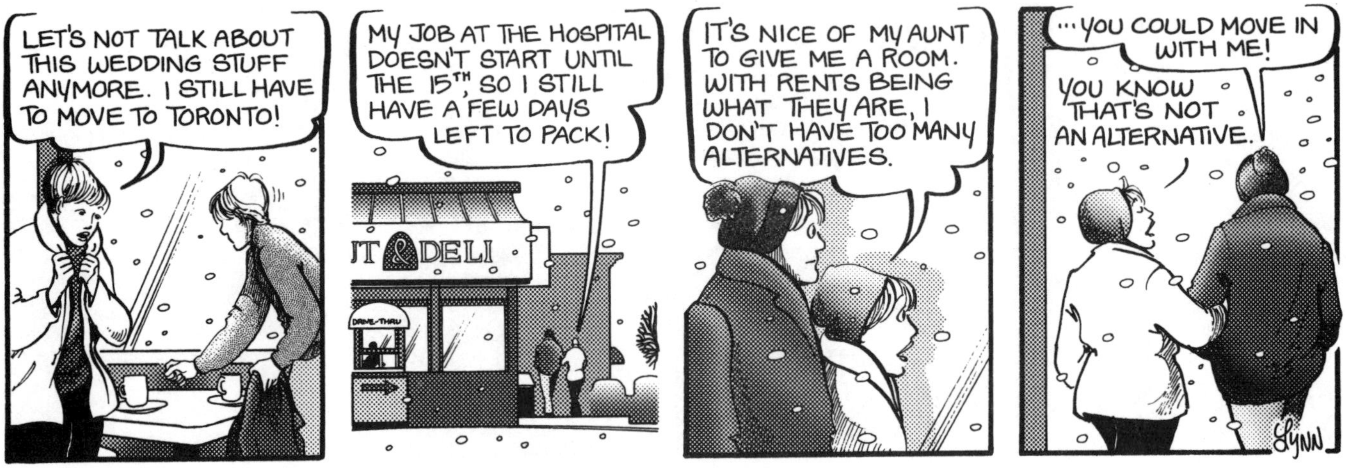
LET'S NOT TALK ABOUT THIS WEDDING STUFF ANYMORE. I STILL HAVE TO MOVE TO TORONTO!
MY JOB AT THE HOSPITAL DOESN'T START UNTIL THE 15TH, SO I STILL HAVE A FEW DAYS LEFT TO PACK!
DELI
IT'S NICE OF MY AUNT TO GIVE ME A ROOM. WITH RENTS BEING WHAT THEY ARE, I DON'T HAVE TOO MANY ALTERNATIVES.
...YOU COULD MOVE IN WITH ME!
YOU KNOW THAT'S NOT AN ALTERNATIVE.
LYNN

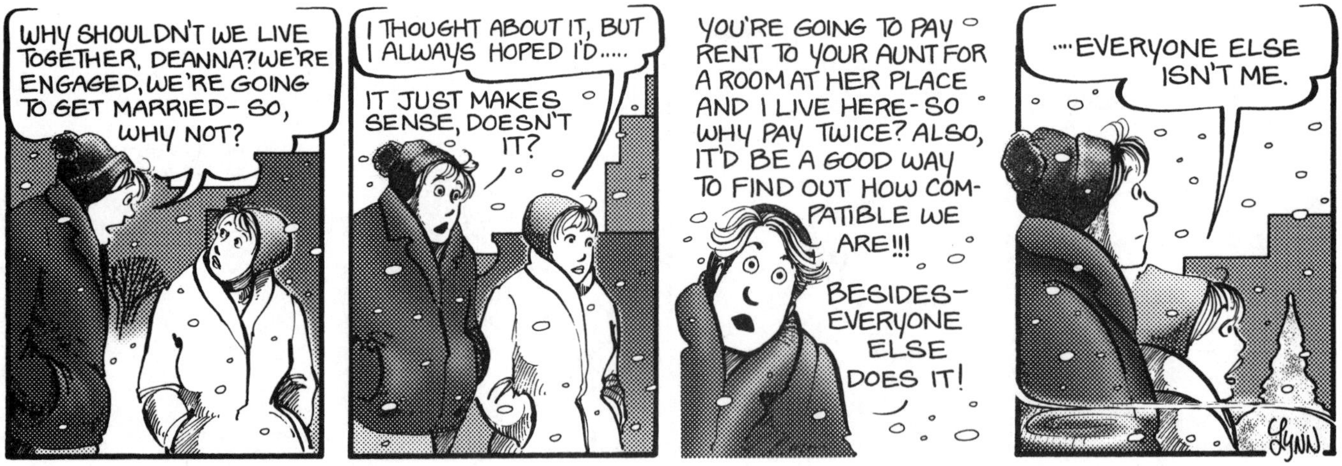
WHY SHOULDN'T WE LIVE TOGETHER, DEANNA? WE'RE ENGAGED, WE'RE GOING TO GET MARRIED- SO, WHY NOT?
I THOUGHT ABOUT IT, BUT I ALWAYS HOPED I'D.....
IT JUST MAKES SENSE, DOESN'T IT?
YOU'RE GOING TO PAY RENT TO YOUR AUNT FOR A ROOM AT HER PLACE AND I LIVE HERE- SO WHY PAY TWICE? ALSO, IT'D BE A GOOD WAY TO FIND OUT HOW COMPATIBLE WE ARE!!!
BESIDES- EVERYONE ELSE DOES IT!
....EVERYONE ELSE ISN'T ME.
LYNN

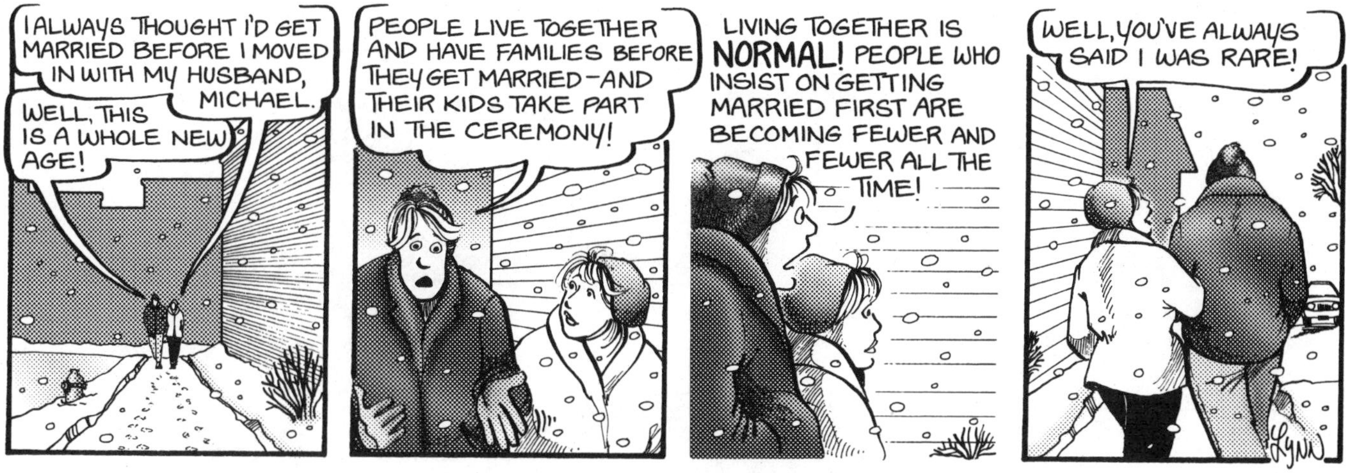
I ALWAYS THOUGHT I'D GET MARRIED BEFORE I MOVED IN WITH MY HUSBAND, MICHAEL.
WELL, THIS IS A WHOLE NEW AGE!
PEOPLE LIVE TOGETHER AND HAVE FAMILIES BEFORE THEY GET MARRIED—AND THEIR KIDS TAKE PART IN THE CEREMONY!
LIVING TOGETHER IS NORMAL! PEOPLE WHO INSIST ON GETTING MARRIED FIRST ARE BECOMING FEWER AND FEWER ALL THE TIME!
WELL, YOU'VE ALWAYS SAID I WAS RARE!
LYNN

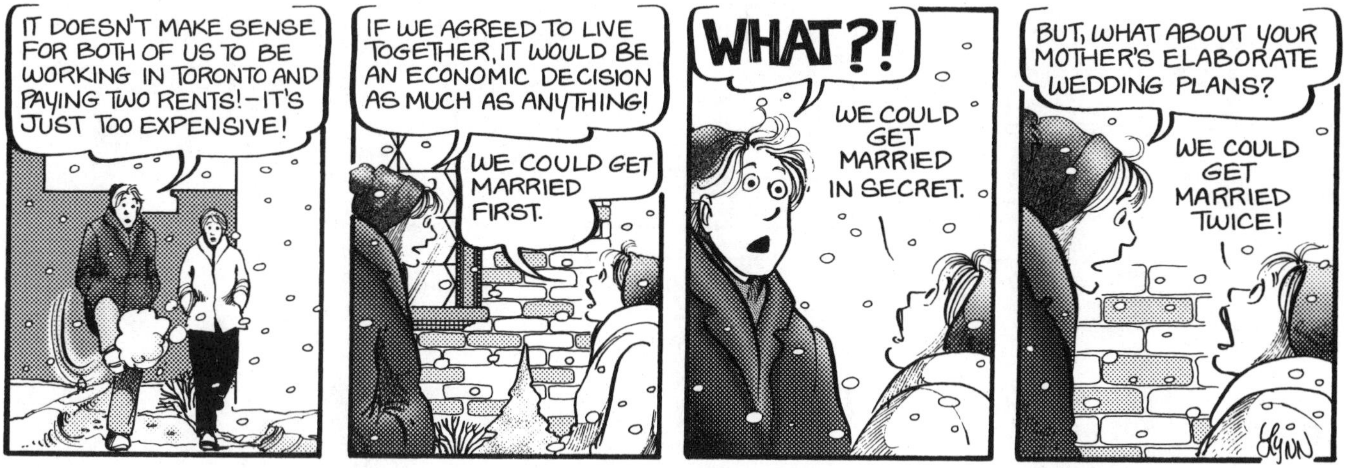
IT DOESN'T MAKE SENSE FOR BOTH OF US TO BE WORKING IN TORONTO AND PAYING TWO RENTS!—IT'S JUST TOO EXPENSIVE!
IF WE AGREED TO LIVE TOGETHER, IT WOULD BE AN ECONOMIC DECISION AS MUCH AS ANYTHING!
WE COULD GET MARRIED FIRST.
WHAT?!
WE COULD GET MARRIED IN SECRET.
BUT, WHAT ABOUT YOUR MOTHER'S ELABORATE WEDDING PLANS?
WE COULD GET MARRIED TWICE!
LYNN

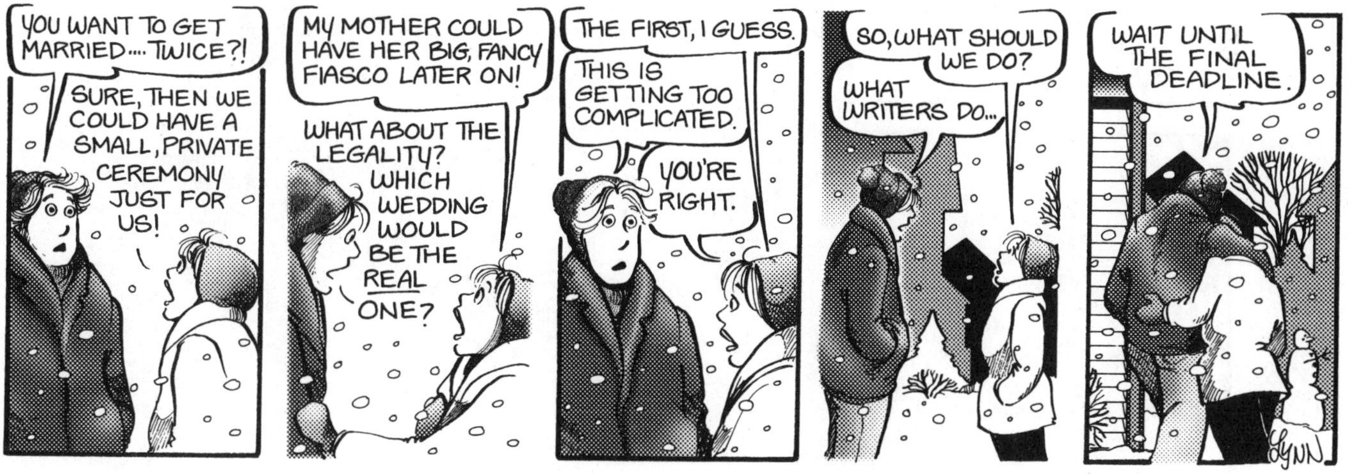
YOU WANT TO GET MARRIED.... TWICE?!
SURE, THEN WE COULD HAVE A SMALL, PRIVATE CEREMONY JUST FOR US!
MY MOTHER COULD HAVE HER BIG, FANCY FIASCO LATER ON!
WHAT ABOUT THE LEGALITY? WHICH WEDDING WOULD BE THE REAL ONE?
THE FIRST, I GUESS.
THIS IS GETTING TOO COMPLICATED.
YOU'RE RIGHT.
SO, WHAT SHOULD WE DO?
WHAT WRITERS DO...
WAIT UNTIL THE FINAL DEADLINE.
LYNN

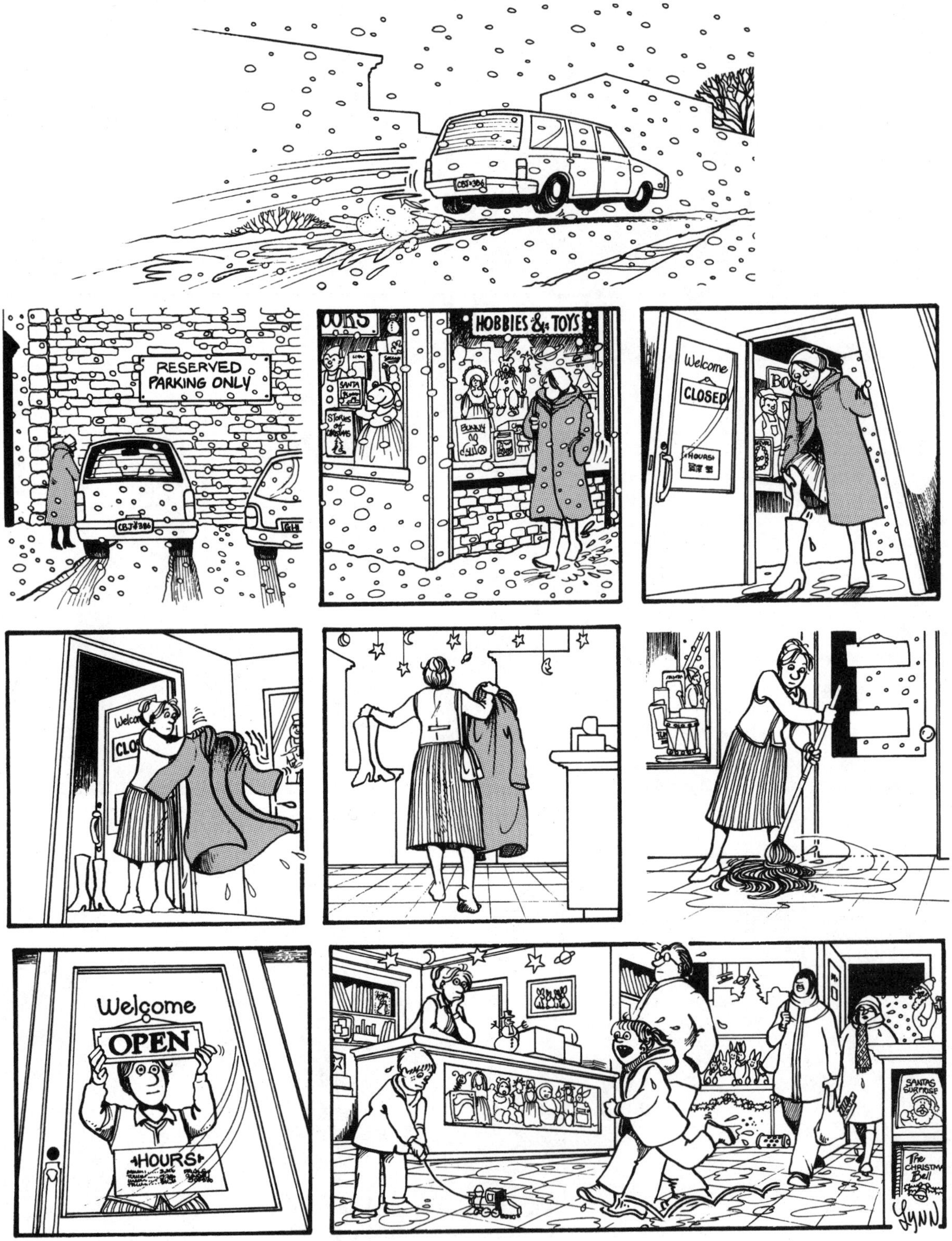
RESERVED
PARKING ONLY
HOBBIES & TOYS
Welcome
CLOSED
HOURS
Welcome
OPEN
HOURS
SANTAS SURPRISE
The CHRISTMAS Bell
LYNN

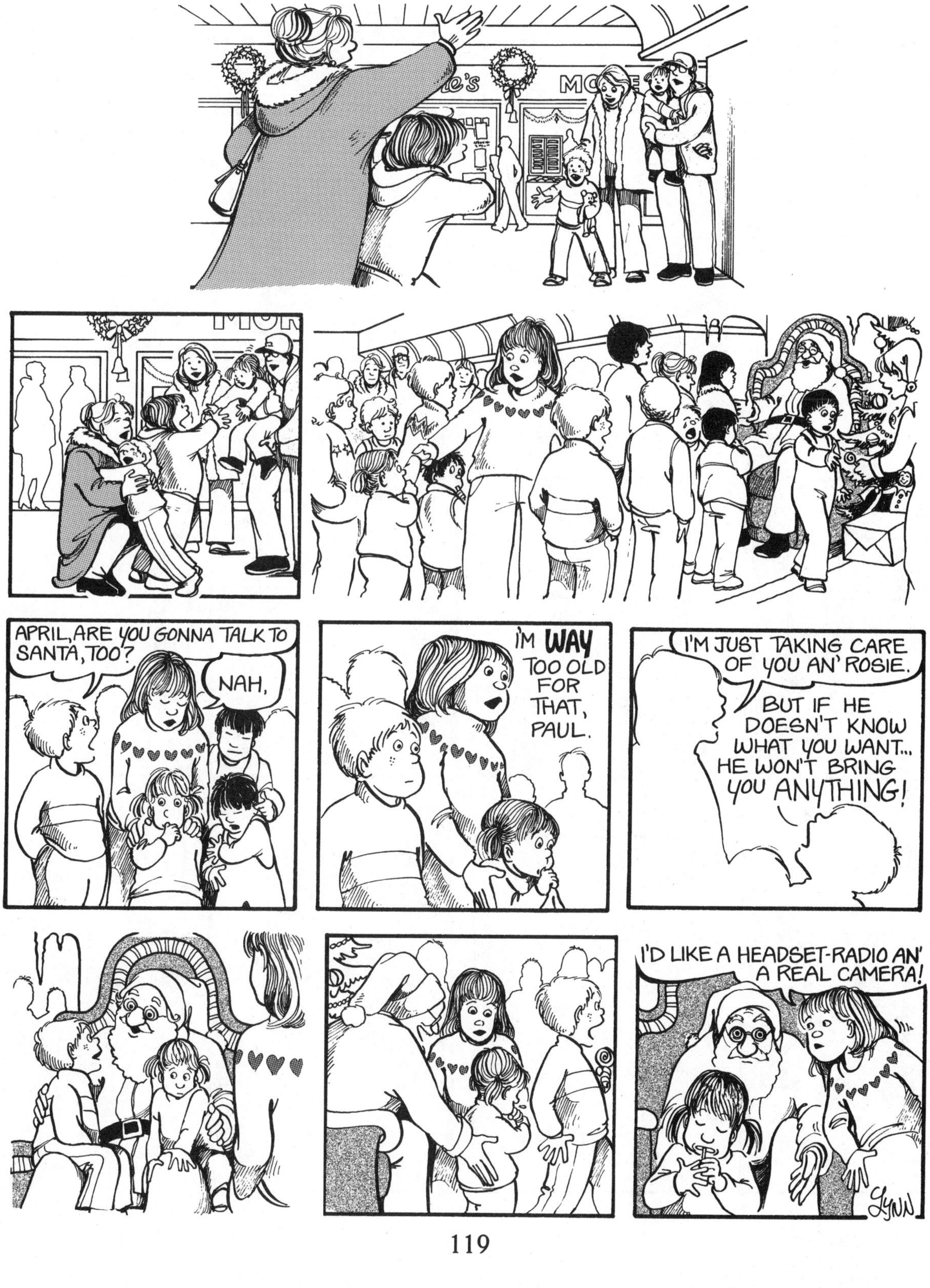
APRIL, ARE YOU GONNA TALK TO SANTA, TOO?
NAH,
I'M WAY TOO OLD FOR THAT, PAUL.
I'M JUST TAKING CARE OF YOU AN' ROSIE.
BUT IF HE DOESN'T KNOW WHAT YOU WANT... HE WON'T BRING YOU ANYTHING!
I'D LIKE A HEADSET-RADIO AN' A REAL CAMERA!
LYNN

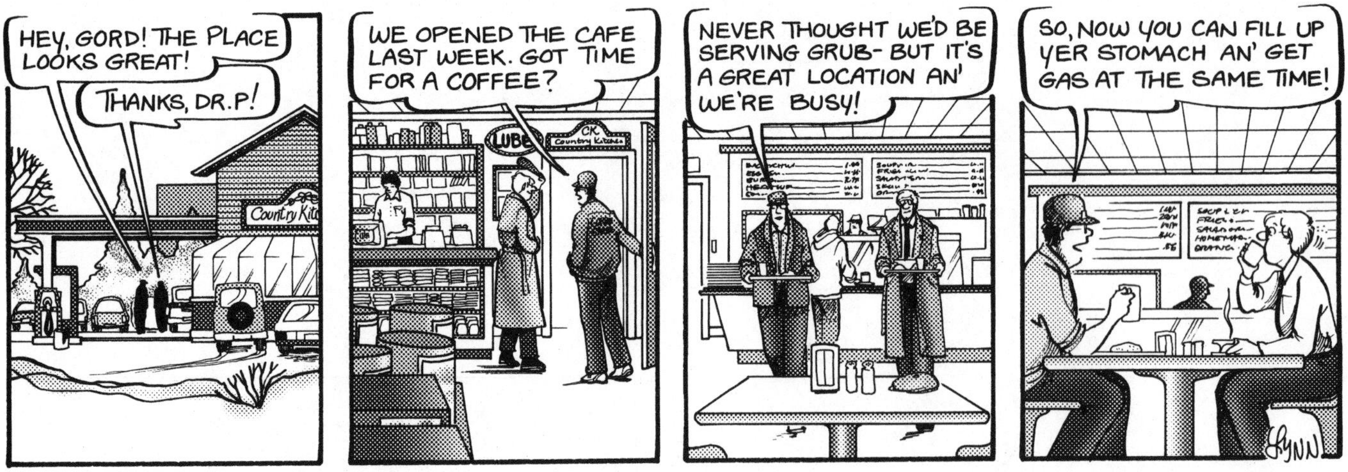

HEY, GORD! THE PLACE LOOKS GREAT!
THANKS, DR. P!
WE OPENED THE CAFE LAST WEEK. GOT TIME FOR A COFFEE?
LUBE
NEVER THOUGHT WE'D BE SERVING GRUB- BUT IT'S A GREAT LOCATION AN' WE'RE BUSY!
SO, NOW YOU CAN FILL UP YER STOMACH AN' GET GAS AT THE SAME TIME!

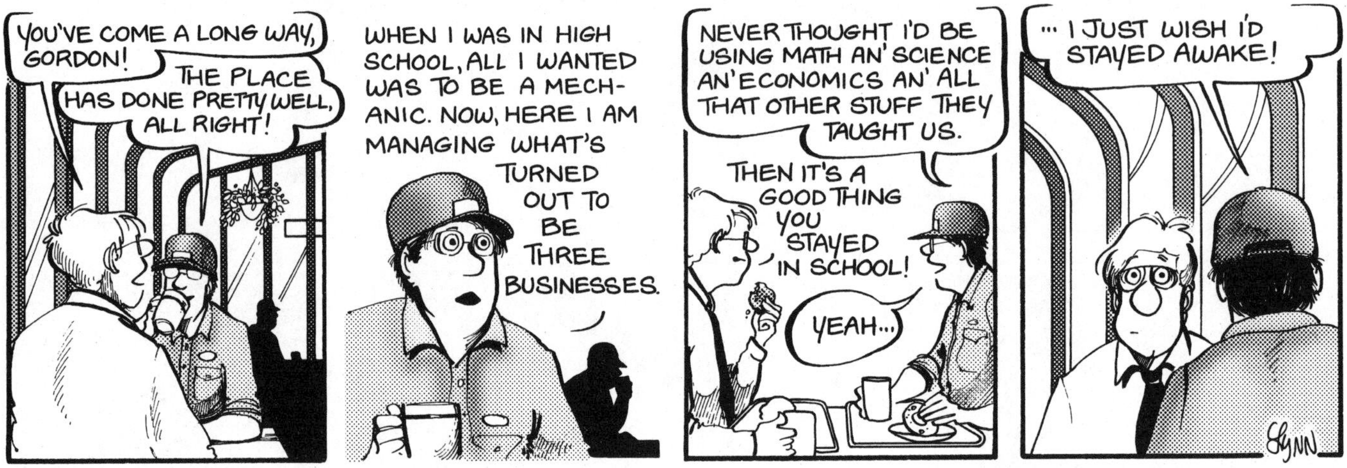

YOU'VE COME A LONG WAY, GORDON!
THE PLACE HAS DONE PRETTY WELL, ALL RIGHT!
WHEN I WAS IN HIGH SCHOOL, ALL I WANTED WAS TO BE A MECH-ANIC. NOW, HERE I AM MANAGING WHAT'S TURNED OUT TO BE THREE BUSINESSES.
NEVER THOUGHT I'D BE USING MATH AN' SCIENCE AN' ECONOMICS AN' ALL THAT OTHER STUFF THEY TAUGHT US.
THEN IT'S A GOOD THING YOU STAYED IN SCHOOL!
YEAH...
... I JUST WISH I'D STAYED AWAKE!

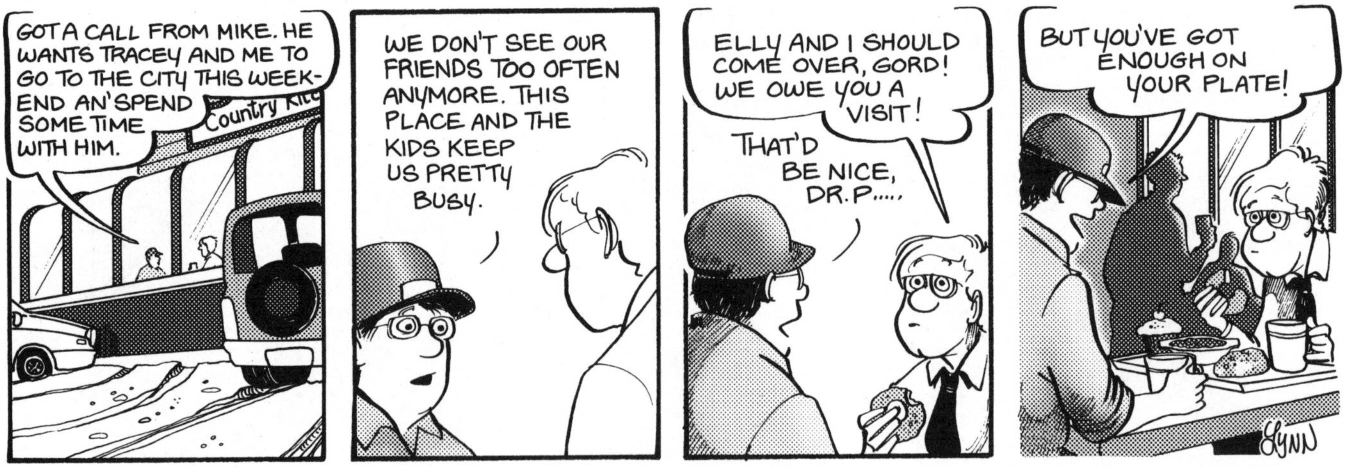

GOT A CALL FROM MIKE. HE WANTS TRACEY AND ME TO GO TO THE CITY THIS WEEK-END AN' SPEND SOME TIME WITH HIM.
WE DON'T SEE OUR FRIENDS TOO OFTEN ANYMORE. THIS PLACE AND THE KIDS KEEP US PRETTY BUSY.
ELLY AND I SHOULD COME OVER, GORD! WE OWE YOU A VISIT!
THAT'D BE NICE, DR. P....
BUT YOU'VE GOT ENOUGH ON YOUR PLATE!

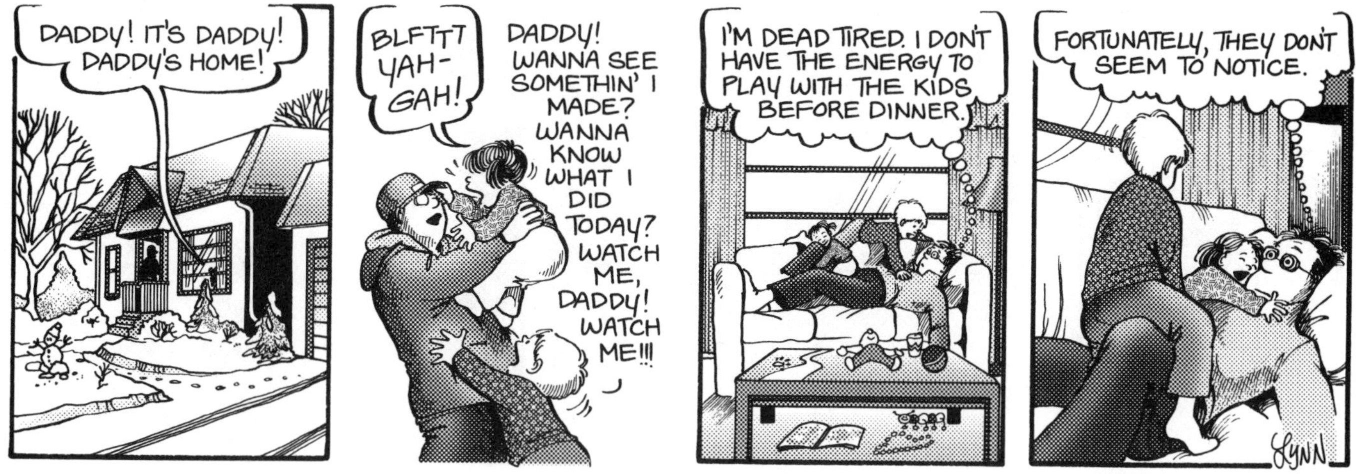
DADDY! IT'S DADDY! DADDY'S HOME!
BLFTTT YAH-GAH!
DADDY! WANNA SEE SOMETHIN' I MADE? WANNA KNOW WHAT I DID TODAY? WATCH ME, DADDY! WATCH ME!!!
I'M DEAD TIRED. I DON'T HAVE THE ENERGY TO PLAY WITH THE KIDS BEFORE DINNER.
FORTUNATELY, THEY DON'T SEEM TO NOTICE.
LYNN

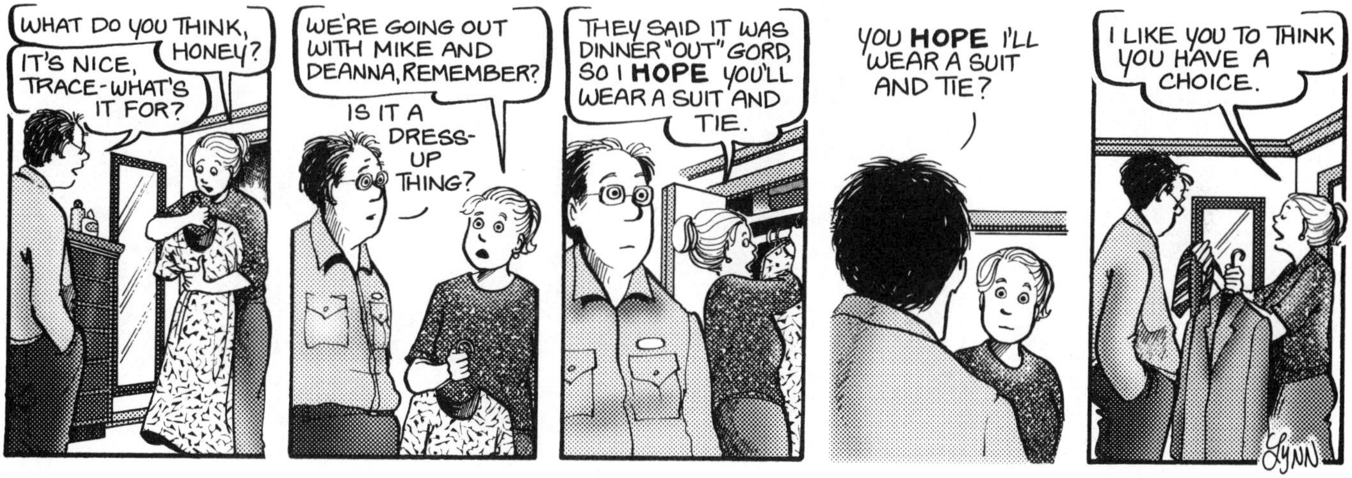
WHAT DO YOU THINK, HONEY?
IT'S NICE, TRACE-WHAT'S IT FOR?
WE'RE GOING OUT WITH MIKE AND DEANNA, REMEMBER?
IS IT A DRESS-UP THING?
THEY SAID IT WAS DINNER "OUT" GORD, SO I HOPE YOU'LL WEAR A SUIT AND TIE.
YOU HOPE I'LL WEAR A SUIT AND TIE?
I LIKE YOU TO THINK YOU HAVE A CHOICE.
LYNN

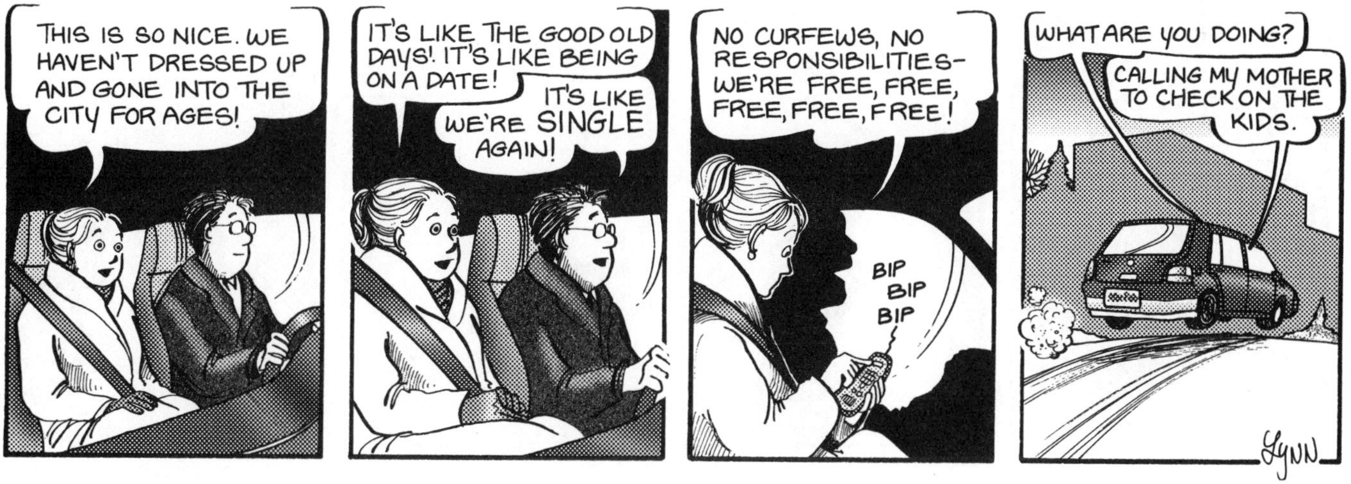
THIS IS SO NICE. WE HAVEN'T DRESSED UP AND GONE INTO THE CITY FOR AGES!
IT'S LIKE THE GOOD OLD DAYS! IT'S LIKE BEING ON A DATE!
IT'S LIKE WE'RE SINGLE AGAIN!
NO CURFEWS, NO RESPONSIBILITIES- WE'RE FREE, FREE, FREE, FREE, FREE!
BIP BIP BIP
WHAT ARE YOU DOING?
CALLING MY MOTHER TO CHECK ON THE KIDS.
LYNN

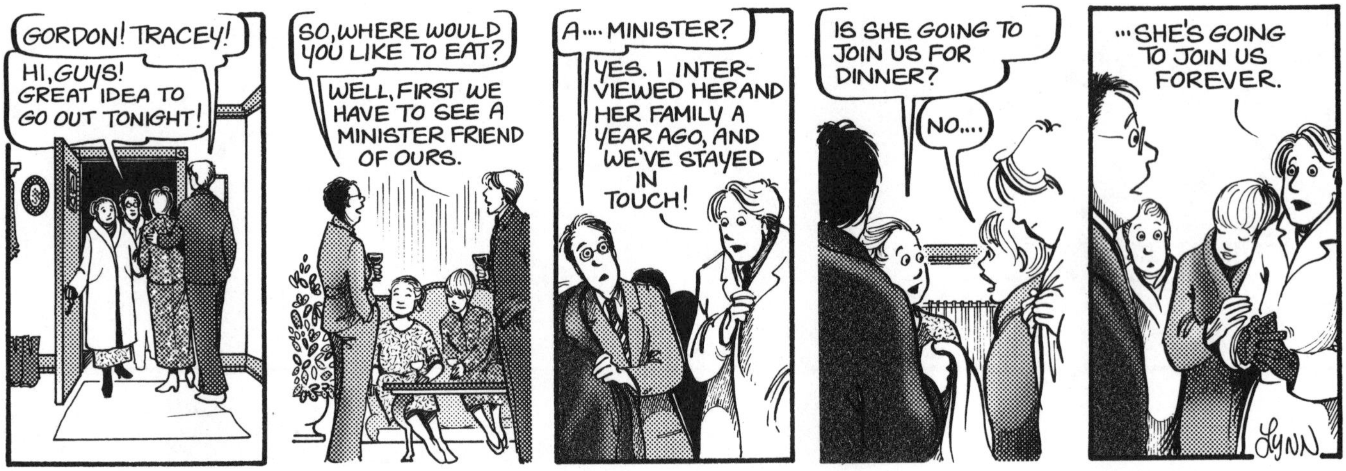
GORDON! TRACEY!
HI, GUYS! GREAT IDEA TO GO OUT TONIGHT!
SO, WHERE WOULD YOU LIKE TO EAT?
WELL, FIRST WE HAVE TO SEE A MINISTER FRIEND OF OURS.
A.... MINISTER?
YES. I INTERVIEWED HER AND HER FAMILY A YEAR AGO, AND WE'VE STAYED IN TOUCH!
IS SHE GOING TO JOIN US FOR DINNER?
NO....
...SHE'S GOING TO JOIN US FOREVER.
LYNN

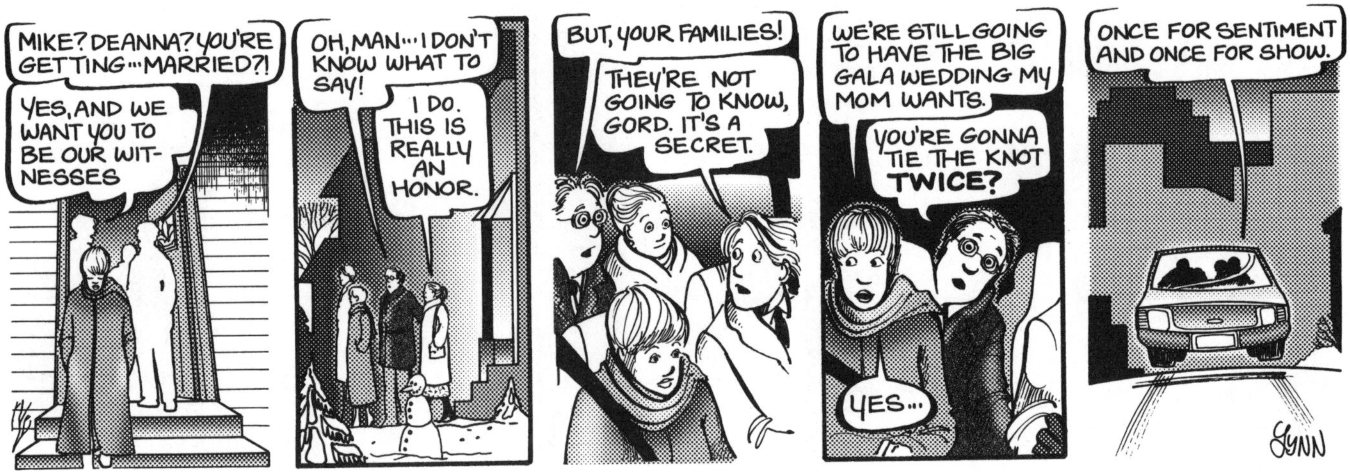
MIKE? DEANNA? YOU'RE GETTING...MARRIED?!
YES, AND WE WANT YOU TO BE OUR WITNESSES
OH, MAN... I DON'T KNOW WHAT TO SAY!
I DO. THIS IS REALLY AN HONOR.
BUT, YOUR FAMILIES!
THEY'RE NOT GOING TO KNOW, GORD. IT'S A SECRET.
WE'RE STILL GOING TO HAVE THE BIG GALA WEDDING MY MOM WANTS.
YOU'RE GONNA TIE THE KNOT **TWICE?**
YES...
ONCE FOR SENTIMENT AND ONCE FOR SHOW.
LYNN

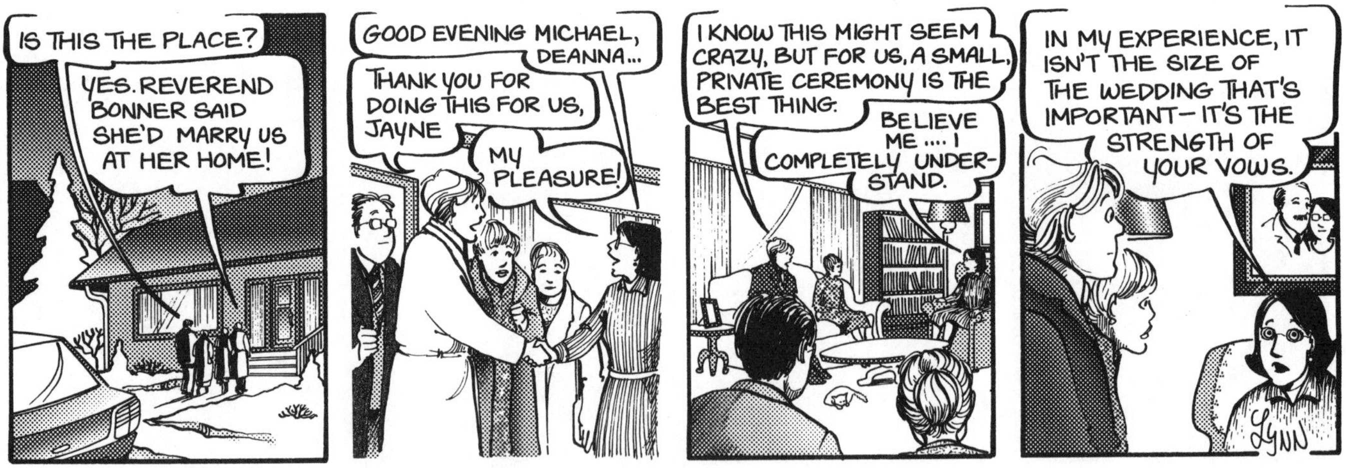
IS THIS THE PLACE?
YES. REVEREND BONNER SAID SHE'D MARRY US AT HER HOME!
GOOD EVENING MICHAEL, DEANNA...
THANK YOU FOR DOING THIS FOR US, JAYNE
MY PLEASURE!
I KNOW THIS MIGHT SEEM CRAZY, BUT FOR US, A SMALL, PRIVATE CEREMONY IS THE BEST THING.
BELIEVE ME .... I COMPLETELY UNDERSTAND.
IN MY EXPERIENCE, IT ISN'T THE SIZE OF THE WEDDING THAT'S IMPORTANT— IT'S THE STRENGTH OF YOUR VOWS.
LYNN

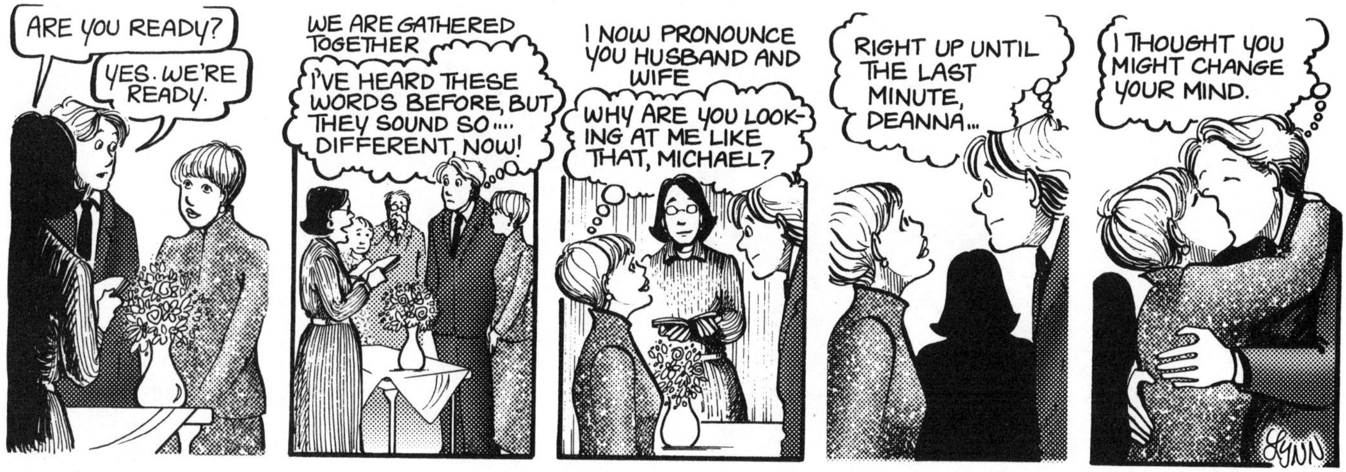
ARE YOU READY?
YES. WE'RE READY.
WE ARE GATHERED TOGETHER
I'VE HEARD THESE WORDS BEFORE, BUT THEY SOUND SO.... DIFFERENT, NOW!
I NOW PRONOUNCE YOU HUSBAND AND WIFE
WHY ARE YOU LOOKING AT ME LIKE THAT, MICHAEL?
RIGHT UP UNTIL THE LAST MINUTE, DEANNA...
I THOUGHT YOU MIGHT CHANGE YOUR MIND.
LYNN

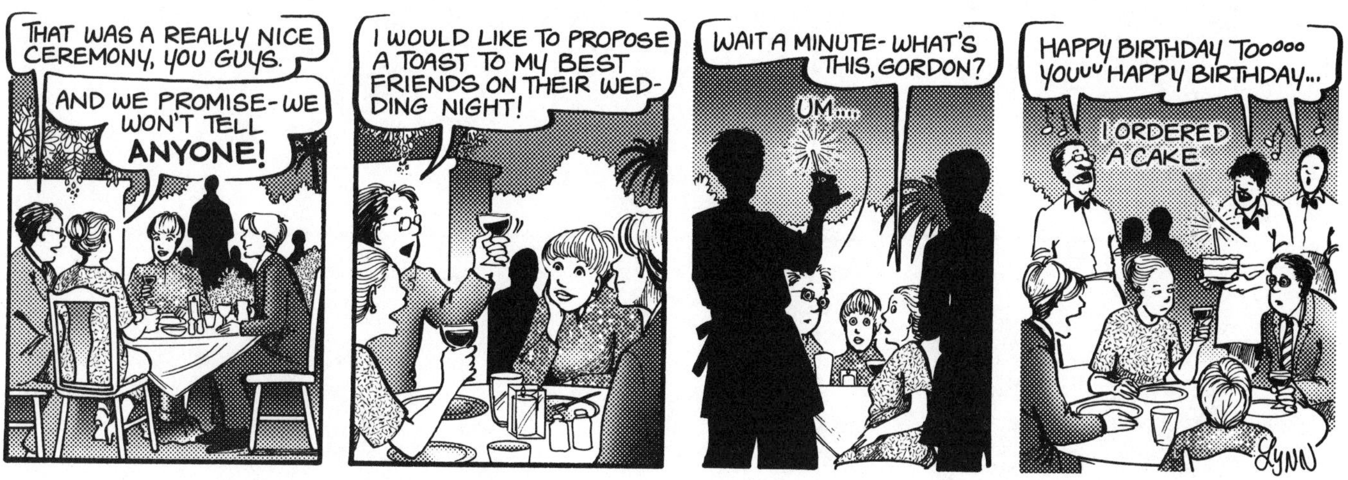
THAT WAS A REALLY NICE CEREMONY, YOU GUYS.
AND WE PROMISE- WE WON'T TELL ANYONE!
I WOULD LIKE TO PROPOSE A TOAST TO MY BEST FRIENDS ON THEIR WEDDING NIGHT!
WAIT A MINUTE- WHAT'S THIS, GORDON?
UM....
HAPPY BIRTHDAY Tooooo YOUUU HAPPY BIRTHDAY...
I ORDERED A CAKE.
LYNN

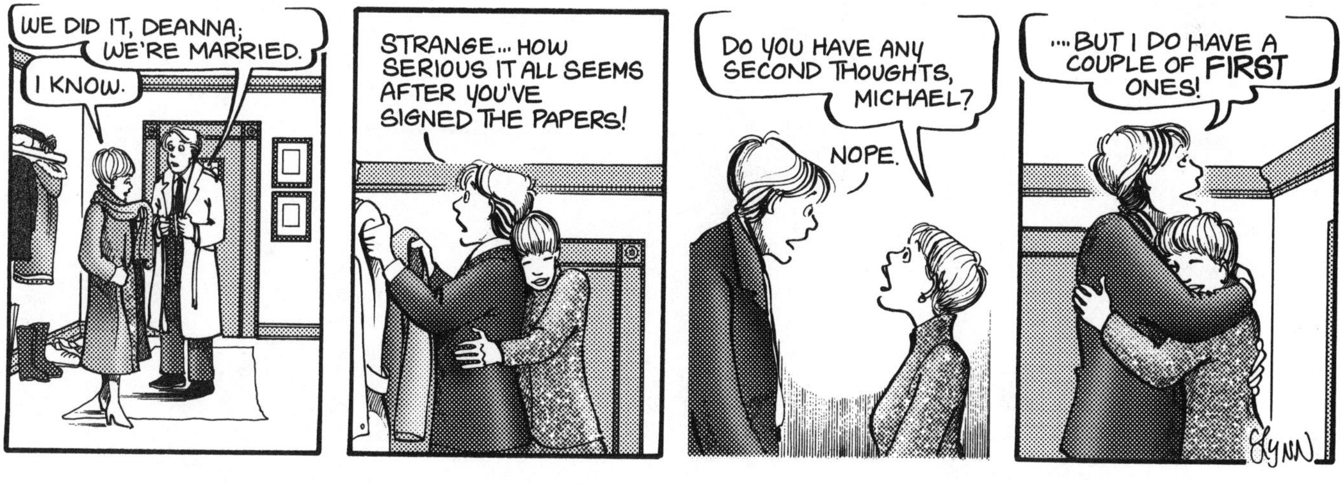
WE DID IT, DEANNA; WE'RE MARRIED.
I KNOW.
STRANGE... HOW SERIOUS IT ALL SEEMS AFTER YOU'VE SIGNED THE PAPERS!
DO YOU HAVE ANY SECOND THOUGHTS, MICHAEL?
NOPE.
....BUT I DO HAVE A COUPLE OF FIRST ONES!
LYNN

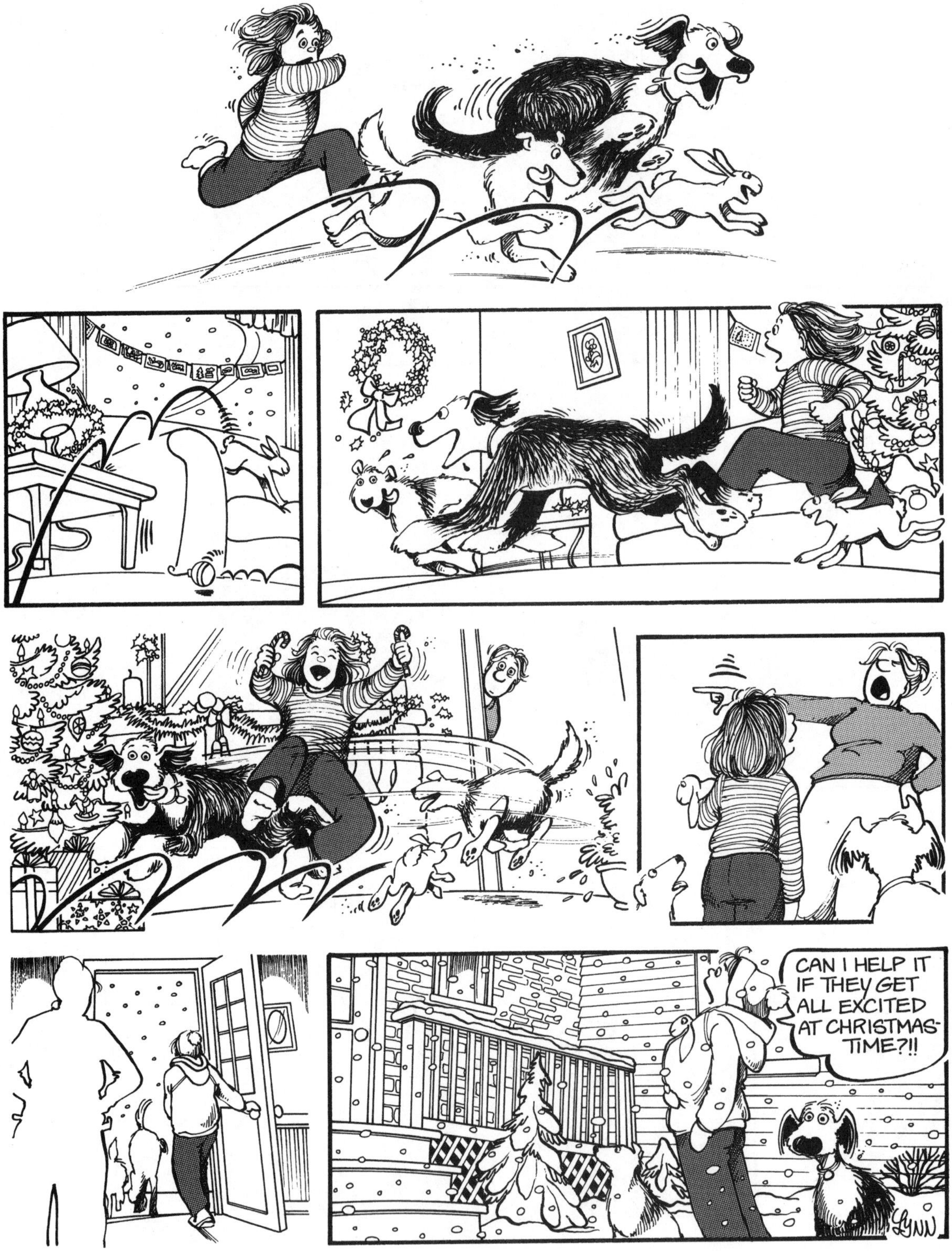
CAN I HELP IT
IF THEY GET
ALL EXCITED
AT CHRISTMAS-
TIME?!!
LYNN

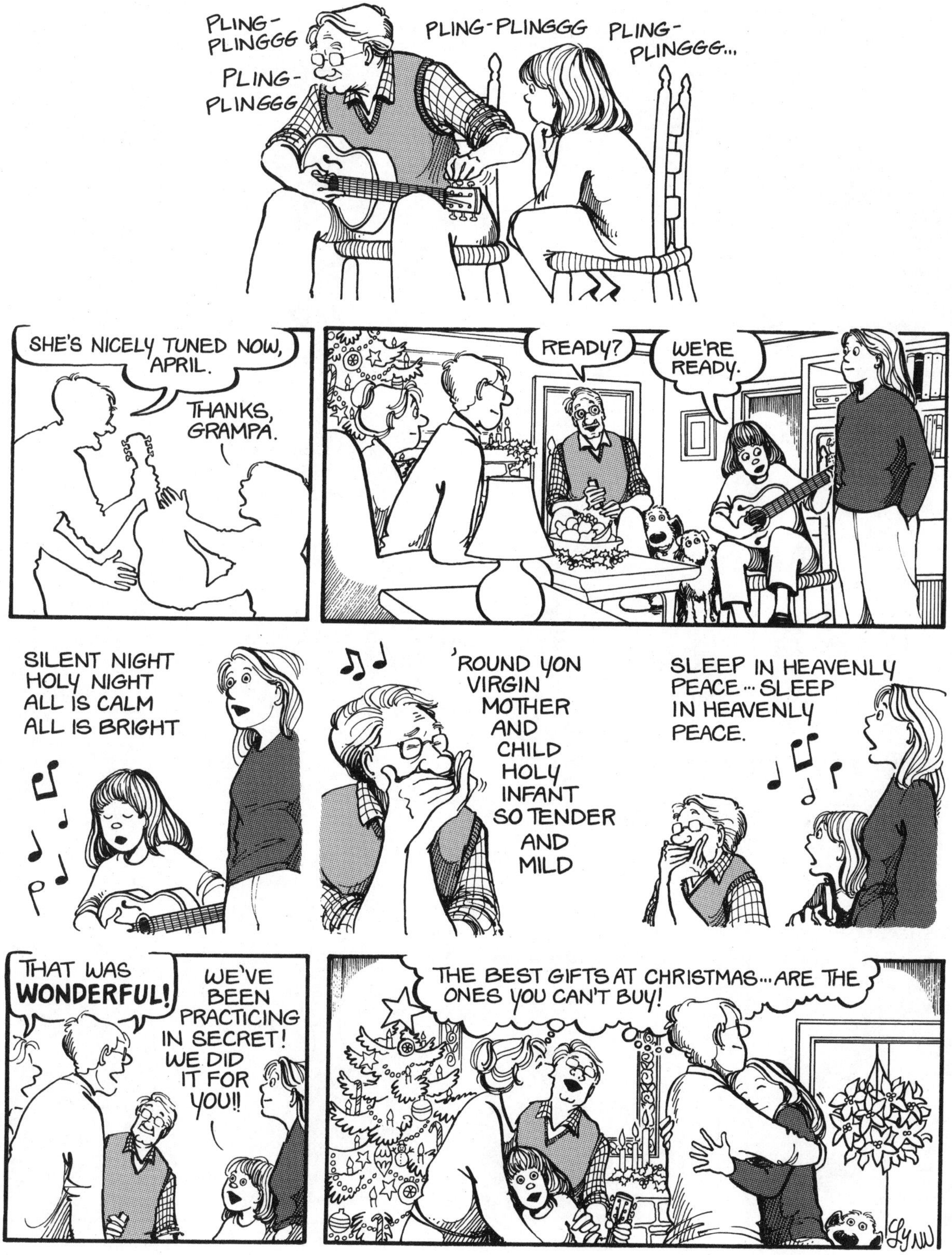
PLING-PLINGGG
PLING-PLINGGG
PLING-PLINGGG
PLING-PLINGGG...
SHE'S NICELY TUNED NOW, APRIL.
THANKS, GRAMPA.
READY?
WE'RE READY.
SILENT NIGHT HOLY NIGHT ALL IS CALM ALL IS BRIGHT
'ROUND YON VIRGIN MOTHER AND CHILD HOLY INFANT SO TENDER AND MILD
SLEEP IN HEAVENLY PEACE... SLEEP IN HEAVENLY PEACE.
THAT WAS **WONDERFUL!**
WE'VE BEEN PRACTICING IN SECRET! WE DID IT FOR YOU!!
THE BEST GIFTS AT CHRISTMAS... ARE THE ONES YOU CAN'T BUY!
LYNN

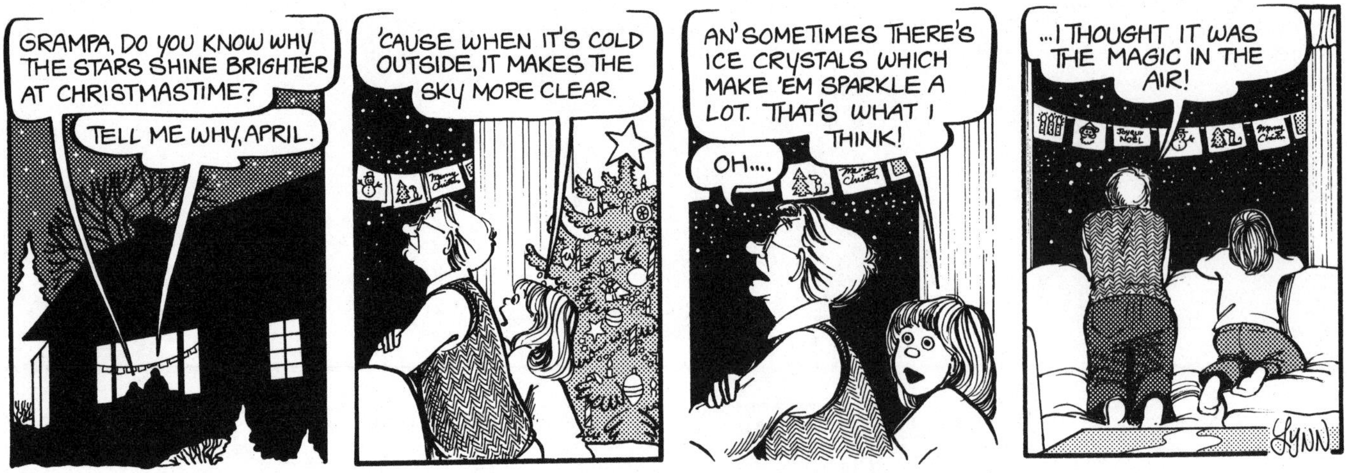
GRAMPA, DO YOU KNOW WHY THE STARS SHINE BRIGHTER AT CHRISTMASTIME?
TELL ME WHY, APRIL.
'CAUSE WHEN IT'S COLD OUTSIDE, IT MAKES THE SKY MORE CLEAR.
AN' SOMETIMES THERE'S ICE CRYSTALS WHICH MAKE 'EM SPARKLE A LOT. THAT'S WHAT I THINK!
OH....
...I THOUGHT IT WAS THE MAGIC IN THE AIR!
LYNN

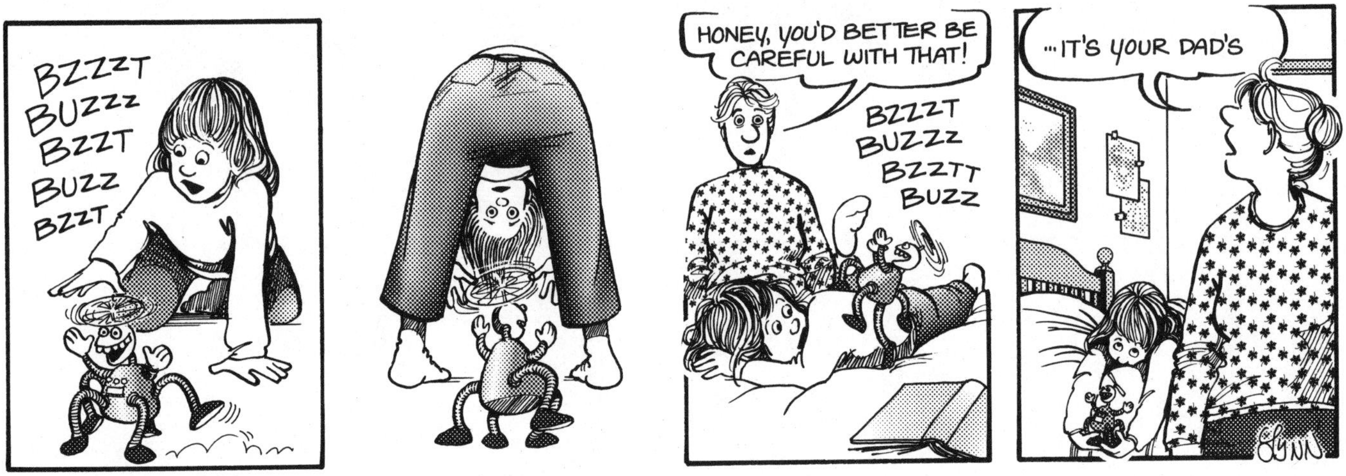
BZZZT
BUZZZ
BZZT
BUZZ
BZZT
HONEY, YOU'D BETTER BE CAREFUL WITH THAT!
BZZZT
BUZZZ
BZZTT
BUZZ
...IT'S YOUR DAD'S
LYNN

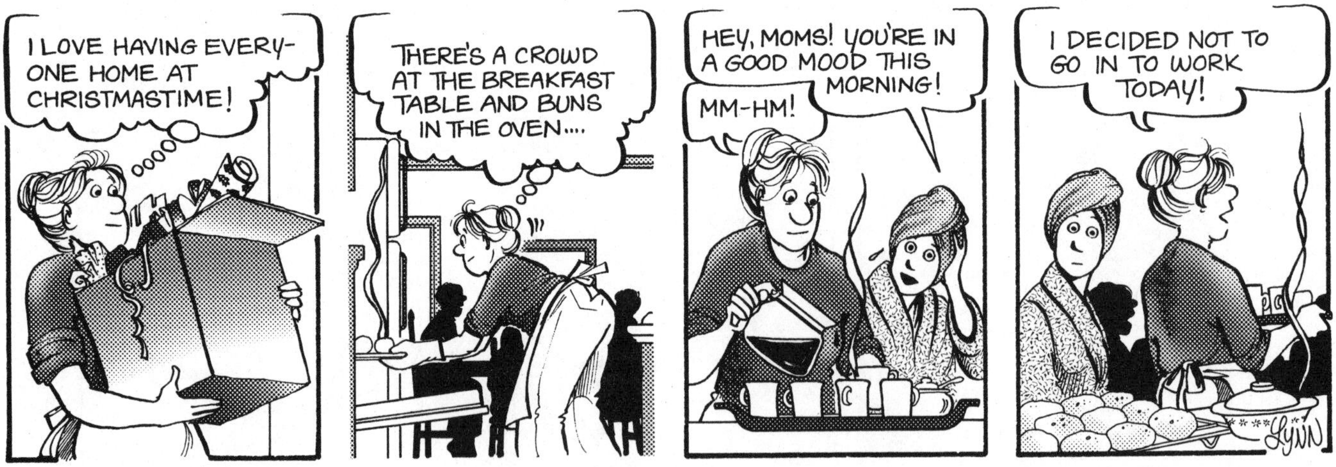
I LOVE HAVING EVERY-ONE HOME AT CHRISTMASTIME!
THERE'S A CROWD AT THE BREAKFAST TABLE AND BUNS IN THE OVEN....
HEY, MOMS! YOU'RE IN A GOOD MOOD THIS MORNING!
MM-HM!
I DECIDED NOT TO GO IN TO WORK TODAY!
LYNN

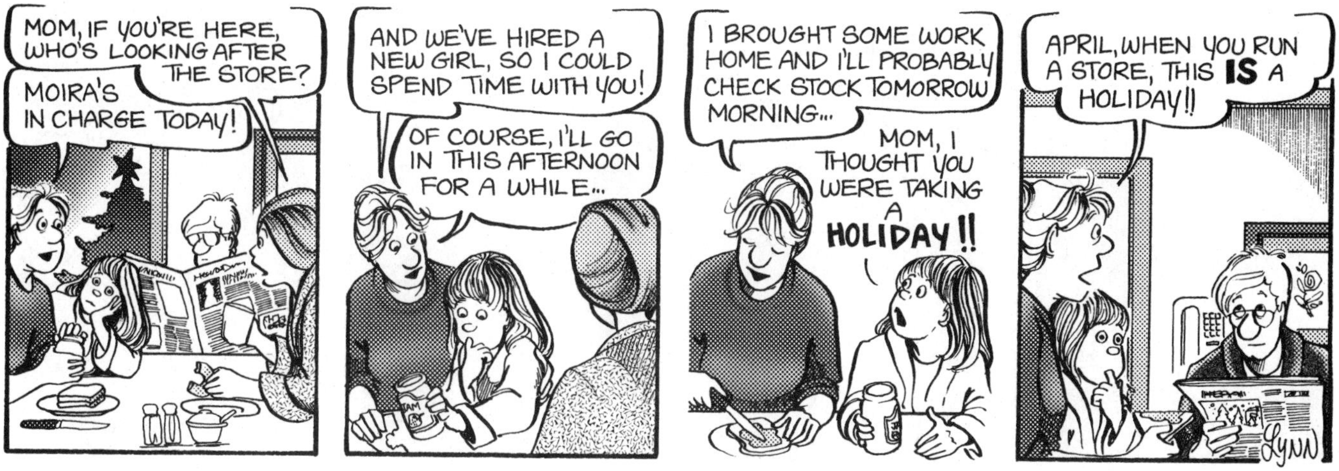
MOM, IF YOU'RE HERE, WHO'S LOOKING AFTER THE STORE?
MOIRA'S IN CHARGE TODAY!
AND WE'VE HIRED A NEW GIRL, SO I COULD SPEND TIME WITH YOU!
OF COURSE, I'LL GO IN THIS AFTERNOON FOR A WHILE...
I BROUGHT SOME WORK HOME AND I'LL PROBABLY CHECK STOCK TOMORROW MORNING...
MOM, I THOUGHT YOU WERE TAKING A **HOLIDAY**!!
APRIL, WHEN YOU RUN A STORE, THIS **IS** A HOLIDAY!!
LYNN

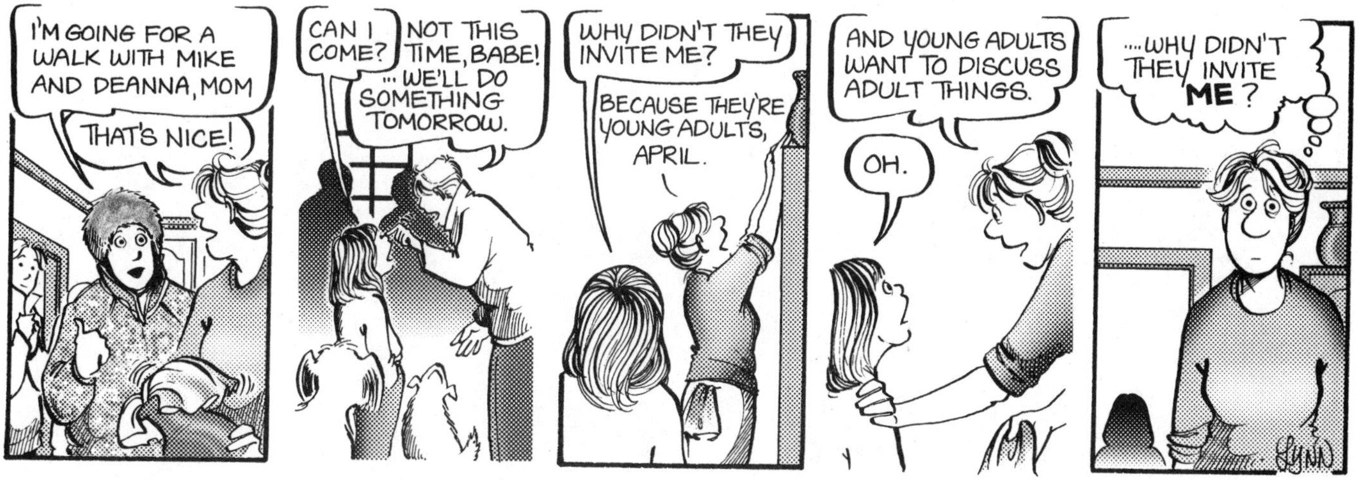
I'M GOING FOR A WALK WITH MIKE AND DEANNA, MOM
THAT'S NICE!
CAN I COME?
NOT THIS TIME, BABE! ...WE'LL DO SOMETHING TOMORROW.
WHY DIDN'T THEY INVITE ME?
BECAUSE THEY'RE YOUNG ADULTS, APRIL.
AND YOUNG ADULTS WANT TO DISCUSS ADULT THINGS.
OH.
...WHY DIDN'T THEY INVITE **ME**?
LYNN

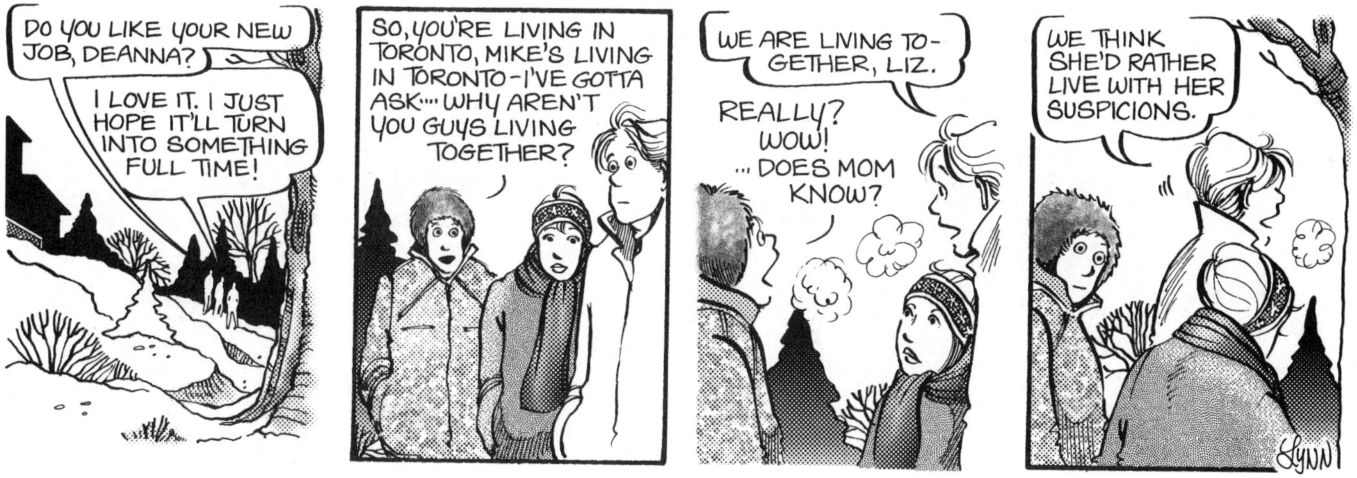
DO YOU LIKE YOUR NEW JOB, DEANNA?
I LOVE IT. I JUST HOPE IT'LL TURN INTO SOMETHING FULL TIME!
SO, YOU'RE LIVING IN TORONTO, MIKE'S LIVING IN TORONTO - I'VE GOTTA ASK.... WHY AREN'T YOU GUYS LIVING TOGETHER?
WE ARE LIVING TO-GETHER, LIZ.
REALLY? WOW! ...DOES MOM KNOW?
WE THINK SHE'D RATHER LIVE WITH HER SUSPICIONS.
LYNN

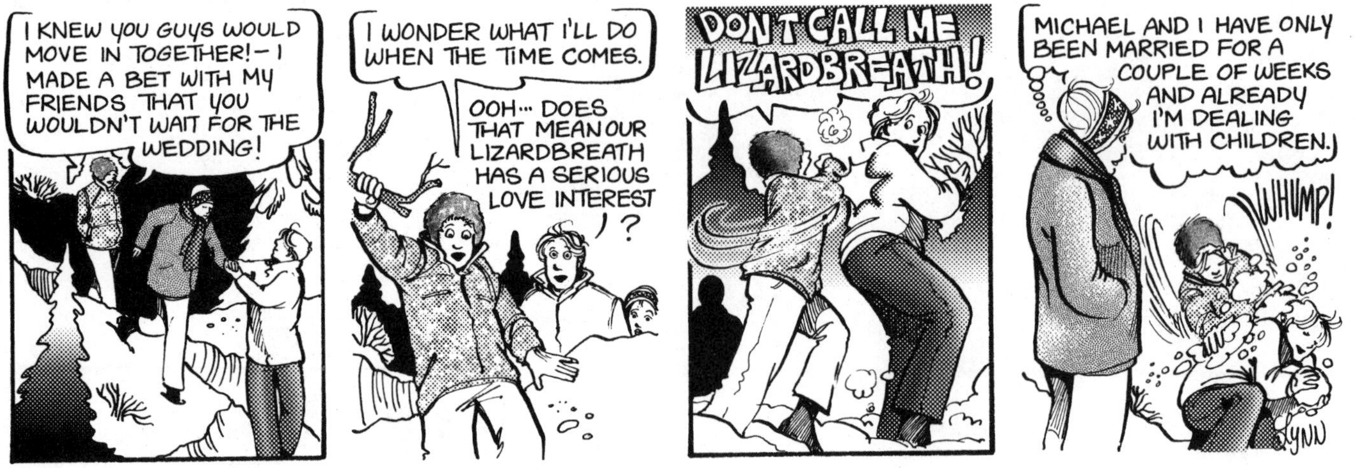
I KNEW YOU GUYS WOULD MOVE IN TOGETHER! – I MADE A BET WITH MY FRIENDS THAT YOU WOULDN'T WAIT FOR THE WEDDING!
I WONDER WHAT I'LL DO WHEN THE TIME COMES.
OOH··· DOES THAT MEAN OUR LIZARDBREATH HAS A SERIOUS LOVE INTEREST?
DON'T CALL ME LIZARDBREATH!
MICHAEL AND I HAVE ONLY BEEN MARRIED FOR A COUPLE OF WEEKS AND ALREADY I'M DEALING WITH CHILDREN.
WHUMP!
LYNN

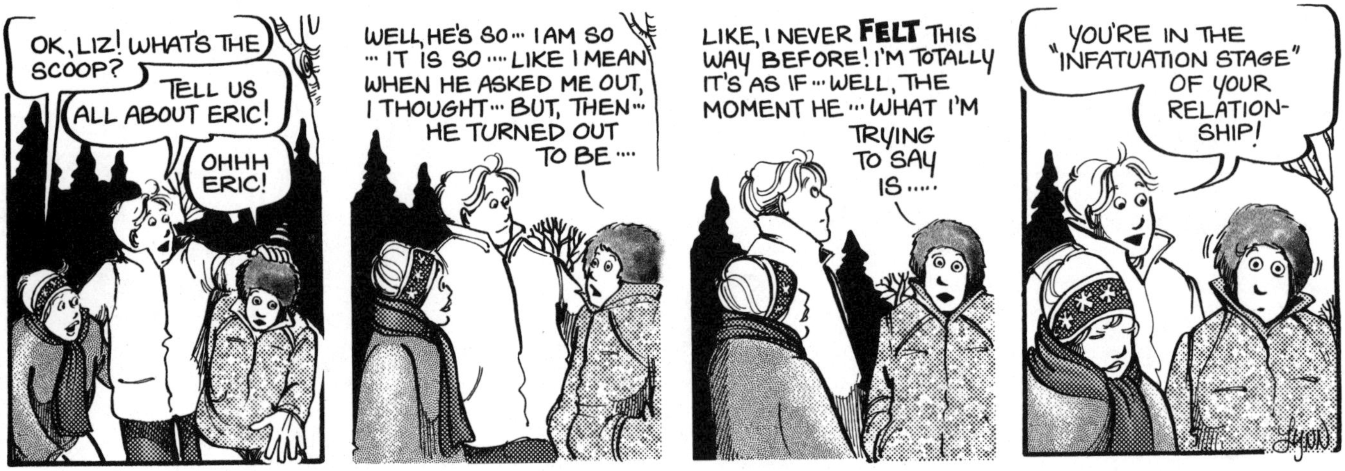
OK, LIZ! WHAT'S THE SCOOP?
TELL US ALL ABOUT ERIC!
OHHH ERIC!
WELL, HE'S SO··· I AM SO ··· IT IS SO···· LIKE I MEAN WHEN HE ASKED ME OUT, I THOUGHT··· BUT, THEN··· HE TURNED OUT TO BE····
LIKE, I NEVER FELT THIS WAY BEFORE! I'M TOTALLY IT'S AS IF··· WELL, THE MOMENT HE··· WHAT I'M TRYING TO SAY IS.....
YOU'RE IN THE "INFATUATION STAGE" OF YOUR RELATION-SHIP!
LYNN

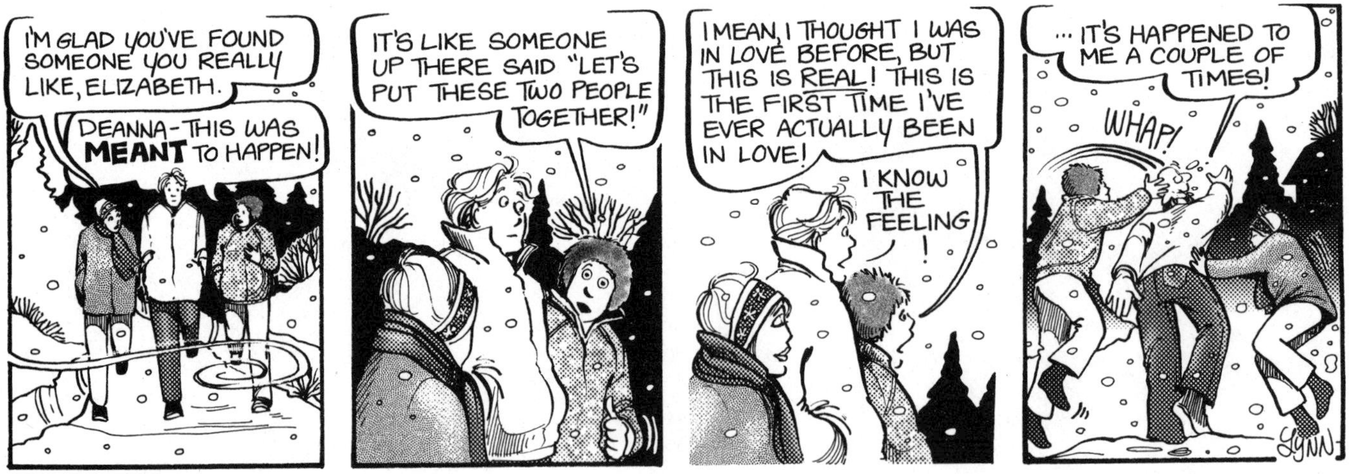
I'M GLAD YOU'VE FOUND SOMEONE YOU REALLY LIKE, ELIZABETH.
DEANNA-THIS WAS MEANT TO HAPPEN!
IT'S LIKE SOMEONE UP THERE SAID "LET'S PUT THESE TWO PEOPLE TOGETHER!"
I MEAN, I THOUGHT I WAS IN LOVE BEFORE, BUT THIS IS REAL! THIS IS THE FIRST TIME I'VE EVER ACTUALLY BEEN IN LOVE!
I KNOW THE FEELING!
... IT'S HAPPENED TO ME A COUPLE OF TIMES!
WHAP!
LYNN

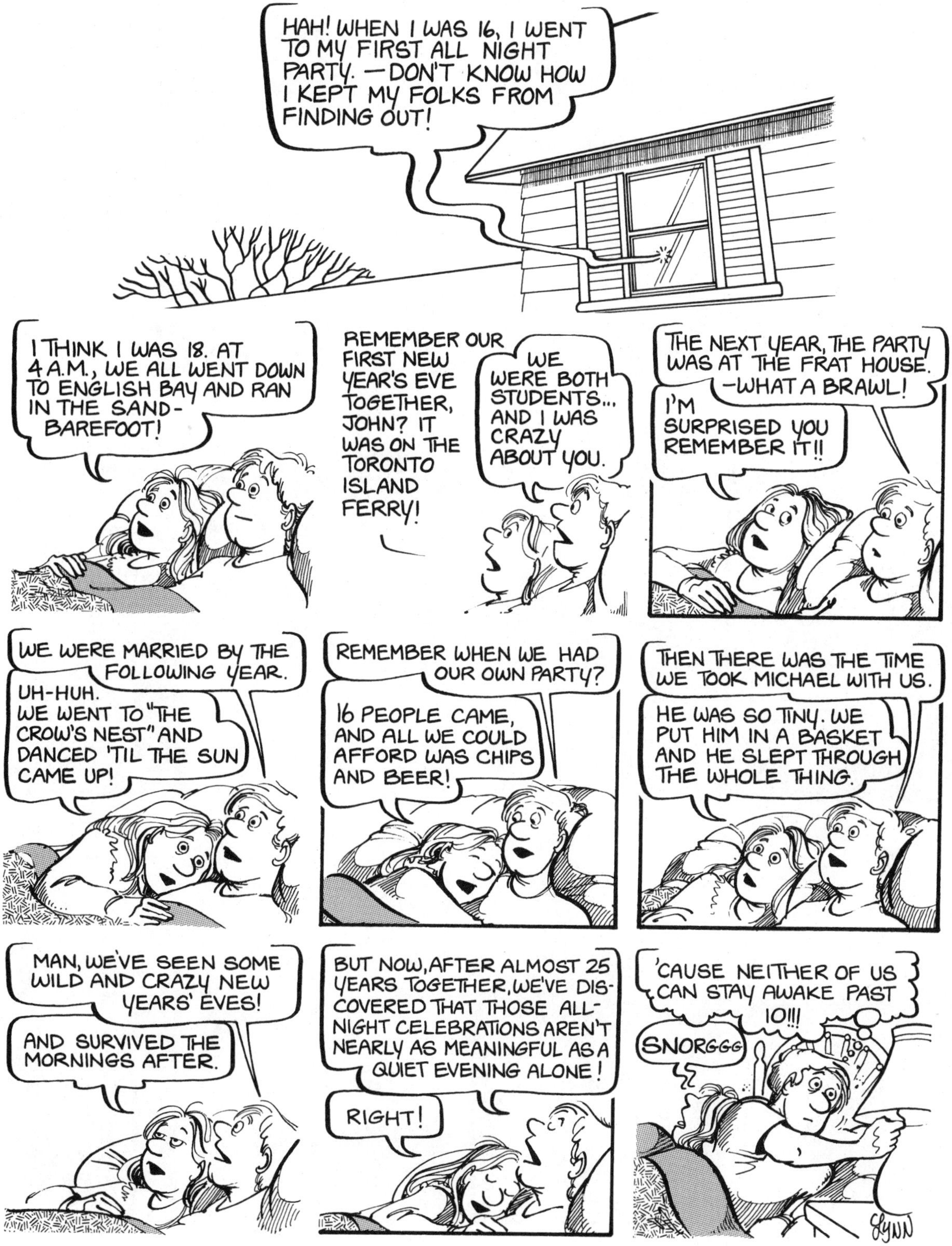
HAH! WHEN I WAS 16, I WENT TO MY FIRST ALL NIGHT PARTY. —DON'T KNOW HOW I KEPT MY FOLKS FROM FINDING OUT!
I THINK I WAS 18. AT 4 A.M., WE ALL WENT DOWN TO ENGLISH BAY AND RAN IN THE SAND-BAREFOOT!
REMEMBER OUR FIRST NEW YEAR'S EVE TOGETHER, JOHN? IT WAS ON THE TORONTO ISLAND FERRY!
WE WERE BOTH STUDENTS... AND I WAS CRAZY ABOUT YOU.
THE NEXT YEAR, THE PARTY WAS AT THE FRAT HOUSE. —WHAT A BRAWL!
I'M SURPRISED YOU REMEMBER IT!!
WE WERE MARRIED BY THE FOLLOWING YEAR.
UH-HUH. WE WENT TO "THE CROW'S NEST" AND DANCED 'TIL THE SUN CAME UP!
REMEMBER WHEN WE HAD OUR OWN PARTY?
16 PEOPLE CAME, AND ALL WE COULD AFFORD WAS CHIPS AND BEER!
THEN THERE WAS THE TIME WE TOOK MICHAEL WITH US.
HE WAS SO TINY. WE PUT HIM IN A BASKET AND HE SLEPT THROUGH THE WHOLE THING.
MAN, WE'VE SEEN SOME WILD AND CRAZY NEW YEARS' EVES!
AND SURVIVED THE MORNINGS AFTER.
BUT NOW, AFTER ALMOST 25 YEARS TOGETHER, WE'VE DISCOVERED THAT THOSE ALL-NIGHT CELEBRATIONS AREN'T NEARLY AS MEANINGFUL AS A QUIET EVENING ALONE!
RIGHT!
'CAUSE NEITHER OF US CAN STAY AWAKE PAST 10!!!
SNORGGG
LYNN

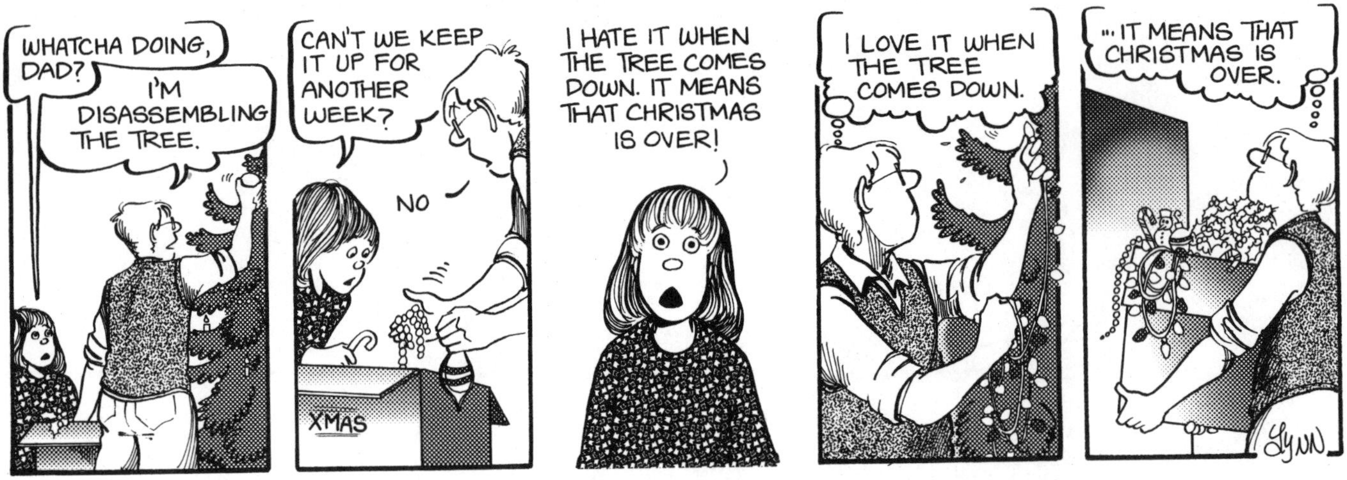
WHATCHA DOING, DAD?
I'M DISASSEMBLING THE TREE.
CAN'T WE KEEP IT UP FOR ANOTHER WEEK?
NO
XMAS
I HATE IT WHEN THE TREE COMES DOWN. IT MEANS THAT CHRISTMAS IS OVER!
I LOVE IT WHEN THE TREE COMES DOWN.
...IT MEANS THAT CHRISTMAS IS OVER.
LYNN

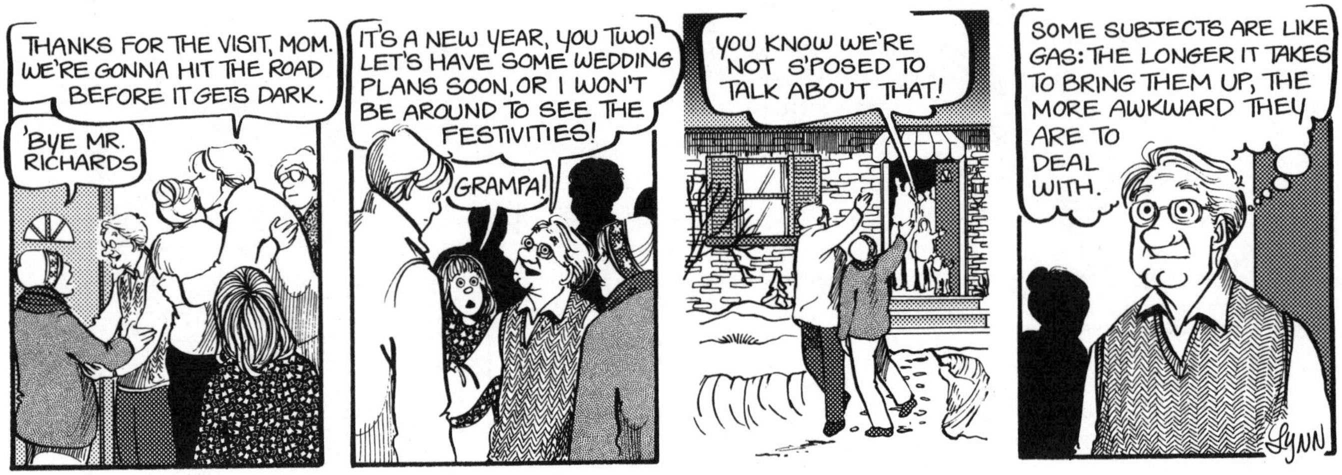
THANKS FOR THE VISIT, MOM. WE'RE GONNA HIT THE ROAD BEFORE IT GETS DARK.
'BYE MR. RICHARDS
IT'S A NEW YEAR, YOU TWO! LET'S HAVE SOME WEDDING PLANS SOON, OR I WON'T BE AROUND TO SEE THE FESTIVITIES!
GRAMPA!
YOU KNOW WE'RE NOT S'POSED TO TALK ABOUT THAT!
SOME SUBJECTS ARE LIKE GAS: THE LONGER IT TAKES TO BRING THEM UP, THE MORE AWKWARD THEY ARE TO DEAL WITH.
LYNN

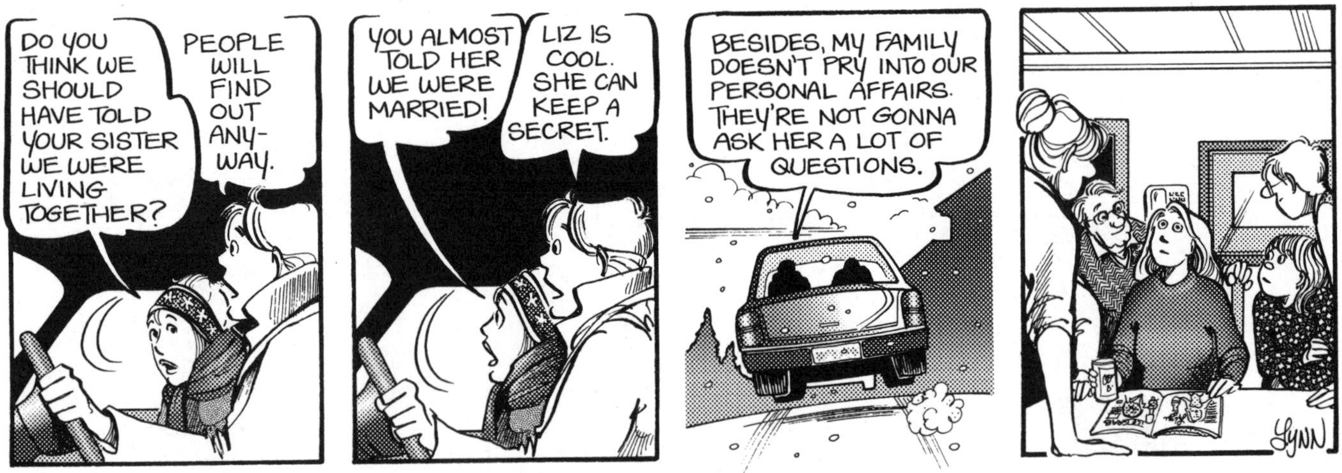
DO YOU THINK WE SHOULD HAVE TOLD YOUR SISTER WE WERE LIVING TOGETHER?
PEOPLE WILL FIND OUT ANY-WAY.
YOU ALMOST TOLD HER WE WERE MARRIED!
LIZ IS COOL. SHE CAN KEEP A SECRET.
BESIDES, MY FAMILY DOESN'T PRY INTO OUR PERSONAL AFFAIRS. THEY'RE NOT GONNA ASK HER A LOT OF QUESTIONS.
LYNN

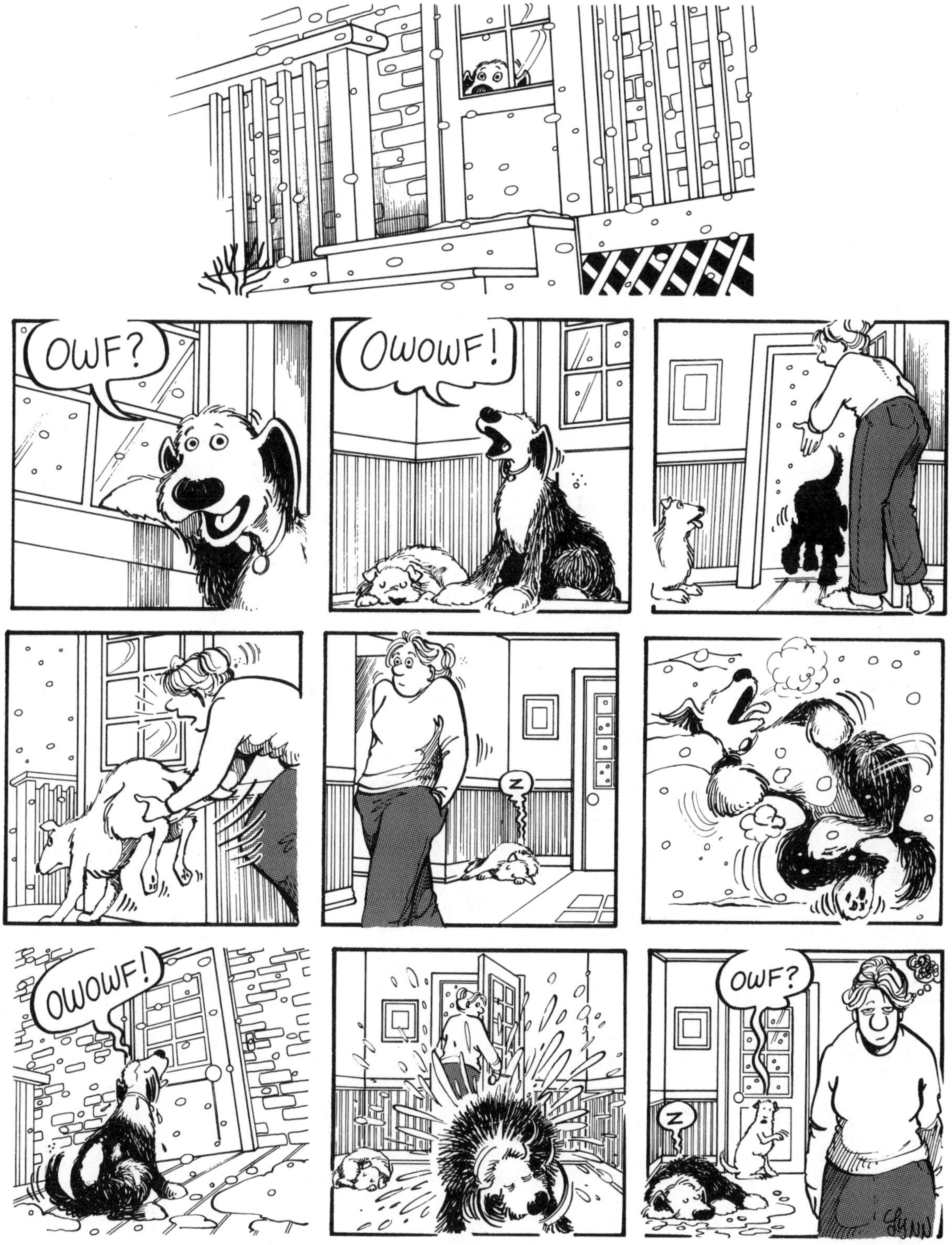
OWF?
OWOWF!
OWOWF!
OWF?

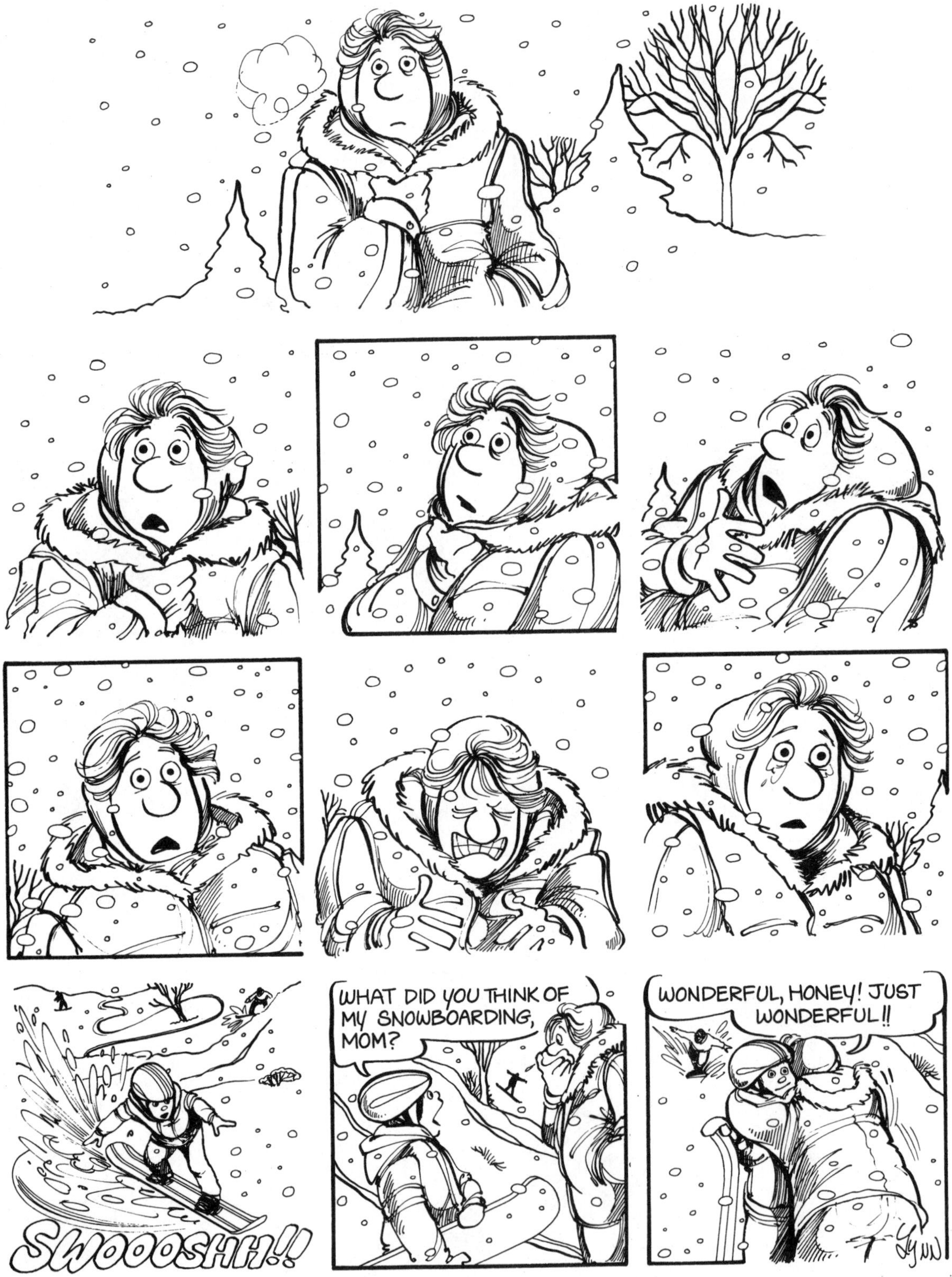
SWOOOSHH!!
WHAT DID YOU THINK OF MY SNOWBOARDING, MOM?
WONDERFUL, HONEY! JUST WONDERFUL!!
LYNN

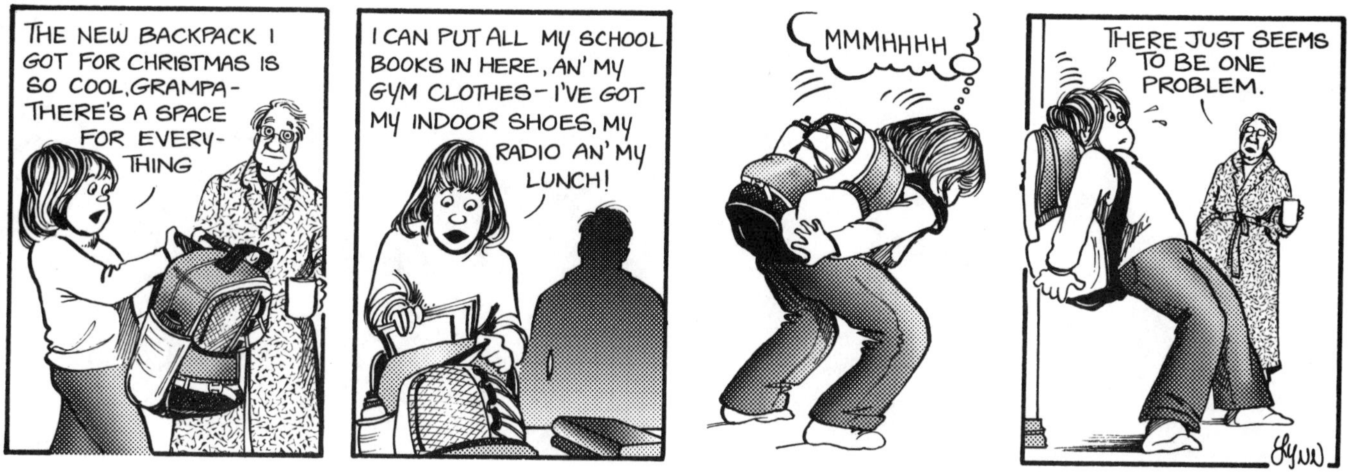
THE NEW BACKPACK I GOT FOR CHRISTMAS IS SO COOL, GRAMPA - THERE'S A SPACE FOR EVERYTHING
I CAN PUT ALL MY SCHOOL BOOKS IN HERE, AN' MY GYM CLOTHES - I'VE GOT MY INDOOR SHOES, MY RADIO AN' MY LUNCH!
MMMHHHH
THERE JUST SEEMS TO BE ONE PROBLEM.
LYNN

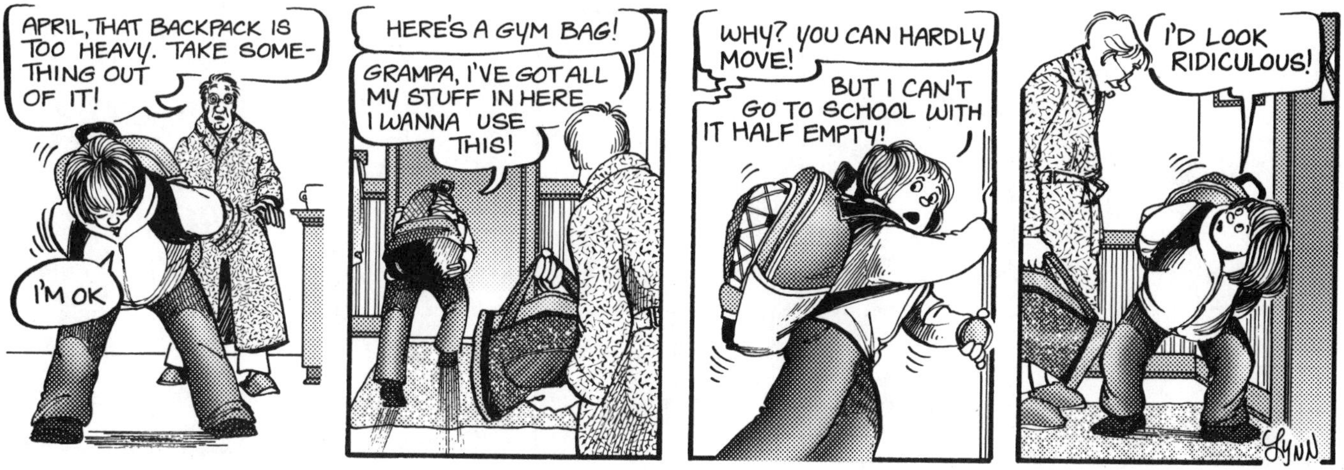
APRIL, THAT BACKPACK IS TOO HEAVY. TAKE SOMETHING OUT OF IT!
I'M OK
HERE'S A GYM BAG!
GRAMPA, I'VE GOT ALL MY STUFF IN HERE. I WANNA USE THIS!
WHY? YOU CAN HARDLY MOVE!
BUT I CAN'T GO TO SCHOOL WITH IT HALF EMPTY!
I'D LOOK RIDICULOUS!
LYNN

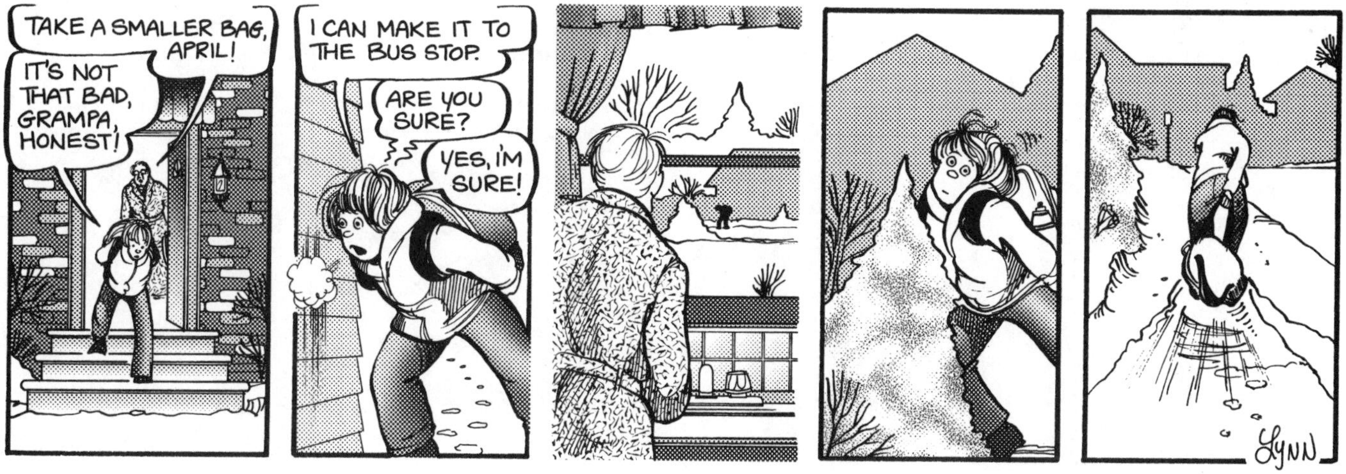
TAKE A SMALLER BAG, APRIL!
IT'S NOT THAT BAD, GRAMPA, HONEST!
I CAN MAKE IT TO THE BUS STOP.
ARE YOU SURE?
YES, I'M SURE!
LYNN

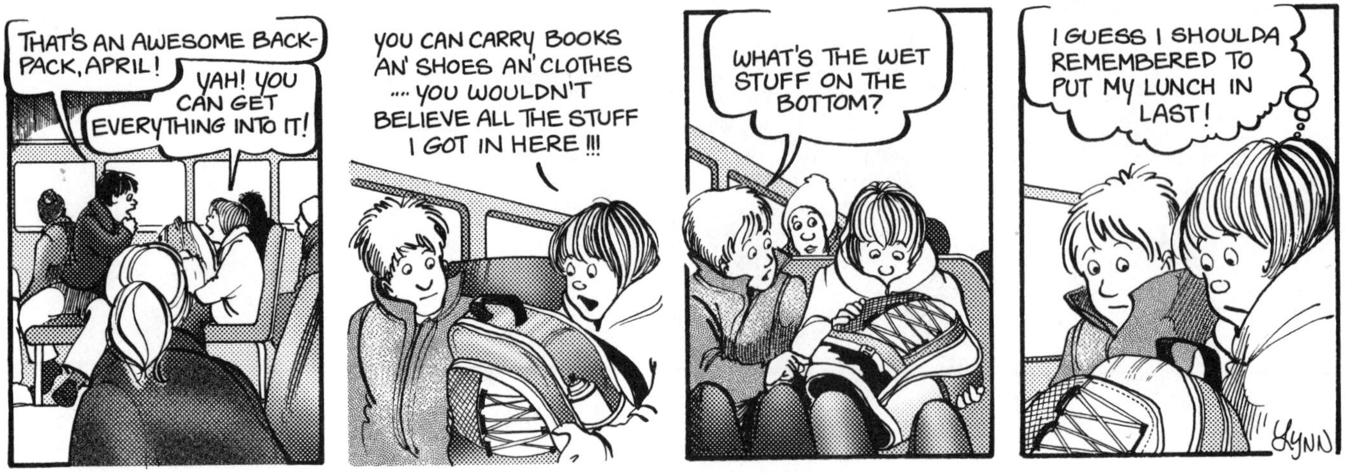
THAT'S AN AWESOME BACK-PACK, APRIL!
YAH! YOU CAN GET EVERYTHING INTO IT!
YOU CAN CARRY BOOKS AN' SHOES AN' CLOTHES .... YOU WOULDN'T BELIEVE ALL THE STUFF I GOT IN HERE !!!
WHAT'S THE WET STUFF ON THE BOTTOM?
I GUESS I SHOULDA REMEMBERED TO PUT MY LUNCH IN LAST!
LYNN

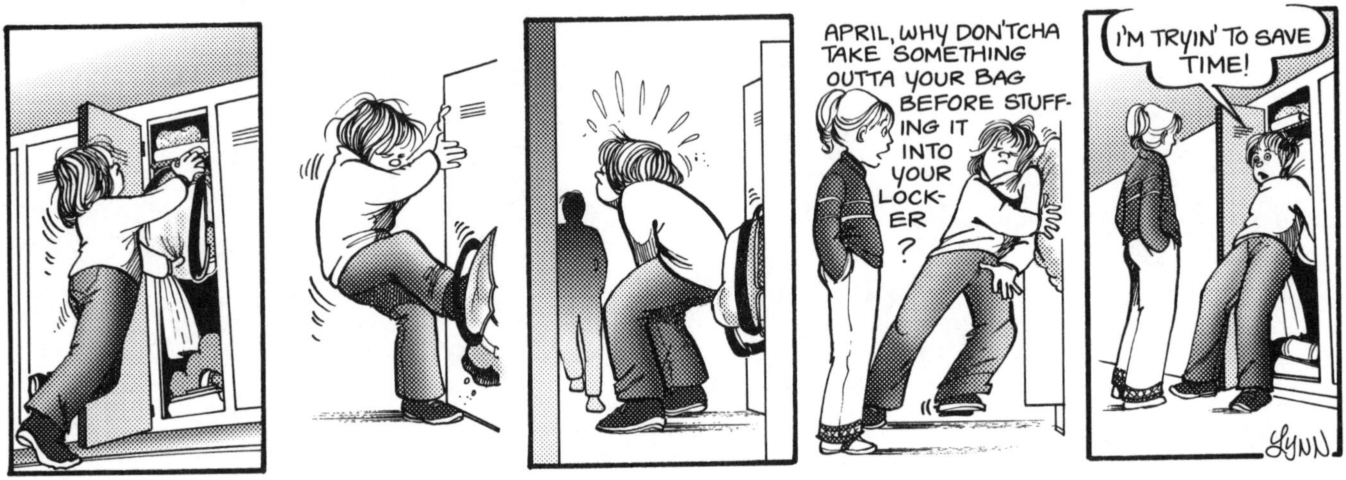
APRIL, WHY DON'TCHA TAKE SOMETHING OUTTA YOUR BAG BEFORE STUFF-ING IT INTO YOUR LOCK-ER?
I'M TRYIN' TO SAVE TIME!
LYNN

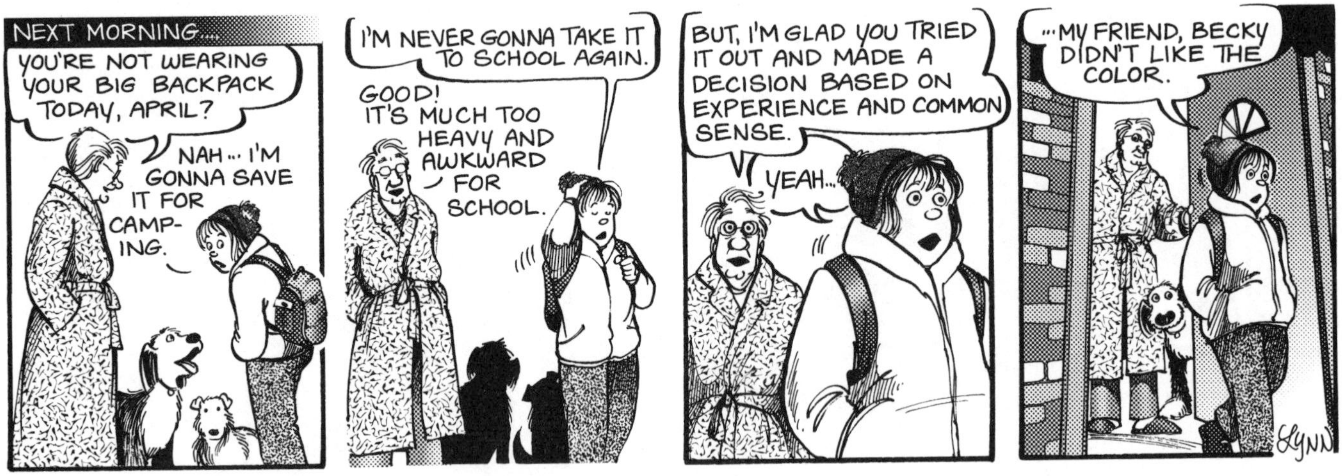
NEXT MORNING....
YOU'RE NOT WEARING YOUR BIG BACKPACK TODAY, APRIL?
NAH... I'M GONNA SAVE IT FOR CAMP-ING.
I'M NEVER GONNA TAKE IT TO SCHOOL AGAIN.
GOOD! IT'S MUCH TOO HEAVY AND AWKWARD FOR SCHOOL.
BUT, I'M GLAD YOU TRIED IT OUT AND MADE A DECISION BASED ON EXPERIENCE AND COMMON SENSE.
YEAH...
...MY FRIEND, BECKY DIDN'T LIKE THE COLOR.
LYNN

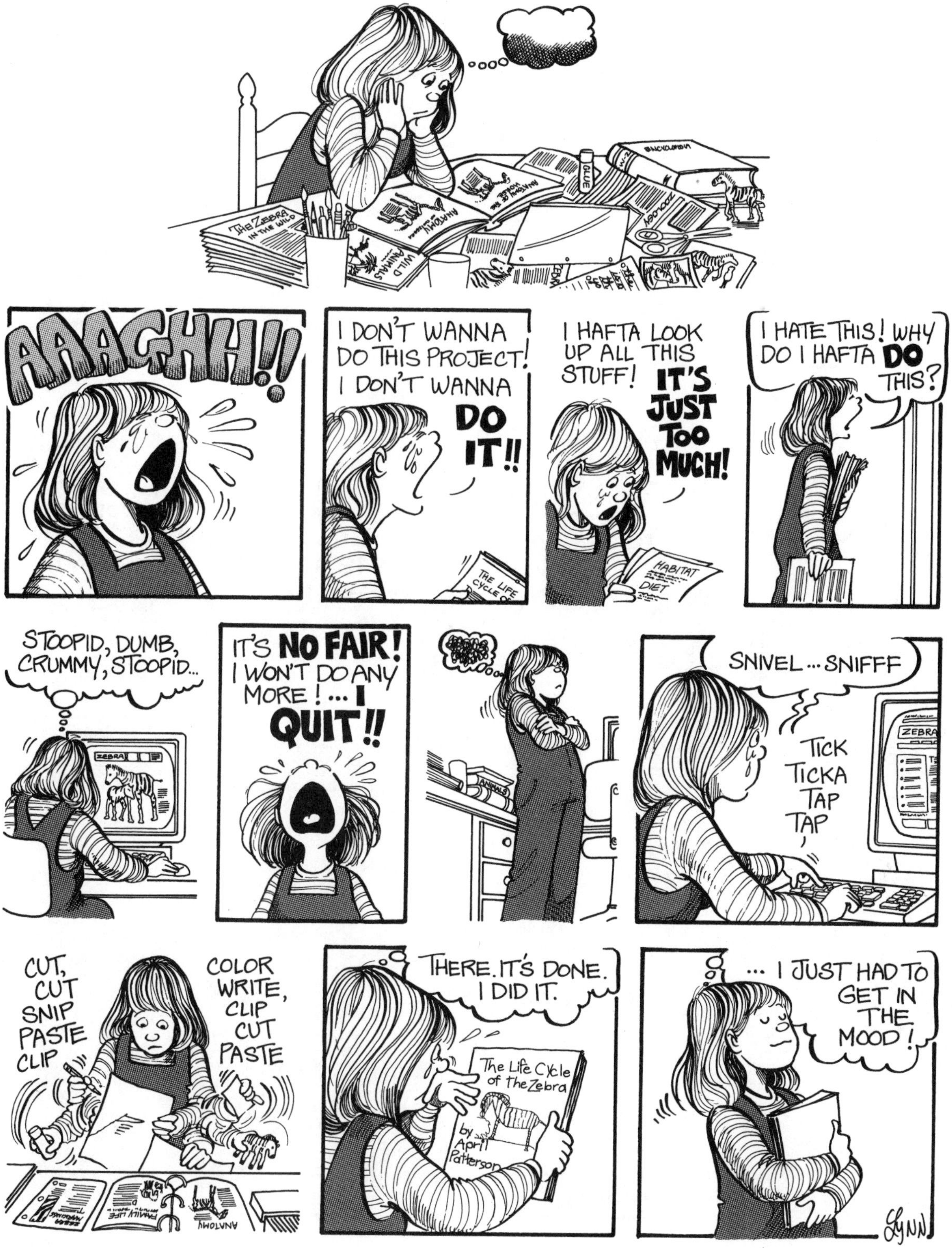
AAAGHH!!
I DON'T WANNA DO THIS PROJECT! I DON'T WANNA DO IT!!
I HAFTA LOOK UP ALL THIS STUFF! IT'S JUST TOO MUCH!
I HATE THIS! WHY DO I HAFTA DO THIS?
STOOPID, DUMB, CRUMMY, STOOPID...
IT'S NO FAIR! I WON'T DO ANY MORE! ... I QUIT!!
SNIVEL ... SNIFFF
TICK TICKA TAP TAP
CUT, CUT SNIP PASTE CLIP
COLOR WRITE, CLIP CUT PASTE
THERE. IT'S DONE. I DID IT.
The Life Cycle of the Zebra by April Patterson
... I JUST HAD TO GET IN THE MOOD!
LYNN

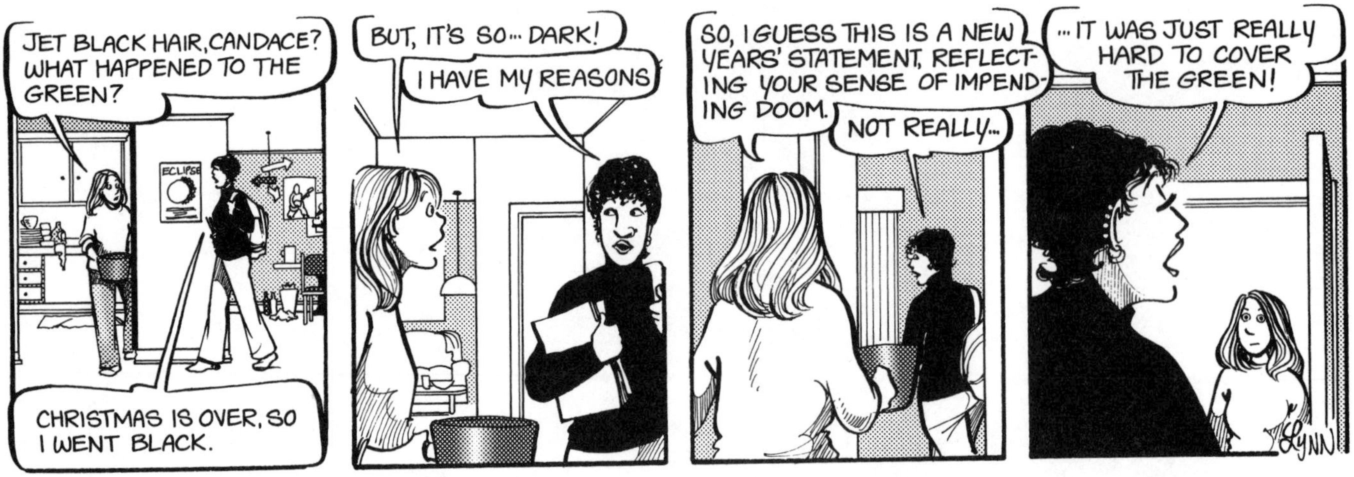
JET BLACK HAIR, CANDACE? WHAT HAPPENED TO THE GREEN?
ECLIPSE
CHRISTMAS IS OVER, SO I WENT BLACK.
BUT, IT'S SO... DARK!
I HAVE MY REASONS
SO, I GUESS THIS IS A NEW YEARS' STATEMENT, REFLECTING YOUR SENSE OF IMPENDING DOOM.
NOT REALLY...
...IT WAS JUST REALLY HARD TO COVER THE GREEN!
LYNN

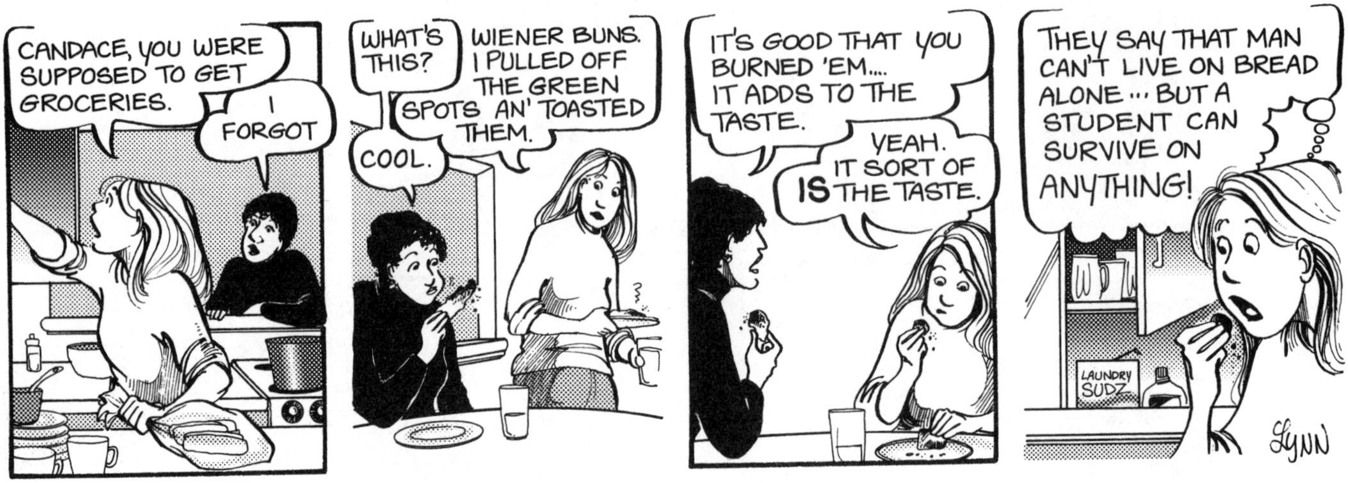
CANDACE, YOU WERE SUPPOSED TO GET GROCERIES.
I FORGOT
WHAT'S THIS?
WIENER BUNS. I PULLED OFF THE GREEN SPOTS AN' TOASTED THEM.
COOL.
IT'S GOOD THAT YOU BURNED 'EM.... IT ADDS TO THE TASTE.
YEAH. IT SORT OF IS THE TASTE.
THEY SAY THAT MAN CAN'T LIVE ON BREAD ALONE... BUT A STUDENT CAN SURVIVE ON ANYTHING!
LAUNDRY SUDZ
LYNN

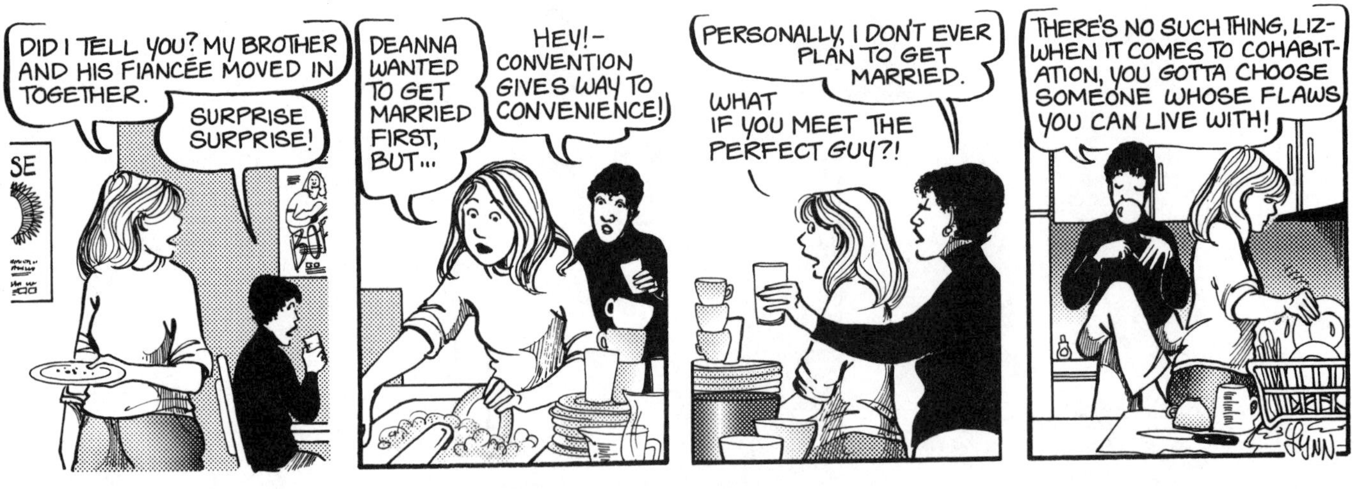
DID I TELL YOU? MY BROTHER AND HIS FIANCÉE MOVED IN TOGETHER.
SURPRISE SURPRISE!
DEANNA WANTED TO GET MARRIED FIRST, BUT...
HEY! - CONVENTION GIVES WAY TO CONVENIENCE!
PERSONALLY, I DON'T EVER PLAN TO GET MARRIED.
WHAT IF YOU MEET THE PERFECT GUY?!
THERE'S NO SUCH THING, LIZ - WHEN IT COMES TO COHABITATION, YOU GOTTA CHOOSE SOMEONE WHOSE FLAWS YOU CAN LIVE WITH!
LYNN

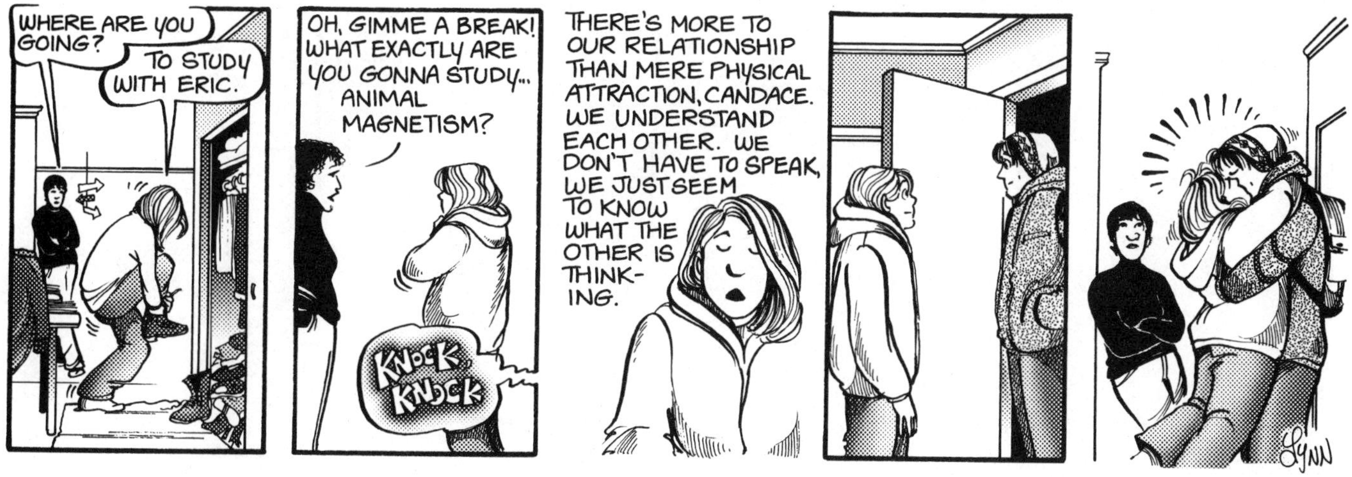
WHERE ARE YOU GOING?
TO STUDY WITH ERIC.
OH, GIMME A BREAK! WHAT EXACTLY ARE YOU GONNA STUDY... ANIMAL MAGNETISM?
KNOCK, KNOCK
THERE'S MORE TO OUR RELATIONSHIP THAN MERE PHYSICAL ATTRACTION, CANDACE. WE UNDERSTAND EACH OTHER. WE DON'T HAVE TO SPEAK, WE JUST SEEM TO KNOW WHAT THE OTHER IS THINKING.
LYNN

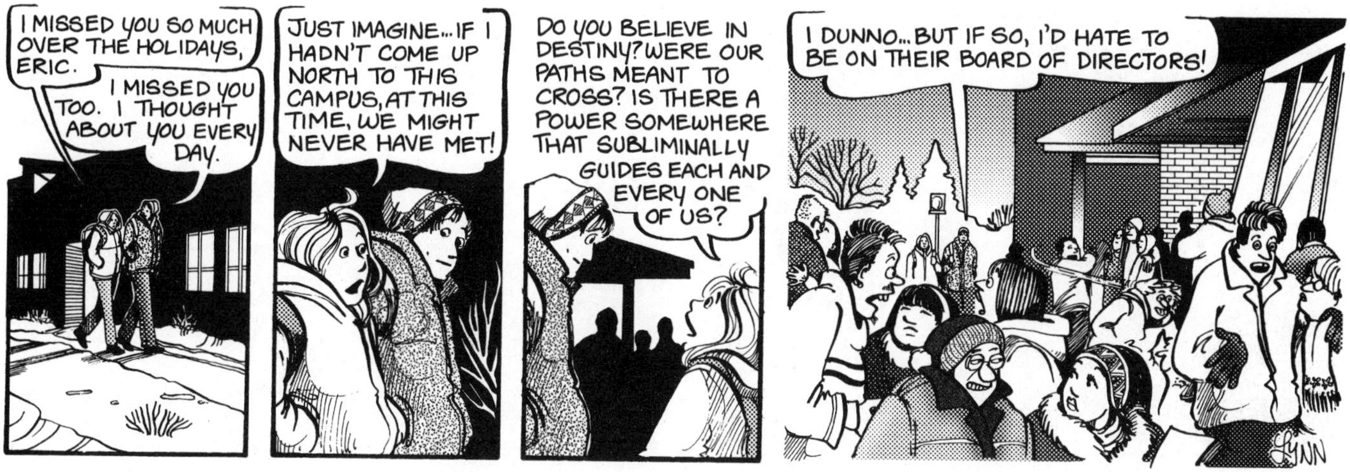
I MISSED YOU SO MUCH OVER THE HOLIDAYS, ERIC.
I MISSED YOU TOO. I THOUGHT ABOUT YOU EVERY DAY.
JUST IMAGINE... IF I HADN'T COME UP NORTH TO THIS CAMPUS, AT THIS TIME, WE MIGHT NEVER HAVE MET!
DO YOU BELIEVE IN DESTINY? WERE OUR PATHS MEANT TO CROSS? IS THERE A POWER SOMEWHERE THAT SUBLIMINALLY GUIDES EACH AND EVERY ONE OF US?
I DUNNO... BUT IF SO, I'D HATE TO BE ON THEIR BOARD OF DIRECTORS!
LYNN

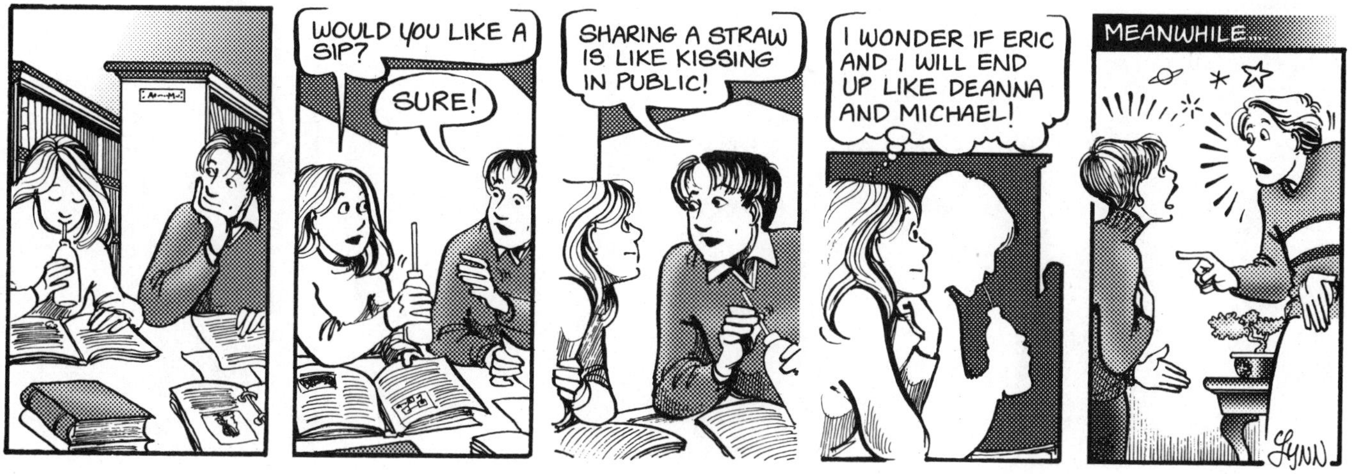
WOULD YOU LIKE A SIP?
SURE!
SHARING A STRAW IS LIKE KISSING IN PUBLIC!
I WONDER IF ERIC AND I WILL END UP LIKE DEANNA AND MICHAEL!
MEANWHILE...
LYNN

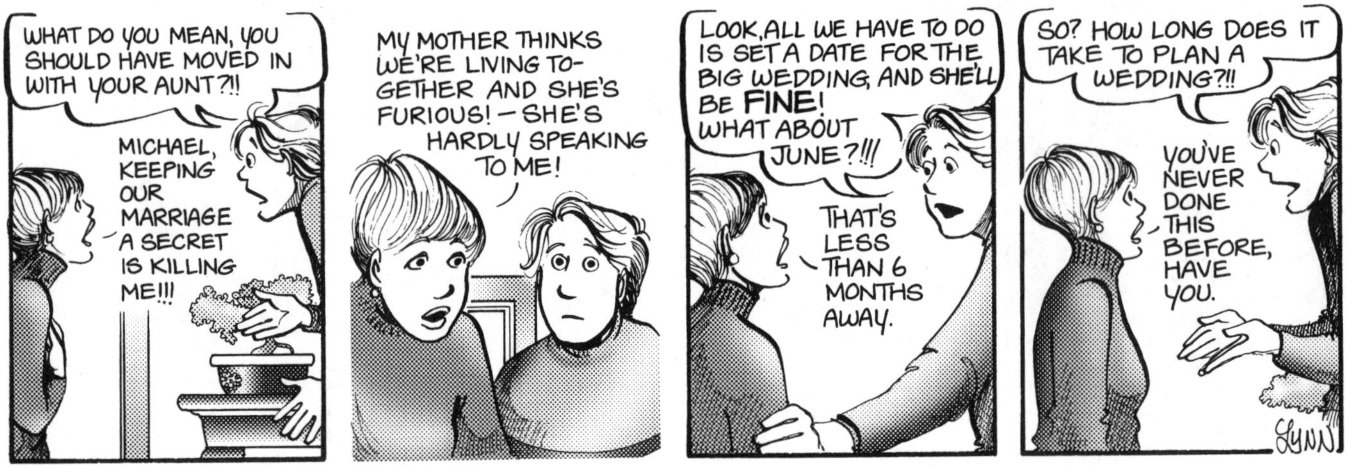
WHAT DO YOU MEAN, YOU SHOULD HAVE MOVED IN WITH YOUR AUNT?!!
MICHAEL, KEEPING OUR MARRIAGE A SECRET IS KILLING ME!!!
MY MOTHER THINKS WE'RE LIVING TOGETHER AND SHE'S FURIOUS! — SHE'S HARDLY SPEAKING TO ME!
LOOK, ALL WE HAVE TO DO IS SET A DATE FOR THE BIG WEDDING, AND SHE'LL BE FINE! WHAT ABOUT JUNE?!!!
THAT'S LESS THAN 6 MONTHS AWAY.
SO? HOW LONG DOES IT TAKE TO PLAN A WEDDING?!!
YOU'VE NEVER DONE THIS BEFORE, HAVE YOU.
LYNN

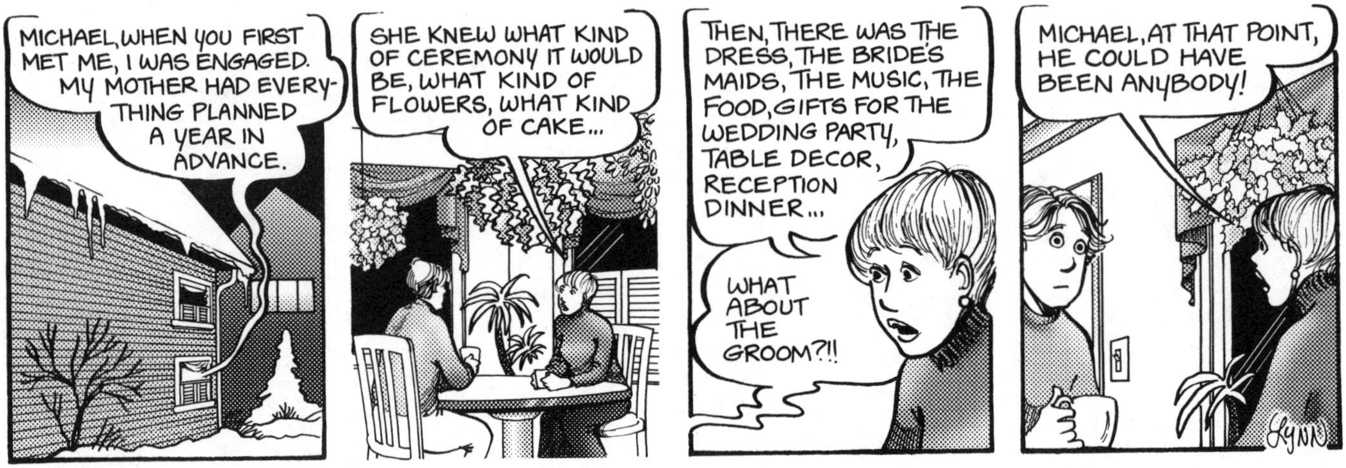
MICHAEL, WHEN YOU FIRST MET ME, I WAS ENGAGED. MY MOTHER HAD EVERYTHING PLANNED A YEAR IN ADVANCE.
SHE KNEW WHAT KIND OF CEREMONY IT WOULD BE, WHAT KIND OF FLOWERS, WHAT KIND OF CAKE...
THEN, THERE WAS THE DRESS, THE BRIDE'S MAIDS, THE MUSIC, THE FOOD, GIFTS FOR THE WEDDING PARTY, TABLE DECOR, RECEPTION DINNER...
WHAT ABOUT THE GROOM?!!
MICHAEL, AT THAT POINT, HE COULD HAVE BEEN ANYBODY!
LYNN

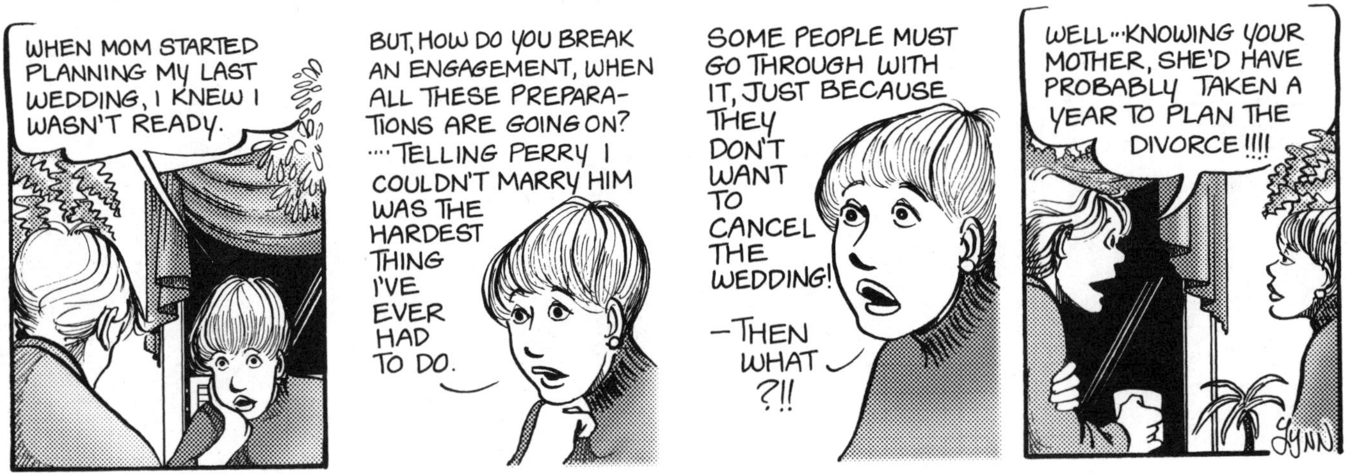
WHEN MOM STARTED PLANNING MY LAST WEDDING, I KNEW I WASN'T READY.
BUT, HOW DO YOU BREAK AN ENGAGEMENT, WHEN ALL THESE PREPARATIONS ARE GOING ON? ....TELLING PERRY I COULDN'T MARRY HIM WAS THE HARDEST THING I'VE EVER HAD TO DO.
SOME PEOPLE MUST GO THROUGH WITH IT, JUST BECAUSE THEY DON'T WANT TO CANCEL THE WEDDING!
—THEN WHAT ?!!
WELL...KNOWING YOUR MOTHER, SHE'D HAVE PROBABLY TAKEN A YEAR TO PLAN THE DIVORCE!!!!
LYNN

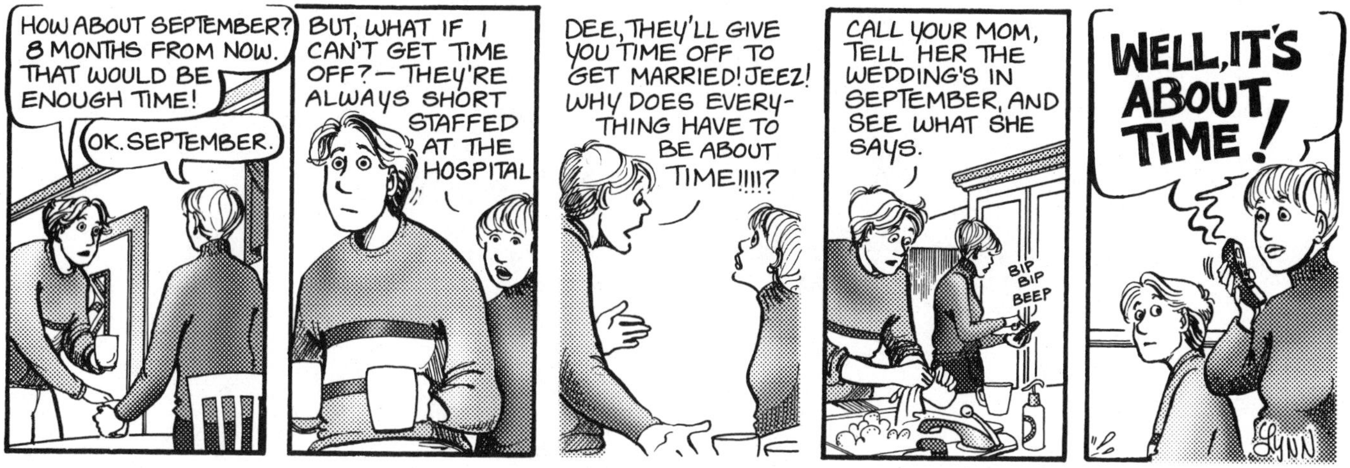
HOW ABOUT SEPTEMBER? 8 MONTHS FROM NOW. THAT WOULD BE ENOUGH TIME!
OK. SEPTEMBER.
BUT, WHAT IF I CAN'T GET TIME OFF?—THEY'RE ALWAYS SHORT STAFFED AT THE HOSPITAL
DEE, THEY'LL GIVE YOU TIME OFF TO GET MARRIED! JEEZ! WHY DOES EVERYTHING HAVE TO BE ABOUT TIME!!!!?
CALL YOUR MOM, TELL HER THE WEDDING'S IN SEPTEMBER, AND SEE WHAT SHE SAYS.
BIP BIP BEEP
WELL, IT'S ABOUT TIME!
LYNN

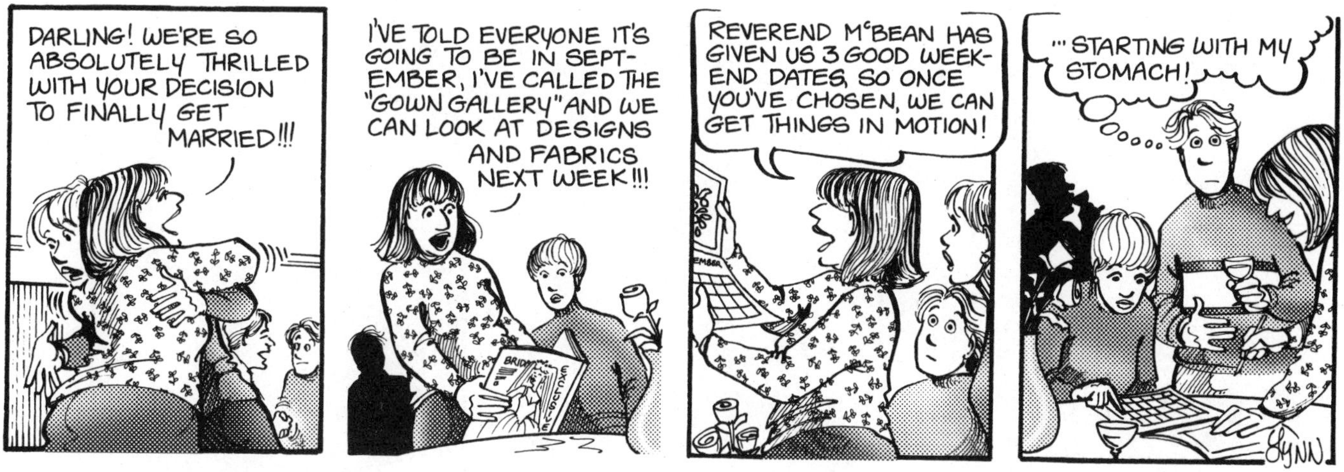
DARLING! WE'RE SO ABSOLUTELY THRILLED WITH YOUR DECISION TO FINALLY GET MARRIED!!!
I'VE TOLD EVERYONE IT'S GOING TO BE IN SEPTEMBER, I'VE CALLED THE "GOWN GALLERY" AND WE CAN LOOK AT DESIGNS AND FABRICS NEXT WEEK!!!
REVEREND M^cBEAN HAS GIVEN US 3 GOOD WEEKEND DATES, SO ONCE YOU'VE CHOSEN, WE CAN GET THINGS IN MOTION!
...STARTING WITH MY STOMACH!
LYNN

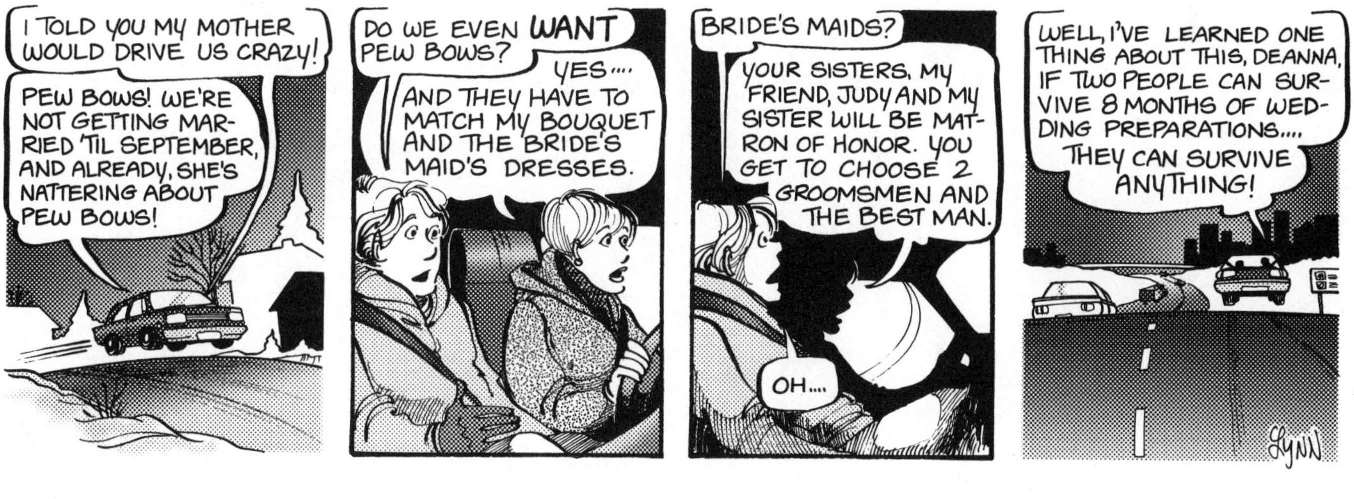
I TOLD YOU MY MOTHER WOULD DRIVE US CRAZY!
PEW BOWS! WE'RE NOT GETTING MARRIED 'TIL SEPTEMBER, AND ALREADY, SHE'S NATTERING ABOUT PEW BOWS!
DO WE EVEN WANT PEW BOWS?
YES.... AND THEY HAVE TO MATCH MY BOUQUET AND THE BRIDE'S MAID'S DRESSES.
BRIDE'S MAIDS?
YOUR SISTERS, MY FRIEND, JUDY AND MY SISTER WILL BE MATRON OF HONOR. YOU GET TO CHOOSE 2 GROOMSMEN AND THE BEST MAN.
OH....
WELL, I'VE LEARNED ONE THING ABOUT THIS, DEANNA, IF TWO PEOPLE CAN SURVIVE 8 MONTHS OF WEDDING PREPARATIONS.... THEY CAN SURVIVE ANYTHING!
LYNN

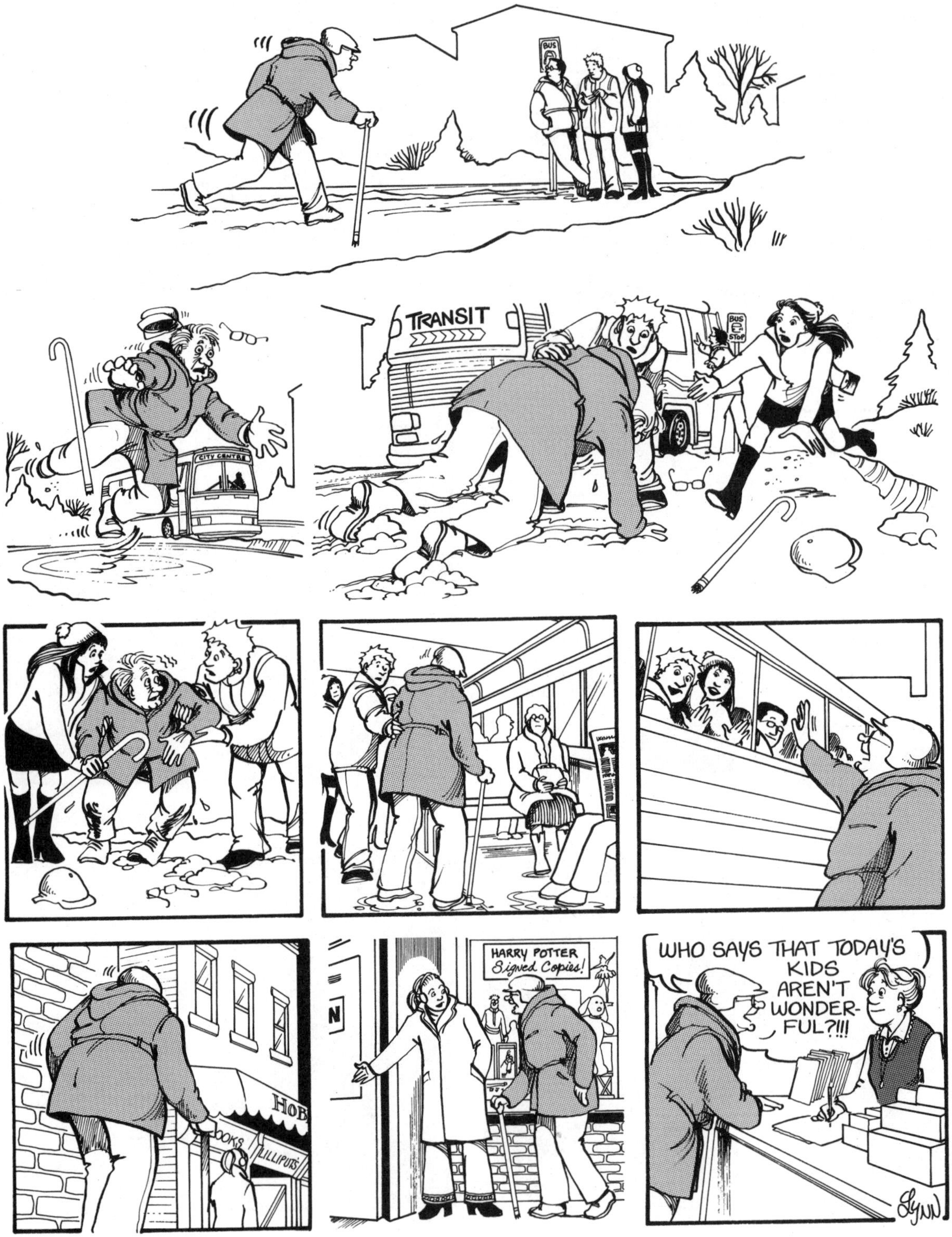
BUS
TRANSIT
CITY CENTRE
BUS STOP
HOB
BOOKS
LILLIPUTS
HARRY POTTER
Signed Copies!
WHO SAYS THAT TODAY'S KIDS AREN'T WONDER-FUL?!!!
Lynn

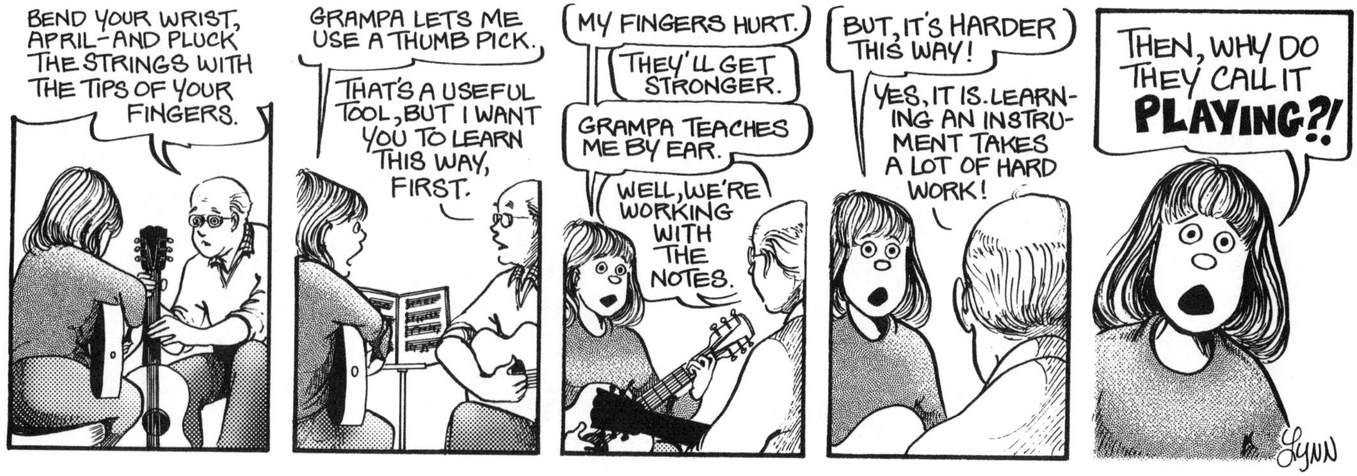
BEND YOUR WRIST, APRIL-AND PLUCK THE STRINGS WITH THE TIPS OF YOUR FINGERS.
GRAMPA LETS ME USE A THUMB PICK.
THAT'S A USEFUL TOOL, BUT I WANT YOU TO LEARN THIS WAY, FIRST.
MY FINGERS HURT.
THEY'LL GET STRONGER.
GRAMPA TEACHES ME BY EAR.
WELL, WE'RE WORKING WITH THE NOTES.
BUT, IT'S HARDER THIS WAY!
YES, IT IS. LEARNING AN INSTRUMENT TAKES A LOT OF HARD WORK!
THEN, WHY DO THEY CALL IT PLAYING?!
LYNN

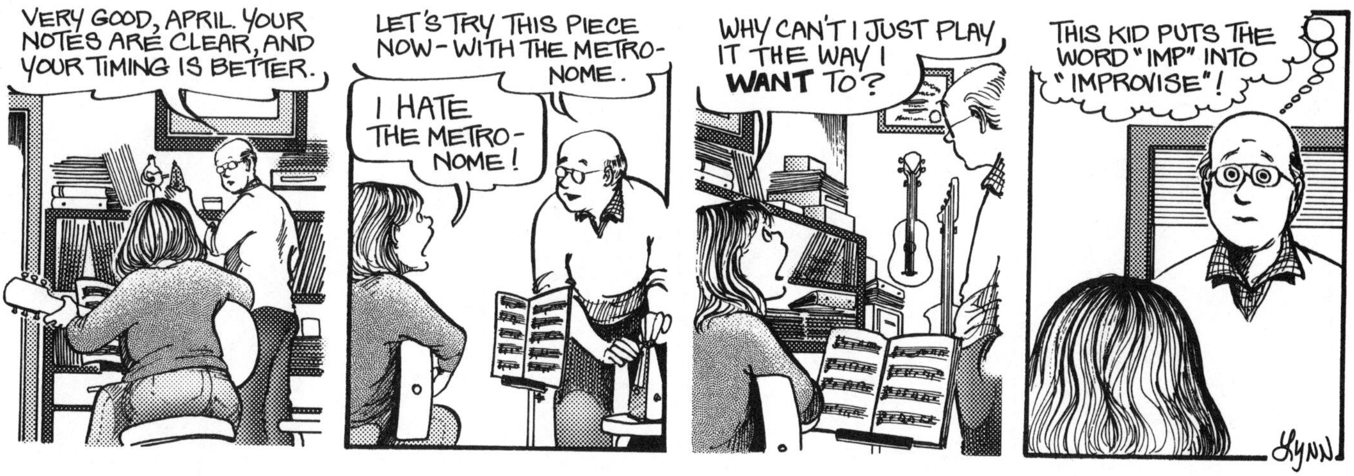
VERY GOOD, APRIL. YOUR NOTES ARE CLEAR, AND YOUR TIMING IS BETTER.
LET'S TRY THIS PIECE NOW-WITH THE METRONOME.
I HATE THE METRONOME!
WHY CAN'T I JUST PLAY IT THE WAY I WANT TO?
THIS KID PUTS THE WORD "IMP" INTO "IMPROVISE"!
LYNN

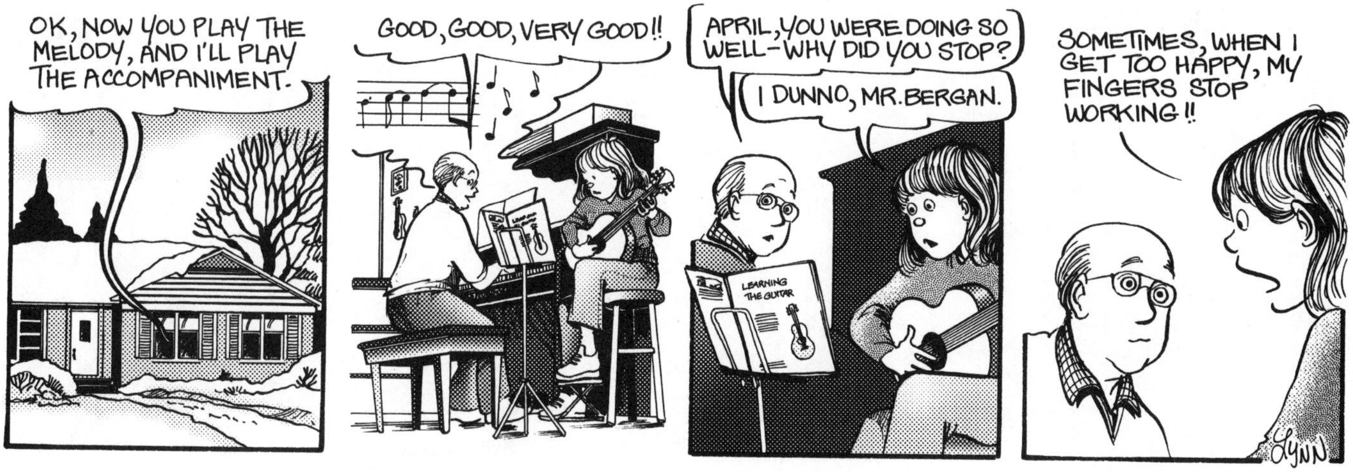
OK, NOW YOU PLAY THE MELODY, AND I'LL PLAY THE ACCOMPANIMENT.
GOOD, GOOD, VERY GOOD!!
APRIL, YOU WERE DOING SO WELL-WHY DID YOU STOP?
I DUNNO, MR. BERGAN.
LEARNING THE GUITAR
SOMETIMES, WHEN I GET TOO HAPPY, MY FINGERS STOP WORKING!!
LYNN

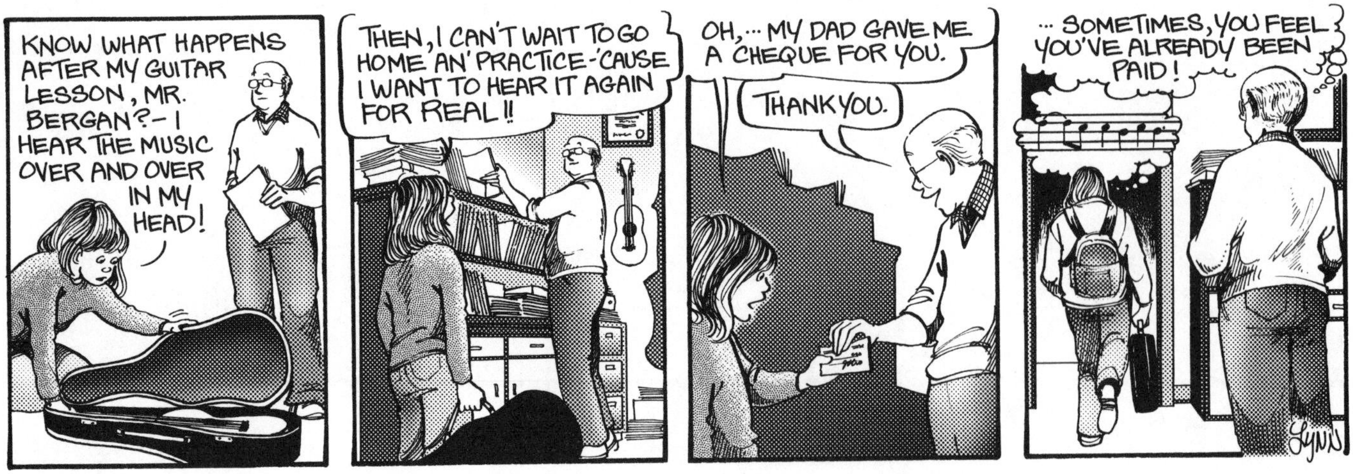
KNOW WHAT HAPPENS AFTER MY GUITAR LESSON, MR. BERGAN?- I HEAR THE MUSIC OVER AND OVER IN MY HEAD!
THEN, I CAN'T WAIT TO GO HOME AN' PRACTICE-'CAUSE I WANT TO HEAR IT AGAIN FOR REAL!!
OH, ... MY DAD GAVE ME A CHEQUE FOR YOU.
THANK YOU.
... SOMETIMES, YOU FEEL YOU'VE ALREADY BEEN PAID!
LYNN

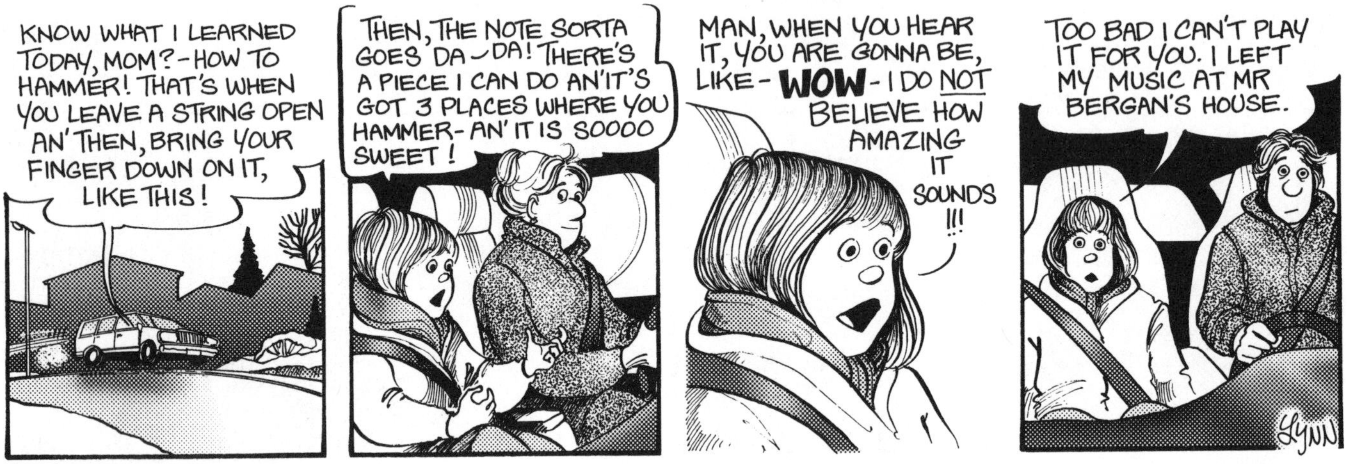
KNOW WHAT I LEARNED TODAY, MOM?- HOW TO HAMMER! THAT'S WHEN YOU LEAVE A STRING OPEN AN' THEN, BRING YOUR FINGER DOWN ON IT, LIKE THIS!
THEN, THE NOTE SORTA GOES DA-DA! THERE'S A PIECE I CAN DO AN'IT'S GOT 3 PLACES WHERE YOU HAMMER- AN' IT IS SOOOO SWEET!
MAN, WHEN YOU HEAR IT, YOU ARE GONNA BE, LIKE- WOW- I DO NOT BELIEVE HOW AMAZING IT SOUNDS!!!
TOO BAD I CAN'T PLAY IT FOR YOU. I LEFT MY MUSIC AT MR BERGAN'S HOUSE.
LYNN

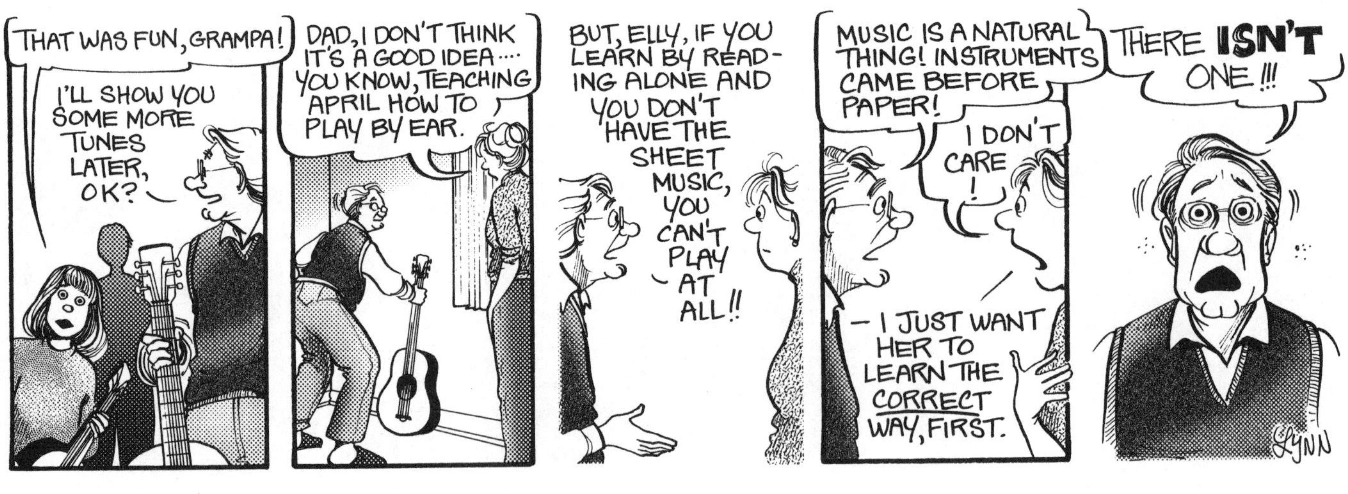
THAT WAS FUN, GRAMPA!
I'LL SHOW YOU SOME MORE TUNES LATER, OK?
DAD, I DON'T THINK IT'S A GOOD IDEA.... YOU KNOW, TEACHING APRIL HOW TO PLAY BY EAR.
BUT, ELLY, IF YOU LEARN BY READING ALONE AND YOU DON'T HAVE THE SHEET MUSIC, YOU CAN'T PLAY AT ALL!!
MUSIC IS A NATURAL THING! INSTRUMENTS CAME BEFORE PAPER!
I DON'T CARE!
- I JUST WANT HER TO LEARN THE CORRECT WAY, FIRST.
THERE ISN'T ONE!!!
LYNN

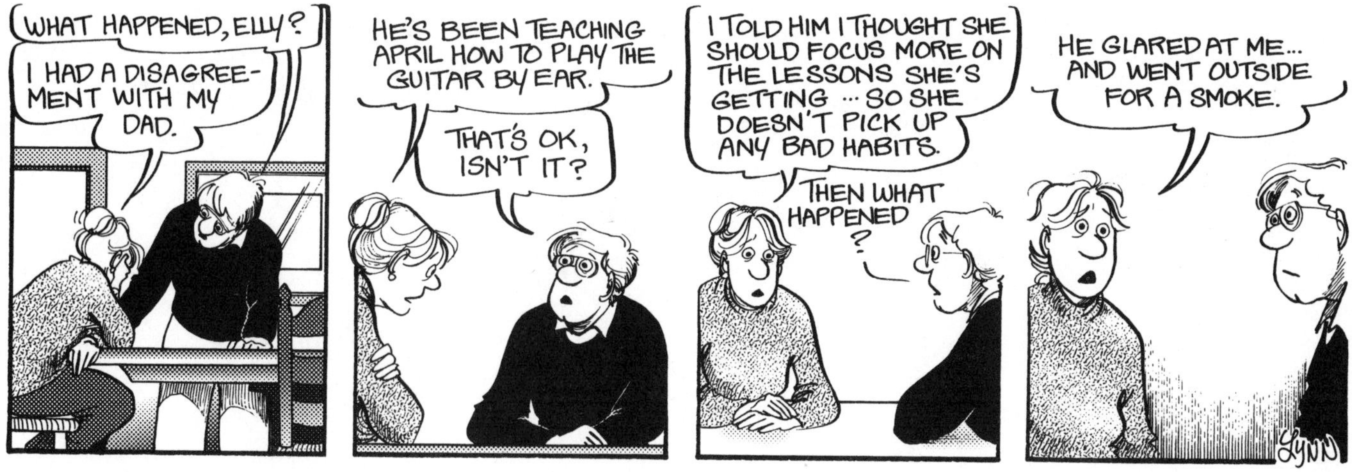
WHAT HAPPENED, ELLY?
I HAD A DISAGREE-MENT WITH MY DAD.
HE'S BEEN TEACHING APRIL HOW TO PLAY THE GUITAR BY EAR.
THAT'S OK, ISN'T IT?
I TOLD HIM I THOUGHT SHE SHOULD FOCUS MORE ON THE LESSONS SHE'S GETTING ... SO SHE DOESN'T PICK UP ANY BAD HABITS.
THEN WHAT HAPPENED?
HE GLARED AT ME... AND WENT OUTSIDE FOR A SMOKE.
LYNN

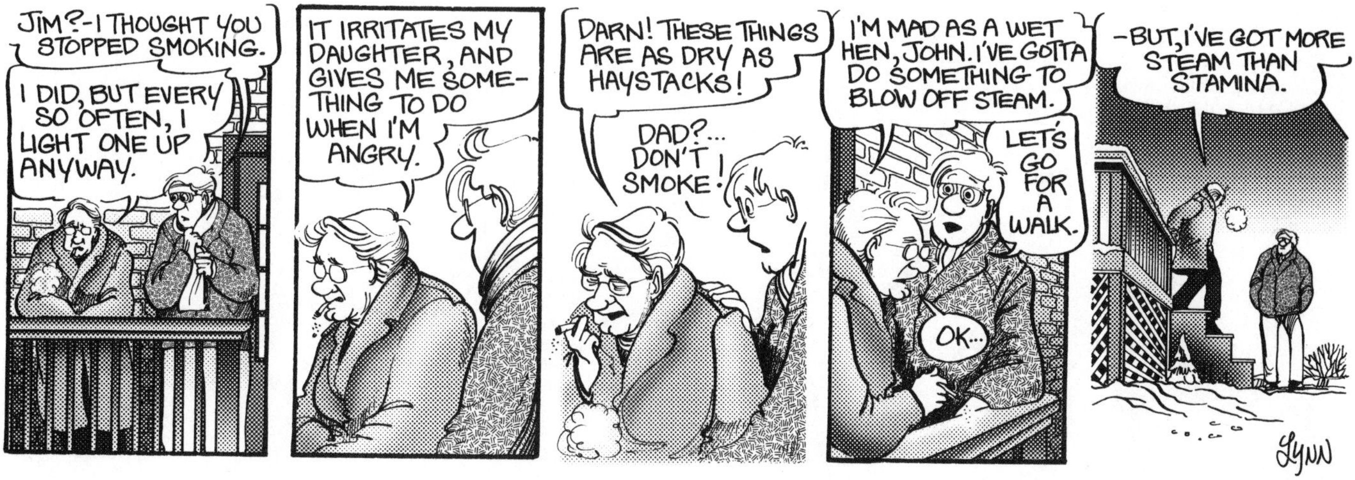
JIM?-I THOUGHT YOU STOPPED SMOKING.
I DID, BUT EVERY SO OFTEN, I LIGHT ONE UP ANYWAY.
IT IRRITATES MY DAUGHTER, AND GIVES ME SOME-THING TO DO WHEN I'M ANGRY.
DARN! THESE THINGS ARE AS DRY AS HAYSTACKS!
DAD?... DON'T SMOKE!
I'M MAD AS A WET HEN, JOHN. I'VE GOTTA DO SOMETHING TO BLOW OFF STEAM.
LET'S GO FOR A WALK.
OK...
-BUT, I'VE GOT MORE STEAM THAN STAMINA.
LYNN

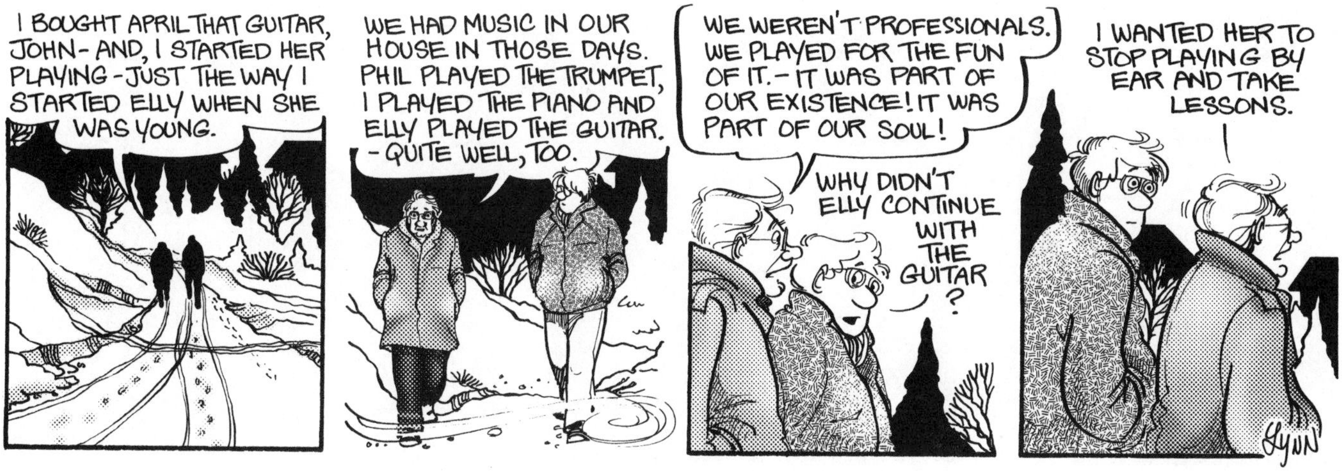
I BOUGHT APRIL THAT GUITAR, JOHN- AND, I STARTED HER PLAYING-JUST THE WAY I STARTED ELLY WHEN SHE WAS YOUNG.
WE HAD MUSIC IN OUR HOUSE IN THOSE DAYS. PHIL PLAYED THE TRUMPET, I PLAYED THE PIANO AND ELLY PLAYED THE GUITAR. -QUITE WELL, TOO.
WE WEREN'T PROFESSIONALS. WE PLAYED FOR THE FUN OF IT.-IT WAS PART OF OUR EXISTENCE! IT WAS PART OF OUR SOUL!
WHY DIDN'T ELLY CONTINUE WITH THE GUITAR?
I WANTED HER TO STOP PLAYING BY EAR AND TAKE LESSONS.
LYNN

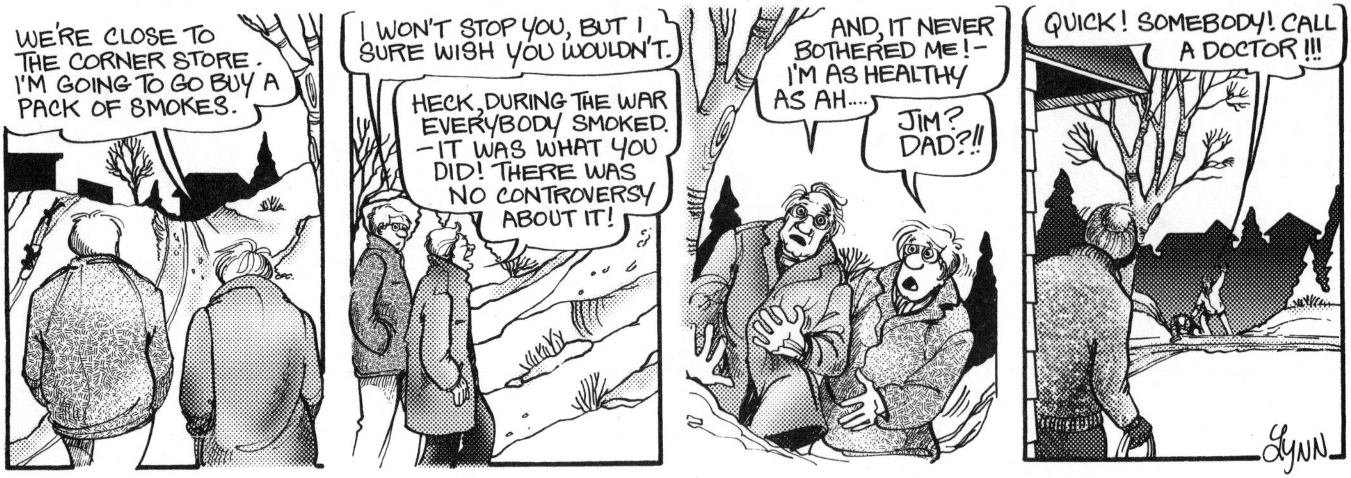
WE'RE CLOSE TO THE CORNER STORE. I'M GOING TO GO BUY A PACK OF SMOKES.
I WON'T STOP YOU, BUT I SURE WISH YOU WOULDN'T.
HECK, DURING THE WAR EVERYBODY SMOKED. -IT WAS WHAT YOU DID! THERE WAS NO CONTROVERSY ABOUT IT!
AND, IT NEVER BOTHERED ME! - I'M AS HEALTHY AS AH....
JIM? DAD?!!
QUICK! SOMEBODY! CALL A DOCTOR!!!
LYNN

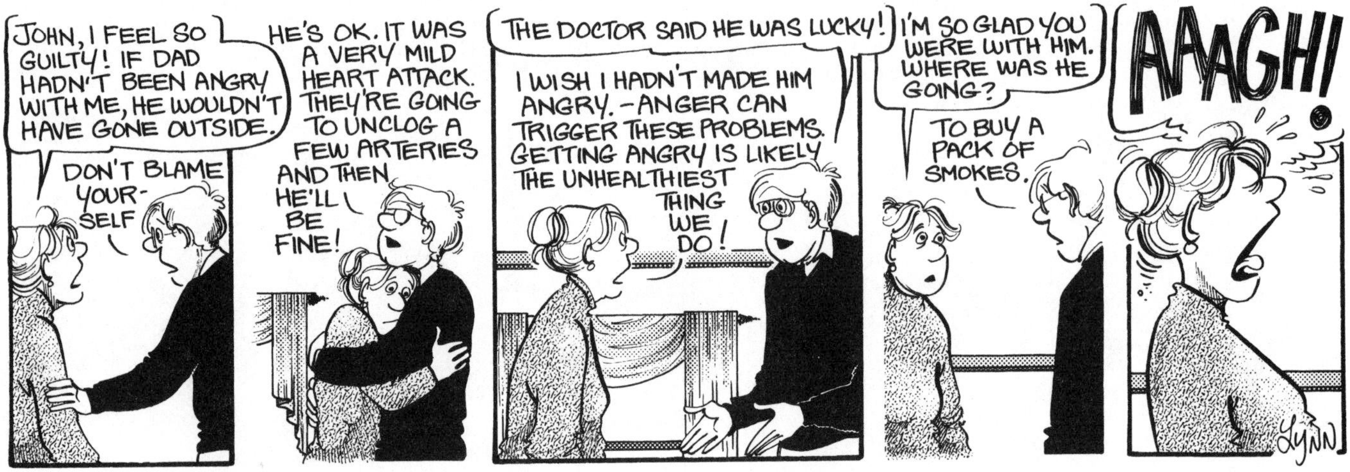
JOHN, I FEEL SO GUILTY! IF DAD HADN'T BEEN ANGRY WITH ME, HE WOULDN'T HAVE GONE OUTSIDE.
DON'T BLAME YOURSELF
HE'S OK. IT WAS A VERY MILD HEART ATTACK. THEY'RE GOING TO UNCLOG A FEW ARTERIES AND THEN HE'LL BE FINE!
THE DOCTOR SAID HE WAS LUCKY!
I WISH I HADN'T MADE HIM ANGRY. -ANGER CAN TRIGGER THESE PROBLEMS. GETTING ANGRY IS LIKELY THE UNHEALTHIEST THING WE DO!
I'M SO GLAD YOU WERE WITH HIM. WHERE WAS HE GOING?
TO BUY A PACK OF SMOKES.
AAAGH!
LYNN

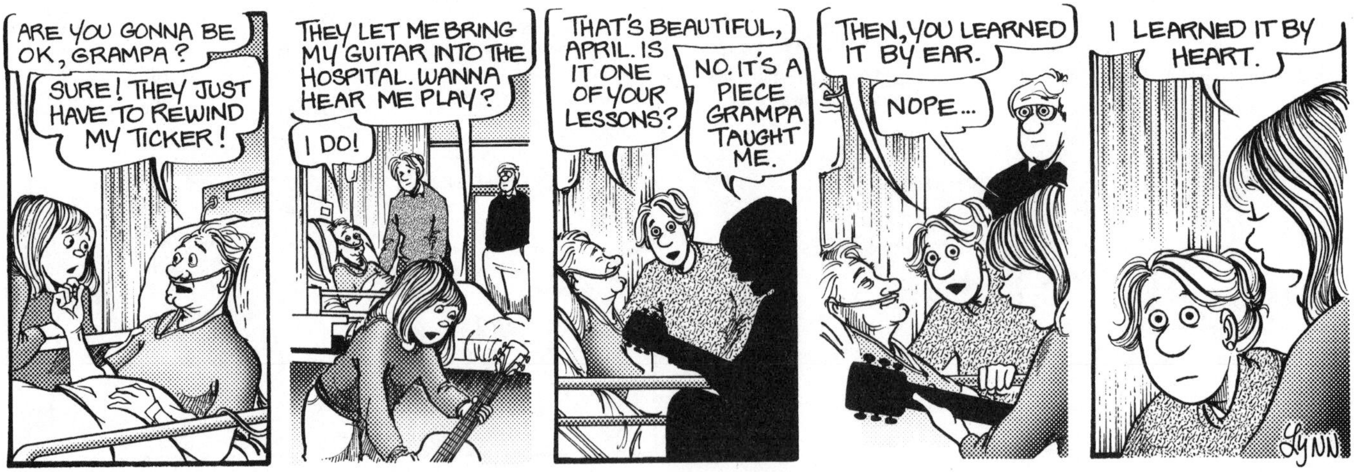
ARE YOU GONNA BE OK, GRAMPA?
SURE! THEY JUST HAVE TO REWIND MY TICKER!
THEY LET ME BRING MY GUITAR INTO THE HOSPITAL. WANNA HEAR ME PLAY?
I DO!
THAT'S BEAUTIFUL, APRIL. IS IT ONE OF YOUR LESSONS?
NO. IT'S A PIECE GRAMPA TAUGHT ME.
THEN, YOU LEARNED IT BY EAR.
NOPE...
I LEARNED IT BY HEART.
LYNN